LEEDS UNITED

It's more than just a game!

Adrian Taylor

Grosvenor House
Publishing Limited

This book is published by
Grosvenor House Publishing Ltd
Link House
140 The Broadway, Tolworth, Surrey, KT6 7HT.
www.grosvenorhousepublishing.co.uk

A CIP record for this book
is available from the British Library

ISBN 978-1-83975-360-2

For Andy, Katherine, Michael and James.

ACKNOWLEDGEMENTS

I would like to thank Andy and Katherine for their time, patience, kindness, and technical support when I was lost! Thanks also to Michael, James, Nick and Lou, for their encouragement and support at all times. And to Melanie Bartle at Grosvenor House for helping to make this project a reality.

Adrian Taylor
August 2020

CONTENTS

INTRODUCTION

So probably, a bit like you, I have always wanted to write a book, any book. And I guess, like so many others, I have dreamt of coming up with the different idea, the 'must read' story that would become a best-seller and make my fortune. On occasions, I have even had some good ideas; some remarkably similar to others who would later – through their hard work, talent, and determination to succeed – develop their thought processes, find their niche, and hit the jackpot. Sadly, I never quite had the staying power.

When I was a young teacher in the 1970s, working in a primary school in Morley, Leeds, I despaired of the quality of children's literature, and especially poetry. Much of the stuff in the school library was the same as I had been made to learn by rote fifteen years earlier. So, I started writing poems in an old exercise book that I thought would appeal to 10 and 11-year-olds. I remember one was about young footballers nervously waiting for their opponents to arrive for a school match, which I called, 'Aren't they big?!' In my entire playing career, the opposition always looked like giants compared to the teams I was playing for, and it seemed I had hit a nerve because the kids really appeared to enjoy the poem as I read it to them. On a roll, I wrote more and more. One about the 'Head' with the hooked nose and the shiny shoes that squeaked out a warning as he approached; another about the 'Dentist' with the smell of antiseptic and the shriek of the drill that filled my senses as I waited fearfully for my name to be called.

They were generally just little stories and rhymes that I thought would appeal more to the children than the rote learning of stuff like 'Quinquireme of Nineveh from distant Ophir' that I had endured, however good John Masefield's poem was.

I even found the name of a publisher and sent them a few samples of my work. But nothing; no response at all, not even a 'thanks but no thanks!' And there I left it, just as I had when, as a 14-year-old I came up with the idea of writing a diary called 'Growing pains!'. I kept it up for a few months, scribbling away about the private fears of a young adolescent boy trying to make sense of his world, parents, teachers, siblings, school, and girls – especially girls. And then I just stopped, lost interest, and moved onto something else, another scheme another dream. And 14 years later, Sue Townsend came up with *The Secret Diary of Adrian Mole, Age 13¾*. I couldn't believe it! It was almost as if she had read my mind, as if she knew my inner feelings. And then she followed up this huge success with *The Growing Pains of Adrian Mole*! Didn't she know I was Adrian, for chuff's sake?

A lack of staying power, a lack of confidence or ability? Perhaps all of those. There was no doubt that I was brilliant at talking about ideas, and pretty good at making notes and checking out details for accuracy on the internet. But, just like when I was faced with preparation for exams at school or college, and could spend hours drawing up a neat schedule of revision times, I somehow never quite got round to doing any actual revision. And so it was with 'the book' – lots of talk, lots of preparation, lots of hot air. So, I spent a lifetime in schools, watching as every celebrity from The Duchess of York to David Williams and Frank Lampard turned their hands to writing children's literature, yet never found the time to compete with them.

And then, suddenly I had the time. Suddenly there were no excuses and, newly retired with my teacher's pension and a pretty empty diary, it was *my* time – not Sue Townsend's or Sarah Ferguson's, not David Williams or even Frank Lampard's, but mine. I had even taken the pressure off myself by no longer planning the bestselling blockbuster, no longer thinking of publishing, but just proving to myself that I could actually sit down and write. Now I would write my story and it would be a labour of love.

I have followed Leeds United since the early 1960s, first going to Elland Road on Boxing Day 1964 (we drew 1-1 with Blackburn), and I remember standing in the famous 'Scratching Shed' and being terrified I would get lost when Dad pushed me to the front so I could see.

Throughout my life, they have been a constant, always there like a special friend, a true love who can raise you to the highest of heights and leave you in the depths of despair. We have, as they say, 'had our ups and downs.'

In the 60s, we were to embark on a period of time that would see us marked as one of the greatest teams in the world. Don Revie's side has ultimately never received its rightful acclaim from a sporting press obsessed with the image of 'Dirty Leeds'. And it seems the club is inevitably linked with, perhaps unfairly, the attacks on Revie which followed his departure (before he was sacked) from the England job, which he held having left Leeds as Champions of England in 1974.

And so to the book!

It was a simple idea really. Just write about my love for Leeds, the important part they have played in my life, maybe mention some great games of the past, and basically track their progress through this, their Centenary season. Obviously I would mention some of my own life highlights, particularly those of a sporting nature, trying very hard to steer away from my career as a headteacher of both state and independent schools – that story is for another time.I just wanted to write down my own thoughts and feelings about our progress through the season; a season that would hopefully see the 'Mighty Whites' at last return to prominence. I would write a few words about the games, make a note about team selection, and offer my own view of the team's performance. I would record the scorers and add a few story lines from the past about family, work, my fairly unremarkable progress through school, and the part Leeds United has played in all of it. Always there for good or bad, through thick and thin, championships and relegation, always offering the opportunity to 'escape' from the pressures of life just for a couple of hours every week.

At the end of the season, I would tidy the notes up and share my musings with the family, my wife Andy, and children Katherine, Michael and James – all well brought up to be massive Leeds fans, all aware of the agony and ecstasy of supporting this very special club. So, that was the plan. And hopefully, in early May when we played Charlton at ER in our last game of the season (surely this was a sign, as Charlton had been the last home game before our relegation in 2004), we would find time to celebrate together our return to the Premiership after a gap of 16 years – too long for one of England's great clubs.

And then came the Coronavirus!

CHAPTER 1

BACK TO THE FUTURE

So now everything is back to front, and my story becomes a record of very changing times where football becomes irrelevant when compared to illness and horrendous loss of life. Writing in lockdown, we are encouraged to stay home and busy ourselves with home working, house chores, gardening, and other activities, painting, reading, and in my case writing. Writing a sometimes painful labour of love about the story of a season. It was a season which had started so promisingly on a sunny Sunday afternoon in August, when Bielsa's boys blew away Bristol City – themselves predicted to be part of the promotion race – winning comfortably 3-1.

Now seven months on, and just nine games from the end of the season, everyone was beginning to sense trouble. Top of the table after a fine 2-0 home win over near neighbours Huddersfield, there was a feeling that at last this year we were going to do it; we were going to be back where we belong in the top flight of English football. We had survived a distinctly worrying period in January and February, losing four of five games. And despite our unpredictable goalkeeper Kiko Casilla once again giving away a disastrous goal, we had hauled ourselves back into the game at Brentford, earning a point – which should have been more – against a team who, along with Fulham, had whittled a nine-point lead down to nothing.

So, why the unease? Well, we are Leeds, aren't we? Any Leeds fan over the age of ten knows that nothing is guaranteed with our team, and just as last year and the implosion in the last few weeks of the season, the clouds were gathering. Only this time, the problem wasn't on the pitch. This time, everything was out of our control. This time, it wasn't Bamford, Harrison or Roofe missing chances, or Casilla charging out of his area on some Kamikaze mission known only to himself. No, this time no-one was to blame. This time, the problem was worldwide, and it was serious.

In mid-December, we were enjoying a winning run of seven games. On Saturday, December 14th, we quickly found ourselves leading Cardiff City – a real bogey team for us – 3-0. But we conspired to throw that lead away, eventually drawing 3-3 with a Lee Tomlin-inspired Cardiff team, which was symptomatic of the nervousness on the pitch and in the crowd that always lurks just beneath the surface at Elland Rd. But there were other symptoms festering not so far away which would have a devastating effect on the lives of so many across the globe. I guess most of us listened with some concern when, in December, the news media reported the outbreak of a virus known as Coronavirus in Wuhan, in the Hubei province of China. Quite a focus of the early reporting centred around British nationals living in the region who, along with their whole communities, were having to isolate themselves to prevent the spread of the virus.

At that time back in December, this virus seemed a long way away, and life in England carried on at pace as the country prepared for the Christmas celebrations. It was not our year to host the family. Katherine and Michael were due to be 'Christmassing' with the in-laws, and James was free to be with us or to enjoy the holiday with friends. Andy and I were due to stay with my brother Andrew, his son Ben, our sister Janet, and her husband Steve, at Andrew's cottage in Sussex. My biggest concern was making sure I didn't miss any fixtures over the festive period, which for us started with our much anticipated away trip to Fulham, followed by a home game on Boxing Day against Preston. The Christmas games concluded with two away trips to the Midlands – Birmingham City on 29th December; and a top of the table clash with West Bromwich Albion (WBA) on New Year's Day.

Fulham is always a great away trip. And with Katherine and Nick living in Bishops Stortford and James in Wandsworth, it always provides us with the perfect opportunity to catch up with at least two of our children. Unfortunately, this year Fulham were redeveloping their ground, so what is usually designated a 'neutral' end of the stadium, next to the visiting fans, was now reserved for home fans only. In previous years, all the neutral end tickets were snapped up by Leeds fans, giving us a vociferous backing of some seven thousand fans. This year James will struggle to get a ticket for the away end. We haven't played at home that often on Boxing Day in recent years, so I was looking forward to the visit of Preston and the chance to take the three points off the visitors that we should have comfortably done in the corresponding game at Deepdale. I love watching football on Boxing Day; it reminds me of my childhood, when we gathered in the morning at Headingley to cheer on the mighty 'Trin' before heading to Elland Rd and becoming 'Leeds' fans for the afternoon.

For Wakefield fans, supporting Leeds R L would be a little bit like a proud 'white' supporting that lot from Old Trafford! As for the trips to Birmingham… well, St Andrew's is one of my least favourite away trips for lots of reasons. It's a scruffy old place, their fans can be really 'arsy', the accent is surely one of the 'naffest' in the UK, and even worse, we generally don't seem to play well there. I hadn't been to WBA before, and it looked like it would be tricky this year, as we host my brother and sister on New Year's Eve in the return leg of our family festivities.

Such problems as these were quickly overtaken, though, by the virus that knew no boundaries and was spreading rapidly throughout the world. The first cases of the illness reported in England were on 31st January, when two people from the same family were hospitalised in York. On 7th February, Dr Li Wenliang, an ophthalmologist who had been working to save people's lives in Wuhan, died of the virus. He was just 34 years old and had warned colleagues in January of the very real dangers of an epidemic. In Womersley, this suddenly all seemed much closer to home. We were regular visitors to York, where Andy had weekly Spanish lessons, and both of us had a commitment to one of the York schools. Also, my reading around the spread and effects of the virus suggested that the risk was mainly for the older age group with underlying health concerns. Yet Dr Wenliang had been only 34.

On Saturday, 8th February, the final repatriation flight from Wuhan to Britain took off with over 200 passengers on board, heading to a 14-day quarantine in the Wirral. Later that evening, a desperately misfiring Leeds side was beaten 2-0 at a buoyant Nottingham Forest, whose fans, management and players celebrated as if they had won the league. In truth, it was a tale of two keepers. Casilla continued a dreadful run of form by letting a shot from Sami Ameobi squirm past him, while Brice Samba at the other end saved brilliantly from a point-blank Liam Cooper header. Forest added a second in extra time, as we desperately tried to find an equaliser. We were beaten, but even though we had played poorly, there was no doubt we should still have gained a point.

The rest of the results that weekend didn't favour us either, with Fulham winning at Blackburn and Brentford pipping 'Boro' 3-2. WBA won at Millwall on the Sunday to pull four points clear of us, and we held onto second place only on goal difference from Fulham. Forest were now only a point away from us, and Brentford – where we headed to next – were just two points off our total. Our nine-point lead over the third placed team had evaporated, and we were heading into the last 15 games of the season with it all to do again. The media were full of Leeds blowing up again and running out of steam, while opposing fans delighted in singing 'Leeds are falling apart again'. Yet we were still capable of playing some beautiful football. We just needed some big performances… and soon. And come they did, as I will explain in more detail later. Leeds dug deep, stopped the rot with that draw at Brentford, and one way or another won their next five matches, finishing with an important win at Elland Rd against a dangerous and improving Huddersfield team. But that Saturday, 7th March, would be the last action for some time. And at that stage, I had no idea when football might return. No-one did.

Thursday, 12 March

Well, we should have been in Rome today. We had planned a short break away to one of my favourite places, and were going to finish the week's holiday with a few days in Florence – a city Andy very much had on her bucket list to visit. It looked like being a super trip, with my love of history and Andy's passion for art both being catered for, along with sampling lots of Italy's fantastic restaurants and bars. I wouldn't have to go without my sporting weekend either, as we had tickets for the Italy v England Six Nations rugby match at the Stadio Olympico, where we would meet up with James and his mates – another bonus – and enjoy the atmosphere of a sporting occasion, even if rugby union does not top my list of exciting sports to watch.

For me, the rules just get in the way of the game, stopping any hope of a free-flowing spectacle. I pull my hair out watching how much time is wasted, with largely over-fussy referees setting and resetting the scrums, only for one of the sides to bring it down again, making sure they waste as much time as possible while staying just the right side of being penalised. The game would be so improved if the refs, as they do in so many sports, just stopped the clock until the match was ready to resume. That way, the players would very quickly get the message and be ready to play. Anyway, we weren't expecting much of a spectacle as England were strong favourites to win comfortably against a struggling Italian team. However, one thing rugby union can do well is stage big international games in some fabulous stadiums in cities such as Dublin, Wellington, Cape Town, Paris, and Cardiff. These games almost always sell out and not necessarily to people who regularly support rugby. Often the tickets are snapped up by corporate groups and those who have the money to pay quite ridiculous prices to go out for an afternoon of socialising and fun. The build-up given to such games on TV is often much more creative and interesting than the entertainment on show during the actual contest. Starting with the anthems – and the 'Haka', when the All Blacks are around – the pre-match theatre is just superb.

Once, in a pub surrounded by 'rugger' types, I rather drunkenly argued that for an upcoming World Cup, all that was really needed to separate the teams was the ref, a place kicker for each side (to score points from the plethora of penalties seemingly randomly awarded), and of course, and critically, the anthems. Following these rules, it was clear to me that the semi-finals would feature Ireland v France and South Africa v Wales, because to my ear those countries' anthems are the liveliest and most passionate. Ultimately, the South Africans and Irish would be eliminated, because no matter how stirring their anthems, they also seem to sing at least a couple of songs just to make sure they have been heard. This would be deemed cheating! So, to a final between France and Wales, and I suspect a fantastic atmosphere with fans singing their hearts out for their countries. In the end, it would be a narrow victory for the French and their *Marseillaise*!

My friends were not impressed with my theory, but then they themselves were not much for flowing rugby. Most of them preferred to see England score a 'push over' try from five metres, while bellowing out the dirge like *Swing Low* and spilling their plastic glasses of Guinness all over the people in front of them, than to watch fast passing, an incisive break, and a thrilling race to the line!

So, while for me the game can be hugely frustrating, that is not to say I am simply against it. I am not. Who could be when it has produced so many fine athletes, including the entire Welsh back division from the 1970's team, headed up by the incredible Gareth Edwards, Barry John, and Phil Bennett – all schoolboy heroes of mine? Indeed, attending a rugby union playing school, I had captained our sixth form team, won the school prize for rugby, and had been picked as a travelling reserve for a Yorkshire Schools' trial. It's something I was totally proud about, but absolutely gutted not to get the chance to play in.

Not knowing that in later life I would become a teacher fully supportive of all school sport, the day of that trial taught me a great deal about manners, respect, and the kind of small-minded people involved in school sport at that time. I had travelled from my home in Wakefield to the Army apprentices' ground in Harrogate, where the trial was due to be held. This had meant an early start, a bus to Leeds, then a train to Harrogate, and finally a taxi to the Army college. Sitting in the changing room, I wasn't sure what to do. Should I change with the others? Go out and warm up? Even though this was an age before substitutes, I asked the teacher in charge, hoping that he might ask me to change. I knew from my own teacher that I had been close to selection, and I had seen him angrily leave the selection meeting when I had not been included in the starting XV following the previous trial. So, I was hopeful this guy might remember me. But nothing; no sign of recognition at all. He just looked at me and said, 'You can go home.' Unbelievable… Though that's not the word I muttered under my breath at the time!

I never forgot that lesson, and throughout my teaching career made sure that I never humiliated anyone in this way. I know my parents and teachers were astounded when I related the story to them later. I didn't play a lot of rugby union after that, preferring to play football at college and in later life. I preferred to watch football, too, though I did have one or two memorable visits to Cardiff to watch Wales v England games.

In the early 80s, my brother Andrew was living and working in Wales with my Uncle Phillip, and lodging in a local pub in a typical Welsh village called Llanelleth. Phillip was a former England international, gaining six caps in the late 1950s and early 60s. He gave legendary service to the Northampton club and played many times for his home county of Yorkshire, when county rugby really mattered.

Phillip gave Andrew two tickets for the match at the old Arms Park, and I was to drive down early on the Saturday from Yorkshire, pick him up at the pub, then drive to Cardiff for the afternoon kick-off. In the days before mobile phones, I had real trouble contacting my brother when my little Triumph Spitfire started to lose power as I reached the border. Not in the AA or any other breakdown organisation, I limped along until eventually stopping at a local garage where a totally brilliant mechanic diagnosed the problem as a knackered alternator. He could sort it, he told me, but it would take some time. I rang Andrew from the garage and we agreed if I couldn't get to him before 1.30, he would raffle my ticket in exchange for a lift to and from the ground, and I would watch the match with Frank, the landlord in the pub.

Amazingly, my friendly mechanic saviour got the job done in record time, and I was left with a race to the pub to make the deadline. I think it was about 1.25 when I eventually arrived. I did know the Welsh loved their rugby, but I had not expected the scene I witnessed when I opened the doors. There were no cars in the small car park, but wow, the pub was heaving – a bit like our local on New Year's Eve. It was totally rammed, with a massive old telly at the far end of the bar. It was like a scene from one of those Wild West films, and when I stepped in the bar, it was as if I was the gunslinger. Everything suddenly went still and completely silent! And then a very large man came lurching towards me and said slowly, 'You're Andrew's brother, aren't you?' I just had time to notice lots of bits of paper being ripped up before Andrew hit me like a rugby tackle and made it pretty clear we were leaving town – and now!

I don't remember much about the game, other than the usually reliable Dusty Hare missed a late penalty which would have given us a narrow victory. I do remember the anthems, because Andrew and I sang *God Save the Queen* with gusto before being accosted by a huge bear of a man sitting behind us. 'Where are you from, boys?' he thundered. 'Wakefield,' we replied. To which he responded, 'Then you're not bloody Englishmen; you're bloody Yorkshiremen, aren't you?' Noticing a lady nearby, he immediately apologised, saying to the woman, 'I'm sorry, dear, for my language, but then again YOU shouldn't be here!' It wasn't something that he would get away with today, but the guy was great fun and we enjoyed a real banter throughout the game, eventually declining his invite for dinner as Andrew was keen to get back to the pub and his friends.

We chatted away as we snaked our way through the traffic of Cardiff and headed out to the countryside. I told Andrew I would probably have a quick beer, then have a nap and bath before hitting the bar. He just laughed. When we got back, if anything the pub was busier than it had been earlier, and we enjoyed a night of great fun and far too much alcohol. Later that night, we were invited to sing to the assembled masses who had for much of the evening been bawling out rugby songs, accompanied by a little guy playing an electric piano. There wasn't a lot of choice, so we nervously began to sing Cliff Richard's *Living Doll*. The pub fell silent again, as if in disbelief, but soon the choirs started to sing and we brought the house down. We followed up with *Summer Holiday* and a lively rendition of *Lucky Lips*, and then quit while we were ahead.

As we left the makeshift stage, a guy pushed a dark-haired, quite attractive older woman towards us. 'Here, boys, av'er!' he said. We couldn't quite believe it and politely declined, but as the evening finished with a rousing rendition of the Welsh national anthem we knew we'd experienced a very special night with some hugely friendly and special people.

I have since visited Cardiff twice more to attend sporting fixtures, both held at the brilliant and atmospheric Millennium Stadium, built to replace the Arms Park as the home of Welsh Rugby. In March 2007, Mike was home from Exeter University for a few days, and I had managed to get two tickets for the 'Welsh' game from our school allocation. It proved to be a good day out, despite the fact England lost 27-18. In truth, I can hardly remember the game, but this wasn't as a result of a fading memory. It was mainly because I spent most of the match running back and forth to the toilets, courtesy of the amount of Guinness we had consumed before the game kicked off. For those of you unfamiliar with the ground, the Millennium is right in the heart of the city and only a couple of minutes' walk from the railway station. As Mike and I got off the train from Euston, pretty much directly across the road was the 'Great Western' pub where Katherine, James, and I had enjoyed a beer before the Watford play-off final game on an earlier visit to the Welsh capital.

It was packed with loads of rugby types, all in good humour and enjoying a good drink before the match. Mike spotted a couple leaving from a table near one of the screens which was showing one of the early matches. Scotland were playing and, as is the way of these things, I strained to see the score, hoping they might be losing. Mike instructed me to grab the table while he headed to join the scrum-like queue at the bar. He seemed to be gone forever, so when I saw him weave into sight carrying a tray full of Guinness, I assumed he'd bumped into some friends. When he sat down, I counted ten pints on his tray and enquired who he'd met. 'No-one,' he said. 'They're ours. Have you seen the queue?'

By the time we left, I was probably feeling as beat-up and groggy as the Scots who had been smashed in Paris. We needed food, and it wasn't hard to find an outlet as we walked to the ground. I do remember Mike steering me across fairly busy roads and telling me off as I made various hand gestures at exasperated drivers. The food helped, and we had a laugh with the girls who served us, Mike embarrassingly apologising for the state he had got his father into.

And so to the ground, and what a fantastic stadium – and one with fortunately many well situated loos. I do remember hearing the Leeds score at some point in the afternoon (we drew 1-1 with Southend on our way to relegation to League 1), and for some reason a brilliant break by our scrum half Ellis to link up with Jason Robinson to score one of our two tries. My abiding memory, though, was of the atmosphere. With the roof closed and the Welsh hordes singing on their team, the stadium felt more like a football ground than a venue for rugby. So, despite the result (it never hurts like Leeds losing), we had a great day out and it was good to spend time with Mike and catch up on his news.

It wasn't quite the same as my only other visit to the Millennium, a year or so earlier, in May 2006. On that occasion I was accompanied, as mentioned, by Katherine and James. This time it was serious: the Championship play-off final, with Leeds up against Aidy Boothroyd's Watford to see who would be playing in the Premiership the next season. It had seemed a long time since we had been relegated in 2003/4, when the club imploded following Peter Ridsdale's disastrous financial mismanagement as he desperately fought to keep the club in the Champions League places. I really don't want to dwell on this painful moment, except now with a return to the Premiership a mere 90 minutes away, it was good to be heading to Cardiff with Katherine. She had been with me for that last terrible home game when we had drawn with Charlton, and Alan Smith, the fans' hero, was mobbed at the end of the match as we said our farewells to the top tier. We knew we were saying goodbye to Alan as well. We understood that, but we didn't realise where he was going, which was a good job for him, too, as the emotional mob that surrounded him and cheered him from the field might just have turned into one of the lynching variety! Alan was

10

destined to sign for Manchester United, our greatest rivals, and for as long as I live I won't understand why he made this move.

I loved Alan, the way he wore his heart on his sleeve, and his sheer bloody mindedness. I never thought he was a natural goal scorer, but his shock of blond hair and his battling nature marked him out as a true Leeds legend, born and bred. I am sure there would have been a queue of big clubs hoping to get Alan signed up, and most would surely have been a better fit for him than Man U. I don't know him or anyone that does, but I would be surprised if he hadn't found time to regret his decision in later years, especially as – along with the equally unpopular Harry Kewell and the Frenchman, Eric Cantona – he has been left out of fans' celebrations of great players of the past, and wasn't included by the club when they asked fans to vote on the 'Bremner X1' for the greatest players of the past. It was a sad end for Alan, and in some respects unfair, because players like Joe Jordan, Gordon McQueen, and Arthur Graham made the same journey, yet have been welcomed back.

I guess the love affair with Alan was just too great because he was, as they say, 'One of our own'! Sadly for Alan, the move didn't work out so well, and he struggled to hold down a regular starting place before his career in the top flight was effectively ended when his leg and ankle were seriously damaged blocking a John Arne Riise free kick in a game at Anfield.

It has to be said, the movement between Manchester and Leeds was not just one-way. And while many would say that Cantona was the greatest of these, I would argue that he was no better and had no greater effect on the team he joined than Johnny Giles and, later, Gordon Strachan. Both of them left Manchester and both went on to inspire Leeds to become champions of England, and in so doing finish ahead of their former employers.

Now we were heading to Cardiff and driving round the M25 to pick up the M4 to the Welsh capital. We were living in Berkhamsted at the time, where I was the Head of the prep school. James, aged 14, was my regular football companion and travelling partner, and – at least when we won – was really good company. When we lost, he was pretty good as well, as neither of us was bothered by the other's complete silence.

Katherine had followed her passion for the club by winning a place to read History at Leeds University, so she was able to meet up with us when we could make the journey up the M1, which we tried to do as often as possible. One of the benefits of her living in the student-dominated area of Headingley was that she had been able to join the queue overnight to guarantee we got tickets for the final. I wasn't worried for her safety, because I knew she would be looked after. In fact, as we waited for the kick-off in the Millennium, we met the group of lads who had 'protected' her in the queue. Had she failed, I knew we would have got tickets in the Watford end, as I worked with people who often went to Vicarage Road. As it turned out, there looked to be hundreds of empty seats at their end of the ground that day, which was a shame when so many Leeds fans were left without tickets.

Watford started as favourites, and had beaten Crystal Palace in their semi-final. We had overcome Preston, drawing 1-1 at Elland Rd, before goals by Hulse and Richardson in front of an ecstatic travelling support took us through to the final. Incidentally, that home game against Preston showed how much the family cared about the club and what an effort they made to support them. The match was played on a Friday evening and Katherine, already in Leeds, was hopefully going to meet up with James and me before kick-off.

We had to travel up the M1, which is a nightmare most evenings, but especially on Fridays. I usually left my office about 6pm, when the last children had all been picked up following after-school clubs. Obviously, this would have left us with no chance of making the game, so I told my deputy I had to be on my way for 4pm. James was not happy, as he had wanted to set off at lunchtime. 'For God's sake, Dad,' he told me, 'you're the chuffin' boss, just leave!' Meanwhile, Mike down in Exeter rang through at lunchtime to say he had got a ticket and was grabbing a lift with a fellow student who was heading to Leeds that weekend for a wedding. We had a race along the motorways – him heading up from the West Country; James and I battling along the M1. The boys kept in touch by mobile, laughing and joking with each other as we got nearer to Leeds.

We made it… but only just. We were in the East Stand – or Lowfields, as I still think of it. As the players came out, I turned and saw Katherine a couple of rows behind us and then, amazingly, there was Mike almost in the roof, waving and shouting. I was so proud of my kids that night.

CHAPTER 2

WORRYING TIMES

So now we were heading over the Severn Bridge, flags covering the rear window, and scarves bashing the roof of the car as they swirled in the wind. I loved being on the road with Leeds, knowing that from all over the country our fellow fans would be travelling to the same destination. It didn't matter which division, what the ticket allocation, we would be there, and always sold out. It was such a buzz to follow this club, as I had done all my life, and there was something special about arriving at a venue, any venue, and knowing that we would out-sing and chant the opposition fans.

No Leeds fan will ever forget, for instance, the fantastic day we sang 'We can see you sneaking out' to the hordes of supposed Manchester United fans as they left Old Trafford early. It was the day, as a League 1 club, when Jermaine Beckford scored the second most important goal of his career as we 'knocked the scum out of the FA Cup', as the song goes. (Beckford's most important goal was to come a few years later when his strike against Bristol Rovers sealed our return to the Championship and ensured the striker's immortality among Leeds fans.)

As we neared Cardiff, the motorway messages were giving details of out of town parking and park and ride, separating the Leeds fans from the Watford supporters. We ended up travelling beyond the city, which led to huge traffic problems after the match as we queued and queued just to get to the M4, and then queued again around the city. Once parked, we got a bus into the city and ended up in the 'Great Western', which was a designated Leeds pub. It was rammed, and not just with our fans, but also those of Munster who had won some rugby cup the day before. We all got on great together, especially with those

Munstermen who could still stand! Leeds have a huge Irish fan base, and I guess most of them were in that pub. I couldn't have much to drink, knowing I had to drive back, so we had a couple of beers and then headed up to the ground.

To be honest, the traditionalist in me was disappointed that the game wasn't at Wembley, which was being redeveloped. I had watched a few cup finals from the Millennium, but it didn't feel special, even with the fantastic 'Gerrard final'. But as we passed through the turnstiles and headed into the ground, I have to say the stadium was hugely impressive. There were loads of bars and eateries, and lots of space on the concourse. We had a great view slightly to the right of goal and roughly halfway up the stand. We took some pictures – one of Katherine and James remains a favourite, and still hangs in the family kitchen. As the ground filled, so did the atmosphere. The roof was closed, and with the floodlights on, the pitch looked vividly green, almost as if it was synthetic. As we waited for the entry of the players, the ground literally bounced to the sound of 'I predict a riot' by the Leeds group Kaiser Chiefs, named after the South African club that Lucas Radebe, another all-time Leeds legend, had played for.

A huge Leeds following then screamed out a fantastic rendition of our song, 'Marching on together' and then... and then nothing. Watford had sprinted out of the tunnel as if they meant business, and sadly we never caught up with them. We huffed and puffed, but from the minute De Merit scored from a first half corner, there was only going to be one winner. In the end, Watford won the game 3-0 – a massive disappointment, but sadly a feeling we had experienced too often over the years.

We left the Watford fans to their celebrations and headed to the buses and car parks for the painful, silent drive home. As we queued, a car full of Watford 'scallies' tried to overtake the cars in front of us, and one of them hung out of the window screaming abuse at some Leeds fans. In my experience, it is so often smaller clubs that travel with hooligan fans, and I had experienced the same taunting at Vicarage Rd a few years later. In this case, the lad hanging out of the car got lucky, as a police motorbike rider came along just as the Leeds lads were getting out of their car to 'talk some sense' into the youngster. We took a lot of stick from Watford fans as we headed back to Berkhamsted, which is a small town about 15 miles from Watford, and James was dreading going into school on the Monday morning. His problem, and mine, is that so many people say they follow a football team but they don't really get it. They're like Roy Keane's prawn sandwich brigade, so it doesn't really matter to them if their team loses. But proper fans, those who follow their team through thick and thin, know just how we were feeling.

I don't know quite how James's Monday was, but as I entered school, I passed an always smiling Richard, our excellent caretaker and a big QPR fan, who put his head down and muttered good morning. He knew how I was feeling. I was feeling a lot worse a few minutes later when I opened up my office to find the whole room festooned in Watford scarves and colours. There was no-one around, so I pulled a few of them down, grabbed my notes, and headed to the Hall to take assembly. One of my deputies – a female with no interest in football – met me by the door and gave me some notes, and then I went into the room. I guess there would have been around 300 children and God knows how many staff in that hall, and a very large percentage of them were wearing Watford colours! Bastards. I behaved impeccably, smiled through clenched teeth, and got on with an assembly about the importance of being a good loser. Naturally. The kids loved taunting me that day and I took it all on the chin, but later got my own back by banning the wearing of Man U shirts every time we had a 'no uniform' charity day!

Three visits to Cardiff, three losses, and another visit due – probably, the way things are looking, the most important of all. We are due to play Cardiff City on 15th March, and initially my plans were to miss this game as we would have been in Rome for the rugby international. I didn't mind agreeing to this little trip as I knew there were bigger fish to fry before the end of the season. Also, Cardiff are one of those teams that we just don't like, nor they us, especially since they attacked us – revved up by Sam Hamman, their chairman – as they knocked us out of the cup in 2002.

The Coronavirus and the devastating outbreak in Northern Italy put paid to our Italian holiday, so it seemed logical to plan to go down to the Welsh capital after all. However, it was becoming apparent that this virus was coming to our shores, and just as in China and Italy, it was going to wreak havoc and tragically lead to many deaths. When we had played our game against Huddersfield on Saturday, 7th March, there was little sign of worry or fear among the fans, as we mixed in pubs and cheered loudly as an out-of-form Bristol City hung on to draw against Fulham in the lunchtime kick-off. The players did dispense with the traditional handshake before the game, as indeed would be the case in every match being played that weekend. But I noticed that Liam Cooper shook hands with the referee and the Huddersfield captain before the kick-off, and the Leeds players celebrated both goals exactly as usual. That said, I already knew that Andy would probably call me stupid for even thinking of going down to Cardiff. I decided to enjoy the victory and a Saturday night where I could sink a few beers, tape the Championship highlights from Quest for later viewing, and generally be relaxed company rather than the angry frustrated figure I usually cut when another Saturday was ruined by defeat.

Even though we had been in the top two for much of the season, Leeds had actually gone from 30th November – when we beat Middlesbrough 4-0 – to 15th February, when we defeated Bristol City 1-0, without a home win on a Saturday afternoon. That's an awful lot of pretty moody, quiet, and fairly 'dry' Saturday nights! Events moved pretty quickly from this point on, in relation to the ever-deepening Coronavirus crisis and family reactions to it. Two days after the victory over Huddersfield on 9th March, Italian Prime Minister Giuseppe Conte imposed a national lockdown on his country, which was being ravaged by the virus.

Despite this, on Thursday, 12th March, at one of his daily news briefings, Boris Johnson – flanked by his senior medical advisers Professor Chris Whitty and Sir Patrick Vallance – confirmed that UK schools would remain open and there would still be no ban on large gatherings. At that time, I think I wasn't alone in our country in not quite understanding the threat of what was about to happen. And certainly, feeling quite fit and well, and with the Prime Minister's support, I mentally made my plans to head to Cardiff. I discussed it with Andy, who was herself preparing to spend a week in York supply teaching, so she didn't get it either. But our children did, and they were about to let us know. As I went to bed on Thursday, 12th March, I was planning the best way to sort the Cardiff game. It was a long journey, and I had earlier booked a seat on one of the official club coaches that would be heading to Wales. The Fourways coach was due to leave Elland Rd at around 7am, as this was a lunchtime kick-off. I didn't really like coach travel, as it obviously limited your freedom to move at your own pace, but it was usually cheaper and you could read, tune into the radio, and enjoy a bit of a chat with some of the other fans heading to the game.

As you will see later, this season I'd only travelled by coach to Luton, Preston, and Birmingham – grounds that could be difficult to park near, and slow to get away from. The coaches usually got pretty close to the ground, and often once they were all ready to go, got a police escort away from the ground which put them ahead of most of the queuing traffic. I was still wondering whether to forget my coach ticket and get to Cardiff early by car, when Andy told me of a text she had received from Katherine. Our family WhatsApp messages were usually warm and light-hearted, often accompanied by family video clips or some funny link from YouTube… but not this one. Basically, Kath put paid to my Cardiff trip by asking Andy to stop me going, because of the risk of me catching the virus. She didn't want me to get ill and was worried about me.

This was typical of Katherine to have such worries about our welfare, and she had done it before when, as a teenager, she badgered me to stop smoking. When I had asked her what the problem was, she'd said simply, 'I don't want you to die.' At a stroke, her words achieved what all my half-hearted promises to myself about 'stopping next week', drifting from cigarettes to cigars, which I ended up smoking just as frequently, and what I found the hopelessly ineffective nicotine patches, had all failed to do.

Now I knew I just couldn't go to Wales. I would feel too guilty. And anyway, the game was on telly, and Kath often scanned the crowd to find me and send pictures to the WhatsApp group, so I would be rumbled! And it wasn't just me, and it wasn't just Kath. Later that week, Mike had phoned to tell Andy that he didn't think doing the supply teaching was a great idea, and that she should really think very hard about going into the school. It seemed that our children were taking this unfolding tragedy a lot more seriously than their parents. And they were right. On Friday, 13th March, just a few hours after the Prime Minister had said that large gatherings could continue, the Premiership and EFL suspended all football fixtures in England... and Wales. It wasn't just Cardiff that was off now; everything was.

As if to emphasise the impending disaster, on Saturday, 14th March, the Prime Minister of Spain Pedro Sanchez joined with the Italians in announcing a total lockdown in his country. On the same day, Karren Brady, the deputy CEO of West Ham Utd, used her column in the *Sun* newspaper to suggest that the only fair and moral thing to do right now was to 'void' the football season. I was amazed at her insensitivity, and she was roundly criticised for the article. It was cheap and thoughtless journalism and brought more shame, if that were possible, on a once proud but now struggling club. Sadly, no-one was in the slightest bit surprised. West Ham were in trouble on and off the pitch, and their loyal fan base had consistently railed at the work of Brady and the club's owners, David Sullivan and David Gold. No surprise then, with West Ham facing possible relegation, that Brady took the first opportunity possible to try and save her club from the financial disaster that eventuality would bring.

Not many were fooled by the timing, with the excellent Henry Winter writing later in the *Times* of Brady's 'venal self interest'. I just seriously hope when all this is over and we are back to normal, that West Ham and that awful woman get the relegation their selfish behaviour deserves. Suddenly the Coronavirus was beginning to affect us all, and not just those poor souls who had contracted the disease. James and his friends, frustrated at not being able to go to Rome, had rescheduled their trip and had headed instead to Krakow for a long weekend. As it turns out, it was probably not their best move. Now they were struggling to get a flight back to the UK, as their original carrier Wizz Air had informed them that their scheduled return flight was cancelled. It was impossible for them to speak to any airline, as we ourselves found out, so they booked a flight with Ryanair, scheduled to return to Stansted on Wednesday, 18th March – the night we should have been playing Fulham at Elland Rd. They asked us to try and confirm that this flight would indeed take place, and with the impossibility of trying to get someone to speak to, we decided to drive to Leeds Bradford Airport to see if we could talk to someone from Ryanair there.

We knew the airport well and had often used it to fly to Girona and Dublin, so I figured the journey would probably take an hour each way and I was hopeful to get back to watch Castleford play St Helen's in the Super League later in the afternoon. The people at the airport were incredibly helpful and not just the Ryanair staff, but those from Jet 2 as well. With so many flights cancelled, they had more time on their hands. But for all their efforts, even with direct numbers to access, no-one could let us know if the Wednesday flight would actually happen. We fudged our answer to James, telling him they 'thought' it would, but that it would be sensible for them to follow their plan to go to the British Embassy on the Monday morning. We headed home frustrated that we couldn't do more to help him, and I settled down to watch Cas. beat Saints 28-14 in front of a crowd of over seven thousand at the awfully named 'Mend a hose Jungle'! The healthy attendance probably reflected the lack of concern that still existed in our country about the dangers of the virus, but the next day the super league was suspended.

The same day, Monday, 16th March, James and his friends headed to the Embassy, only to find – rather unhelpfully, given the numbers of stranded Brits in Krakow – that it was shut! The message advising Britons to head to Warsaw was not particularly welcomed or helpful. Fortunately, they decided to head to the airport, where amazingly and without any prior knowledge, they found a Ryanair flight due to return to Stansted that morning. They were allowed to change their tickets from the Wednesday flight without charge, and so it was with much relief that I received the text from James that confirmed they were on the plane and that it was airborne. As it turns out, they had been very lucky. Later that week, with all flights cancelled, there were 50 kilometre queues of traffic forming at the Polish borders. With every day now bringing news of more and more deaths throughout Europe, and particularly in Italy and Spain, the pressure from a revved-up media grew on the government to take more punitive actions. At that stage, I think a lot of people agreed with the government's handling of the unfolding nightmare and the explanations of the key medical advisers as to how their strategy would unfold and support us. There seemed little doubt, however, that the country would have to brace itself for an appallingly high death rate, perhaps as high as twenty thousand or more.

The clear emphasis was on protecting the seventy-plus age group and those with underlying health issues. We all knew now the importance of regular and lengthy hand-washing, and some people took to wearing masks. As we listened to the press briefings, it was clear the government were planning to create as many hospital beds as possible and planning for an epidemic that would strike down thousands. Much of the press coverage was intelligent and supportive, rightly quizzing the Prime Minister and his advisers, and trying to help us as a country understand the kind of problems we were due to face. As always, the BBC tried to create rather than report the news, and their coverage thus far had been, in my opinion, poor and hugely negative. Laura Kunsberg and her 'oppo' Beth Rigby on Sky News seemed to relish the opportunity to report aggressively, desperately trying to find someone to blame for something, anything, as long as they could have their scapegoat. It was almost as if they were in competition with each other to see which of them could be the rudest, stirring the pot like the witches in the opening scene of *Macbeth:* 'Fair is foul and foul is fair.'

They had been the same during the Brexit crisis, always seeking to undermine and pit one view against another. They and many of their colleagues seemed to revel in the chaos enveloping the country, and I often wondered if only a total collapse would satisfy them. I'm certain that on 12th December, when election night came and Boris Johnson was elected with a majority of 80 seats and a Labour Party, led by the despairing Jeremy Corbyn, suffered their worst electoral defeat since 1935, the pair of them must have been devastated. The country had voted decisively and I think, despite the efforts of the liberal left media – particularly, as mentioned, the BBC – it was a result that could easily have been predicted if only the media and the Labour leadership had been more in touch with the feelings of the people. That together they contrived to send Boris Johnson back to Westminster with such a healthy majority is something that history should judge them harshly for.

Now, as we prepared to fight this terrible virus, we needed certain elements of the media to behave more responsibly, and focus on reporting the facts openly and honestly and be less interested in causing division and furthering their own views and opinions. It seemed to me that we also needed a more intelligent opposition, and one which could challenge the government for the good of the country, rather than to promote some outdated political ideology. It was time for our parliament to come together for the good of the people it served.

On Wednesday, 18th March, Boris Johnson announced that schools in England would close at the weekend. It was a decision he had been under pressure to make, but I could see good reason for the closure of schools being delayed, particularly as children were seen as low risk in terms of the viral illness and parents would have problems finding childcare. Grandparents, the obvious people to turn to for support, were likely to be at greater risk of serious illness than parents or teachers. And children were surely safer at school than being left to walk the streets or survive at home on their own.

Now the decision was made, and as the pandemic took hold it was swiftly followed on Friday, 20th March, by the request to avoid restaurants, theatres, and pubs. And finally, on Monday, 23rd March, the Prime Minister announced a total lockdown of the country. We were all urged to stay at home, except for key workers such as doctors and nurses or for essential travel to get food or medicine. Before the end of the month, we would experience food frenzy in supermarkets as people sought to panic buy such items as toilet rolls and cleaning agents, while there was a rush on tinned stuffs and bread and milk. And with every day that passed, the numbers of the infected and, sadly, the dead grew ever more rapidly. And then it was confirmed that Johnson himself was a victim of the virus and was self isolating.

As I write, I don't know what the future holds, how many families will suffer grievous loss, when this virus will leave us, and when the lockdown will finish. No-one does, and all the talk about sport and when it will resume seems to become more and more unimportant as the pandemic rages. Except, hopefully one day soon things will return to relative normality and we will once again rejoice in the freedom to follow our hobbies and pursuits, and just maybe, despite the efforts of La Brady, the season will be completed and Leeds will return to the Premiership. So, with nothing left to report as of 27th March and my life in lockdown, I can only return to August and go 'back to the future' and the start of this upside-down diary, and hope that I will be able to bring the season to a proper chronological and successful conclusion when this devastating pandemic has passed over us.

CHAPTER 3

THE SEASON BEGINS

Bristol City…1; Leeds United…3
Sunday, 4th August

Girona Airport I am sitting in the cafe next to the entrance to Gate One, and watching the queue for the flight to Leeds grow. People are arriving stressed, realising that the gate was scheduled to close at 6.10am. They needn't have worried; the border police haven't manned their passport desk and the Ryanair check-in team are nowhere to be seen. I would normally have been stressing with them, trying to be at the front of the queue. Not because of any wish to be first on the plane but simply to make sure my bag could be in the overhead locker relatively close to my seat. I fly regularly, and those that know Ryanair also know the chaos of boarding; there is nothing positive about cheap flight travel – no style, no luxury, and little comfort. What is generally true, though, is that you can get cheap seats and, in my experience, the flights are usually pretty much on time. I am happy to accept all this providing some officious stewardess does not make me move my bag from one end of the plane to the other. Hence my need to queue!

Today, though, I am travelling light. No bags, no wife (she has just dropped me off), and no reason to stress at the length of the queue. I have long since stopped playing 'try to spot the terrorist', and as I have a seat randomly chosen, I don't know who I will be sitting next to. I pray that it isn't someone who is on the rather large size or, even worse, someone who simply smells. Ryanair have lots of conditions, and for me one or two extra wouldn't go amiss, like you shouldn't pay for one seat and then fill two, and you should be clean!

To be fair, my wife Andrea would normally stop me talking in this way, and it is one of the reasons we never sit next to each other on short haul flights. Andy likes to enjoy the experience, take her time and stroll through the airport, checking out perfumes, sunglasses, etc, and generally spinning out the time until boarding. I am the total opposite – keen to be at the front of the queue, as previously mentioned, and watching for all those 'queue jumpers' who join the priority queue when they absolutely know they haven't paid for it. These people are also the type who board at the front of the plane when their seat is at the back and cause total carnage as they bash their way from front to back. I have studied this behaviour long enough to be able to pick them out fairly easily, but I would get into trouble for describing them here. Suffice to say that it works for both of us if we don't sit together.

The plane is due to take off in 20 minutes and the check-in team arrive flashing their airport passes at the border police guys who have been lazily checking passports for some ten minutes. A family arrives with two children – a toddler in a pushchair and a little boy, probably about five years old. They are carrying loads of stuff and desperately searching for passports and check in papers. It's not their panic that takes my attention, but rather that the boy is wearing an Aston Villa shirt. Suddenly they realise they are in the wrong queue; suddenly I realise that the pain hasn't left me yet.

The pain of seeing my team Leeds United, who I have supported for nearly 60 years, throw away a two-goal lead on a balmy night in May, and thus lose all chance of promotion back to the top flight of English football. I can still remember the incredible sight of a full, all-white Elland Rd and the huge noise that followed Stuart Dallas's goal, which put us effectively two up following our 1-0 win at Derby the previous Saturday. I remember looking at my watch and thinking, *Just a few minutes to half-time, and if we go in two up there is no chance Derby can beat us. They have offered nothing so far in nearly a game-and-a-half.* And then. And then… we gift them a goal. There is no danger, a loose ball heading to our area which should be easy to deal with, but our keeper Kiko Casilla gets it completely wrong and the ball falls to Marriott, who joyfully steers it into the empty net. From nothing, from no creative play of their own, they are back in the game. The half-time whistle blows, and I look at James, our youngest, who has travelled up from London to be here. And we both know what is going to happen. We have been here before; it's enshrined in our song 'and we've had our ups and downs'.

The second half brings us the downs – goals from Mount, Wilson, and Marriott again, send Derby to a play-off final, despite a fine, desperate effort from Dallas. We lose 3-4 on aggregate. I am completely gutted. James and I travel home in silence, gone is the lively chat and expectancy of the outward journey, the lunchtime BBQ a distant memory. Poor Andy. She is waiting for us, bright as ever, but she already knows that nothing she can do will change this mood. I can't watch the highlights; I can't buy a paper; I'm not interested in football – not the end-of-season play-offs (I'm no Villa fan, but I secretly hope they stuff Derby for their over-long and ridiculous celebrations at the end of the game. And they do!), nor the European finals and international fixtures. I have always been the same, ever since the 1967 cup semi-final against Chelsea, when Peter Lorimer's stunning equalising free kick was unaccountably ruled out by referee Ken Burns. It was the first of sadly too many inexplicable and horrific refereeing decisions that cruelly robbed such a wonderful football team of so many trophies, including the European Cup in 1975.

The only cure is time! Day by day, through the long summer, the aching will begin to ease. Sadly, I know this from painful experience; the last time being the League One semi-final play-off defeat by Millwall. It's just such an awful way to end a season. The excitement and hope of reaching the Premiership, by way of Wembley, suddenly dashed away and then just nothing... nothing until the new season in May. Well actually, there is the release of the new fixture lists in June. The Premiership first. Norwich go to Anfield, Sheffield United to Bournemouth, and Villa visit Spurs. This is just too much to deal with; my recovery is still in its infancy, still too raw. It's not just devoted Leeds fans who think we should have been promoted, but so many experienced football pundits also agree. It should have been us out-singing the 'Scousers' at Anfield, sunning ourselves in Bournemouth, or reminding the Spurs fans just what the Premiership has been missing, as we serenade them at White Hart Lane, or whatever their ground is called now. The truth is we blew it: Wigan at home; Brentford away; Derby in the play-offs. The Premiership was in our grasp and we threw it away.

The Championship fixtures are released the week after the Premiership, and at last the pain begins to ease. We can pencil in plans for fixtures at Christmas and Easter and, if not automatic promotion, the dreaded play-offs in early May. But first there is Bristol City, the opening game of the season – a tough one, if they perform as they did last season, just missing out on the play-offs. And a long trip for starters. Not helped, of course, by Sky moving the match to a Sunday afternoon kick-off. Sky, who desperately need teams like Leeds in the Championship to swell their viewing figures, yet reward the travelling fans by arranging fixtures at ridiculous times like Sunday afternoon at 4.30!

And that is why I am here, watching the queue at Girona Airport. I need to be there when the boys run out at Ashton Gate; need to exorcise the pain of defeat; need to embrace a reincarnation and share the emotion with the rest of the fans, and indeed the players and management. There is unfinished business and everyone knows it. I like to believe it is why our manager, Marcelo Bielsa, remained at the club, and why Kalvin Phillips – a Leeds boy and our best player – is still with us despite supposed interest from Premiership clubs. If they stay and we are promoted, they will live in the history of the club forever. The boy in the Villa shirt has long gone, his family eventually finding the gate for the Birmingham flight. I join the end of our queue which, as always, is held up on steps between the departure lounge and the plane. Eventually, I get on the plane and experience a sense of relief to see I am sitting between two normal-sized women who don't appear to be terrorists or even to smell. They both have earphones on, so I don't even have to make polite conversation!

It's a fairly uneventful flight. My neighbours sleep most of the way and I try to do so, too, but it's difficult in the centre seat, and every time my head flops forward, I wake myself up. I'm re-reading *About a Boy* by

Nick Hornby, who famously wrote *Fever Pitch* – the first football book to become accepted by the liberal elite. I've been a couple of times to the Emirates and can see why Hornby would feel so at home, given the library-like atmosphere that pervades there. Maybe I am getting older, but the book seems very dated and twee, and I drift off to sleep again.

With a plane full of people, many of whom have had little or no sleep, why on earth would the cabin crew ensure that every few minutes or so one of them makes a tannoy announcement? Extra drinks, perfumes, scratch cards, etc. Shut up, for fuck's sake! The approach to Leeds is smooth, and we are on time; with the hour back, it is just after eight o'clock. With no bags to collect, I should be on my way fairly quickly – that is, if the buses are waiting. Leeds is one of those airports that buses people from the plane to the terminal, even if you are actually only 50 metres from the building. Andy and I once sat on a plane waiting for the buses' arrival for longer than the actual flight from Dublin took us to reach Leeds!

Today, I am in luck. The buses are there waiting, and it's not long before we are passing through passport control – something where Leeds scores highly, given that they use humans rather than technology to check the validity of the passport. I am in a good mood and happily thump the smiley face to give feedback on 'what my experience was like today'. Now to find the Tiger 757 bus service that will take me to the centre of Leeds, where I can get my connection to Pontefract and on to my home village of Womersley. I haven't been on a service bus for a long time, but with all day to get home and a couple of papers to read, the journey of just over 50 minutes passes quickly and only costs me £3.80! Once in Leeds, I find myself amazed at just how much bus stations have changed. Numbered gates and electronic timetables make it very easy to find your way around, and there are a good selection of eateries and food shops, including Greggs, which makes my favourite tuna crunch sandwich.

The bus, when it comes, is heading to Chequerfield but stops in Pontefract enroute. It's not the most comfortable, but again the journey passes quickly until the route decides to take us through the 'Junction

32' shopping centre. Eventually free of the shops, the bus enters the town, going past the racetrack and the new housing estate built on the wasteland that was once the Prince of Wales Colliery. I see the sign for Pontefract Colliery AFC on the left, and my mind takes me back to the day I played and scored in a charity match against the ex-Leeds United players as they sought to raise money for St. James's Hospital. I was headteacher of the local St. Joseph's RC primary school at the time, and some contact at the school managed to get the Leeds team over to Pontefract to play the game, in return for our support of their charity. Our team was a mixture of staff and parents, and as I remember we enjoyed a couple of practice sessions which proved to be good value in getting the dads more involved in the life of the school.

We could have trained for a year, but we still wouldn't have got close to winning the match! I can't remember all of the Ex-Leeds players who turned out that day, but certainly Peter Lorimer and Eddie Gray started, and I remember Byron Stevenson and Arthur Graham were about, too, while the legendary John Charles was there supporting from the touchline. Once, on our way into Elland Road, my eldest son Michael dropped the change he had been given by a programme seller. A very tall man stooped over, collected the money and, as he gave it back to Mike, told him to make sure he looked after the pennies and they would grow into pounds. It was Charles, the gentle giant, recently voted the greatest overseas player the Italian giants Juventus had ever signed. Mike never forgot his advice becoming a City banker following University.

In the charity match, we chased shadows for a while as Leeds hardly broke a sweat, keeping the ball and passing it between them. They had already scored two or three when, in a rare attack, the ball cannoned off their goalkeeper as he cleared a shot at the edge of his area. I was running right towards the ball and realised the keeper, one of his defenders, and one of our forwards, were all lying in a heap just inside the box. I can still see it now, and I knew all I had to do was chip the ball up and over and into the empty net. I hit it perfectly from about 15 yards and watched joyously as it hit the back of the empty net. I'd scored against my boyhood heroes! There was quite a sizeable crowd of parents, staff, children, and friends watching the match, and given the pasting we were taking, my goal was greeted with quite a cheer. As headteacher, my street cred had never been so high, so it was a shame that later that week I would leave St Jo's – my first headship and a brilliant school – to take up a new appointment. Someone made a video of the match, and I still have it!

Finally back in Pontefract, I busied myself while waiting for the last bus of my journey from the airport. I got some money and went into the indoor market to buy a couple of small pork pies for lunch – in my opinion, the best I ever tasted. I was going to waste a little time checking out the old CDs in the music shop opposite the station but was disappointed to see it had shut. The guy who ran it was brilliant and always seemed to be able to find any 'record' you were searching for. The last CDs I bought there were Slade's Greatest (aren't they due a revival?), and Badfinger's *If You Want It Here It Is*. Only, sadly, it no longer was.

I get home just after midday. A journey, with some shopping stops, of just over three-and-a-half hours, it had cost me about £12 instead of the £45 pounds a taxi would charge. I would spend the savings on a pie and chips in Bristol and wash it down with a pint of lager. Having been in Spain for four or five weeks, it was great to enjoy some typical English fayre. The house is great – no problems, and it is lovely to feel carpet under my feet again, rather than the tiles on the floor in Spain. We bought a ground floor apartment in Calella de Palafrugell for a song in 1997, and it was the best investment we've made – all the family love it. In a small community of just 12 and with stunning sea views, it has paid us back over and over again in terms of the money we would have spent on family holidays, trying to find a coastline as beautiful as the one that runs from Calella to Begur.

I would head back there on Monday, after my trip to Bristol. But I simply couldn't miss the chance of seeing my team again and getting rid of all the angst of that awful evening in May. I tried to sleep during the afternoon and dozed my way through bits of cricket and lots of Sky Sports News. The Championship starts tonight with a live TV game between Notts Forest and WBA – both of them will be challengers for the play-off spots, I reckon, though possibly more likely Albion. They were strong last season, and although they've lost Gayle and Rodrigues, they've recruited well and brought in Slavic Bilic as their manager. I enjoy a deep bath, ring Andy in Spain, join in with some of the family banter on WhatsApp, and make some beans and cheese on toast before settling down to watch the match. It's a good game, and though Forest take an early lead, Albion fight back to win 2-1, though their equaliser looked a bit of a mis-hit cross. I crawl off to bed at the end of the match and sleep deeply, not even waking for a midnight visit to the loo – unusual for a man of my age!

Saturday is a truly lazy day. I enjoy a cup of tea in bed and then make some toast for breakfast. I FaceTime my brother Andrew down in Sussex and catch up with his news. I hadn't seen him since 15 June, when the whole family came together at The Mermaid Inn in Rye to celebrate his sixtieth birthday. It was a great celebration – obviously particularly for Andrew, surrounded by all his family and especially his boys, Ben and Josh. It had been a desperately difficult time for them since the tragically early passing of Tricia, my sister-in-law, who died of cancer in France a little over a year ago.

Today, we talk about holidays. He's just returned from a week in Portugal with an old friend, Paul Ryan, and obviously given this first weekend of the season, we talk about our chances and likely team news. Leeds have been quite busy in the transfer window, and brought in some useful looking players, particularly signing Helder Costa from Wolves and, resigning on loan, Jack Harrison from Manchester City. He is a player we had last year and who, unlike the majority of the team, had been playing better and better towards the end of last season. We've also signed on loan a young centre half Ben White, from Brighton, but no-one seems to know much about him at this stage. I must admit to being slightly worried about this. Brighton struggled to avoid relegation last season, just missing the drop, and sacking their long-serving manager Chris Hughton – someone I have always admired for his honesty and dignity, particularly when commenting on matches his teams have been involved with. Brighton certainly didn't look solid at the back, so any defender they are sending out on loan might not be at the level we need.

We'd sold our centre back Pontus Janssen to Brentford. I am a Leeds fan, and I have my opinions based on what I have seen at the matches and heard in discussion with friends and family. I don't have any contacts within the club, and am not privy to insider information, so all I can say about this sale is that I am not completely surprised. Janssen has been a supporters' favourite for a couple of years and seemed to enjoy the relationship with the fans and hearing his 'Pontus Janssen's magic' song. He's been a strong player for us and has in previous times been linked with sides in the lower reaches of the Premiership. He does have his faults, though, and often loses the ball in the wrong places when trying to dribble out of defence. He also seems to have a low pain threshold, as on quite a few occasions he has gone to the ground in apparent agony before recovering to play a full part in the game.

Towards the end of last season, in a bad-tempered game with Aston Villa, Leeds gained some notoriety by playing on while a Villa player lay on the ground injured. The move finished with Mateus Klich scoring a fine goal before the game erupted, with Villa players responding manically to the situation. I was there that afternoon and felt for Klich. He was running towards the vociferous Kop end of the ground, and when Leeds looked as if they were going to put the ball out of play, the crowd urged them to play on. This was in part because of the frustration of seeing Villa players falling over and wasting time at every opportunity. It is a problem every football fan is aware of, and part of the 'professional cheating' that all teams employ. Once the referee had restored some kind of calm (a Villa player was sent off for 'striking' Patrick Bamford, who was later banned for conning the ref), our manager Bielsa took control of the situation and ordered his team to let Villa equalise direct from the kick-off. While many in the ground, including me, felt Villa had got what they deserved, the Leeds players followed their manager's instructions, as they must do. Except for Janssen, who made an ungainly attempt to stop the attack before Adomah eventually rolled the ball across the line. Janssen was injured later in the season and missed the first leg of the play-off final at Pride

Park, before being chosen as sub for the second leg. I don't want to revisit that dreadful occasion, save to say Janssen sat on his own in desolation at the end of the game. So, for me it was no surprise in the summer to hear rumours that he might be sold. In the end, though, the fact that he went to Brentford seemed strange, particularly after all the Premiership rumours.

In terms of transfers out, we have also sold Jack Clarke to Spurs for a rumoured £10million and then immediately brought him back on loan. Again, I am a little surprised by this move, though it seems a win-win from our point of view. Clarke burst onto the scene with an assist at Sheffield United and a delicious curling finish in the Christmas fixture at Villa. He also ran the Derby defence ragged in a televised fixture, which brought him rave reviews. Then in an away fixture at 'Boro, he suffered a collapse on the bench after being substituted at half-time. There was clearly a serious problem, and he was treated on the pitch for some time before being taken to hospital for tests and observations. Clarke was out of the team for some time before coming back into the squad towards the end of the season. To me, he never seemed the same, so I do hope that this season he will recover and help fire us to the Premiership. We end our FaceTime, as Andrew has to go and walk his dogs, and I am ready to go online and search out the excellent 'away fans' guide in preparation for my trip to Bristol. I've been a couple of times before and usually park at the Bedminster cricket ground which, unlike the parking at most football grounds, is really quite a pretty venue, especially in the spring and summer months. And it's only a ten-minute walk from the ground.

Incidentally, by far the worst charges for any football club parking I have experienced is the FIFTEEN pounds to park at Brighton. Robbing bastards –and that was a couple of years ago, before their promotion! They do sell fantastic meat pies in the ground, though, and at reasonable prices! I'm looking forward to a lazy afternoon in front of the telly, watching Jeff Stelling and the boys talk us through the first Saturday of the new EFL season. Who would ever have thought in days gone by that such a programme could be so informative and entertaining? I remember the days when BBC Sport reigned supreme, with wonderful commentators such as Bill McLaren, Ken Wolstenholme, and David Coleman, enhancing our enjoyment of rugby, football, and – among other sports for Coleman – athletics. No Leeds fan will ever forget Coleman's classic commentary when we defeated Arsenal to win the 1972 cup final, "Clarke... One Nil!"

The cutting-edge excellence and innovation of BBC Sports heyday has long since past, with the corporation vainly trying to keep apace with the brilliance and invention of Sky Sports and weakly imitating such superb programmes as Stelling 's Soccer Saturday. Today he is back on our screens in top form, leading the team in discussion and debate, and keeping us up to date with goals and events as they take place up and down the country. He has a lightness of touch that means the programme is hugely enjoyable, and has long linked players' names with other parts of society to bring a smile to the viewers' faces, even when saying such things as 'and if you Leeds fans thought it couldn't get any worse... well, look away now!'

Stelling lets us know that Peterborough have taken the lead; the scorer being their new forward Mohammed Eisa. Jeff goes into overdrive, making puns of the striker's name: hasn't taken him long to open his 'account', and that he seems to be to be at 'top rate', and on and on. It's not difficult to see how the opposition – Jason Mohammed, Garth Crooks, and among others, Martin Keown – seem so dull and pedestrian. If Stelling's genius makes the programme work so well, then it can only be matched by which ever Sky producer came up with the idea that viewers would sit and listen to comments about matches they couldn't see! At a stroke bringing the experience of listening to the excellent BBC radio programme, Sports Report, into our living rooms.

With Leeds playing tomorrow, it will be interesting to see just how the Championship results pan out. And actually, from a Leeds' point of view, they look pretty good. Fulham lose at Barnsley, Cardiff at Wigan, and Brentford at home to a Birmingham side I expect to be in trouble this season, having lost their manager Gary Monk and two top players, Atkins and Jota, in the close season.

I've been watching developments from Spain through the long close season, and I expect Fulham, WBA, and Brentford, to be our closest challengers from a football point of view, and think Bristol City, Preston, and Forest, will also be in contention for a top six finish. I think Cardiff and Huddersfield may well struggle following their relegation, and I very much hope that Derby County also struggle – mainly for their ridiculous overlong celebration following the play-off semi-final and Frank Lampard's hysterical reaction to 'Spygate'. On Bank Holiday Monday, the day of their play-off final at Wembley against Villa, James and I had enjoyed breakfast together at a coffee shop in Wandsworth. We had been planning a weekend of sport – going to the Twickenham Sevens on the Sunday and, hopefully, the play-off final on the Monday. But as you know, that was not to be. We suddenly found ourselves sitting next to some Derby fans getting ready to go off to Wembley. We couldn't let them know our pain, so we sat in silence listening to them talk about their support of their club.

One of the group explained to the others how, because he'd attended one game at Derby during the season, he qualified for a Wembley ticket! It made me smile, and I wondered just how many loyal club members at Leeds wouldn't have qualified for a ticket if we'd have made the final.

At last the day dawns, and I am so looking forward to my trip to the West Country. Despite having been to Ashton Gate a few times, including last season when a lone Bamford strike ensured all three points, I have got all the 'away day' info sorted. Sat-nav tells me I'm looking at a journey of just over three hours. Maybe, as it's a Sunday, it might not be too bad. The game kicks off at 4.30 and of course, given such a ridiculous timing, it's obvious it's on Sky. I set the recorder on the television as I always do when Leeds matches are covered (frequently!), so that I can enjoy watching again the key moments of a win. Obviously, I delete these recordings if we lose!

Just before turning off the M1 to pick up the M69 towards Birmingham, there is a service station with a Greggs outlet, so I pull in and get a tuna crunch for lunch and buy one of those very tasty bacon pastry wraps for a late breakfast. I get a *Sunday Times*, hoping that Rod Liddell is on form, be it in his writing on football or his hugely funny and searingly truthful and honest observations about the 'PC' nature of the society we live in at the moment. Although I don't necessarily like them as people (Liddell is a Millwall fan – ugh! Say no more!), the country needs writers like him, Jeremy Clarkson, Camilla Long, and Piers Morgan (wasted on that 'frothy' breakfast television show) to be brave enough to point out the shallowness and dishonesty of those in public office.

I love the way these writers expose the self-interest of some of our politicians, particularly those Labour MPs who bang on about a fair society and then send their children to private or grammar schools, at a stroke betraying their own high-held principles and the people who elected them! Liddell also calls out particularly those MPs of all political parties who speak passionately about defending our democratic rights and then vote in Parliament against the views of the constituents who elected them. Like Liddell, I believe that such politicians should resign and prove themselves to be honourable and respectful of the democratic process by declaring their voting intentions and letting their constituents know they can no longer in good conscience represent them in the House of Commons.

I am making good time and it's a lovely August day. I'm looking forward to a cold lager once parked at the cricket club, and a read of the sports section. I come off the motorway beyond Bristol and drop down towards Bedminster, avoiding Bristol city centre which, according to friends I meet at the game, appears to be being dug up! I spent much of last night trying to pick my starting eleven for today. Roofe is injured, as it seems he always is, so Bamford will start up front. But what of the new arrivals? White must make his debut, as Ayling and Baradi are injured and suspended respectively. I would like to see Costa start, but where? I suspect he is the long-term replacement for the excellent Pablo Hernandez, but surely not today? It's possible he could come in for Harrison.

By far my biggest concern is our goalkeeper Kiko Casilla, who so damaged us with his untimely rush out of his area in that horrid play-off semi-final. It's not just because of that game, or even a few weeks earlier when he did exactly the same thing, gifting Ipswich an undeserved winning goal. I have felt almost since his first appearances in the New Year that he is a weak link; to me, he seems to have no presence and little judgement. There were rumours throughout the summer that he would be sold, but it is Peacock -Farrell who will leave the club, heading to be an understudy at Burnley.

In terms of goalie recruitment, I wonder who is advising the club. The last one – the German, Wiedwald – was also hopeless, eventually losing his place to Peacock-Farrell after a series of gaffes, and was finally sold on within the year! Today, Casilla starts, and I seriously hope someone has been working hard with him during the close season. We can't afford him undermining the defence like last season.

In other areas, I hope that Alioski plays at full back in preference to Douglas, who to me seemed to lose all confidence after a bright start last season. The left back was injured towards the end of the season and is now back in contention to reclaim his place. The midfield will be key, and with Roberts still injured, I suspect Forshaw, whose form was up and down last season, will partner Klich, with the key man Phillips holding everything together. The transfer window has yet to close, but to me and many others, Phillips is the key to promotion and the one player we can ill afford to lose. The rumour is that Villa and Spurs are keen on him, and certainly I wouldn't swap him for someone like Dyer, even if he is an England international. Phillips will be soon, surely.

Leeds team: Casilla, Dallas, Cooper, White, Douglas, Phillips, Klich, Forshaw, Hernandez, Harrison, Bamford.

So, Bielsa stays loyal to the majority of players who served him well last year. Only the youngster Ben White comes in, and Douglas is preferred to Alioski at full back. We are in a new kit that is grey, but it looks brown to me! The travelling fans are in good voice, though it seems Bristol have reduced our allocation from last season and there are rows of seats at the front taken out. No matter; we will make ourselves heard!

I had read the Bristol manager Lee Johnson's programme notes about his team's excellent pre-season – part of which was based in Miami. Johnson claimed that through all the hard work in high temperatures, his side was fit and ready for battle. However tough their training camp, it can't have matched Leeds'; to me, the Bristol players looked drained after 20 minutes. Leeds started at high tempo and moved the ball and the Bristol team around the pitch with ease. Dominant from the start, it was so important for us to turn the early possession into goals, and that's just what happened in the 27th minute when Hernandez drifted into a central position and curled an unstoppable shot past the Bristol keeper Bentley from the edge of the area. I was right behind in the away end and saw immediately that the ball was goal-bound! Cue explosion of noise from the visiting fans – always such a fantastic feeling!

A little later, Forshaw curled another excellent effort narrowly wide, and Leeds were good value for at least a one goal half-time lead, though it has to be said Bristol caused some trouble down our left flank, and Douglas seemed a little lost on occasion. Casilla made one early dash out of his area, but fortunately managed not to foul the Bristol player, and the ball was cleared. He did make one good stop low to his left, but later on television, Paul Robinson – a former Leeds and England keeper – claimed his bad positional play at a corner led to the Bristol player having time to shoot. In the second half, our excellent play was rewarded with two further goals. First, Hernandez skipped past his marker and crossed from the right. I was following the expected flight of the ball and looking in the centre of the penalty area, when suddenly it was in the net! Patrick Bamford, a striker who has had his ups and downs with the fans, moved brilliantly towards the near post and headed the ball cleanly and with power past the helpless Bentley. I was right behind the goal, no more than 20 metres from the action, and Bamford's movement and speed of thought beat me as well as the home defence! A third goal – scored by Harrison following a Klich shot and a super run by the impressive Dallas – wrapped the points up for Leeds, though they did concede a sloppy goal when Costa, on as a sub, lost the ball and a scuffed shot by Weimann beat Casilla – in my opinion, too easily.

The players came and celebrated happily in front of us. Phillips looked such a part of this; surely there is no way he will leave. Why go to a lower end Premiership team when, hopefully, at the end of the season he will be back there with a huge club and his hometown team? I head out of the ground full of confidence and sure that this season we will do it and at last return to the top division, where of course all Leeds fans, and quite a few others, feel we belong. It's a lot easier leaving the ground than getting in. On entry, Bristol seem to funnel all visiting fans through several 'search checks', which leads to much queuing and far too much congestion and confusion, in terms of getting to the right entrance. It's a small point, but the experience could be so much better for visitors. Or is it just something kept for us visiting Leeds fans?

I pass a policeman who I chatted to on the way to the ground, and he smiled and asked about the game. I think sometimes over-zealous policing can often cause unnecessary problems at football fixtures, but this chap was excellent, as were a whole group of fierce-looking officers, all kitted up and shepherding Leeds fans into Bramall Lane last season. They reacted brilliantly when a young visiting fan ran along the entire group, high-fiving them, and all responded with smiles and high-fives back to the little chap!

Back to the car, and a fairly rapid escape, straight into moving traffic and ready for the long journey home. I guess all football fans will agree with me that driving home from a match, particularly a long away fixture, is immeasurably more fun when you have won! Today I can enjoy listening to the end of 'sports report', catching up with all the news, and then listen to the '606 phone' programme. This evening, it is Chris Sutton with Alastair Bruceball. Sutton can be a bit stroppy, in my view, but he has strong opinions and seems to get along well with Bruceball. I also don't mind Ian Wright in the 'expert's' role, but when Robbie Savage is teamed up with Jason Mohammed, I find their 'joshing relationship' just too irritating so usually swap channels.

I suspect Savage has done in his broadcasting career pretty much what he did as a player, and that is to make a lot out of a limited talent. He used to wind me up beyond belief when I watched him in action, so nothing has changed there. That said, he must be given great credit for his professionalism and hard work in achieving success in two very different forms of entertainment. Some of the callers tonight are bonkers, especially those calling for managers to be sacked before the season has started! Solskjaer at Man U seems to be a popular target. I quite like Solskjaer, in that he seems an honest broker and has clearly inherited a nest full of vipers in the United changing room. As a Leeds fan, I really don't care about that lot from Old Trafford and obviously hope they get relegated, but some of these callers to the footy programme clearly know absolutely nothing about the game. There is also an obsession with the top Premiership clubs, especially the aforementioned Man U, City, Liverpool, and the London three of Arsenal, Chelsea, and Spurs. This limits the depth of discussion and range of topics, and ultimately the enjoyment of the programme. Certainly, Man U and the London clubs attract a lot of 'passing fan' support, which becomes obvious in the limited knowledge of the game – and even about their own clubs – displayed by the callers.

I drift off back to the game and think about the team for the coming weeks. We play Forest next Saturday, which should be a good test against opponents who I think will challenge for the top six and follow that with an away Carabao Cup match against Salford. I can't say I'm much bothered about the cup game at Salford, though obviously losing to Gary Neville and the Gang of 92, or whatever they are called, would not be fun. I hope we play our new arrivals and some of the youngsters coming through our excellent academy. In terms of the Forest game, I can't see Bielsa making many changes, but personally I would bring back Alioski for Douglas.

Today was a strong performance and particularly from the debutant Ben White, who looked a really excellent prospect and fitted in well with the ever-improving Cooper. I am home just after 10pm, make some toast, then pour a cold John Smith's and settle down to watch the Sky coverage of the Bristol game. I love it when we win and the game has been on telly; it's great to watch the key points over and see if your impression at the time is what actually happened when you can watch slowed down replays of events. Mine are pretty accurate: it was a great strike from Hernandez; it was a poor goal to concede; Weiman definitely seemed to scuff his shot; and the team did play really well. Bamford's excellent movement for the crucial second goal still surprised me, as it clearly did the Bristol defence. A great day out and a really important win. Just another 45 to go!

Monday: Back to Girona today to carry on with the holiday. It's an evening flight from Leeds, which means I have all day to get to the airport, so it looks like the service buses for me again! Andy will meet me at Girona, but by the time we get home it will be midnight, so I will get a sandwich at the airport and then enjoy a few cold beers on our terrace when we eventually arrive home. I get a couple of papers, the *Times* and *Telegraph* – both produce useful sporting, and particularly football-related, sections on Mondays. I always enjoy reading well written football commentary, and have a number of articles about Leeds framed in my study, that for me capture the spirit of what it means to be a Leeds fan – or indeed any football fan with a passion for their club. Henry Winter and Rick Broadbent clearly get this, and I wonder how long it will be before they are writing about the woes of supporting Bolton or Bury, two clubs who have started the season (or not, in Bury's case) in total disarray.

The journey is uneventful, only enlivened by one total fruitcake who, though he was wearing headphones, blasted his booming music throughout the Leeds bus from Pontefract. Oblivious to the rest of us and dressed from head to foot in light grey, accompanying himself with weird dance moves, he more than entertained the rest of the passengers for the short time he was on the bus. I so hope I never end up next to anything similar on a Ryanair flight, that's for sure. Tonight, I am in luck. The flight is on time and there are just a few 'hens' heading to Barcelona via the link coaches from Girona. As usual, the 'girls' are all dressed in team t-shirts bearing the final destination, the bride-to-be's name, and their own 'moniker' for the week. There is a spread of age range, and some of the older hens are sat behind me. It's difficult not to hear their conversation, which is drink- fuelled and over-loud. To be honest, it's not unlike the type of chatter on a 'stag do' – fairly basic, and often very funny. All conversation is broken off when one of the younger hens staggers down the plane calling out to the more mature hens for help. She explains that she's desperate to use the loo and has been waiting outside the toilet door for some minutes. It says vacant,' she whines. 'What does that mean?' Vacant loo, vacant minds. Only in Yorkshire, I think!

Andy is waiting for me at the airport and we chat about the few days I have been away as we drive back to the flat. As always, she has busied herself with the garden and house chores, particularly preparing for the arrival of Mike, his wife Lou, and our granddaughter Margie, on Wednesday. We carry on the chat over drinks on the terrace. The Estrella lager is cold and goes down very well – a lot better than my update on the boys' performance at Bristol. I see Andy's eyes glazing over... it's time for bed.

CHAPTER 4

CALELLA, FRIENDS AND FOREST

Thursday, 8th August

We woke up this morning in a boarding house in Claira, a small village just outside Perpignan. We've been celebrating our good friends Dave and Wanda Parkinson's 40th wedding anniversary with them and their family – children Kate, Robert, and Alice, and their partners Dan, Sophie, and Chris. They are our oldest friends, and it was their invitation to join them for a holiday in Spain that led to us buying our apartment in Calella all those years ago. Previously, we had always much preferred to take our summer holidays in the South of France, and as we were both teachers we had been able to spend at least a month at our caravan in Agay, not far from St Raphael on the Esterel.

We had built up a great friendship base there with lots of couples and families who, like us, headed to the same spot every year. I guess we had holidayed there every August for seven or eight years and always had great fun, so when the Parkies invited us to join them in Calella, we were reluctant to give up on our summer idyll to head to Spain. We were also, if I am honest, a bit put off by the 'Luton Airport brigade' image of Spain and didn't want to be surrounded by 'kiss-me-quick hats' and adverts for English breakfasts. Not that I am not a fan of the 'full English'; I love it. But it's more a case of 'when in Rome'.

Anyway, Agay was also perfect for our young, growing family, so we hit on the idea of meeting up with the Parkies at Easter time as a compromise. At the time, I was the Head of a boarding school, and in the Spring we were fortunate to get the best part of a month off. It was important to get away as well – not just to recharge the batteries, but because the school was often leased out to various groups and organisations during school closures. This provided much needed extra funding to help balance the accounts but made it difficult for us to stay in our own school accommodation, especially when visitors, who didn't always respect the facilities, dominated the site.

The Parkies were right about Calella. It was, and remains, beautiful and from that first Easter visit we fell in love with it. A year later, in May half term, we bought a ground floor apartment in a small community with stunning sea views. The apartment had three bedrooms, a family bathroom, and a master ensuite; it was perfect, and amazingly had been on the market for the best part of a year. We paid £47,000 in 1998, and as I have already said, have had our money back in spades since that time. We visited every holiday, in the early days (before Ryanair) piling the kids in the back of the car and just keeping the car going, swapping drivers every now and then, and doing the 1000-mile journey in around about sixteen hours. We would often leave home about midnight and arrive the next day in late afternoon, however uncomfortable it was for the kids. Andy once made them travel with a new headboard across their laps, but it was always worth it when we finally arrived. They loved it as much as we did, and of course there was usually the benefit for them of having Kate, Robert, and Alice staying in the village, too. Perfect.

Now, though, it was time to leave the Parkies and head back to Calella. We called in at Robert's to say our farewells. It had been a lovely few days, hosted by Rob and his girlfriend Sophie in the house he was provided with as part of his contract as Head Physio to the Catalan Dragons rugby league team. We had stayed with them earlier in the summer when the Dragons had played a hopelessly out-of-touch Trinity, but the less said about that the better, I think! We would see them all again soon, but now it was time to hit the motorway and head back to Spain. Given that it was peak summer season, we were expecting heavy traffic, especially at the Spanish border and La Jonquera – the first peage in Spain, where often there are lengthy queues. But today we were in luck, and pretty much sailed through.

The last time we had driven back this way, we had found ourselves in four queuing lanes of traffic trying to converge into one, following an accident. It was slow going, but with the normal give-and-take, gradually the four lanes were becoming one. As we neared the damaged vehicles, it became pretty obvious to us that a few cars in front of us, as the lanes came together, there were two vehicles that were not going to give way. And unbelievably, in front of our eyes, neither did! They just drove very slowly into each other and then kept moving, causing more and more damage to both vehicles as they bumped and scraped along together! When eventually they had to stop, there was a moment or two where nothing happened, before one of them got out and started shouting and gesticulating wildly. Not knowing too many Spanish swear words, I guess it translated loosely as, 'What the fuck are you doing?' The other driver just sat motionless with his head on the steering wheel. Muppets!

This time, it wasn't long before we reached Salida 6, came off the motorway, and headed for Palamos. Mike and Lou had arrived yesterday, getting a taxi from Girona Airport to the flat – a journey of about 45 minutes. It would be great to see them again and our granddaughter Margie, just 17 months old. They were up at the parking spaces waiting for us when we arrived. Lots of hugs and kisses, and especially for Margs, before enjoying a lovely salad meal Lou had put together and a few cold San Miguels – the perfect welcome home. As Andy and Lou chatted babies (Lou was pregnant with number two), Mike and I talked about developments at Leeds! I had been following 'Leeds Live' on my mobile while we had been in France, anxious to see if we had held onto Phillips or added to the squad since the weekend. Mike had watched the Bristol game on the telly and agreed with me that it had been a super performance.

There had been some movement, but thankfully Kalvin, despite continued rumours about offers from Villa and Spurs, was still at the club and still apparently in 'positive' negotiations about a new contract. Roofe, though, was leaving, heading to Anderlecht for 7million euros. I wasn't too disappointed, even though he had had by far his best season last year. He was very injury prone and, for me, a bit hit and miss. I also couldn't figure out why he would go to Belgium, even though Vincent Kompany had just become manager of the club. Surely it was a backward step for Roofe, which made me think the club must have been happy to let him go.

One of the most important upgrades I had overseen as we developed the apartment was in paying for a satellite dish to be discreetly fixed on a side wall, well out of view of other flats. This allowed me to bring my Sky box with me from home and keep up-to-date with happenings in England, and especially sporting events. I love being in Spain and we have spent so much time in that wonderful country over the last 20 years or so. But unlike many compatriots who feel that the television intrudes on their enjoyment of a different culture, I simply couldn't exist without Sky.

Mike and I tuned into the Sky News channel to pick up on key developments and to hear more about our replacement for Roofe – Eddie Nketiah, a young striker signed on loan from Arsenal, and who had a number of clubs interested in signing him, particularly Bristol City. It looked a smart move and he seemed, while only young, a very real talent, already capped by England at U-21 level. He would be an interesting addition to the squad and provide a challenge to Patrick Bamford who, after an injury-hit season last year, had started so promisingly and in goal scoring mood at Bristol. Mike and I, quite happy with the business so far, headed outside to join the girls and watch Margie splashing about in the paddling pool.

The kids had all got the 'Leeds bug'. Katherine, now 35, Mike 33, and James 28, not only loved going to Elland Rd whenever they could, but had their own memories of childhood visits and great games watched. I hadn't forced them; they just took to the atmosphere the first time I took them along to a game and were hooked. I remember Katherine excitedly standing on her seat to see her heroes as they went past the family stand on an end of season farewell lap of honour. I guess at that time she was probably about nine years old. I would take her and Michael to matches when I could – usually at school holidays and midweek games. As Saturday was a major sports day for Barlborough Hall, the boarding school I was leading at that time, it was impossible to go to weekend matches on a regular basis.

We didn't always get to see the boys at Elland Rd, but once famously they did come to see us at the school! Most of the places I worked, once I left the Leeds area, soon got the message that I was a big Leeds fan. And most of the people I worked with couldn't care less, either having no interest in sport, or being 'trophy' fans of Man U or some such club. BHS was a Jesuit boarding school, set in extensive grounds and the Prep school to Mount St Mary's College, situated just a few miles away in the village of Spinkhill. When the job was advertised, I didn't think I would have a chance of being successful, but the school had experienced some difficulties and the move from Jesuit priests to lay heads had not gone well. By the time I was interviewed, the school had had three heads in a year and had launched its own enquiry as to what was required moving forward to secure its future. That, as they say, is another story.

I was appointed, and now some two years into my headship there, the governors, my senior team, and Andy and I, had all worked hard to improve the atmosphere and image of the school. One of my key projects away from the education of the pupils, training of staff and recruitment of both, was to try and enhance the quality and appearance of the grounds. First impressions matter, as they say. The actual Hall where much of the teaching took place was quite an attractive building, built in 1584 by Sir Francis Rodes, though he himself never lived there. The Hall remained in the Rodes' family until 1935, when the Jesuits bought it as the Prep to MSM. The grounds immediately in front of the Hall, especially the lawned areas, were well kept and almost like a bowling green in appearance. There were cricket fields to the side and rear, and a cinder running track, so facilities near the school in truth were not that bad. But away from these areas and certainly going up the half mile drive to the gated entrance from the village of Barlborough – apart from a couple of rugby pitches – there was a huge amount of the grounds that was basically unkempt and growing wild.

As this was the first sight visitors had on entering the school grounds, it was a pet project of mine to enhance it. And being football daft, it was obvious to me that I had the chance to create my very own Wembley. Massively helped by our superb Chairman of Governors, Kevin Fox SJ (and a Spurs fan!), we set about plans to fund and upgrade this part of the school and grounds. Kevin started the process by supporting the development of a hugely impressive new drive and car park; the drive running from the gates right down the half a mile or so slope to the school. With this done, and at not inconsiderable cost, it was up to the bursar and ground staff to oversee the levelling and seeding of two football pitches at the top of the drive.

When I was young, I had always loved to play Subbuteo, and took great pleasure in spreading out the pitch and setting up the players before a game. We had great fun and many battles as we developed a full-on league that led to many full-on fights, full-on pitch invasions, and games abandoned by hosting parents, full-on fed-up and sick of the noise, arguments, and bad language of so many warring children. Now I could create my own ground, set up my own pitch, and relish the thought of planning and playing matches on it. I know lots of people who loved creating their own Subbuteo grounds, but how many people get to create their own pitch? I was so excited about the project.

Eventually - it seemed to take the frigging bursar ages to mobilise his teams - I was to have the same Subbuteo experience with my very own pitches at BHS. When finally finished, with new gleaming white posts and nets in place, they looked fantastic, and often after work had finally ended, I would head up there and practise my shooting and footy skills. We would play some great games there over the years and I relished the opportunity to coach our first X1, who were tactically aware, and mixed the qualities – technical and spiritual – of pupils from all over the world. And with an all-Spanish midfield, a bullocking, old school-style English centre forward, a crazy Mexican keeper, and a classy African centre-half, we didn't lose many of the games we played.

With the drive finished and the pitches in place, things were looking much better all round, and the school itself was picking up, too, with more and more families interested in joining as we began to develop not only the resources, but also the quality of staffing. I went back to St. Joseph's to recruit some proven teachers, and appointed Elaine Izon – a wonderfully calm presence and a gifted teacher, who was to sadly pass away at a tragically young age. I also brought in our friend Wanda Parkinson as a senior member of staff, and someone I knew I could trust to help me raise standards and improve the profile of the school. Indeed, a few years later, as we moved south to Berkhamsted, Wanda was appointed Head of the school and went on to lead it very successfully for the next 13 years.

The school was headed in the right direction, and then one day as I returned to my office from some task or other, my secretary Vicki casually mentioned that Leeds United had been on the phone! It was obviously too late for them to be offering me a trial – I was 40, for goodness sake! So I quizzed her about the call: what did they want, etc; who did they want? Unhelpfully, she didn't really know, but helpfully she did have a contact number. I told her it would probably be my brother or one of my friends taking the Mickey so I asked her to ring the number and ask them to send a fax from the club explaining what they wanted. And they did!

On headed paper as well, and signed by the manager Howard Wilkinson's right-hand man, Mick Hennigan. Basically, they were looking for somewhere relatively private to hold a light training session before a league cup tie with Mansfield! Howard Wilkinson lived in Sheffield and knew the school and grounds, and as we were literally within a mile of junction 30 on the M1 (you can see the Hall on the left as you drive south), it would be the perfect place to break their journey, being just a short distance from the Mansfield turn-off. It didn't take me long to respond and agree to the visit of my team to my school; I was beyond excited. I had some discussions with Wilkinson about the organisation and asked him if he would mind if the children were able to watch. Howard was brilliant and so were the players. He just wanted a short private session and then said they would be happy to sign autographs and pose for photos, and that's exactly what happened.

There were some pretty famous players who rocked up to BHS that day, among them Gary McAllister, Gary Kelly, Brian Deane, Tony Dorigo, and Gary Speed. Gordon Strachan was missing, but it was fantastic for me to watch their training session and then see how brilliantly they treated the children and staff. They were such good ambassadors for the club, and for this Leeds fan it was a very special day. Sadly, it didn't end well for the team, as Mansfield knocked them out of the cup later that night. The next morning, Vicki wondered if the result might have been something to do with all the sandwiches and cakes we offered the players, but then quickly forgot about it. For her, as for most of the female members of staff, what she really remembered was the shape of Gary Speed's legs.

Following the visit, Howard Wilkinson wrote a warm thank you letter and invited me as his guest to a match of my choice at Elland Rd. It didn't take me long to respond and, because of my work commitments, the match would have to be in the school holidays. There was one very obvious fixture, a real stand-out game – home to Manchester United on Christmas Eve. Howard gave me four tickets and I shared them with my dad, my brother-in-law Chris, who I used to go to all the matches with when I was a teenager, and Dave Parkinson. What a Christmas present as a full and rocking Elland Rd celebrated the holiday a few hours early as we blew the old enemy away 3-1, with goals from McAllister (pen), Yeboah, and Deane. The seats were brilliant – in the West stand, and about in line with the penalty area at what I always think of as the 'Shed' end of the ground.

I can still see in my mind Steve Bruce and Schmeichel arguing fiercely with each other after we were given the penalty, and Yeboah breaking free to score with ease as he so often did. I remember a very young Phil Neville – a sub that day– warming up on the touchline in front of us and looking quite frankly terrified, and Tomas Brolin, who with two assists, played possibly his best game for the Whites. I also can't forget the passion and noise as the whole ground erupted at the final whistle, with every Leeds fan in the ground seeming to point their fingers at the visiting fans huddled in the corner and loudly telling them what we thought they were! It had been an amazing experience the day I had entertained my heroes on my own version of Wembley. And as I write these notes, I am looking at the signed Leeds football the players left us as a memento of that fabulous day in 1994.

Sitting with Mike all these years later, we laughed about the BHS days and the first game of football he had ever seen live – a Sheffield derby at Bramall Lane, where we had been invited as guests by one of the parents at the school. He must have been 'well in' because we had excellent seats, and after the match we were introduced to some of the Wednesday players – Chris Waddle, David Hurst, and Des Walker among them. I can't remember the score of the match now, possibly 1-1. I do remember there was quite an atmosphere, as you would expect, but above all I remember a very young Mike tugging at my sleeve and pointing excitedly to the electric scoreboard shining brightly at the far end of the ground. It was showing that Leeds had scored in their match being played simultaneously at Elland Rd, some 40 miles down the M1. I had brought them up well.

We only had a few days with Mike and family, as they were flying back to England on Sunday morning, but there was some time to get to know our lovely granddaughter again, especially when we babysat on Friday to allow Mike and Lou to enjoy dinner out at La Blava, one of our favourite restaurants. We learned that Margie, just like our other two grandchildren, Oliver and Lucy, was a bundle of fun and had a real sense of humour. I was always amazed how these little ones seemed to just sense that they were in safe hands with us, especially as Lou had said Margie was terribly clingy when visitors were around. My own theory was that there must be some sense of animal smell that just instinctively told them they were ok. I realise that might be total rubbish, but that's my opinion, so there. Margie was fine playing and pottering about but was less sure when we put her in her cot! She was happy while one of us stayed nearby, but the minute we tried to leave the darkened room, she pulled herself up on the cot rails and made it clear we should stay. Eventually, after much patting of back and 'shushing', she gave up the fight and fell deeply asleep. In fact, so deeply asleep was she that we couldn't hear her breathing on the monitor in her cot. These monitors were modern technology we didn't possess when we were bringing our own children up, and thank goodness is all I can say! I couldn't settle till I could hear some kind of noise. There is a clear difference between the responsibility of being a parent and that of being a grandparent, and I was beginning to feel it right now.

Andy was more relaxed and told me to stop fussing, but then she too found she couldn't hear anything on the cursed monitor, so I decided to have a little peep into the room to see if I could see any signs of life. I was as quiet as I could be, and as the light from the living room sent a shaft of light into the bedroom, it enabled me to see the soft rise and fall of Margie's frame breathing. Mightily relieved, I was gently leaving the room when I thought I heard a different sound. I carefully reopened the door and there, standing up and smiling at me through the cot rails, was Margie. Andy was not pleased, but it was nothing that Peppa Pig couldn't sort out, and I actually think Mike and Lou were pleased to see her when they came in from their romantic night out.

We sat drinking and chatting into the night, watching the moonlight falling on the sea and lighting up some of the fishing boats from the town. Then around midnight, we turned in; it was a big day tomorrow. We were playing Forest in the first home game of the season. I hated missing games, especially at the start of the season when the weather was usually good, the pitches looked fantastic, and all around there was a sense of expectation about what lay ahead. This, of course, was true of all teams, but after going so close last year and with an excellent start at Bristol last week, it seemed particularly hard not to be at ER today.

I am a season ticket holder with an 'away season ticket' as well, guaranteeing me entry to all Leeds matches home and away throughout the season. But with a place in Spain and in the height of the summer holidays, it's difficult to argue with my wife's stance that we 'can't stay at home all year just to watch football'. Absolutely, I can hear some readers shouting out 'course you can'. But it would be football or the divorce courts, and anyway I could fly home from Girona to Leeds probably as cheaply as an away trip to one of the London clubs or places like Cardiff would cost. Even as I renewed my season tickets, I was aware that I would have to miss some matches during the campaign. The trick was trying to make sure 'family trips away' coincided with international breaks and games that were not so exciting.

Or if they were, then away trips were not to grounds that I hadn't yet visited, though to be fair that was only the two Welsh clubs and, for some odd reason, WBA. I could also, to make sure I wasn't just throwing my money away, try and see if one of the kids could go in my place, so the ticket wasn't wasted. I guess this is frowned upon by the club, but all three are 'proper fans' and all three 'gold members', but sadly all three struggle to get tickets as they can't even consider buying a season ticket due to work and family commitments. This wasn't the case when we were in League One, when a hard core of around 15-20,000 made sure the club still received great support, and you could always get a ticket at least for home games. One of the problems of our success, like any club in the country, is the 'glory fans' who only join in to watch a winning team. I would never sell my ticket, as many fans do, particularly for away games. I have been at away fixtures standing next to 'Leeds fans' who have told me it's the first time they've watched the club, and others who didn't know who the players were. I know the club do their best allocating, particularly away tickets which are like gold nowadays, but it's so unfair on the real fans when other fans sell on their tickets to touts.

I bought my season ticket when I retired, and I bought the seat my youngest was giving up when he finished his time at university in Leeds – an education chosen obviously so that he could go to ER as often as possible. James, still single, often travelled to away games to meet up with me. Sometimes he would give up a ticket he had managed to get in the home areas because he had met people outside the ground who had sold him a ticket for the away end. Usually these would be from Leeds fans who, for whatever reason, had a spare ticket, and often they would be sold at face value. But I know there have been games where he has had to pay way over the odds. I really don't know what the club can do to stop this practice; I guess it's up to the fans to sort it all out, but certainly I would only give my ticket to my children, who I know would behave responsibly and support the team passionately. There were compensations obviously for being away from the UK, not least the sun and sea and a wonderfully relaxed lifestyle. There was also Sky TV – hated by Leeds fans for making us travel all around the country on odd days and at daft times, and for rescheduling matches, which was a total bugger for me and often wreaked havoc with my travel plans. But in terms of the Spanish situation, Sky was a lifeline I couldn't do without. And if I were ever on 'Desert Island Discs', it would be without any hesitation the luxury I would take with me.

Leeds United…1; Nottingham Forest…1
Saturday, 10th August
James's birthday!

I suppose not surprisingly, Bielsa has kept with the same side that did so well at Bristol. I don't suppose anyone could complain, but Douglas had certainly struggled a bit before half-time in that game, and Casilla didn't fill me with confidence. But with Peacock-Farrell gone to Burnley, it looked like we were stuck with him. It looked a glorious day in Yorkshire as we settled down with some chilled San Miguel to watch the game. I could imagine the build-up at ER, and missed the pre-match chat with Miles, Vic, and his sister Julie, who had all looked after James so well during his student days and had now become friendly with me in the years since I had taken over his season ticket. There were also the brothers, Chris and John, who sat next to me; Dave and his friend, who always asked about James; and Mick, a good-natured guy who sat in front of them and who has a pretty similar sense of humour to me. They are good people and hugely loyal fans who have travelled the length and breadth of the country for years supporting the Whites. In truth, I couldn't believe their level of support. It was ok for people like me, retired with a pension and a grown-up family. If I had been somewhere like Reading for a match, which is a rubbish ground to get away from and almost always a midweek game, I wouldn't get home until about 2.30 in the morning, and I live a few miles south of Leeds. I could have a sandwich and a beer, watch the highlights, and then sleep in the next morning.

That wasn't the case for these guys, though. They were all significantly younger than me and all had to go to work or, in the case of Julie's daughter, to school the next day. I often asked them how they could afford to do it, both in terms of time and, of course, money. It's an expensive business being on the road with your team. They pretty much just all shrugged their shoulders; it was their passion and escape, and just like me and all other true football fans, if there was a way to be there then they would be there.

The importance of 'being there' was summed up one Saturday afternoon when one of the guys that sat near us was describing the difficulties he was going through as he separated from his wife. He couldn't stop talking about his frustrations even as we all kept our eyes firmly on the action unfolding in front of us. 'She's teken' everything,' he moaned, 'f**king everything.' Then silence, followed by a bit later, 'She's teken car.' Then, 'She's teken carpets.' Followed by, 'She's even teken f**king curtains!' More silence, more watching the match, and then one of our number tried to put a positive spin on it for him. 'Well,' he said, 'it's not all bad, is it? I mean. she hasn't taken your f**king season ticket, has she?'

James and I fell about laughing, not at the poor man's expense, but at the brilliant cutting edge of terrace humour – so funny yet tinged with a truth that we all understood. I sometimes wonder if the players and those that run the clubs, and not just Leeds, have any idea about the sacrifices and hardships the fans supporting them go through to be on those terraces when their heroes run out onto the pitch.

We generally don't like Forest. As with Derby, there are historical reasons that go further back than Derby's misplaced, and ultimately pointless, celebrations following their play-off victory over us last May. Brian Clough and the miners' strike link both these Midland clubs with us, and James asked me once, 'Why are we chanting "Scum" at the Forest fans? I thought that was our name for Man U?' I explained as briefly as possible the history of the miners' strike, and that what they were really chanting was 'Scabs' with reference to the fact that the Nottinghamshire miners' union, while officially supporting the strike, found many of its members continued to work. It's difficult to explain to someone born in 1991 – six years after the strike ended officially in 1985.

Difficult to explain how such an event literally tore families apart, as the Yorkshire miners particularly suffered huge deprivation and sacrificed much to support their union. One of our best friends was a policeman in the South Yorks. force and found himself on the opposite side of the picket lines to his brother – a miner fully supporting the union position. It was a complete nightmare situation for the family to deal with, especially their poor parents. Difficult also to explain how Arthur Scargill, the miners' leader, was demonised in the press and media. Yet just a few short years after the strike, his worst prophesies of what would happen to the mining communities would come to pass, with the closure of so many pits and the crushing of the towns and villages of which the pits had been the life blood. It's probably true to say that the deeply unpopular image of Scargill and his brash and aggressive public persona, even if he was proved to be right, caused much damage to the miners' cause. For many, he was the wrong man with the right message.

Which brings us to Clough and his personal characteristics, so similar to those of Scargill, over-confident, outspoken, brash, and confrontational. I remember Clough coming into ER and bringing with him key players from his Derby squad, such as John O'Hare and John McGovern. They were good professionals but not in the class of Bremner, Giles, Clarke, and Joe Jordan. I was a student teacher at the time, on holiday from St Mary's – a teacher training college in Twickenham – and working for Wakefield parks department, mainly cutting privet hedges on the local council estates. I read that Clough wanted to replace our goalie, David Harvey, a Scottish international, with a new keeper Pete Shilton, who was in those days an understudy to Gordon Banks at Leicester. What was he thinking of? I don't know the ins and outs of Clough's time at ER, but I heard later that he told the team, who were league champions when he took up the position of manager, that they should throw their medals in a bin because they were cheats. It was not hard to see how he only lasted 44 days.

Of course, Clough was wrong. The team he labelled 'cheats', went on – under the management of Jimmy Armfield – to reach the final of the European Cup that very season, only to be cheated themselves by a referee who turned down two clear penalty shouts and disallowed Peter Lorimer's second half volley. It's why to this day Leeds fans still regularly chant, 'We are the Champions, Champions of Europe'. I know we are; I was in Paris to witness it.

Clough himself famously went on to take a previously largely unsuccessful club like Forest to two European Cup victories, which was an outstanding achievement. They were captained by John McGovern, who later visited BHS and was most complimentary about my football pitches, but only passed a wry smile when I told him I was a Leeds fan. He seemed a really nice man, though, and like Clough himself, in terms of his Leeds career, was probably the right man at the wrong time.

We dominated Forest for much of the game and created numerous chances, but they were defensively strong. And when we did open them up, particularly in the second half, we were wasteful in a way we hadn't been last week at Bristol. Bamford missed a couple of good chances. Nicely set up by Harrison from the left, he hit a volley into the ground which bounced up and off the bar. A little later he brilliantly controlled a ball coming in over his shoulder and, having done the really hard bit, sent his chip over the advancing keeper and wide of the right-hand post.

At last, on 59 minutes the deadlock was broken, as Klich superbly set Hernandez racing through the middle of the Forest defence. If we had to have one Leeds player in this kind of position, it would be Pablo. Very much in the later stages of his career, he was still in my eyes the most creative and talented player in the team. And he didn't disappoint, veering to the right of goal before firing a delicious shot into the left-hand corner of the net. Cue huge eruption in Hernandez's home country, as Mike and I showered San Miguel over each other and much of the living room, jumping with joy, while at the same time almost instantly realising Margie was asleep, and managing to silence ourselves in mid-celebration. There was half an hour to go, which hopefully would see us double the score and mean we could enjoy seeing out the last ten minutes or so before celebrating a lovely Saturday night with the girls, with that warm feeling of knowing we were 100%, two wins from two. Unfortunately, it was not to be. Forest, as they had to, tried to force themselves back into the contest. They never really created much, but they did force a couple of corners. From the first, their centre back Dawson headed over the bar when finding himself unmarked in the penalty area. Everyone in the ground and everyone watching on telly knew he should have scored.

From the second corner, awarded after it appeared Grabben had fouled Cooper in the build-up, they scored. It was a scruffy goal. No-one seemed to take control in the Leeds defence and the ball pinged about before deflecting off Grabben's shin and rolling in off the base of the post. 'For f**k's sake, what were we playing at?' was the general consensus heard in Spain, before settling back into the sofas, aware that as a Leeds fan anything was possible in the last ten minutes.

Bielsa responded by replacing Klich with Costa, and Leeds responded by forcing their opponents back. Forest gave up any ambition to win the game, realising a point was, given the way much of the game had panned out, much more than they deserved. In truth, we huffed and puffed and tried hard to get past them, especially down our right flank. Costa had two shouts for a penalty – both, in my opinion, rightly turned down – but then Dallas was clearly kicked by a desperate Forest defender, and unaccountably the referee waved away the desperate appeals of the Leeds players and a packed Elland Rd.

I have found the standard of refereeing in the Championship to be generally poor, and not just when decisions have gone against Leeds. And I don't know what the reason is. I do understand that the game is played so quickly that referees and linesmen only have a split second to get their decisions right, and clearly some calls are going to be incredibly difficult to get right. But there are other decisions that are just hopeless and clearly wrong, and these are the ones that cause so much uproar in the grounds and so much frustration on the pitch, often changing the nature of a game.

My own theory is that some refs have little empathy with the playing of the game, and very much appear to enjoy stamping their authority on proceedings. They are often described as being 'Headmasterly', but as I was one of those for nearly 30 years, I would have been very disappointed if this is the way my manner was perceived. My own solution, given that refs are so critical to the game, would be to make it an attractive option for players coming to the end of their careers to study for, just as rigorously as they prepare for coaching badges. They would obviously be well rewarded, but it would be a demanding role and carefully monitored to ensure only the best would be officiating at the highest levels.

It will be interesting to see how the use of VAR in the Premiership goes down with the football community when it is introduced this season. Certainly, from my watching of rugby league, it has added to the fairness of the competition over the awarding of tries, especially as the referee has to indicate whether he believes a try has been scored as he hands over to the video ref. I'm not sure about the use of technology in rugby union, though, with too much interference from their video refs and quite often, and unbelievably, the wrong decision being reached even after slow motion viewing. Forest hold on for their point, and there isn't a Leeds fan on the planet who won't be thinking we should have taken all three points. Still, we remain unbeaten, though worryingly, Fulham, Brentford, and Cardiff all won, and Lee Bowyer's newly-promoted Charlton have six from six. WBA, like us, drew at home with Millwall. Early days.

Mike and Lou are heading back to the UK tomorrow, and the Parkies have turned up at their apartment with Robert and Alice, Sophie and Chris. So, after the match we head down to theirs. It's just a ten-minute walk, and we have a lovely session sitting on the lawns by their pool, chatting, drinking, and easing the frustration of the dropped points as the alcohol takes hold. We finish the evening enjoying a lovely meal on the terrace back home, and when Lou calls it a night, Andy and I have an interesting 'work' chat with Mike, who is in the early stages of a demanding new job in Dublin.

The next morning, it's time for them to head off, and Andy is sad as she hugs them all goodbye, but we will be heading to Dublin soon. And for now, the job is to get them to Girona Airport safely. It's a journey we have made countless times, and we are all chatting happily until Margie decides to throw up. Fortunately, we were able to pull off the road and park up on some wasteland, and Mike and Lou were able to clean her up and change her so she wouldn't stink the plane out later. I wasn't sure about the car, though. And as most of the stuff she'd thrown up was on her clothes and the baby seat, we put the whole lot in the boot and did the best we could to clean the back seat down with baby wipes.

Mike didn't need me to remind him about how dreadful an experience it is to drive in a car that is full of the perfume of puke. Once, on one of our family journeys heading home from the South of France, James had with little warning done exactly the same as Margie. In those days, we put James in a child seat in the middle of the car, separating Mike and Kath so they couldn't either drive us mad with their silliness or alternatively kill each other. We all heard the explosion, and again fortune favoured us as we were close to a motorway services on the approach to Lyon. We were lucky. A few more miles further on, and we would have been stuck in queueing traffic for the city, and the stench from James's stomach would have meant we would probably have had to sell the car on our eventual return home. I guess we were in part to blame, as in an effort to bribe the kids into silence so that we could travel as far as possible in one go, we would give in all too easily to their requests for sweets, drinks, and goodies. Sometimes when we stopped, they were all stuck to the seats, and the back of the car resembled a crisp packet that had been sat on – literally 'salt and shake'. Amazingly, the next year and at exactly the same stage of the journey – and certainly being far too young to realise this – James repeated his performance in some style.

Sad to wave Mike and Lou off, nonetheless I was quite looking forward to a lazy afternoon on my return to the flat. It had been quite a busy time since leaving to head home for the Bristol game, and now there was a chance to put my feet up and enjoy a few days' chilling before we began the long drive back to England in a little over a week's time. There were two more games to take in, too, with a Carabao Cup match away to Salford, and our second away league game at Wigan the following Saturday. Despite the attraction of defeating a team like Salford, with their connection with Gary Neville and a number of former Man U players, I wouldn't have gone to this game. Indeed, if it hadn't been for the Man U link, I wouldn't have been bothered if we'd lost. In fact, I hoped we'd take the opportunity to give a few of our younger players a run out. As far as I was concerned, I was only interested in going for promotion, so I didn't want any of our key players getting injured in a competition that was long past sell-by date.

The Wigan game was one of those I'd calculated we should win comfortably and give them some payback for the disastrous loss they had inflicted on us last Easter, as we imploded and blew automatic promotion. It was also at a ground I had visited many times, so it fit my criteria for matches I was prepared to miss. I remember the first time I went to the 'DW Stadium'. Spotting a Wigan fan waiting by the roadside, I rolled my window down to ask him directions. 'How do you get to the ground?' I shouted and laughed with him as he shouted back, 'In my brother-in-law's car!' Now, instead of doing battle with the M62, I would enjoy the last few days of the summer holiday and get back to England in time for the Brentford game and the return of Pontus Janssen to ER.

In the event, Bielsa played a strong team at Salford, and there were first starts of the season for Baradi, Alioski, Shackleton, Clarke, Costa, and Nketiah. I half watched the game on telly, but after Nketiah scored the opener in the 43rd minute after good work from Costa, there was little doubt who would be progressing to the next round. We added further goals in the second half from Baradi and Klich, and it was good to put one over on those old Manc boys Scholes, Butt, and the Neville brothers, who were watching from the stands. The main thing for me was that it appeared we hadn't suffered any injuries to key players, Nketiah had played and looked more than useful, and Phillips was outstanding. I just wished he would hurry up and sign that contract. I wasn't happy that so far this season every game we had played had been on the television for everyone to see what an outstanding prospect he was.

CHAPTER 5

SPEED TRAPS, SUSPENSIONS,
HOME AT LAST

Wigan…0; Leeds United…2
Saturday, 17th August

Obviously, for the afternoon, I would have loved to have been able to 'magic' myself to the North West, but given I had identified this as one of those games that would have to be sacrificed, there were compensations! For example, it was another beautiful day in Calella, and with the extra hour in Europe, the games in England didn't get going until 4pm, so there was plenty of time to enjoy the day before the tension of tuning into 'Soccer Saturday'. I had always loved the opportunity to try and get fully fit, mentally and physically, when spending the summer in Spain. Throughout my teaching career it had been a vital bolthole and my escape from the pressures of headship. I loved the freedom to be me again and not just some figure of authority who was praised and criticised, loved and hated, depending on the whims of a shifting population of parents, teachers, governors, and of course children. Though I never particularly worried about the children; they were usually totally honest and upfront. I always felt throughout my teaching career that the children were with me, even those who on occasion I had to discipline.

Maybe that was because I had experienced being the victim of some fairly brutal teachers in my own school career. Maybe because I knew that empty feeling of being humiliated by my academic failures. Obviously, my lack of hard work contributed significantly to these disappointments, but so too did a disproportionately high number of fairly crap teachers. And maybe it was because I remembered those teachers who saw enough in me to encourage me to try – a small number admittedly, but their encouragement and trust was hugely important to my development.

One John 'Jack' Canning so frightened me in my early encounters with him that I could hardly speak when he asked me a question. This was at a time when in French lessons we regularly pretended to be the Glenn Miller Orchestra, standing to belt out *In the Mood* on imaginary trombones every time the teacher turned to write on the board. Some teachers demanded respect and some… well, they got Glenn Miller.

Sometimes I don't think teachers realise just how much their interventions can affect students, both in a negative and a positive way. I pretty much gave up on understanding Maths when one of my teachers thought it would be funny to copy out onto the board one of my quite wrong answers from a recent test. I think he hoped to further add to my humiliation by getting my classmates to join in the fun with him. But my classmates all turned their backs on him – even the 'good girls' sitting at the front who acted as his monitors, collecting in books and answering all his questions. I wonder now how proud of himself he was, looking at all those backs defiantly sending the message that he was bang out of order, a real bully, and a total loser with a sad sense of humour.

The damage this particular cretin did in that lesson was not fully corrected until many years later when, as a student, I finally had the understanding and confidence to attempt and pass the necessary Maths qualifications required for me to embark on life as a teacher. Funnily enough, I believe that my understanding of what it was like to fail, and the embarrassment of feelings that experience can bring, ultimately helped me to be a much better teacher all round and particularly of Maths.

Jack was different again, taking me from a decidedly dodgy set of 'O' level results (I pretty much passed anything I liked or didn't have to revise for, which wasn't very much) to successful 'A' level passes and even more 'O' levels two years later. One of the 'A' levels I studied was

History, which Jack taught, and which – so the legend said – no-one had ever failed. I so respected what he had done for me in supporting me through Sixth Form that I couldn't bring myself to attend school on results day just in case I let him down.

I took up the option of having my results posted to me, saying that I would be on holiday with my grandma in Hastings on results day, when in reality I was at home in Wakefield. So, I went to the pub in town where we had all agreed to meet up, either to drown our sorrows or to celebrate, and I just sat there and waited for my friends to arrive. Being Catholics, we were 'bussed' to school in Bradford, so I knew it would take some time for them to get back, and I waited and waited until at last a few of them dribbled into the pub. One of the boys who had arrived was in my History group, and I asked him how things had gone. He had passed and had got the grades he needed for university; in fact, he had done better than he expected and was quite elated. He couldn't stop chattering, and then he said, 'Jack's really chuffed.' I asked why, only to be told that the group had achieved the best results anyone could remember. 'So, everyone passed then?' I asked fairly nervously. 'Oh yes,' he said, 'everyone did really well. Jack's buzzing!' And with that, I left him, walked out of the pub, headed to the bus station and caught the first bus to Bradford.

By the time I reached the school, Jack was just locking up his office. 'What the bloody hell are you doing?' he asked, and I told him. I just came out with the fact that I literally couldn't face him if I had let him down. I'm not sure if he understood the effect he had had on my school career, nor for that matter on my future, but I do know if I hadn't had the good fortune to run into him I would never have achieved what I have managed to do in my professional life. His trust in me changed my whole school life round, taking me from a lazy failure to a young student with a plan, and a dream to become a teacher, just like Jack, trying to help young people have the confidence and belief to unlock their talent and potential and not to be frightened by cynical and negative teachers, but to have the freedom and trust to simply do their best, to have a go. So, these two very different teachers helped me form my own philosophy about how to relate to young people, and how important it was to treat all of them with respect, even when on occasion the law had to be laid down.

Jack could certainly do that when he had to. But even then I found myself agreeing with him, even though on one occasion it led to me being temporarily 'suspended' from school. It had to be football. It had to be Leeds. Jack absolutely knew which of us supported the Whites, and he absolutely acted on 'intelligence', probably whispered to him by some 'snakes in the grass', Valley Parade type. On one occasion, when the country was being ravaged by the earlier mentioned miners' strike, there were times when power had to be saved or couldn't be guaranteed, and one of the casualties was floodlit football matches. Unfortunately, this meant that our FA Cup replay with Liverpool, following a hard fought 0-0 draw at Anfield, would kick off at 2.30 on the Wednesday afternoon, rather than 7.30pm which was the norm at that time. The problem for me and my friends with that was that we should have been at school at 2.30; in fact, we should have been doing my favourite lesson – double games. No matter, it was far too big a game to miss. I bamboozled Mum into thinking I had some revision to do; after all, 'A' levels were just around the corner. And I never really bothered about Dad, as he was rarely home early in those days. We found out later that year just why he was absent so much, when he left the family home, having conducted a lengthy affair. But that is another story and for another time. The main point now was that I never even thought to ask his permission to stay off school.

The next day, I got up and enjoyed breakfast with Mum, Janet, and Andrew, and when they had all gone off to work and school, I took the paper and went back to bed. Then the phone rang. I guessed it would be one of my friends wanting to check out meeting times, so as I was nice and warm, I decided to ignore it. I ignored it the next time, too, but when the phone rang again a few minutes later I threw the paper down, stormed down the stairs, picked up the phone, and shouted, 'What?' down the receiver. I nearly froze when I heard the reply. It was Jack, and he was telling me the times of buses that I would be on to make sure I was in school before eleven! I responded in that pathetic croaky voice that people put on when they are trying to pull 'a sicky' and put the phone down. What should I do? I rang Dad at work and explained the situation, but he simply told me what I already knew: in 'A' level year I couldn't do without Jack's support, so I would have to go to school.

I was gutted, to use a modern parlance, and was just hanging up when Dad asked about the ticket and kick-off times. He told me to leave my ticket on the telephone table and he would go to the match. Double whammy! But at least we won the game, and I could see the highlights on telly later. It was a great game, too, between two great sides, and settled by two great strikes from Allan Clarke, who would go on to get the winner in the cup final a few months later.

And it was after that game that I did get into trouble. History shows that we won the cup, beating Arsenal with the aforementioned Clarke 's brilliant diving header. I hadn't, despite all best efforts, been able to get a ticket for the match, with Mum banning my plan to queue overnight at ER when they came on sale. So, along with a few friends from school, I was determined to go to Wolverhampton on the following Monday when we needed just a point to become champions and complete the double.

Again, the problem was school. To get to the ground in time to get a ticket would necessitate leaving school before the end of the day. One of the boys in our English group, who had absolutely no interest in football but who did have a car, was persuaded to drive, and we all chipped in to make it very worth his while. When we checked our timetables, we were all supposed to be in reading groups, which basically meant private study and preparation. Everything was perfect, and we slipped away in early afternoon. I only have fleeting memories of the game, but I know Molyneux was rammed and that most of the people there seemed to be Leeds fans.

I remember we should have been given a penalty for a blatant hand ball, and I remember they scored just before half-time. Sadly, they scored again through Dougan, who had been put through by John Richards – a forward I had always rated. Not all hope was gone, though, as Billy (who else?) scored almost straight afterwards, pumping the night air right in front of us with his passionate celebrations. We tried to get the draw needed, but their keeper Phil Parkes was in outstanding form, and right at the end a goal-bound Yorath header was deflected agonisingly just over the bar.

We had fallen short, and our tired and injury-hit team (Mick Jones was missing, having famously dislocated his shoulder in the last minutes of the cup final) just couldn't find the legs to get the point required. So, the title went to Derby, who were already on a pre-season holiday, with spadeloads of help from the FA for making us play the game just a day after the cup final. Disgraceful.

We went for a beer somewhere after the match and then headed home. Fed up and tired, we showed our lack of support for our driver by falling asleep, and he showed his lack of map reading skills by ending up in Blackpool! Eventually, in the early hours, I quietly let myself into the house and was having some cornflakes when I heard the front door open. It was Dad. It was half three in the morning. For some reason, he took the high ground and demanded, 'Where have you been?' I took the match programme out of my jacket, showed him, and then challenged him in the same way. 'So then, where have you been, eh?' And with a great flourish, he reached into his pocket and pulled out the self-same match programme. We both just started laughing. The tears would all come later.

The next day, Jack made another phone call – only this time it was to Mum. They had to bring me into school to meet with him, and until they did I was suspended. Blimey! Of course, it all worked out. I apologised, took my telling off from Jack, and felt I had let both him and Mum down a lot. I would make it up to them a few months later, though, when I at last managed to pass some exams.

Calella certainly provided the necessary breathing space for recuperation from the stresses of headship, as well as so many opportunities to get fit. For many years, I jogged miles and miles, usually in early evening before enjoying a shower and some cold beers ahead of our evening meal. We also walked miles along the country roads and the beautiful coastal paths, and with 127 steps from the lower road to our apartment, regular trips into town also kept us on our toes.

In recent years, with my knees suffering from the wear and tear of too many football matches and too many miles run on hard roads, I had taken up cycling. I bought an absolutely beautiful second-hand racing bike for 500 euros. Light as a feather and with a built-in timer, it was my escape to fitness, and I worked really hard, setting myself tough targets and time trials to achieve. My favourite route took me from the apartment down minor roads to the sleepy village of Ermedas, and from there along tiny country lanes all the way to the stunning beach of Castell and the sea. Sometimes I would lay the bike down on the sand and just throw myself into the water – still in my cycle kit – splash around for a bit and then hit the tougher uphill ride home.

I always knew when I was getting fit because I made the end of the time trials without my lungs bursting. I could also tell by viewing my profile as I passed various windows. I used as my cycle top one of the yellow elasticated Leeds 'away' shirts which certainly didn't hide any excess bulk, and when my tummy started to look a little flatter, I knew I was winning. Leeds didn't wear the yellow kit at Wigan, choosing to play in the classic all-white strip introduced all those years ago by Don Revie. There was little doubt that this was an important game for us, and especially after the dropped points against Forest. Bielsa once more stayed with the same side, and while there was little or no talk of revenge for the damaging defeat of last April, we couldn't afford to be as profligate in front of goal as we had been last week. We started well and Phillips dragged a free kick from the left across the six-yard box with no-one, attacker or defender, able to get a decisive touch. Then Joe Williams recklessly cut across Stuart Dallas, needlessly earning a yellow card, before a Lee Evans free kick seemed to trouble Casilla more than it should have done. From the resulting corner, there was the kind of confusion in our penalty area that had proven to be so costly again Forest.

Unfortunately for Wigan, after twenty minutes Williams lunged into a challenge with Patrick Bamford, leaving the referee with little option but to award another yellow card and send the Wigan man off. He left the field protesting his innocence when really, he should have been apologising to his team mates and manager for being so stupid. So, just like in April at ER, Wigan found themselves down to ten men. But there seemed little likelihood of a repeat performance, partly because their outstanding player that day, Reece James, had returned to Chelsea. And partly because, after 34 minutes, Bamford scored to settle Leeds nerves. It was only what Leeds excellent approach play deserved and came after Hernandez had shot weakly into the side netting a few minutes earlier. The hard working Klich crossed from the right and Forshaw, who had started the season brightly, headed against the post when it seemed easier to score. Fortunately, the ball fell to the unmarked Bamford, who prodded it home from close range. Leeds made and squandered several more chances before Douglas crossed well for Forshaw once again to be denied.

It would not be long, though, before the second goal that we just could not score last April, would come along and secure all three points. From another corner by Douglas, confusion reigned in the Wigan defence, and Bamford literally pushed the ball in as all around him did a passable impression of an under-eights' school game, all chasing the ball in a tight group with only Bamford seeming to know where it was! In the end it was a comfortable win, and the team and their legion of fans could head back across the Pennines knowing they stood top of the league on seven points – a total shared by Charlton, WBA, Swansea, and Millwall. I was getting ready to head home, too. Our holiday in Calella was coming to an end tomorrow before the long drive home, starting on Monday. In a few days, I would be back at ER for the first time since that dreadful evening in May, and I was already looking forward to the excitement.

I always hated leaving the apartment. It didn't matter if we'd been for just a few days or for several weeks, it always felt like a major operation, packing, tidying, cleaning, and getting ready for the journey home. Usually that meant getting the hire car to Girona and then a two-hour flight to a UK airport. But today, as it was the end of our long summer holiday stay, it meant packing our own car for the 1,200 miles' journey home. Andy and I were always better company once the flat was locked and we were on our way than we were in the preparation to leave, when we could occasionally rub each other up the wrong way. Andy needed to leave the apartment as clean as possible and, without a deadline, would simply clean all day. I, on the other hand, was aware of the upcoming journey and wanted to be on the road as soon as possible. We had learned to leave each other be, busying ourselves with different tasks until it was time for me to call a halt on cleaning. This I would usually do once I was happy the car was packed well enough, with an overnight bag easily reachable for our stopover. The biggest worry was making sure all the beer and wine we had bought at ridiculously cheap prices was: a) out of sight; and b) covered away from sunlight, to avoid any explosions or ruining of produce. Once the car was packed, I would usually be wet through with the effort of running up and down the steps from the apartment to the car park. I always took time out to sit and take in the view from our little garden while drying myself down and putting on one of my favourite Leeds shirts for the drive home. As it was still August, it would be a sparkling hot day to travel, and my usual clothing would be shorts and t-shirt. I plumped for a black and grey centenary shirt and went in to tell Andy it was time to go.

There isn't a great deal to talk about with the journey, other than it's one we've done countless times, and it's long. I always try to get as far as possible, while Andy prefers to build in hotel stops to break the journey up. Andy also can, on occasion, be a bit of a 'backseat 'driver, and regularly lets me know when I am going too fast or getting too close to the car in front. The journey time halves when she is dozing and I can make good progress, though not the type that it was possible to make before the advent of speed cameras. The last part of the journey, from Reims to Calais, is almost all motorway with hardly any traffic and would easily see us driving perfectly safely at 100 mph. Alas, those days for us are long gone. In truth, they were over before the advent of speed cameras; in fact, they were over the day we got snared in a police trap just by the exit to the town of Bethune.

We saw the police car hidden in a clearing by the hard shoulder just as we passed him, but it was too late. Even as we slowed down, we could see the police roadblock by the exit sliproad. They took me from the car and put me in a police minibus while they checked my papers. I wasn't alone; there were another four drivers in the bus, all English. We had been caught in a racist speed trap! They told us how fast we had all been going, that we would have to pay a fine, it would have to be cash, and it would have to be paid now. If necessary, they would take us to the bank to get money. I was told I had been doing 100, and the copper just laughed when I asked if that was kilometres. Fortunately, we had the money, and I wanted to pay it quickly and get on my way. I was really very worried that they would breathalyse me, as I had had quite a bit to drink at the hotel stop in Reims the night before. I needn't have worried, though; they just wanted the cash. As one of the English guys said, 'I bet it's all for their Christmas bash!' Thinking about it, he was probably right. Anyway, from that day onwards, we always give a 'victory wave' every time we pass the Bethune exit.

Today, however, we will stop at Beaune – a pretty French town in the wine region, and roughly the halfway point of our journey. We both love to enjoy a few beers in the sun as soon as we have checked in, and then head to the town to get something to eat. I usually end up getting an omelette and chips or something simple, as quite often the food for my taste can be overpriced and, for instance with steak, not particularly high quality. I understand the French have a worldwide reputation for their culinary dishes, but my experience of the country, unless you are in a top-class restaurant, is that the food can often be crap. And worse, it's frequently served by pretentious and miserable waiters.

For some reason, I hate the journey between Dijon and Reims, where for mile after mile you seem to be travelling in the middle of nowhere, rarely passing anywhere that looks interesting enough to stop. Andy usually makes brilliant sandwiches from the breakfast we enjoy in the hotel, and always seems to provide a very good value lunch with bread rolls, ham, and cheese, etc, smuggled out in handbags and pockets. We eat as we drive and listen to music endlessly. This long stretch of the journey always reminds me of driving south with a car full of kids,

71

listening to stuff like the Lightening Seeds' greatest hits, the Beatles, and sixties greatest hit compilations. Before they were old enough to have their own music and headphones, the children – strapped into their seats – had to simply listen or fall asleep. I guess in some senses it was a case of child abuse. Even today, the youngest, James, is always playing the Lightening Seeds; in fact, the line 'Put your foot down and drive' is almost an anthem for the journey. Calais usually brings the same conversation of things we've missed about England – almost always fish and chips – and we realise we will have to wait a little longer till we get north to really fully enjoy this treat. It's not worth being tempted by the food on the ferry, particularly fish and chips, and tensions develop again between us when I start to discuss the journey home from Dover to Yorkshire.

There is always a bit of bounce about getting up to Calais, and even going through Dover and climbing the hill out of the old town makes you feel a bit nearer to journey's end. The reality, however, is that it's still 250 miles, and we have already done something like 400 plus. Andy doesn't enjoy my need to break the journey down into sections and times, and especially can't bear my rants about time lost on the M25 and particularly the Dartford Tunnel, which amazingly you have to pay to pass through or over, usually having queued for four miles in slow moving traffic for the privilege.

We always seem to land in England in time to get up there for rush hour, and there's always a lengthy delay. We have options, as Katherine and Nick live in Bishops Stortford, just a couple of stops up the M11. We haven't seen them since they stayed a week or so at the apartment in early July, and we have missed them and our grandchildren, Oliver and Lucy. By the time we have battled our way up to London, got through the frigging tunnel and fought our way through to the M11, the traffic is beginning to ease and flow. So, we usually, as we do this time, plump to head on up the A1 to Yorkshire and home. It's a long run, and we are knackered when we finally arrive, having managed from somewhere to pick up an Indian takeaway meal and some milk and bread to get us through to the next day.

The house looks good, and I'm glad I didn't leave any rubbish in the bins from my flying visit home for the Bristol game. Again, it's brilliant to feel carpet under our feet rather than the tiles of the flat, and it's also great to get the sense of space in the house. There are no disasters awaiting us in the piles of mail which Adrian, our friendly postie, has kindly hidden in the garden shed for us. And there are no demanding voicemail messages, though I usually turn this feature off when we are away. We text the kids that we are home safely, then it's time for a beer and food.

Leeds United...1; Brentford...0
Wednesday, 21st August

I love going to Elland Rd, and I especially love the atmosphere at night matches. There are so many great games, so many great memories stretching back down the years. A creature of habit, like many football fans I always follow the same routine. I always park up in Beeston in exactly the same place that my dad used to do when he took me to occasional matches in the days I was too young to go on my own. Walking down the steps between the bus depot and the school, you get the first sight of the ground, with the huge East stand rising up above the rest of the stadium, and the lights of the city shining out in the distance. Once down the steps, and before joining ER itself, you now go past the car park entrance to the swish-looking headquarters of Leeds City Police. In days gone by, it was the greyhound stadium, and in the 1970s the home of the New Hunslet rugby league team.

Elland Rd itself has not changed, still running as it does right past the ground at the South Stand, previously the famous 'Scratching Shed'. The road may remain the same, but the approaches left and right have seen great change, with the police building dominating on the right as you approach from Morley, and the old training grounds on the left now replaced by car parks and even a park and ride for the city. Further down, opposite the ground, there is still the parade of shops and Gravely's fish and chips shop, which proves so popular – and not just on match days. The New Peacock pub still gets rammed before the games, so has now created an extra drinking area outside of the main building, but it's still difficult to get in unless you are very early. On the stadium side, the club have developed their own 'Billy's Bar' for season ticket holders and members, and at the end of the ground is the club Superstore, selling all types of club merchandise.

In front of the store is the famous statue of Billy Bremner, a true legend of the club. In my opinion, he was the greatest player in the club's modern-day history, the player who sums up more than anyone the spirit of the club and its modern-day image of 'side before self'. There are always flowers, scarves, and tributes around the statue, sadly often placed there in memory of fans recently departed. To me, it's a place of pilgrimage; there is just something hugely personal about being in the area. Now renamed 'Bremner Square', fans can have their own tributes etched onto stones of varying sizes that surround the statue. I haven't done this yet and probably won't, for the memories of the man and the fantastic times spent watching all those great players at different times will always stay with me wherever I might be. There will be more from me about Billy before these notes are finished.

Across the Geldard Rd, another statue stands, proudly facing the impressive new frontage of the stadium. Don Revie was the visionary who led the club to greatness, from the near disaster of relegation to the old Third Division in the early sixties, to possibly being the greatest club side in the world in the later years of the decade and early seventies. Don's reputation has been a little tarnished, mainly because of the way he departed his role as manager of England to take up a post in the Middle East, one that would have made him financially secure for life. The fact that he was on the brink of being sacked has not saved him from the attacks of many sports journalists, many of whom simply resented the success of Revie's amazing Leeds team.

He is still loved in Leeds, of course, and revered by his former players; without him, Leeds would not be the huge club we are today. And yet, even though I know all this and the evidence of his success is written in the football history books, am I being naive or greedy in saying I think we should have won so much more? I never met Don, so I can only form opinions from reading or listening to TV and radio interviews, but to me his quite dour public image most definitely hurt us on occasion, by helping to turn so many against us. I think there can be little doubt that someone like Alex Ferguson would have always held the upper hand with Don, with his mind games and teasing, much as Brian Clough and Bob Stokoe did so disastrously as far as Leeds were concerned. To me, there is a sadness about the statue that possibly reflects Don's character. I can't help thinking that if he had been less tense on occasions, less defensive, and more free spirited, with the players at his disposal he could have sent them out to play without fear and to crush the opposition with the quality of their football – something we saw in wonderful glimpses, but not as often as we could have. Certainly, the dismal defeat to Sunderland in the 1973 Cup Final is a game we should never have lost, despite Jim Montgomery's heroics.

I usually aim to get to my seat about ten minutes before kick-off and have a catch up with the group who sit/stand around me. It's always good to see them after the long summer break, and there are always smiles, hugs, and handshakes. This time, the greeting for me is accompanied by some suggestions that because I wasn't at the Forest game I might not have renewed my season ticket, so crestfallen had I been at the cruel way our season ended last May. Although I bought the ticket and seat previously owned by James, it is a view from the part of the ground I always stood in as a teenager. The seat is in the Revie Stand, slightly to the right of the goal and in the upper levels; it's a great place to watch the match, a great atmosphere, and surrounded by great people. While the atmosphere has always been good, the stadium is barely recognisable from the one of my early teenage years, and even the pitch looks different. Today it looks like a bowling green, while in the past it sometimes resembled a paddy field.

I remember one game against Newcastle years ago, where there was a diamond of mud the length and breadth of the surface, with just green bits growing up in the four corners off the ground. In those distant days of my youth, the 'Kop' – or Revie Stand, as it is now – was open to the elements; just a terraced banking, pitted with metal crash barriers. If you stood right at the top, you could look out and watch the InterCity trains making their way into Leeds or heading south to London. I have seen some fantastic matches from this vantage point, and some stay so fresh in my mind despite the passing years. I remember a freezing cold night when we played Partizan Belgrade in the Cities Fairs Cup , and I should have been at home revising; the night we were crowned champions for the first time and beat Forest with a late Giles' goal; the despairing afternoon we were robbed of the title by the 'offside goal' against WBA; and the fantastic day we beat Bristol Rovers to claim promotion from League One. More of those games later, and more memories of games gone by and watched from different parts of the ground.

The huge East Stand, which dominates not just the ground but much of the local area, was always the 'Lowfields Rd'. I often stood here when taking Andrew, my younger brother, to matches, as it has always been a relatively safe place even before becoming the 'family stand' in more recent years. His first game in 1969 was a sensational 2-1 win against the enemy from Salford. He got to see Best, Law, and Charlton, and he got to see them well beaten with goals by Mick Jones and Mike O'Grady – not a bad start! It was from here I watched as Rod Belfitt claimed a hat trick against Kilmarnock on my thirteenth birthday, and I got trapped on a crash barrier as we beat Rangers 2-0 in the Inter Cities in a febrile atmosphere with an official attendance of 50,498, which must have been several thousand more given the number of Rangers fans who tried every which way to get into the ground! The South Stand, which stands on the site of the old Scratching Shed, is somewhere I haven't stood that often since that first game against Blackburn on Boxing Day, 1964. Dad pushed me down to the front, as all the old tales of football past said should happen to 'nippers' so they could see the action better. The romantic notion certainly didn't work for me. I was frigging terrified I was lost and made a note there and then that I would never let him do this to me again. It was, of course, the part of the ground where the fans who loved to sing and chant used to congregate before the 'Kop' was built. From my standing place in the Geldard End, I used to watch in awe of the guys who were hoisted on the shoulders of their friends to lead the singing of the choirs. Nowadays, and especially in recent seasons as we have fought ourselves back to prominence, the fans who love to chant have returned to this area, making Leeds one of the few grounds in the country where the noise comes from all parts of the stadium.

The West Stand, as previously mentioned, was not somewhere I have seen many matches from, with the exception of that famous victory over Manchester when Howard Wilkinson had given me the tickets. I don't know why I haven't used it that often; maybe it's more expensive, or maybe there is less atmosphere and less enthusiastic support. I'm not sure. It was, however, the area of the ground where people ran onto the pitch in protest at the West Brom goal, when inexplicably referee Ray Tinkler allowed Tony Brown to run on, even though Suggett was yards offside. Even Brown thought so, stopping to look round at the ref before running on and slipping the ball to Astle, who scored. The pitch invasion that followed started in the West Stand, and an abiding memory I have of the afternoon is of a guy in a suit, shirt, tie, and all, being led off the field by two policemen. Not the look of the usual hooligan of the time. It was one of unfortunately too many huge decisions that have gone against Leeds over the years; gone against them in big games, too, with trophies and titles at stake.

To this day, a chant of 'the football league's corrupt' rings round Elland Rd, and while this might not be true, it is certainly the case that the football league and the FA have employed, at best, incompetent officials who have cost the club dear, both on and off the field. So many memories, so many ups and downs. And we have had them against tonight's visitors, again suffering at the hands of incompetent referees. In our last home game against Brentford, they scored from the penalty spot after their forward Watkins had conned the referee with a clever dive. And last season, in a game we simply had to win as our promotion bid faltered, referee Keith Stroud denied us a stonewall penalty. I guess all supporters of all clubs will claim they are the victims of such injustices, but surely none as frequently or as heartbreakingly as those that far too often have penalised us.

Elland Rd was full again as it always is at the moment, and there was a good atmosphere, though I didn't hear too much chanting either for or against the returning Janssen. Bielsa has made the change I wanted to see, in that tonight Alioski starts in place of Douglas. The crowd around me make fun of me because Casilla is still in goal; they absolutely understand what a weak link I think the goalkeeper is. Good or bad, he was well beaten early on when a fierce left foot strike from Mbeumo struck the inside of the post. I was dead in line with the shot which flew past Casilla, and it seemed goal-bound until thankfully the post intervened. Leeds went close, too, with Bamford heading a couple of chances narrowly wide. One of them was nicely created by Alioski, who often puts an early ball into the penalty area from a midfield position. It's good to see him back, as his pace and tenacity add to the team going forward and he seems to have forged a good understanding with Harrison. Perhaps, like Douglas, he can be exposed defensively, but he is a trier – and Elland Rd has always loved one of those.

We are the better team in the second half, and find ourselves frustrated by Janssen and his colleagues. The crowd are keen to see Nketiah, especially after his goal-scoring debut at Salford, and Bielsa gives them what they want when the youngster replaces a tiring Hernandez after 77 minutes. And four minutes later, he scores the decisive goal. It's a good move started down the right. Klich moved the ball onto Costa, whose superb cross takes out the Brentford defence and finds Nketiah running free to tap the ball home from a yard or so. A great goal, and one that sums up Leeds style of play – crisp passing, great movement, and all at pace. Brentford couldn't keep up, and ultimately Costa's pass ripped the heart out of their defence, Janssen and all. As always, we seem to fall back, and I am not the only one in the ground who has his head in his hands when it seemed Benrahma must score with a late chance in injury time. Fortunately, the forward blazed over, and we can head home with the three points safe and look forward to our weekend trip to the Potteries. We are still top of the table on goal difference from Swansea, but in these early days things are tight, with only three points separating first and ninth.

I love it when we win at home, and especially a night fixture. By the time I get in, Andy is usually in bed, which means that instead of being thoughtful and asking her about her evening, I can make something to eat and tune into Sky Sports News, catching up with all the fixtures and goals in our division. I write up some notes, pour myself a can of John Smiths, and enjoy the end of the evening. The difference between winning and losing. It's so good to be home.

CHAPTER 6

THE BOYS OF '66, WEMBLEY LEGENDS AND THREE POINTS IN THE SUN

Having stayed up late enjoying the victory over Brentford, I suffer a bit this morning, as we are up early and heading down to do some babysitting duties in Bishops Stortford. Katherine and Nick are due at a friend's wedding, and we are in charge of Oliver and Lucy till late. Despite the distance, we are regular visitors, and looked after Oliver every Monday and Tuesday for a school year when Katherine returned to her teaching duties after maternity leave. It meant we got to know him well. Our ability to be able to travel worked for all of us – we had some definition to our week; we got to see Kath and Nick; we got to help them out with childcare; and most importantly, we got to know our grandchildren.

We also got to know the A1 pretty well, and the A14 and M11, and learned the pressure points and times when traffic would be at its worst. Generally, even with all the huge redevelopments on the A14, we managed to get there in time, and today we had a good run. We decided to take the kids for a trip to the caravan park in Ashwell where we often stayed when visiting. This was a godsend for all of us, because it meant that when our 'babysitting' duties were over, we could escape and enjoy an evening without the hassle of bedtime, or worse once Lucy was born, the disruption of being woken up at one, three, and five in the morning. We also got to enjoy a drink and chill, which is exactly what Kath and Nick got without having the grandparents hanging around all night.

The kids knew the caravan and the village of Ashwell, and always saw it as a treat when they came over for the afternoon. They loved playing in the little park at the far end of the cricket/ football pitch and going on to the sandwich shop. It also sold fresh cakes, which they loved, and which meant we could bribe them into doing what we wanted. It's about a 45-minute journey from Stortford, and while it can be frustrating getting stuck behind slow-moving vehicles (why is it that old people think they become safer drivers by going at such a slow speed that they have almost stopped?!), the final part is quite quick with dual carriageways and eventually the A505 from Royston to Baldock.

We park up at the caravan site and go and book a few days down there in late September, when we will be back to celebrate the children's birthdays. The kids enjoy a run round then we walk them into the village and let them play on the swings and slides. We know that Lucy still has an afternoon nap, so we are fairly quickly back in the car and on our way. It is a central theme to all successful childcare that you sleep when they do, if you possibly can, thus avoiding being totally knackered later in the day.

Being grandparents, we decide to treat them for lunch and pull in at the McDonalds on the A505 before Royston. It's still the school holidays so it's carnage in there, but it's too late to turn round because Oliver is likely to strop big time if he can't get his toy with the Big Mac. I manage to find a space big enough to fit us all in, while Andy joins the queue. The children devour their meals and Lucy manages to get ketchup all over herself, we all have too much Pepsi, and I feel ridiculously full and vaguely nauseous watching all these kids stuffing food down their faces while stupid parents try to negotiate them back into cars.

It's different being grandparents; you have to be careful. You are not the parents, and so when they fall and hurt themselves, you feel more guilty than you used to as parents when you just had to rub it better and get on with life. Grandparents can't do this so easily, and every bump or bruise the little ones grow feels like a badge of shame hanging around your neck. As grandparents, you are supposed to be calmer and kinder, running around tidying up after them and cleaning hands and faces;, as grandparents, you are old enough and experienced enough in the ways of life to understand child development; as grandparents, you should be able to coax the little ones gently around to doing the right thing. As grandparents – as Andy gently reminded me – you should not need to shout out loud, 'Get in the fucking car!'

Lucy slept in the car and Oliver was happy to be home to play with his toys. They are both really good and neither of them mention Mummy and Daddy, which is a relief because they're not due home till late and are likely to be well-oiled and in happy mood when they do return. The kids are great at bedtime, and while Andy takes the brunt of nappy changing and bathing, I tidy round the kitchen and put the toys away until tomorrow.

It has been a successful day, no great traumas, no serious injuries, and we have booked the caravan site and survived McDonalds. I hear Lucy cry in the night and the sound of doors opening, so we know they are home and back on duty. It's time to go back to sleep. We are up and off early tomorrow, and I am back on the road on Saturday for our game at Stoke. I take a bit of time to drift off, and I spend some time trying to pick our best team and review our progress thus far this season.

It's early days, obviously, but there are clear pluses. Ben White, who I hadn't really heard of before his signing, has been outstanding, as too has Kalvin Phillips. But worryingly, even though the transfer window closed weeks ago, there are still clubs circulating and he still hasn't signed his contract. Stuart Dallas who, along with Harrison, finished last season strongly, has again impressed. As has Forshaw, who I felt got caught in possession too much last season. He looks fitter and has had a number of good attacking efforts, being unlucky not to score a few goals, particularly against Bristol and Wigan. The way he is playing, I am sure that elusive first goal can't be far away.

Patrick Bamford has also looked much sharper, and clearly has benefitted from a full pre-season. I am still seeing his movement and speed of thought for that headed goal at Bristol. Pablo Hernandez is our most talented player and he has again started well, with his ability and speed of thought helping to keep him ahead of most players in the division, despite his advancing years. All in all, a positive start, despite the frustration of dropping home points against Forest. Even Casilla has looked more focussed, and so far has only made one hair-raising run out of his penalty area. Hopefully they have been working hard with him in the close season, and he will be more consistent this year and less likely to unsettle the defence. That said, there remains a nagging doubt over his involvement – or lack of it – in the two goals we have conceded so far.

Stoke City...0; Leeds United...3
Saturday, 24th August

I seem to have spent a lot of the last week in the car, and having said our farewells to Kath and the kids, we are pretty keen to hit the road and get home before the roads get too busy with the usual Friday night weekend traffic. It's a good journey – just over two-and-a-half hours, so quick as well – and it's good to be home again, even if tomorrow I will be in Stoke, and next Sunday we will head up to Thornton le Dale in the caravan. James is home tomorrow as well, and disappointed he hasn't been able to get a ticket for the 'away end' at Stoke. Usually, he would turn up and try and get one before kick-off, but today he decides just to head home from London and chill for a few days. He could have caught the train up from London to Stoke and met me at the ground, but he didn't think there would be much chance today.

I check out the 'away fans' guide for details of travel and parking, trying to find a better parking space than the last time I was there when I seemed to be queuing for ages to get away from the ground. The stadium isn't well situated really. Quite close to the town, but off the main through road, it's almost built on a business park and there is little or no off-street parking. There are buses that come up from the town, but I can't be bothered sorting all that, and you still have to park before you get the bus. I find a place called Longton Rugby Club, about a 15-minute walk from the ground but which has parking for the match and a clubhouse where you can get food and drink. It also has big screen televisions and Sky. It seems perfect, and though it's actually past the stadium, it's clear that you can get away quite easily after the match and don't have to come back towards the ground.

I am off bright and early, and it's a really beautiful late August day. I'm in good spirits, looking forward to the match and hoping for three points, as Stoke have been on a bad run and their manager Nathan Jones is under increasing pressure. It's a fairly straightforward journey, and as usual I try and spot a 'Greggs outlet' to pick up a tuna crunch sandwich and get hold of a paper from somewhere. I always try to get to away games quite early, to try and find a good parking spot and enjoy some food, listen to the radio, a read of the paper, and then have a good look round the ground before kick-off. I get to the ground just before 1pm, and drive past it on my way to the rugby club. There are a few people around, but the traffic is light and I turn right at the signpost and drive up a lane to the entrance to the car park. There isn't a rugby match today, so there's loads of space, and I spin round a few times till I think I am strategically well placed for getting away after the game.

It's really very hot now, so I go and find the loo and have a look round the clubhouse. They are doing food and beer, and there's a few Leeds fans already enjoying a pre-match drink. One of them is Chris, who I sit next to at ER. He is with his dad, as John – his brother and usual travelling partner – is at a friend's wedding today. They are already eating, so I just have a quick word and leave them in peace to enjoy their meal watching the lunchtime Premiership match. Normally I would have joined them, but it's such a sparkling day it's far too nice to be inside.

I get a lager and take my Greggs sarnie and the paper and settle down on one of those bench-style seats you see in pub beer gardens. Everywhere looks lovely in the sunshine, and this is just an ace place to spend an hour before kick-off; a lot like the cricket club set-up in Bristol. I wander down to the ground around 2pm, and see all the police minibuses lined up by the entrance to the 'away end'. There are loads and loads of Leeds coaches from all over the country parked up there, too, and the coppers mingle with the fans or just hang around in groups looking menacing and probably wishing they could swap their cumbersome riot gear for the shorts and t-shirts most of the fans are wearing. I try to start a conversation with one of them around the lines of him being too hot, but he's not interested. Obviously, I am a Leeds

fan and in his eyes, at least for the next few hours, I'm the enemy.
Usually I try and get a photo on my mobile of the grounds I visit, and
today I know the shot I want. So I leave the away fans zone and the
overheated police officers, and head up the road a bit until I reach
the statue of Gordon Banks – a true Stoke hero. But more than that, a
true English hero. A World Cup winner and of course the keeper
who probably made the most famous save ever when deflecting Pele's
goal-bound header up and over the bar in a World Cup match in Mexico
in 1970.

I stand a while looking at the statue, thinking of times gone by and
how, just like Leeds United, the man in front of me has given me
some special moments. I was 12 when we won the World Cup, and
I loved everything about it. For a start, all the matches were on telly –
something quite unusual at a time when the only live game shown on
television was the Cup Final. And it was a chance for me to watch the
great players of the world, players I read about avidly as I bought
up loads of papers and magazines dedicated to the World Cup. Players
like Pele and Garrincha from Brazil; Eusebio and Colouna from
Portugal; and Beckenbauer and Seeler from West Germany, as they
were at the time.

For a 12-year-old, this competition was like a month of birthdays,
watching some great matches and some improbable performances. I
will never forget the look of the Italians leaving with their tails between
their legs, knocked out in the group stages and beaten 1-0 by North
Korea – the minnows of the tournament. Such upsets are part of what
makes football, for me, the greatest game on the planet. The Koreans
almost went one better when they raced to a three-goal lead inside 25
minutes against the might of Portugal, before Eusebio showed the
potential to snatch Pele's world crown with a four-goal blast which sent
the plucky Koreans home.

My heroes, other than of course England, were Brazil – winners in
1958 and 1962, but not destined to be champions in 1966. I watched in
horror as Pele was injured against Bulgaria and didn't feature in what I
felt was the best football match of the competition. When Hungary ran

out 3-1 winners over the World Champions, I knew I had watched some seriously good football. And while the Brazilians fielded some fantastic young talent in Gerson and Tostao, whose time would come in Mexico four years later, they were outclassed by some fabulous play by the talented Hungarians.

I hadn't heard before the kick-off of Bene, Farkas, and Albert, but boy, it was impossible not to see their class during this game. Bene scored first, cutting in from the right to fire left-footed into the net. Brazil equalised before half-time, but the match was sealed by Farkas, the Hungary number ten, who ran onto a cross from Bene on the right to hit a first-time, right foot volley in his stride, high into the roof of the Brazilian goal. It was a fantastic piece of skill and I remember practising hitting that volley again and again on our house driveway, throwing the ball high up against the house and swivelling to volley the rebound into the goal. Obviously, it wasn't really a goal – it was a garage door, but it served as a goal, and as long as we played with a light ball it didn't cause too much damage. The light ball also moved through the air, bending and dipping and making us think we had the powers of Pele or Garrincha to hit a 'banana' shot. Dad would not be happy if we played with the old leather ball, heavy and misshapen, that would certainly disfigure the garage doors without any problem. Once my brother Andrew hit a pile-driver from only a few yards, and I heard the crack as it flew past me. We looked at each other in horror and both took a deep and fast intake of breath, then spent all afternoon with a hammer trying to restore the 'goal' to its natural state.

Sadly, the Hungarians lost out in the quarter finals to Russia, who ultimately would be beaten in the semi-finals by the Germans. The Portuguese, with Eusebio fast becoming the player of the tournament, and having eventually disposed of the plucky N Koreans, were waiting for us in the semi-final. But not before we had to play the talented but emotional Argentinians. During the competition, I had realised I was having the same problem watching England as I did with Leeds, namely being unable to bear the tension. I just wanted them to win; I wanted it to be all over so that I could enjoy the celebrations. I was finding it difficult to watch, taking over long visits to the loo in a desperate effort to make the time pass more quickly. We had started quietly with a goalless draw against Uruguay, and Jimmy Greaves got injured, receiving a nasty gash down the shin. In the second game, we played Mexico and the game was defined by a brilliant goal by Bobby Charlton, who gracefully glided left and right before unleashing an unstoppable shot into the top left-hand corner. I practised that one a few times, too, veering to the left of the shed and back to the coal bunker, before slamming the ball into the garage door.

The Charlton goal seemed to calm England, who went on to win the match 2-0 and repeat the performance and score against France in the last group game. If Charlton's goal had calmed his teammates, it had also had the same effect on me, and strangely I didn't feel worried about our upcoming games against Argentina and an eventual semi-final with Portugal. Everyone now knows how awful the game with Argentina was. What can be said? At best, a clash of styles, a misunderstanding of intent, a meeting of total opposites, an accident waiting to happen. The game exploded into World Cup infamy when the Argentine captain Rattin was sent off, and the dreadful scenes and delays that ensued as he refused to leave the field tarnished the Argentinians' football reputation for many years to come. The game would also mark the first in a number of bitter and controversial clashes with the South Americans in the years to come, with the sending off of Beckham in France 1998, and Maradona's infamous 'hand of God' in 1986 almost certainly costing England two further World Cup appearances. England eventually won the game with a finely taken goal from Geoff Hurst, the injured Greaves' replacement. His header, flicking the ball on the run so it sliced across the keeper and into the opposite corner, was another of those skills that I tried hard to practise after the game had finished. I have to say, over the coming years it became my favourite way of scoring headed goals, especially from corners, running from deep to attack the ball from around the near-post area. I found if I got it right and there wasn't a defender on the far post, I would score more often than not.

The semi-final and the spirit in which it was played couldn't have been a greater contrast from the Argentina game. The Portuguese, playing in their first World Cup, had some serious talent – and it wasn't just Eusebio. The nation's nerves, and certainly mine, were eased when a Roger Hunt shot was blocked by the keeper but the ball ricocheted straight to Bobby Charlton on the edge of the area, and with great skill and precision he simply passed the ball side-footed into the net. The Portuguese were always a threat, and for once Eusebio lost Stiles, his shadow, and hit a firm shot goalwards, only for the man whose statue I am standing in front of to save brilliantly down by his right-hand post.

In the second half, England went two up when Hurst brilliantly held off his marker before turning to set up Charlton for his second goal. There was still time for Portugal to threaten, and from a looping header by Torres, Jack Charlton handled the ball to prevent the rangy forward scoring. In today's game, Charlton would certainly have received a red card for the offence, which would have probably meant one Leeds legend missing a World Cup final and another – Norman Hunter – appearing. Such is life. Eusebio sent Banks the wrong way from the penalty spot, and as he gathered the ball which bounced back to him from the net, he put his arm round the defeated Banks and patted his head.

It was an action this incredible athlete and sportsman would repeat on the same ground in the final of the 1968 European Cup final. With the game between Benfica and Manchester United coming to a close and the two sides locked at 1-1, the great Portuguese got through the United defence. I remember it well, watching at home. I was on my feet. He had to score. But his stinging shot was saved by Alex Stepney. Eusebio must have realised he had just missed the chance that would almost certainly have won the game, but again he held out his hands to Stepney, applauding the keeper's save. It was the defining moment of the final which Manchester would eventually win in extra time, but it was also a defining moment in sport when one of the greatest players who has ever kicked a ball showed his class as a person and not just as a player.

Of course, we won the World Cup final as everyone knows, and Geoff Hurst became the only player ever to score a hat trick in the world's greatest game a feat that has still even today not been repeated. How life's moments are created. Would Hurst have even played if Greaves, who was England's greatest goal scorer at that time, not been injured against Uruguay? It matters not. It is history, though it changed the lives of those two players forever, with Greaves going on to fight battles with depression and alcoholism, and Hurst receiving a knighthood. England fully deserved their triumph, winning the game twice, as their manager Alf Ramsey had urged them to do.

I had missed the Germans' equalising goal in the closing minutes of the game. I just couldn't bear the tension. And after Martin Peters had given us a 2-1 lead in the 78th minute, I went for a walk. I walked into Wakefield and was amazed to see the normally busy town centre completely deserted; the shops were still open, but most of the assistants were gathered round radios or little black and white televisions. The whole country, I reckon, had come to a halt so we could all get behind our team. I felt like I was letting the side down wandering round this deserted city. Maybe because I hadn't stayed to watch, in some way I would be punished from above for deserting them in their hour of need. Even worse, the team might be punished, and all because of me! I began to think of all those religion lessons when Jesus rebuked his apostles for falling asleep in his time of greatest need. Oh my God, I had let them down! I ran home as fast as I could, saying Hail Mary's as I went.

Mum was coming out of the kitchen door as I arrived home breathless and full of anxiety. 'They scored,' she said, quite matter of factly. Then she quietly added, 'The Germans.' I couldn't believe it, but fortunately things were already getting better by the time I got back to the telly. We were in front, and Hurst had scored the controversial third goal. It was nearly over, and this time I knew I had to stay and support the boys. I didn't have long to watch, for almost as soon as I sat down, the incomparable Bobby Moore launched a superb long ball over the German defence which Hurst fastened onto. And almost as if he knew it was his destiny, he barrelled forward and fired past the helpless Tilkowski in the German goal. We had won, we were the Champions of the World – and now I was standing thinking of all these wonderful times, right in front of the statue of Gordon Banks, one of our country's footballing heroes.

His moment of true legend would come four years later in Mexico, with that incredible save from Pele. Sadly, a stomach upset meant he missed our quarter final – again, against Germany – when incredibly we squandered a two-goal lead and Peter Bonetti, the Chelsea keeper and Bank's replacement, had endured a difficult introduction to the World Cup. I have little doubt that if Banks had played we would have won that game and gone on to face the fantastic Brazilians in the final. The Brazilians destroyed the Italians and produced one of the truly great performances in football, with many still today claiming that the team who won the cup in Mexico that Sunday evening in 1970 was the greatest team that has ever played the game.

And yet, Banks, Moore, Ball, and Charlton, were all world class players, and that 1970 final-that-never-was could have been one of the greatest of all-time. Instead, we hung our heads in disappointment, and mine was doubly depressing as I had given up all hope of passing 'O' levels by staying up half the night watching all the matches from Mexico. And, fairly stupidly from an exam point of view, even those that England were not involved in. It was a fantastic World Cup and some of the play was simply stunning, but which bright educationalist came up with the idea of setting crucial exams in the middle of a World Cup?

I left Gordon Banks and my memories, and wandered back to the ground to join the rest of the Leeds fans. As I passed one of the coaches, a guy stepped in front of me and offered me a ticket for the Leeds end, at face value. James would be spitting feathers if he knew. I passed the overheated coppers slouched on their motorbikes and headed to the turnstiles for the obligatory searching. The guys pass me through without bothering; I can't look very threatening or maybe they think I'm getting too old to lead a riot. While outside Stoke's ground looks like it's been dropped into a business park as an afterthought, inside it generates quite an atmosphere, and the fans don't need a drum to get things going like their neighbours up the road at Derby. They are quiet today, though. Maybe it's the sparkling heat, or maybe they are just not happy; their team is in a run of miserable form, and already so early in the season their manager Nathan Jones appears to be fighting for his job.

I bump into an old friend Eddie, who is disabled and sits in the area of the away end created for disabled fans. We met one New Year's Eve in the Shoulder of Mutton in Kirk Smeaton, when he made some space for Andy to sit while I was at the bar. By the time I had got the drinks, they had already established we had a lot in common: Leeds United, and apartments in Spain – in Eddie's case, further south than us, in the Valencia area. We got on immediately and often bump into each other at venues up and down the country. He always has a smile on his face and today is no exception. We both think we could do well today.

At the Britannia, the players come out to the pitch from the corner near the away fans, which immediately gives us an advantage, and the travelling fans are in good voice today. Alioski keeps his place on the left, but the captain Cooper is missing, replaced by the popular but occasionally suspect Baradi. Stoke have made changes, most notably in goal, where Butland suffers for recent errors and is replaced by Frederici. I have a great view halfway up the terrace and right behind the goal. It's amazing how often I see the same people when we are on the road, and there are a few waves and nods at friends and familiar faces before the game starts. Stoke actually start quite brightly and McClean, their politically controversial winger, has a few runs at Dallas that threaten momentarily but then peter out. Gradually we start to exert our authority. Hernandez has a shot blocked by Federici, and Klich fails to convert the rebound before Dallas fires a long-range effort just wide of the left-hand post. It's clear watching from the terraces that Stoke are getting stretched, and just before half-time we take the lead, and it's a brilliant team goal.

Forshaw, buzzing around in midfield, won possession of the ball and played it quickly to Klich, who found Hernandez out towards the left-hand side and just inside the Stoke half. The Spaniard played the most superb instant diagonal pass behind the Stoke defence, which put the marauding Dallas completely through, leaving McClean chasing his shadow, gulping for breath and looking horrified as it must have dawned on him that this was his man. Dallas took the ball in his stride and struck the ball, side foot, past the helpless Federici. At the other end of the ground, the visiting fans erupted, joyously hugging each other and celebrating a truly great goal.

In the second half, we took over the game completely and played the fast tempo passing game we have become used to under the influence of Marcelo Bielsa. It's wonderful football to watch and it's interesting to see how much fitter we are than our opponents, with players from most of the teams we have played quite often putting their hands on their knees and looking around nervously as if to see where the next attack is coming from.

The football media often talk about great managers and coaches, and it's clear there is no specific template to model and create the perfect manager. People like Ferguson, Mourinho, and Guardiola, each great in their own way, all appear to have different personal strengths and qualities. They have also all had most of their success working with the best players, and for me that is why Bielsa is a great coach, because most of the players on the pitch today had looked distinctly average, finishing in mid-table the season before he arrived at ER. Klich, such a key member of today's team, had even been sent out on loan.

The second goal comes in the 50th minute. Following a foul on Bamford, clever inter-play between Forshaw and Hernandez sends Bamford through on the right, and his superb cross takes out the keeper and finds Alioski speeding in at the far post and firing home, as a tired home defence looked around to see where he'd come from. Then Klich set Harrison up, and the winger's excellent shot flew just over the bar. It was all over a few minutes later when Hernandez (who else?) threaded a fine pass through the heart of the Stoke defence to set Alioski free. The North Macedonian's shot on the run was well blocked by the Stoke keeper, only to fly to Bamford, who volleyed the ball into the ground and up into the far-right corner of the net. There was still time for Costa to have a brilliant effort well saved by Federici, diving to his left, before another sub, Nketiah, set up Forshaw. He should really have scored, but again the keeper did well to block the midfielder's shot. Stoke had offered little, but certainly their keeper had kept the score down, and Etebo and Clucas worked hard for the cause. The home crowd showed their frustration with loud and derisive cheering when substitute Ince at last put a shot – easily saved by Casilla – on target.

At the end, our team came to celebrate with the fans, punching the air and laughing and joking with each other. They knew they had played well, and so did we. It was a near-perfect performance and it guaranteed a very happy journey home and a few celebratory beers later. I chatted with some Stoke fans on the walk back to the rugby club, and understandably they were unhappy with their team's performance. What I didn't quite get is that they thought we were lucky, and that really Stoke should be beating teams like Leeds! It's when you have chats like this that you realise some football fans have absolutely no clue about the game. I like to think I know when we have played well, and when we have been well beaten and hope that however painful the defeat, I can respect the qualities and good play of our opponents. I am sure not all Stoke fans know so little about the game, but these two... well, enough said. I wished them well and headed for the car.

It took a while to get away from the ground, so I reckon next time – and I sincerely hope it won't be next season, as there is absolutely no way Stoke are going to be in a promotion battle – I will possibly look to travel on one of the club coaches and leave the stress of driving and parking to others. That said, there are bonuses to driving, and I listen to the results and general sport chat on the radio.

It's been a good day as the clubs which I think will challenge us have had mixed fortunes. WBA drew at Derby; Charlton, the surprise packet so far, beat Brentford; and Forest had a great win away at Fulham. I can't help thinking that as we should have beaten Forest with some ease, things are beginning to look quite promising. Then I realise we are Leeds and anything can happen, so I banish the thought. And anyway, Swansea play tomorrow, and they come to ER next week. If they beat Birmingham, they will have the same points as us. Once clear of the football traffic, it's a good journey home and I celebrate early by getting another sandwich and buying some midget gems to enjoy on the drive. James is home when I get back, and in great form, so we all head to the' Shoulder' and have a few beers and a really happy chat. Andy has made him his favourite chicken pasta bake for tea, and we continue drinking and catching up when we get home. Eventually, Andy calls it a day, and James and I settle on the sofas and tune in to Sky, catching up with all the goals from around the country. A perfect Saturday.

A pretty perfect Sunday also. Another glorious day, and we have a BBQ and enjoy the bank holiday weekend with the Sunday papers and a few lagers. James doesn't head back to London until tomorrow, so it's really good to catch up with all his news. It's always the same when we have the kids home. Much as we love those rare but special occasions when we are all together, we often find out more about what's happening in their world when they come on their own. A lazy Sunday has its ups and downs on the football front. Manchester Utd lose to Crystal Palace, which is excellent, but Swansea comfortably beat Birmingham, so they will come to Leeds next weekend level on points with us. No matter, it's time to put feet up and enjoy having the family around.

In terms of football, we have a Carabao Cup match on Tuesday and I have decided to go, as the tickets have been reduced. So, I have 'bought' my own seat for this game and, as so often happens with the lottery of fixtures, it's Stoke City again. It's so sad that what was originally the 'League Cup' has become so devalued that even lower league clubs tend to play understrength teams, often taking the chance to give younger players a chance to have a run out. It wasn't always the case, and certainly from the mid-sixties onwards the League Cup was a sought-after prize, with a Wembley final the reward for the successful teams. It was also the first major prize that Don Revie's great team were to win, and fortunately I was there to witness it.

Leeds reached the final with 4-2 aggregate win over Derby and were to face Arsenal in the first of many clashes the two would have in the coming years. It was in many respects a poor game, with both sides perhaps almost too desperate to record a major triumph; in Leeds' case, their first silverware of significance. Terry Cooper struck the winning goal (as apparently he had dreamt he would), firing home a left-foot shot from an Eddie Gray corner in the 20th minute. The Arsenal players claimed their keeper Jim Furnell had been fouled as the ball came across, and replays showed an arm across him from Madeley as he jumped in. It would certainly not have been given in today's game, but back then it was just close. Arsenal huffed and puffed, but it was never one of those games when anxiety took over, and I didn't find myself wishing I could go for a walk until the game was finished. Leeds had the edge, and it showed when McClintock stupidly charged Gary Sprake following a corner, and all hell let loose. I remember the sheer joy at the final whistle, and Billy dancing Nobby Stiles-like in a celebration which showed the release of all the frustration built up after being so close to titles and cups in the recent years.

We broke down on the way home, and had to leave the car at some motorway services on the M1. Dad chatted to some of the many coach drivers ferrying happy Leeds fans back north, and we managed to get two seats on one of them. I don't know if he paid the guy or not; I was just pleased to be on the way home, and wrapped myself in my coat, keeping warm and reliving the game in my mind as we travelled. We had just won our first major trophy, and hopefully it would be the start of many more triumphs. I was chuffed to bits.

I had loved being at Wembley; it was such a special place, enshrined in the history of football – the 'White Horse', the Stan Matthews' final, and of course, the World Cup. So many great games, so many memories. And with my birthday on 18th May, the cup final always seemed such a special occasion – almost part of my birthday celebrations. I reckon I could name every final, competing teams, and goalscorers from 1964 to 1976, but while I might have a good guess in the few years up to the eighties, I would be struggling after that. It wasn't just football that had nurtured my Wembley dream. Every May, there was also the Rugby League Cup Final, and I grew up in the sixties when Wakefield Trinity, my home town team, played in four finals. They won three – against Hull, Huddersfield, and Wigan – and controversially lost to Leeds just a few months after that League Cup victory over Arsenal.

As we moved professionally further south, and friends and colleagues got to understand my passion for all things Leeds United, it was sometimes confusing for them to understand my total apathy at best towards Leeds RL club. For me the 'Loiners' were the Manchester United of rugby league, the big city club always buying up the smaller clubs' best players. But in the sixties, we were by far the dominant side, and with players like Turner, Neil Fox, Poynton, and Holiday, we played an exciting brand of attacking rugby that simply blew most teams away, as we did to Hull in the 1960 final, winning 38-5 and setting a then record score. Trinity returned in 1962 and 1963, beating Huddersfield and Wigan respectively before that infamous day in May 1968 when they faced the old enemy in the 'Watersplash final'. One of the things that often seemed to me to be the case was that the final, be it football or rugby, always seemed to be played on a glorious sunny afternoon. That was the other thing about Wembley. It wasn't just the history that made it special, but seeing the sun light up the immaculate playing surface, the sense of theatre as the teams entered like gladiators marching from the far side of the ground, and the presentation to the Queen or some visiting dignitaries. All of this watched over by the iconic twin towers that guided the thousands of pilgrims, dressed in their clubs' colours, on their walk up Wembley Way to the stadium. The colour, the sense of pageantry and tradition, meant every sports fan in the country – rugby or soccer – knew it was a real achievement to be enjoying the day out here. It was just so very special. But now it's gone and, sadly for me, forever. It's still called Wembley, and both rugby and football cup finals are still played there, crowds still battle their way up Wembley Way from the tube station, and there is no doubt that the comfort, seats, toilets, bars, and food facilities are much better for being upgraded. And yet... There is a reason why the BBC, and every station that broadcasts FA Cup fixtures and the final, still bang on endlessly about the 'magic of the Cup', desperate to enthuse a watching football population in matches between clubs from the lower leagues and the reserve teams of the big Premiership clubs. Desperate to convince us (as they have bought the TV rights) that actually these matches matter to us anymore.

The truth is, they don't matter. The truth is, the magic has gone. Swept away with the old towers, the battered seats, and the iconic goalposts and nets. There are, for me, many reasons why this is so, not least the vast number of televised football matches which means the once-a-year live coverage of the cup final is now just normal and no longer an event to look forward to. The FA have also massively devalued their own tournament by ridiculously staging the semi-finals of the competition at Wembley, thus ensuring that making it to the final is no longer a special occasion. This, at a time when the country boasts modern stadiums in Manchester and London that could easily host a Champions League Cup Final. Sadly, the remodelled ground has also lost that magic, and in terms of design I'm not sure it needed to. I think the architects and planners got it wrong here, losing some of the iconic features of the old stadium.

If I am honest, I do quite like the new Wembley arch, and think in time it will be viewed with the same affection as the twin towers. But that fabulous march of the gladiators has gone, replaced by a come-day-go-day midfield entry point that is the same as most grounds in the country. That beautifully prepared pitch bathed in sunshine has also gone, leaving the few shafts of sun still lighting the pitch fighting a losing battle against the ever-growing heavy shadows that dull the playing area and the senses of those watching. And the kick-off at 5.30pm. Really? And let's not mention the hundreds of empty corporate seats, shamefully placed directly in front of the TV cameras, that seem to scream out the message that football doesn't matter anymore... just the money.

The importance of the cup has also been hugely damaged by the growth of the Champions League in football and the Super League in rugby. Where once clubs saw the double as winning the League Championship and the FA Cup, now it is more likely to be the Premiership title and even Champions League qualification before the cup. In rugby, the event that now really grips supporters is the Super League final in October, which generates an unbelievable atmosphere under the lights at Old Trafford and ensures at least one match at that old ground has some passion around it.

Wembley wasn't bathed in sunshine that May Day in 1968 when the players of Trinity and Leeds marched onto that iconic ground. The area had been hit with huge storms before the game and they continued throughout the match, punctuated by periods of brilliant sunshine. The truth is the pitch was totally unplayable, with large areas of standing water covering the field, and further huge storms at half-time meant that the surface was not only waterlogged but there was a real possibility a player could drown in one of the many areas completely underwater.

But the game went on, with both sides not surprisingly making many handling mistakes, and players from both sides aquaplaning for several metres as they went to ground. Surprisingly, both kickers – Risman for Leeds and Don Fox for Wakefield, picking up kicking duties because his brother, the legendary Neil Fox missed the final through injury – managed to score early penalties, with Risman giving Leeds an early 4-2 advantage. Trinity weren't happy with the first penalty award, and the referee John Hebblethwaite lectured Bob Haigh like an old-time teacher, making sure it was completely obvious to everyone just who was in charge. He would upset Trinity a lot more before the game finished. Don Fox, who had earlier converted a penalty from distance, then kicked brilliantly from midfield and the Leeds winger Atkinson, in trying to stop the ball going into touch, slipped in the water and floated off the pitch, leaving our winger Ken Hirst to kick through and fall on the ball for a try which Fox converted from nearly the touchline.

It was then Leeds' turn to benefit from the conditions when, from a Seabourne kick through, the last defender who would have cleared the ball easily fell victim to the conditions, leaving Atkinson chasing through and trying to claim the ball. As he ran, he was alongside a Trinity defender – I think Fox – who had got back to cover. Both of them seemed to overrun, and as they turned, putting on the brakes, it looked as though they both linked arms as they tried to turn towards the ball. The Trinity player got there first and, interestingly, Eddie Waring's commentary continued unabated as Trinity ran the ball clear. But the referee wasn't following the game; he had unaccountably, and particularly given the prevailing conditions, awarded a penalty try. I think it was the first such award in the history of Wembley finals, and I can only think of one in the 50-odd years since. We were all devastated, but Hebblethwaite wasn't finished yet. He awarded Leeds a dubious penalty for an alleged high tackle by Poynton in the last minute, straight in front of the posts.

There remained only just enough time to restart the game, with Leeds leading 11-7. Fox, already awarded the Lance Todd trophy for man of the match, switched the direction of play and the receiving Leeds winger sensibly tried to trap the ball soccer-style, but it skidded under his foot and into the path of the onrushing Hirst, who hacked the ball on towards the post, wrong-footing several Leeds defenders who simply fell over in the water. Hirst just got to the ball before it crossed the dead ball line, diving for his life and victory. He was mobbed by his team mates as the Leeds players fell to the floor aghast at what they had just seen happen.

And then. And then everyone in sport must know what happened. Don Fox, the man of the match who had converted much harder chances during the game, missed the simple kick from straight in front of the posts, unbelievably shanking the ball way right of the right-hand post. And so such great moments in sport are born, and so sport so cruelly defines the life of those who play the game.

I don't know Don Fox, but I'm pretty certain that that moment, which should have been one of the greatest in his life, must have stayed with him forever, must have been there at his waking and at his sleeping and in his dreams, and must have haunted him for the rest of his days. From such moments are legends created and lives distorted; a game that should never have been played, a try that should never have been awarded, a goal that should never have mattered. How vicious can the fates be.

I was in Wakefield town centre the following Monday when Trinity paraded through to the Town Hall without the cup which was rightly theirs. I wasn't alone. I suspect only those holed up in the local prison and the very, very elderly and infirm weren't standing shoulder-to-shoulder in Wood Street, chanting the name of Don Fox so loudly and continuously, and trying to ease the pain for him that none of us could really understand. I wasn't there that Saturday in May, wasn't there to share the misery of the defeated fans and their despairing journey home. I would share it a few times in the future, though, but not that time. That time, I was at home in Wakefield; well, I was at home that afternoon, but I shouldn't have been.

I had had my share of trips to Wembley, and this time the tickets went to my Uncle Michael visiting from South Africa, my Uncle Phillip, an England rugby union international and still at the time playing for Northampton, Dad, and Andrew – at the age of nine, making his first trip to Wembley. Mum travelled with them but stayed with my Aunty Margaret while they headed to the match. In truth, I didn't put up that much of a fight about being left at home. I was coming up to my fourteenth birthday and my life was changing.

It wasn't a bad time to be growing up. My favourite football team were on their way to being the best side in the country, if not Europe; my rugby team, as mentioned, headed to Wembley four times in the sixties; and there was the music. Oh my, just how good was that? We had always had music in the house as we grew up. Dad loved Sinatra and Mum liked Perry Como and songs from the musicals. Dad used to occasionally bring old records home from the jukebox of the coffee shop that was next to where he worked. I listened to stuff like *Tell Laura I Love Her* from Ricky Vallance, and Michael Halliday's *The Story of My Life*... and then came the Beatles.

I knew that first trip to ER on Boxing Day in 1964 that I was going to love the Beatles. Our house was full of their music and my sister had already seen them twice, coming home with dried tears smudging her face and a voice that was barely audible. She had got the group's latest LP, 'Beatles for Sale', for Christmas and I played it over and over again. *Eight Days a Week, I'll Follow the Sun, Words of Love, No Reply*; I couldn't get enough of it. This music was so different. I wasn't a musician at all. My primary school didn't really offer any instrumental lessons, and if they did it wasn't the likes of me that got chosen. I could sing a bit and that was it, but now I found myself playing what I later knew to be an 'air guitar' in front of the dining room mirror, combing my hair into a Beatles' fringe and wishing it was longer. I didn't really know anything about music, but I knew I loved this Mersey sound; it was just so different. I couldn't really explain why. Maybe it was the harmonies, maybe the charisma of the group themselves, but there was just something so exciting and so much energy about this music. And it made me feel so alive and so happy. It still does.

Now, four years later, the music was alive in me, and it wasn't just the Beatles. The Sound of Motown, the Stones, Kinks, and Hollies, all filled my head, and all helped me play out my dreams of pop stardom as I refined my live act in front of the mirror. I had to move the family photographs out of the way before I took the stage. Black and white pictures of my grandparents smiled out of their black and white world; they were probably only in their early sixties, but they looked a hundred.

The world of my parents and grandparents might have been played out in monochrome, but my world was exploding with colour and new experiences. Everything was so bright, so fresh, and so exciting. As the Beatles sang out *Hello Goodbye*, I kind of understood I was leaving my childhood behind and reaching out for adolescence. And that's the real reason I wasn't with my parents at Wembley. I had met a girl at a church youth club disco. I know I was still very young, but we were allowed to go because the priest would be there, and clearly that meant there was no danger of anything getting out of hand. It wouldn't have done anyway, even if no-one was there; I was too frightened to do more than smile and show off on my racing bike. I showed off all the time, I think, but anyway this particular young lady saw enough to want to return my smile, and so that's what we did.

We smiled at each other on the school bus, we smiled at each other in the playground as I showed off even more with my 'keepie-uppies', and we smiled at each other as we walked through the park nervously moving towards holding hands. The Wembley trip provided the chance to spend a little more time together.

My sister was due to stay with a friend, and at seventeen she was already in a relationship with Steve, the man she would marry a few years later. I, on the other hand, was to stay with my grandparents who lived just about a hundred yards away from our family house. There was absolutely no chance of getting free in the evening, so the only hope was to meet up with my friend in the afternoon. And then it came to me as clear as day: I would invite her to watch the Cup Final at ours. And that's what I did, telling Grandpa that I would shout too much at the telly to watch it at his house.

It was perfect. We met in the park and then walked up to town, had a coffee in one of the cool 'mod' bars, and then headed up to my house in time for the kick-off. I was obviously very wary of our next-door neighbours Pat and John and left my friend at the corner of the road until I could check the coast was clear. The plan was for me to let myself in and then wave to her so she could walk up to the front door unobserved. I have to say this worked perfectly, and before long I was offering her a Pepsi, and we sat together on the sofa as the teams walked out on that stormy day in North London.

I had this awful feeling the house was watching me, or maybe it was my dad peering through the television cameras at Wembley. I ran round closing the curtains, just in case someone might be able to see in. And just as I settled down and tentatively tried to put my arm around her shoulder, I heard the key in the front door. I grabbed her hand and shot into the kitchen and told her to hide in the pantry, I wouldn't be long.

It was Janet and Steve and I don't think they were pleased to see me. Perhaps they had more ambitious plans for the afternoon than I did. Steve did his usual 'go play on the motorway' routine, which often worked, but this time for obvious reasons I wasn't going to shift. They said they had come to watch the match, but as neither of them had any interest in Trinity, I wasn't exactly convinced about this. Anyway, they sat down, and as the game unfolded in front of us, Janet continued to interrogate me about why I was at home and didn't seem to entirely believe my explanation for having two glasses of Pepsi. At half-time I think Steve realised I wasn't budging, so he suggested they go for a drink. I told them I would be going back to Grandpa's straight after the game, and with that they got up and left.

They were very closely followed by my girlfriend who, once freed from the pantry, surprised me with her industrial turn of phrase, and indeed her turn of pace. We never walked together again, and honestly who could blame her!

We eventually lost the Carabao Cup game against Stoke on penalties. Bielsa made some changes to the side that had played so well at the weekend. Shackleton, McCalmont, Bogusz, Clarke, and Nketiah all started, and Douglas came back into the team. We played ok, and Costa and Nketiah scored goals that saw the game finish 2-2. Stoke played a strong team and recalled Butland in goal. They huffed and puffed a bit, and I spent some time watching the antics of Nathan Jones, their under-pressure manager. He was manic, dashing around his allotted space a bit like Manuel from *Fawlty Towers* on speed. I couldn't take my eyes off him; up and down, head in hands, jabbing out hand signals, all at such speed – clearly a man I suspect very close to the edge. In the end, he got the win which probably earned him some kind of reprieve, and he celebrated joyously with his players when Butland saved Phillips' penalty which saw the side from the potteries home by 5-4.

Despite being a side low on confidence, they had scored all their penalties. I must admit, if I had to take a penalty for my life, I would choose Casilla to be in goal against me. While other keepers make themselves big, put their hands up and pull at the crossbar, stride around the penalty area as if protecting their kingdom, Kiko tends to wait before making his move – and unfortunately the ball is usually in the net by then. Still I wasn't unduly worried. I am pleased to be out of this competition, and it was a reasonably entertaining evening. No injuries and a home game to come against Swansea at the weekend. A top of the table clash.

FCOFF WhatsApp group picture

Out with The Parkies

The Boys of '66

Kath, Mike and James in Agay

With Kath at PJ's

James joins me at Fulham

Janet, Andrew and me at Emporda

With the Agay trophy

With Mike and Andrew in the Kop

Early start on Fourways

Mike, Rob and James in Calella

New Wheel AFC
Chris my teenage ER travel pal and now my brother in
law first on the left, front row

The boys at Beeston!

Calella, the view from the garden

Andy escapes the beck

CHAPTER 7

HASTINGS, SWANS, PJs AND CARAVANS

Leeds United…0; Swansea City…1
Saturday, 31ˢᵗ August

There's quite a bit of interest in the match at the weekend, with it being a top of the table clash, and I must admit I am looking forward to it and hoping we can go into the first mid-season break with three points under our belt. Having been on the road quite a bit in recent weeks, it's good to catch up with a few jobs around the house and enjoy some of the beautiful late August weather. We will be heading off in the caravan on the Sunday after the game, but only up to Thornton le Dale – a beautiful village near Pickering in North Yorkshire, nicely situated for the moors and the east coast.

I love going to the English coast, or the 'seaside' as we always called it when we were growing up. The sounds and smells of the seaside resorts remind me of fantastic holidays in my childhood, spent mainly on the east coast in boarding houses, or in Hastings at my Grandma's house. Looking back, I think I preferred to go to Grandma's little cottage off the Old London Rd, though the journey down by car in those days was a nightmare, only slightly softened by the fact that we often would stay there for a couple of weeks. The house had a lovely long garden, if slightly on the narrow side, but it was big enough for Andrew and I to spend hours playing cricket and football while Mum and Grandma chatted away and Janet listened to her music and read her magazines.

One of our visits down there coincided with a massive clash of Mods and Rockers, and I remember a group of lads on scooters driving either side of the rear of our car, smiling and waving at Janet as she sat with us in the back of the car. They stayed on our tail for several hundred yards, and I actually thought Dad was going to kill them. He was so angry, cursing under his breath that he wanted to run them off the road, and worse. Only Mum's strong protests stopped him from achieving his objectives. When Grandma, sat in the front, tried to calm matters by telling everyone Dad didn't mean it, he turned to look at us with such a contorted reddened face that it was fairly obvious that he absolutely did. The Mods didn't give a stuff about Dad, leaving him apoplectic as they sped off, weaving and twisting in front of us, and giving Dad the old two-fingered salute as they disappeared into the night. While mostly the youngsters preened and postured, trying to draw attention to themselves, there were some nasty incidents, and the police reacted strongly, trying rightly to protect the thousands of holidaymakers whose annual leave was being ruined by these gangs of youths. I remember they rounded hundreds of them up and marched them up out of the town and past Grandma's house. I can't believe the police would get away with that kind of action in today's world, but back then it seemed quite a sensible thing to do and it stopped all the trouble in the town.

A year or so later, I returned to Hastings with Chris Morton, my best friend at school and most often my companion at ER. I was only 15 at the time, Chris a year older, but amazingly our parents let us go to Hastings for a week on our own, providing we checked in at Grandma's once or twice during the week. We stayed in a boarding house quite near the centre of town and an easy walk to the pier and beaches. We were too young to get away with drinking in the local pubs, but we did get some cans of beer from a local off-licence where the manager seemed totally disinterested in checking our ages. We drank the beer in our room and on the beach and enjoyed trying to look as cool as possible in our Levi and Wrangler jackets. One night we went to the pictures and took in an X-certificate film our mothers would certainly not have approved of, but which we found surprisingly stimulating.

Some of the other residents staying in our boarding house included an older couple, also from Yorkshire. Each night at the evening meal, the woman would ask us what we'd been up to that day. Rather than tell her the truth, that we'd spent the day on the beach looking at all the fantastic women in various stages of undress soaking up the sun, we would tell her we'd visited Grandma or gone to the museum or something. Her husband sat listening intently, and always at the end of the meal he would make his only comment, 'Remember, lads, say nowt!' One evening we went down on the pier and spent some coins on the amusements, and while we were there we noticed some German girls listening to a radio and laughing and giggling together. There were about 12 of them, and they were obviously part of one of the many European youth or school groups attracted to Hastings by its place in medieval history. There were too many of them for us to try and start a chat with, so we hung around on the edges, leaning on the railings, looking at the sea and chatting.

Then we noticed two of the girls on the steps down to the beach, looking as if they were being troubled by a group of English lads. They were clearly not enjoying this and were trying to make their way up the steps and back onto the pier. Neither of us being particularly brave, we were not inclined to intervene until, as we got closer, it became obvious the youths were only about 12 and the girls had already pretty much broken free of them. Chris had taken his German 'O' level just a few weeks earlier, and as the girls arrived back on the pier he asked them if they were ok. They were, and not only that, they were happy to chat, so we decided to go and get a coke and get to know each other a bit better. They were on a youth club visit from a place called Regensburg in Bavaria, and they were in Hastings for another two weeks. Their names were Jutta and Christina, and they were about our age and, wonderfully, spoke excellent English.

The time flew, and soon they were telling us they had to meet their friends and head back to the hotel. They were on a curfew, and anyone coming in late would be grounded the next day. We arranged to meet them the following afternoon at the pier and smiled as we said goodnight.

Chris and I pretty much floated home, stopping only to get a few lagers to help calm our nerves. We had a date! And try as we might, neither of us could get to sleep that night, so excited were we about the day to come. It was like Christmas Eve, and we couldn't wait for the morning. That said, it took ages for the clock to get round to 2pm – the appointed meeting time.

We survived the usual breakfast time interrogation and I even went out shopping and bought myself the single *Good Morning Starshine* by Oliver, from the musical *Hair*. Amazingly, the boarding house had an old-fashioned gramophone player and I scratched the record beyond repair in my desperation to hear the song. I don't know why I liked the song so much. Certainly, the lyric wasn't great, but I just loved it and still do, and in fact I have just put it on from one of my Spotify playlists as I am writing this now. The girls were on time and so were we, having spent several hours preparing our coolest look. It being a beautiful day, we decided to head onto the beach and the girls had a big bag with books, creams, towels, and a radio. We had a towel each from the boarding house and a copy of the *News of the World* – another thing our mothers wouldn't have been impressed with.

Having waited 17-and-a-half hours for this moment, we found it was one of those occasions when you think, *Now what?* We made small talk. They were going on a day trip to London the next day and wouldn't be around; I told them I was going to my Grandma's. They didn't look impressed. This was an obvious error on my part and I lay quietly, wondering how badly it might have damaged my image. While I was lying there, eyes closed, listening to the Beach Boys singing *Do It Again,* someone else turned up and started chatting to the girls. She was one of the youth group – one of their friends – and she was stunning! Jutta and Christina were both fairly pretty, one dark and one fair, and both funny and really friendly. But their friend was, well, a real looker. The girls introduced us to her, and I shuffled round to say hello and shake her hand. She said she was called Honey, and I heard Chris whimper quietly as he lay listening to the conversation. Later, he would whimper involuntarily again as Honey offered to rub suntan lotion on his back, and I forgot all about my promises to Mum and Grandma as I patiently waited for my turn.

It was then, on the beach, with the radio playing sounds of the summer and the gorgeous Honey rubbing suncream into my back, that I noticed the old couple from our boarding house sitting on a beach blanket just a few yards away from me. The lady was lying down and looked to be sleeping soundly, but her husband was sitting up with a cigarette in his hands, looking intently towards me with the lovely Honey massaging my back. He flicked the ash from his cigarette and a hint of a smile appeared across his face. 'Remember, lad,' he said. 'Say nowt!

The holiday flew past and we met the girls regularly, but too soon it was time for us to head to the station to begin the long train journey home. We had all exchanged addresses and agreed to become penpals. We promised to keep in touch, and the way we had begun to pair off meant that I would write to Jutta and Chris to Christina. What Chris didn't know is that the very next week my mum was due in Hastings with my brother for their family holiday. When it had first been discussed, I had protested strongly that I didn't want to go back to Hastings and that I would try and get a holiday job and stay home in Yorkshire with Dad and Janet. I don't know if Mum ever worked out just why her eldest son suddenly desperately wanted to return to Hastings, but two days after the long train ride home, I clambered into the family car and prepared for the tortuous car journey back to Sussex.

Of course, I made every excuse under the sun to go off on my own, and Andrew couldn't quite understand why his sports buddy kept disappearing, but he would in a few years. I met Jutta a few times and we went to the beach and walked around the parks, then it was time for her to return to Germany. We promised again to write, and in fact we did and regularly, developing a friendship that eventually led to Chris and I travelling the next summer to stay with the girls and their families in Regensburg, but that's a story for perhaps another time. They were lovely girls and great penfriends, and they shared lots of the same interests – music, school, growing up, and generally trying to make sense of life and all the opportunities that stretched out in front of us.

One of the evenings, I went down to the boarding house where they were staying. Honey answered the door and told me that Jutta and Christina had gone on some history trip somewhere, so they weren't home. But she was. She told me to wait for a minute and disappeared inside, only to appear again a few seconds later, pushing me back onto the street and following after me. We set off walking to the town and then cut back across the road towards Old Town then got on the big lift that went up to the cliffs and the castle. There were less people there, and we laughed and chatted a lot as we made our way towards the famous old castle which had fuelled my love of medieval history when I had visited it so often as a boy.

I started to tell her all about William and Harold and the battles of 1066, then I realised she wasn't listening; she was just laughing at me. She ran on ahead and then stopped and waited for me to catch up. She looked simply stunning, wearing jeans and a little Levi jacket with a pink shirt underneath and, as appeared fairly obvious, not a great deal at all under that. As I caught up with her, she reached up and put her arms around my neck. With my heart beating like crazy, I put my arms around her waist. It was right then, as we moved towards each other, that I remembered the old man in the boarding house and his words of wisdom. 'Remember, lad, say nowt!'

I guess, like most football fans, as mentioned earlier I have a routine for home matches. Getting ready, the travel, and pre-match food and drinks, all play a huge part in the build-up and enjoyment of going to the game. And while obviously before the match you haven't got the euphoria of victory coursing through your veins, equally you don't feel the misery and despair of defeat either.

I always prefer to have one of the children or Andrew with me, but as they all live down south or in Dublin and they all have their own family responsibilities, most often I am on my own. That said, I usually meet up with Damien, Dad's eldest from his second marriage and a great guy, and his pal Rick for a quick beer and catch-up before going into the stadium, and then of course there are all the people who sit near me. So, as regular fans will know, you are never truly on your own.

A perfect Saturday will always have a lazy start, and while Andy watches some cookery programme and enjoys some tea and toast, I resist the call for breakfast in case it spoils the fish and chips and beer a little later. I usually tune into Sky Sports News for any early team information, but there is little of interest today. We only lead Swansea at the top of the table on goal difference, so we need to put a little distance between them and us, and I can't see why we shouldn't win comfortably this afternoon.

There is a funny exchange on 5Live when the Leeds fan and comedian Micky P Kerr, who released a reworked 'Bielsa Rhapsody' for charity, rings into the programme to explain in broad Yorkshire why we will be too good for the 'Swans'. I grab my scarf and head to the car; first stop to get a paper, and second to get up to PJ's fish and chip shop on the main Bradford Road, between East Ardsley and Tingley. We discovered PJ's when we used to travel up for games from Berkhamsted and it was the first 'chippy' we came to after leaving the M1. What a find. I think even Southerners would agree that fish and chips in that part of the country just can't compete in terms of taste to those in the north, and PJ's is right up there at the top in terms of taste and excellent portions. I get parked up and ask for haddock and chips in a tray, and then a liberal sprinkling of salt, sauce, and vinegar, and my tongue is almost hanging out. Back to the car, leaving the door slightly ajar so I don't smell fish and chips all week, find something useful to read in the sports section, and turn the radio on for a catch-up with any live matches being played. It's usually a bit early to tune into Radio Leeds and their football programme, which obviously is much more interesting to listen to than the more national and Premiership driven 5Live.

I like the combination of Adam Pope and the ex-player Noel Whelan, and they usually put on a good programme, particularly after the match, when their assessment of how things have gone usually fits that of my own. They are also very good at dealing with fans' phone calls, even though on occasion they must wonder what planet some of the callers exist on. The fish and chips are superb and worth the sacrifice of tea and toast, especially as it will be three weeks before I can enjoy them again, thanks to the stupid international break.

I only just make it to meet up with Damien, as there is quite a queue to get into the Centenary Pavilion, or whatever it is called now. I pay my money and get a can of John Smiths on entry and find the two of them with Rick's son up by the staging, where occasionally former players give their opinions on team selection and performance. It's good to have a catch-up but Rick is keen to get in the ground. So, we arrange to meet in a few weeks, before the Derby game, and I go and find a spare seat to finish my drink and check out the team news. It's as I expected and hoped for, with Cooper recovered to reclaim his centre half role and Alioski staying at full back, with Douglas and Baradi on the bench, joined by Costa, Shackleton, and Nketiah. There is a bit of a clamour for Nketiah to start and he has certainly proved to be a hugely popular addition to the squad with the fans, who can be heard regularly chanting 'Eddie Eddie'. It's a bit tough on Bamford, who has scored four goals in five games so far, and who for me has looked really sharp and worked incredibly hard for the team. I am interested in seeing how Helder Costa will play, once he claims a regular starting spot. I am sure he has been bought, in time, to replace Hernandez, when the Spanish wizard's powers start to wane. Already he has a goal to his name in the midweek match against Stoke and a super assist for Nketiah's match-winning goal against Brentford. Some in the crowd are not convinced, but to me he has that Hernandez-like ability to go past defenders and get to the byeline.

We start well against the side from Wales, and Alioski shoots acrobatically from a Dallas cross only for Woodman in the Swansea goal to save smartly. Dallas, who like Forshaw and Bamford seems to be a different player this season, then intercepts a poor clearance from the keeper and crosses from the right, only for Bamford to steer a header wide of the post when it might have been easier to score. Swansea don't offer much offensively, and Van der Hoorn wastes a free kick from a dangerous position. Just before half-time we almost take a well deserved lead when Cooper hits the bar with a powerful header from a Hernandez corner. The talk at half-time on the terraces is all positive, and surely sooner rather than later we will take one of the chances we have created? I was disappointed with Swansea, who have offered little, and I can't see this side challenging for honours with their limited manner of their play. The second half continues in the same vein, with Woodman saving well from Hernandez following lovely inter-passing between Harrison, Forshaw, and Klich. Nketiah, on as a sub, then sprints free only to shank his shot up and over the bar when he looked certain to score. Surely the goal will come? And when Costa cleverly sets up Hernandez, the Spaniard's shot flashes inches wide of the Swansea goal with Woodman well beaten.

There are the mumblings of concern on the terraces as Leeds seem to squander more and more opportunities. We have all seen this scenario play out before, and sure enough Swansea start to come back into the game, and we almost lose a bizarre own goal when a Celina corner hits an unsighted Phillips and rolls just wide of Casilla's left-hand post. Encouraged, Roberts heads over, and Swansea players shout loudly for a penalty when Casilla challenges Surridge, but referee Bond fortunately waves their appeals away. Then, having given one or two prompts, Swansea score. Harrison concedes a corner on the right, which is swung into the area by Grimes. Confusion reigns, as has been the case a few times this season from dead ball situations, and once again no-one claims the ball. It is only half cleared and falls to Routledge near the penalty spot, and his scuffed shot rolls apologetically past Casilla and into the net, off the left-hand post.

The Swansea players celebrate joyously with the thousand or so fans who have made the journey from South Wales. The goal came in the 90th minute, but there is still time for Nketiah to equalise, when a brilliant cross from Dallas eludes the Swans defence, only for Eddie to send his header into the side netting.

I can't believe we have lost this match – our first defeat of the season and a game we should have won comfortably, even though Swansea did exert a little pressure late on. In his post-match comments, Steve Cooper the Swansea manager was buoyant, claiming his team 'had come to win', that they had a clear 'game plan', and knew areas to 'exploit'. I know he was probably excited but really, what game was he watching? To me, Swansea at best seemed to be a hardworking side who got lucky because we decided once again to miss far too many chances, just like in the Forest game. Only this time we haven't just lost one point, we have lost all three. It's a bad loss and made worse by the fact that Swansea now go three points ahead of us. There are also wins for WBA, a threat, and Charlton, who continue to play above themselves on their return from League One. We find ourselves in third place, three points behind Swansea who are top, and three points ahead of Fulham in sixth. WBA are fourth, just a point behind us and Bristol City, who we have already beaten soundly but are also in the top six. It's obviously early days, but three of the teams that I think will challenge us are already in the top group. Having watched Swansea this afternoon, I don't think they will be one of them, and Charlton will surely fall away. Time will tell.

I hate it when we lose, and I especially hate it when we lose at home and on a Saturday afternoon. It makes the evening so long, and it's not fair on Andy when, instead of responding to discussion about plans for the weekend or how the kids are, I am clearly reliving the game that played out earlier in the day. I'm sure I am not alone in this respect, and many wives and partners up and down the country probably hate the way that football takes over their weekend, particularly if the result doesn't go the right way and leaves them living with a manic depressive. Of course, defeats are even worse when you have to endure an international break, which means two whole weeks before you can fix things and get life back on an even keel again.

I do have to be clear here. I am English and will always support my home country, even getting quite excited and carried away when we are involved in major tournaments like the Euros and World Cup. But there are simply too many 'international breaks' which disrupt the season, and there are too many meaningless games where the broadcasters expect us to get excited about England playing some minnow country whose standard of play isn't much higher than a pub team. I completely get that smaller countries should be able to play in these major tournaments, but surely there should be qualifying stages for smaller nations to play through, a bit like the Rugby Union World Cup organisers put in place. In recent years, the World Cup has lasted so long, even someone as completely football daft as me has lost interest. Plans to increase the number of teams in these competitions must ultimately ruin them as spectacles, turning spectators off until the final stages when competition at last becomes relevant. It's the same with the Champions League – again, far too many meaningless games, where teams from inferior leagues go head-to-head with the big clubs of England, Spain, Germany, and Italy. Given that FIFA and UEFA have been riddled with incompetence, and worse, I don't expect any radical change any time soon; just more expansion and ridiculous decisions like playing the Word Cup in Qatar. No doubt there will be a move to create a European super league, with teams like Real Madrid, Barcelona, Juventus, AC Milan, and others, mixing it with teams from the Premiership. I wouldn't necessarily disagree with such a structure, but there would have to be relegation and promotion from any such league, and there would be the problem of what to do about clubs like Celtic and Rangers, whose standard is more like mid-Championship than top of the Premiership.

A better structure of international fixtures, with teams of similar abilities competing in more meaningful fixtures, has to be the way ahead. That would benefit all true football supporters and allow them to support their national teams in competitive fixtures, while not having the lifeblood of the game – the national leagues – being continually interrupted for meaningless international matches. As it is, we are about to embark on an international break, which effectively means that our league will now stop for two weeks just as it has got up and running. Crackers! Worse, of course, we go into the break on the back of our first league defeat of the season. There is nothing that can be done but take the pain and try and fill the time until 'proper' football returns in a fortnight and we head to play our old Yorkshire rivals at Barnsley. Until then, it's time to get the caravan out and head up to Thornton le Dale.

I guess lots of people have views about caravaners, and probably not universally positive ones at that, especially if you have ever been stuck behind one or two on some single-carriage road in heavy holiday traffic. I completely get that, and of the image of caravaners boiling a kettle outside their van on a tiny little stove, dressed in cords and woolly jumpers, and stuck in some time-warp in a desolate field in the middle of nowhere. It is, to be fair, a picture that I had myself. And even as an experienced caravaner, I have found myself cursing and swearing at the back of a caravan being driven at funereal pace and unable to safely overtake. So, way back in 1987, when Andy and I discussed the possible purchase of a caravan to enable us to take a holiday with two young children, I must admit I was not immediately attracted to the idea. We had always loved holidays, and as students had travelled the Greek islands, spending weeks and weeks away from home in the sunshine and loving the freedom to island hop. This was not so easy to do with a growing family, and anyway we were completely skint as Andy had left her teaching post to look after the kids, so we were soldiering on just on my teacher's salary. With half our income gone and desperate for a summer holiday, we hit on the idea of buying a caravan. That way, we could head to the South of France and the sunshine, and we could take our own things – toys, bikes, food, drink – and get to the sun on the cheap. At least, that was the plan.

Some friends in the next village to us had an old caravan they were looking to sell, so we went to look at it, and half an hour later we were proud owners of an old and fairly basic 'Monza'. It was clean, it was four-berth, and at four hundred quid it was perfect, despite its fairly dodgy brown and cream colour scheme. Our friends agreed to store it for us until we could find a place to park it, and of course we had to insure it and get the fittings in place on the car in order to tow it. Suddenly it wasn't four hundred pounds any more, but with no alternative we pressed on.

Despite its age, colour, and fairly basic level of comfort, it would be a roof over our heads and it meant we could travel. Well, we could, once I had learnt to drive with a caravan on the back of the car.

Once we had negotiated a cut-price deal to park it on the forecourt of my local garage (a year or so later it was, mercifully, nicked from there), I had the chance to hitch up and practise driving with it attached to the car. I went very slowly and headed to a supermarket car park – shut for the evening – to practise manoeuvres. Really, it was all about understanding length, stopping distance, overtaking, and speed, which really meant heading away from the car park and finding a stretch of dual carriageway or even motorway to try and get a better feel for driving with a house attached to your car.

I gave up trying to reverse when I found the caravan almost overtaking me, as I got the manoeuvre hopelessly wrong. Now all these years later, providing I have lots of space to work in, I can just about manage this activity... but only just! I didn't overtake anyone else on that practice run, but I did experience that horrid feeling when the van seems to 'snake', and for a few seconds you feel completely out of control, just as you do when a huge lorry overtakes you and it seems as if it's going to suck you underneath its back wheels. We decided to stay in England for our first holiday, and planned a two-stop holiday at Andrew and Tricia's, then on to a site in the Bournemouth area. I planned to travel on a Sunday, as there would be less traffic and certainly far fewer heavy goods vehicles around. Andrew lived in a pleasant village just outside Ipswich, and most of the route was dual carriageway – the old A1, A14, and so on. It was a good journey, but it wasn't long before I realised my plan of just driving at a steady speed and never overtaking was hopelessly unrealistic.

I don't think we had got much further than Worksop before I was so frustrated with the lorry in front that I just had to pull out and go past him. It took a while, staring in my extended wing mirror, before I felt the cars behind me were sufficiently far away for me to start the manoeuvre. But eventually I gritted my teeth and went for it, keeping my foot down, and watching the lorry as we drew level then eventually surged past it – but not before I was convinced the bastard had put his foot down!

At last beyond him, I watched carefully until I felt it safe to pull in front of him, making sure my speed would take me further away from him. I am sure I stayed in the overtaking lane far longer than I needed to, and I was aware that faster moving vehicles were snarling up in a disorderly queue behind me, but at last I indicated left and pulled in front of the lorry. I had done it; I had overtaken something. And each time I repeated the process on that first journey, I went through the same agonies, so that Andy and the two children found themselves taking the same sharp intake of breath that I did until at last we were safely past the vehicle. Of course, as with everything, practice breeds confidence. And by the time we had left Andrew's and negotiated the M25 enroute from Ipswich to Bournemouth, I was feeling less apprehensive and more in charge. The holiday passed without incident, and though we never bothered to put up the very large and very ugly dark brown awning, we both felt we were getting to understand our new home.

Andy found the cooker fairly straightforward, once I had managed to get the gas supply working and while the gas also lit up our little heater, we made sure we turned it off fairly sharpish once there was some warmth, to avoid poisoning ourselves. We had running water, too. And while we relied on the kettle to provide hot water, we could survive, and with the electrics fixed and giving us light, and the portable loo up and working, we gradually began to feel quite at home.

I must admit to a feeling of quiet satisfaction as I parked the caravan up at its garage base and fixed the fairly primitive lock over the jockey wheel to secure our holiday home until the next time. I have a pathological hatred of all things DIY, having no interest and no ability in fixing things, and usually experience only miserable failure whenever I have been foolish enough to try. The fact that we had survived a whole week in the caravan and got home safely meant that the next time we ventured out for a summer holiday we would be more experienced and more adventurous. The next time we would head to France to the Cote d'Azur and to the sunshine of the Mediterranean we had missed so much in the last couple of years.

CHAPTER 8

HOT DAYS, WARM BEERS AND TITLE WINNERS IN THE SOUTH OF FRANCE

And so a year later, having broken up in late July from my job as Head of St. Joseph's, Pontefract – a post I had been in only since January – we piled the kids (in those days only Katherine and Michael; James was yet to arrive in this world) into the back of the car and set off on our long journey to the South of France.

I guess there are two things you should know straight away. First, my story of a teaching career that ended up with headship is, as I have said, really for volume two of these notes. But yes, the responsibility of the post was just as great in those early days as it was 26 years later when I retired from Berkhamsted Prep School, my third headship in the period. One huge difference, of course, was that back then there was no internet and crucially no mobile phones, though they were on their way. This meant that once I knew that all the children were home safely and convinced myself that the papers on my desk could wait till September, I could leave and not be contactable by work for a whole month. No Inset to plan for, no timetables to prepare, and no School Development Plan to write. How did we cope?!

The second thing you should know is that in order to safely pull our battered old caravan the thousand or so miles down to the Cote d'Azur, we had bought a new car. Well, it was new to us; it was a Talbot Solara, and it was red. The guys who ran the garage where we parked the van up on the forecourt had fitted the towing gear and wired in an indicator to the dashboard, which I really quite liked. It seemed a bit old school to me, and I always felt a huge sense of relief when its brightly flickering orange light let me know it was safe to overtake.

Now, with a few expeditions under our belt, I was a lot more confident as a caravan driver, and the 'new' car gave me a greater sense of security. We made good time down to Dover, where we stopped on a pretty basic site somewhere up on the cliffs overlooking the old town. In years to come we would stay on a variety of sites on both sides of the Channel, the best was by a distance in the village of Guines, just south of Calais. It wasn't just the best site, but it also meant the ferry and all the hassle around that part of the journey was over with and we could look forward to brighter weather and, at least for the first couple of hundred miles or so, quieter roads as we made our way south.

Unfortunately this time we were stuck up in some field, and once we had got the kids to bed Andy and I enjoyed a can of beer and a much-needed cig (yes, for right or wrong we were still smokers in those days. Andy stopped a few years later when she was pregnant with James; sadly, I struggled on until my mid-forties before I finally kicked the habit) or two before we tiptoed into the caravan to get some much-needed sleep. I woke up at about 5am with the light streaming in through the flimsy curtains; no pull-down blinds in those days. Peering out of the window, I was relieved to see there was almost no wind, which would mean a calm crossing. And if conditions were the same in France, we would make good time and wouldn't suffer the scary buffeting that can so unnerve drivers of caravans.

The children, sleeping at the front of the van, were beginning to stir. They were very young to be going on this kind of a trip; Katherine, about to celebrate her fourth birthday in a few weeks, and Michael just two and a couple of months. He still needed a cot, and I had managed to construct something which stopped him rolling off his single bed. It wasn't great; I just wedged one of the sides of his cot from home and somehow managed to trap it behind the cooker at one end and a window handle at the other. I did tell you earlier that I was fairly hopeless at DIY, but this contraption worked once Mike understood that it would collapse if he stood up and tested it with his weight.

In fairness to the children, they were brilliant travellers, and once we had them secured in their car seats with some of their books and toys around them, they weren't much trouble. And if they were, we always had lots of bribes in the form of sweets to keep them quiet. The best ferry we actually found in those early days was the Sally Line, sailing from Folkestone. It was a bit further, but the boat had one of those 'ball parks' on it, which kept the kids busy for the entire crossing and meant that we could sit and enjoy a drink and a cigarette and only occasionally have to intervene in their play.

On that first occasion, though, our sailing is from Dover and, once parked up – always slightly hair-raising with a caravan attached, but especially the first time – I go in search of a paper, taking Katherine with me. It's the first time we have taken them on a boat and it's not that long since the horrific sinking of the *Herald of Free Enterprise*, so once I've got the paper sorted, I find my way to the back of the boat. Holding on tight to Kath's hand, I watch as the rear doors of the boat are firmly closed.

Now with the boat's doors secure, I can relax a bit and ponder the journey ahead. We plan to reach a town called Chalon Sur Marne, just south of Reims and a journey of about four hours, if overall I average fifty miles an hour. That would be an easy 'ask' on today's roads, with motorway connections literally from Calais to the South of France, but it wasn't the case in 1989. For a start, we had to queue all the way round Calais when we left the boat, which was a frustratingly slow start to the holiday. Once free of that traffic, there was at last a stretch of motorway, but it stopped at St Quentin, quite a bit short of the major town of Reims. It was when I was on this single carriageway road that I had to stop for petrol, and for some reason I decided to check all around the car, but particularly under the bonnet.

I don't know why I did this, because just like I was totally useless at DIY I had no mechanical ability either, short of putting petrol in, checking tyre pressures, and oil and water levels. That was it; I couldn't do anything else. So I can only think I was looking to make sure we weren't overheating, that we weren't losing any water. We weren't. It was a lot worse than that: we were losing oil! I mean, frigs sake, losing oil has to be bad. The car was too hot for me to check levels, so I did the only thing I could and got back in the car and set off for Reims. For the rest of the journey to Chalon, I had my eyes totally focused on the oil warning light, expecting it to come on shining bright blue at any time. And then, as if to raise my stress levels to breaking point, as we approached the city of Reims the temperature gauge started to rise... slowly at first, but then as we seemed to spend longer and longer stuck waiting for the endless number of traffic lights to change, it got nearer and nearer to the top of the gauge. We had read somewhere that when a car is overheating, you should turn the car heaters up to try and equalise the heat of the water in the engine. Stuck in endless queues and watching the needle hovering around at the top of the gauge, I cursed the French traffic as Andy tried to cool the children down with 'wet wipes'. It wasn't just the car that was overheating, we were all melting.

Fortunately the traffic began to ease as we left the heart of the city, and as we ran on to a dual carriageway the temperature needle at last began to fall, allowing us to turn the heaters off and carry on to Chalon in a more relaxed fashion. We were certainly all a lot cooler – physically and emotionally – by the time we stopped at the traffic lights waiting to turn right into the caravan site. And that's when Katherine showed how attentive she'd been on the journey when she called out from the back, 'Daddy, how long before these fucking lights change!' We spent the rest of the holiday talking about these 'flickering lights' every time we approached a traffic light, keen to ensure she didn't repeat her observations when back at school or, worse, to grandparents.

It had been a horrible drive but eventually, some six hours after disembarking the ferry, we had at last reached the caravan park at Chalon sur Marne. One thing I had done as part of my holiday prep was to buy some book about French caravan parks, and though I hadn't booked anywhere specific to stay, I had plotted a rough route through the country and down to the Mediterranean. Chalon sur the first planned stop and we had made it. Once we had got the car unhooked and pushed the van into place, Andy took the kids off in the double buggy we had borrowed for the trip, to investigate the site and to try and find an ice cream. I collapsed in a heap, having got the legs down, set up the water and loo, got the gas working, and enjoyed a much-needed cig break in peace. I was stressed about the car but it was too hot to check oil pressures, and anyway, there was nothing much I could do about it at the moment. I had a big plastic bottle of Castrol engine oil with me, and that was at least a tad reassuring. Andy and the kids were soon back, and they brought good news. The site had a children's play area and not only that, it had a little cafe selling stuff like omelette, chips, pizza, and salads. There was also a drinks machine that dispensed, as we were to find out, ice cold lager. We had hit the jackpot at the end of a long day for all of us.

I woke the next morning, pondering in my head the best route to continue our journey south. No-one else was awake, and it was great to stay warm, peaceful, and still, ahead of what I knew was going to be a long day. And of course, there was the oil problem which could change all our plans at the flash of a blue warning light. I decided that it would be best to head to Troyes and then Dijon, all on single carriage roads with sections of dual carriageway, before we would at last pick up the motorway south of Dijon. The children started to stir, and while Andy busied about getting them ready, I made sure the car was set up as comfortably as possible for them for the long journey ahead. Eventually I had to check the oil and water levels. I put it off till last. and if the dipstick showed a clear lack of oil and we had to abort the journey, at least we were safe, off the road, and in a place where we could get pizza and ice-cold beer. The water, which I had finally topped up when the car had cooled down last night, was absolutely fine. And encouraged, I grabbed some tissues and pulled out the dipstick. Well, it wasn't empty, but it was showing a level slightly below the halfway point between the two lines. Sod's law. Really not low enough to abort mission, not high enough to guarantee a stress-free journey. I got the Castrol out of the boot and poured a good amount in. Time to put the bonnet down and get the journey underway.

It was a beautiful day and about 8am we pulled away from the site. Both of us agreed that despite the violent thunderstorm that had curtailed our evening drinks, we would definitely return to Chalon. We made good progress along country roads before stopping in a village where conveniently there was a space big enough for a car and caravan to park up right outside a boulangerie. We stocked up with cold water and those lovely *pain raisins* and Andy bought quite a few bribes for the kids, including those 'Chupa Chups' lollies they loved to suck on. We had loads of tapes to listen to on the journey, ranging from kids' stories to the Beatles, Sixties compilations, and more modern stuff like Wham and the Police. The blue light stayed wonderfully unlit, the sun was coming up, we had food and water, and life for the moment was good. I spent mile after mile working out distances and clumsily trying to remember how mathematically to change kilometres into miles. It was slightly depressing to see that Lyon, roughly the area we were heading to, was 450 kilometres away – less so to think of it as 270 miles or so. I also tried to work out how many miles we were averaging in the hour, which was definitely not an exact science as we got snared up in serious traffic going through Troyes.

What none of us knew at the time was that this was the day we would pull the caravan the furthest without building in an overnight stop; we never again spent so much time continuously on the road. We just kept going and going, and when we did stop for petrol and clean-up breaks, I looked at my AA caravan sites book and tried to find a suitable stopping place for the night. We eventually joined the motorway *'autoroute soleil'* south of Dijon and started to make good time, hugging the slow lane and doing battle with lorries and other caravaners. The kids shouted with glee as we passed the cartoon figures advertising the *'aire de jugy'*, situated every thousand metres or so at the side of the motorway as we headed for Macon. We would say hello to them every year as we passed; we still do today.

Eventually we hit the approaches to Lyon and got into heavy traffic queuing to go through the tunnels that take traffic out of the centre of the city. I suffered agonies watching the temperature gauge rising again, and once more kept it under control by putting the heaters on. We were boiling in the afternoon heat, even with all the windows open; aircon wasn't standard in those days certainly not in a Talbot Solara. After an unpleasant hour or so, we were through the city and heading south again towards the town of Vienne. Just as you pass the city on your left, the motorway bends to the right, and for a moment or two you are driving close to the river. With the sunlight glinting on the water, it lifts the spirits and puts you in holiday mood. It was time to stop and, given that we had already gone further than our intended stopping place, we found a place called Tain Le Hermitage in our AA book that seemed perfect and very close to the motorway exit. We were nearly at journey's end, but not before we spent ages queuing at the peage, and then struggled to pull the caravan up a massive climb. The car at one point almost seemed to be stopping with the effort of pulling us all up hill. It reminded us of the scene in *Dumbo* where the train struggles up the tracks saying, 'I think I can, I think I can', before eventually at the summit shooting downhill shouting out, 'I thought I could, I thought I could.' We made it, and we pulled into the site at Tain, having spent the best part of 11 hours on the road. The kids had been brilliant. They had enjoyed the picnic stops and the bribes, and now they had earned a run and a play. Andy took them off to find some ice cream, and hopefully some cold beers for us. Even at seven o'clock it was still sweltering. I set up the caravan and collapsed on a chair, enjoying a cigarette and already planning the route ahead and the next stopping place on our long journey.

We were heading to a campsite in Cavalaire near to St Tropez, that had been recommended to us by one of the girls in Andy's babysitting group who had stayed there earlier in the summer. In the end, the journey took us three days, and we stayed at a lovely site in Aix en Provence the following day, which put us within easy distance of journey's end. At the start of each day, I checked the oil, and each time it had fallen below the halfway point on the dipstick. I would need some more Castrol for the journey home. As we got further south and the temperatures continued to rise, we found a wonderful thing called *'relais Bebe'* on the motorway services. These were like mobile homes where you could literally give your children a cooling wash-down, change nappies, etc, and be given fresh and ice-cold water. They were fantastic, and we used them every year we travelled to the Med.

Cavalaire was busy. In fact, it was absolutely rammed when we approached the resort around mid-afternoon. We inched our way through the town, looking at the signposts advertising restaurants, hotels, and caravan sites. Eventually we found the place and drove up a slight hill towards reception. There was a little lay-by for caravans to pull into just in front of a formidable red and white barrier that had a sign saying *'Complet'* stuck to it. Andy said, 'Shit' but I didn't know why. But as she explained that *complet* meant full, I got the horrible meaning of what we had done – or rather hadn't done. We hadn't booked a site. In fact, we hadn't booked any of them, and now we were stuck in a layby at the top of a hill with nowhere to go, because I absolutely couldn't reverse.

Andy, who spoke some French, went to plea with the teenagers on reception duty while I just sat with my head on the steering wheel. When she came back, the news wasn't good. Apparently, they were booked every day until September, and we were still in July. The only hope, we were told, was to speak to the boss, who was having his lunch but would be back within the hour. They asked us to move, but I told them I couldn't. We waited where we were and they stared at us, so I stared back. Then they came out gesticulating and asking why we hadn't moved, so I told them I couldn't fucking reverse! It was during this exchange that an older guy, the boss, approached. Andy explained that we had no booking but had come on a friend's recommendation who had asked her to say hello to him. And that's where we got lucky.

The boss wanted to know who the friend was, and when Andy told him the name, everything changed. Apparently, her friend's husband, who was our village Bobby, had helped the owner kick some rowdy English kids off the site during their stay, and helped diffuse a nasty situation. He was called Nev Duke. The owner smiled. 'Any friend of Nev Duke is a friend of mine,' he said, and with that he got on a bike, lifted the barrier, and found us a nice shady spot near all the amenities. How stupid had we been not to realise we needed to book, and how much did we owe Nev Duke? We had a fabulous holiday, even though the site was rammed with younger people and there wasn't that much for families. We were just so grateful to have a base. We learned so much on that holiday about how to plan properly and how to make sure we had the right kit to make living for a month in a caravan comfortable. We didn't even have a fridge to keep the kids' drinks and fruit cold, and worse, there was nowhere to keep our beer cold – absolutely essential for such a long stay.

During the holiday, we visited some of the other sites in my AA book, and we found an absolute cracker near the seaside town of Agay, on the coast between St Raphael and Cannes. We drove over to check the site and realised immediately it was more suitable for families than the one in Cavalaire. It was full when we visited, but they did have a space for the last week of our holiday, which we booked there and then. We returned to Cavalaire to thank the owner and enjoy the last few days at our first stop on the Cote d'Azur. We had found the place where we would spend eight incredibly happy summers, making friends for life, and letting the children enjoy making their own friendships and get involved with lots of different activities, and generally having a ball. We also got to grips with the ins and outs of caravanning in the sun, and made sure for our next visit a year hence that we would: A) have a booking; and B) have a fridge!

I also learned the hard way how to erect our awning for the first time. It was not an easy thing to do, and Andy had to keep her eyes on the children as I threaded the canvas through the runners that ran round the edges of the caravan. It was a fairly basic awning, and in keeping with the colour scheme of the little 'Monza', was an awful brown and orange combination. Worse, once it was fully erected, we found there was a huge grease spot that ran down one side of the structure. We were not exactly caravan fashionistas in those early days. But we got better, and in later years, with a smart new outfit, we bought ourselves a smart new awning to go with it – one in which we could set up camp beds for Katherine and Mike to sleep in once James had joined us. It was brand new with big clear windows and a very fashionable two-tone grey colour scheme.

It took some setting up, though, and with Andy holding onto James to stop him escaping, and Kath and Mike off on jobs filling water containers, I was left to fit it pretty much on my own. I had grown tired of watching other couples turning up on sites and quickly getting everything fixed up perfectly without any apparent problems. In contrast, I was probably more of a sideshow. Indeed, one year when we arrived on our chosen spot, we found two cold bottles of beer and two empty chairs in the middle of the pitch. The beers were for us from our friends Chris and Cherie, who had already arrived, and the chairs were for them so they could come and have a laugh and enjoy the spectacle of me trying to fix up an awning. This was because the previous year they had all heard me shouting in frustration at Andy, desperately asking her if I had lined up the awning correctly. I was standing there with arms outstretched, holding the bloody thing in place, head covered with canvas, sweat pouring down my back, and melting in the searing afternoon heat. And it was then that a passing wasp decided to sting me... Several times. I don't think those in the immediate vicinity have ever heard or seen anything like the war dance of pain and anger that ensued, nor heard quite so many expletives spat out in one incoherent sentence. And that's why Chris was here watching, and laughing, literally selling tickets to our group of friends for the opportunity to watch me set up my caravan. As he said, the best laugh of the holiday, but not the only one. We had so many over the years with such a great group of people. One year, we even won the site football tournament – not an easy thing to do when the competition attracted footballers from football-playing countries all over Europe.

The games were played on the site tennis courts, and each team could have a squad of four players with only three on court at any time. The goals were from the 'water polo' park, so the target was small, and the games were played in the early evening heat. Most of the teams that turned up could 'play', so the standard was pretty good. And while we were all in our late thirties/early forties, some of the entrants were a good ten to 15 years younger than us. It didn't matter. With Chris full of running, Ron a 'Beckenbauer' style libero at the back, and Andrew and me free to roam around generally trying to cause trouble, we quickly found ourselves winning through to the final stages. It was so hot, and I began to realise a little of how terrible it must have been for the England players trying to defend the World Cup in the raw heat of Mexico.

Eventually, at about ten o'clock and with quite a crowd gathering, it was time for the final. We understood why the crowd had gathered when we warmed up and saw our opponents. They were a group of French lads, all about late teens, and they had brought half the campsite out to support them – family, friends, and some quite stunning girlfriends. They were clearly here to win and celebrate with a party, and they were cocky bastards to boot, showing off from the kick-off with fancy flicks and shouts of 'Ole' when they made progress. Ron put an end to one of them, driving him into the plastic fencing that surrounded the court. It was a classic 'they don't like it up them' challenge, and the game soon settled down into a proper match once they realised we were also here to win. The final was scheduled for two five-minute halves, and I could feel my insides burning when we reached half-time, still all square at 0-0. Soon after the break, they went one up when Ron slipped as he went to play the ball, and their striker ran through to score. I wasn't prepared for the roar that followed the goal and realised as darkness had fallen that more and more 'fans' had gathered to cheer the locals on. We only had a minute or so to get back into the game, and our opponents, who had long since given up fooling around, were working their socks off to keep us away from their goal. And then Chris, still amazingly running around, given the heat, stuck out a foot and nicked the ball away from one of their defenders. It broke wide to me, and as I ran in at an angle on goal, the keeper dashed out to challenge me. I heard my brother shouting for the ball and instinctively played it across for him to slide the ball home for the equaliser.

The game finished shortly after Andrew's strike, and there was some question about what we should do now. Everyone seemed happy to just call it a draw, but the organiser wouldn't have this, as they only had one trophy and four winners' medals. There would have to be a penalty shoot-out. which involved each player in the team taking a shot from the halfway line into the empty 'water polo' net. Given the distance involved and the tiny goal to aim at, this was quite a challenge, and there was a huge cheer from around the courts when their first player successfully rolled his penalty home. We managed to stay with them until it came to the last round of penalties and then their final player struck the post with his shot. He followed the shot in and blasted the ball into the goal, but the organiser blew loudly on his whistle, waving his arms to show that 'goal' didn't count. The large crowd vented their displeasure, and the lad who missed was cursing away and shouting at his friends through the fencing. Some of the teenagers watching were getting quite aggressive, shouting insults at us, and generally behaving like total prats. I had the last kick, and they were trying their best to put me off, coughing, and shrieking at silly jokes. I looked at the organiser, who blew his whistle, and I passed the ball into the empty net.

We had won. We were tournament champions, and we received our cup and medals at a special presentation ceremony a few days later, but not before we went back to Ron's and drank so many bottles of '33' that we filled a bin with the empties. What a night! 'We are the Champions, Champions of Europe'. The car eventually made it all the way back to Yorkshire, but just north of Reims on the return journey I had to fill up with oil again just to keep it going. We sold it to the garage I stored the caravan at, and bought a nearly-new Montego, a car I liked very much. And as for the caravan? Well, as mentioned, it got nicked from the same garage, which meant by the time we headed to the Med again, we did so in a better car and a far more comfortable caravan, with a fridge and a proper awning.

CHAPTER 9

BARNSLEY AWAY, OLD FRIENDS, NEW BEGINNINGS AND THE MANTRA

Barnsley...0; Leeds United...2
Sunday, 15th September

I have never caravanned in Barnsley, but I have visited some of the lovely park areas around the town, especially Cannon Hall where we often enjoyed a picnic and let the children run free a bit, particularly in the summer months when school had finished. We used to call it 'Greendale' after the mythical village in *Postman Pat*, which we all enjoyed watching – in the kids' case, over and over again.

Oakwell, the home of Barnsley FC, is no 'Greendale'. It's not a ground I enjoy visiting, even though as the crow flies it's the nearest football stadium to my home. We often seem to lose there and the natives definitely don't like us much, often congregating towards the left-hand corner of the ground to hurl abuse at the visiting fans, which on occasion can lead to outbreaks of violence. I don't understand how the home clubs don't keep certain sections of the ground free of fans and create an effective barrier between home and visiting fans. It happens at a number of grounds, and Barnsley has been one of the worst over the years. Nonetheless, it will be good to get back to 'proper' football after the international break, and there has been some fantastic news since the unexpected defeat against Swansea in our last game. Kalvin Phillips has at last agreed a new contract. It doesn't matter for how much or how long, because we all know he has to leave if we aren't promoted. But what matters is that he is with us for this year, for this season, for the promotion push. If we go up, he will surely stay and become one of the true legends of the club. A home-grown boy leading his home town club back to greatness.

It's a Sunday kick-off, which gives us the benefit of knowing how the results of our rivals have gone. And interestingly, one or two of them played each other. WBA drew at Fulham, which I guess is a point that we would take when we head to Craven Cottage in December. Swansea, so cock-a-hoop with their rather undeserved three points at ER, come a cropper losing at home to Forest, who are beginning to shape up as a tough team to beat. Meanwhile, early pacesetters Charlton lost at home to Birmingham, and Brentford lost at Preston, who may well be a dark horse as the season unwinds.

There is no doubt that we need the three points today, and with Barnsley starting shakily after a tremendous opening day win over Fulham, there is no reason why we shouldn't win comfortably the way we have been playing. I suppose one slight doubt I have running through my mind is the number of ex-Leeds players now playing in a very young Barnsley side. Alex Mowatt, Malik Wilks, and Apoel Halme, have all played for the Whites, and while Wilks and Halme didn't play for us that often, Mowatt enjoyed a number of starts and looked for a time as if he could secure a permanent starting berth, with his passing ability and eye for a goal. Perhaps he lacked a little pace, but certainly he had the ability to open up defences and must have been devastated to be sold by the club, though his talent was instrumental in helping his new club to promotion from League One last season. There is no doubt the three of them will be out to prove themselves this afternoon; out to put one over on their old club. I must admit I always loved playing against former teams, and especially when I had good friends in the opposition camp. Once I had left college football, I had wanted to continue playing at as high a level as possible. I also wanted to keep involved with the social element of the game, which had been so enjoyable in student football. It was important to me that there were facilities after the match to have some food, a drink or two, chat about the game, watch the tv for the professional results, and generally unwind, before heading off to enjoy a Saturday night.

I ended up playing for Leeds Academicals, who played in the Yorkshire Old Boys League. In theory, the club was for teachers in the Leeds area, and while quite a few of the team were local teachers, it wasn't exclusively the case. The club had three or four teams, and played games at Woodkirk school near Tingley, which to be honest didn't have the greatest of pitches or facilities. But for me living in Wakefield, it was much easier to get to home games than to travel to the other side of Leeds, which is where our 'clubhouse' was in a pub in Headingley. The teams in the league, as its title suggested, came from all over Yorkshire. However, other than cup fixtures, most of our league games were played throughout West Yorks, which meant travel to Leeds, Huddersfield, Halifax, Bradford, and Wakefield – still a fair amount of journey time for amateur players.

As you would expect joining a new club, I started off in the lowest of teams, but scored quite a lot of goals in my early games and quickly got moved up from the fourth to the second team. There were four or five leagues, and obviously the standard of play got better the higher up the leagues you played. Our first team were in the top league, so the seconds were probably in division two of five – not bad, but not where I wanted to play. I did pretty well in the seconds and scored regularly, and each Saturday after the matches, when we headed back to the pub, the 'selection committee' would go into a separate room and pick the sides for the following week.

At first, I didn't really expect to make my way straight into the first X1, and I was happy to play in the seconds and get a few goals along the way. But then the 'firsts' stopped winning and they stopped scoring, and I thought it was time I should be promoted. Each week, I waited patiently for the selection meeting to finish, only to find myself still in the 'seconds'. I started to get a bit fed up, and chatted to one of the senior guys, who was a PE teacher at Woodkirk, about what I should do, who should I speak to, what more could I do, etc. I trusted his judgement as he had always been friendly and very helpful, securing me two nights a week 'nightschool' where I coached two local teams and earned some good money to supplement my teacher's salary. He basically told me to keep my head down, keep trying, keep scoring.

I followed his advice and went on a good goal scoring run, but every time I got my hopes up, they were dashed with the announcement of the teams for the following week. Eventually, one of the players took me aside and explained the problem, which I could see now I couldn't really solve. Unfortunately for me, two of the oldest and most senior players were the captain and the centre forward. They were great friends, and basically while neither was playing well, they weren't going to drop each other for some young teacher who had just joined. It would happen in time, I was told, so just keep scoring. So I did. The following week I scored four goals in a match – the most I had ever managed in a game of reasonable quality. Surely this time it would be enough. Surely now they would have to pick me and give me a chance. No, they wouldn't. So I left.

I have always tried to be fair in sport, and indeed professionally, trying to understand the opinions and strengths of others, but I feel I have also always understood my own strengths and weaknesses and what I have offered to a team, or indeed a school. I have never reacted well to being taken for granted, and throughout my life when I have felt snubbed or not valued, I have backed myself to do better and moved on.

In this case, it wasn't too difficult. Chris, my old ER, Hastings, and Germany buddy, and now my brother-in-law, played for a Wakefield club, Old Thornesians, in the same league and same division as Academicals' first team. It was, as they say, a no-brainer. Same standard, best friend, shared travel, and a much nicer bar situated in a local cricket club, which was ours for the winter months. With the club being based in the town I grew up in, I knew a few of the other players, too, and was, as I had been at Academicals, happy to make my way hopefully up through the teams. Chris and I had known each other through school, and we lived closely to each other as well, so we were always playing football on 'The Green' that separated our homes on the Leeds and Bradford Roads. Everyone met up there and we used to play for hours, especially after we had been to ER or in the long school holidays.

As we got older, a number of us went to the church youth club, and football was one of the activities we pursued. One of the younger priests even arranged some friendly matches that we all enjoyed playing in. Then one night, the guy who ran the club told us he'd got a pal who knew a guy who used to play for Spurs, and he thought he could get him to come and train us one afternoon. We were beyond excited, and as the session got nearer we shared our thoughts about the possibility that this guy might have the kind of contacts that might lead us to a professional trial somewhere.

We were due to meet at some local playing fields, and as it was the school holidays I had Andrew in tow, who was then about eight years old. We gathered by the goalposts and were kicking the ball around when a car approached and came to a halt a few yards away from us. Jim, the guy in charge of the youth club, got out, followed by the priest, and eventually our coach for the day. He was quite young; I would have guessed about twentyish, and he was tall, and had jet black hair greased back in position. He was in full kit, and impressively he had a bag full of old footballs which he emptied out in front of us. This was quite amazing for us, as we always had to scratch around to find any kind of ball, and when we did it often got burst when it got kicked onto the road and some car ran over it.

Far more impressive, though, was that the young man was wearing a green goalkeeper's jumper which bore the crest of Tottenham Hotspurs Football Club. Now, this was in the days before you could buy replica kits, so it was clearly a jumper that the young man had earned. He was obviously a proper professional, and we were in awe of him. Jim introduced him and told us that he would put us through our paces for a while, then watch us as we played in small-sided games. It sounded perfect, and as we readied ourselves and checked our kit, our visitor ran off at some pace to the other end of the pitch and did some fairly rigorous exercises. I noticed Andrew, clearly unimpressed by all the fuss, messing with our ball around the halfway line and heard our visitor shout at him to try a few shots. Andrew duly did as he was instructed and started to dribble towards the keeper, who moved from side to side as he approached the penalty area. I thought the guy was looking a tad aggressive, as he decided to rush out of the area to confront Andrew, and I hoped he wouldn't bump into him. But

I needn't have worried. Andrew simply dropped his shoulder, feinted to go one way and then changed direction, slipped past the keeper, and rolled the ball into the goal.

Our guest coach lay floundering on the grass, and it was in that moment that we realised we had been had. He was, in fact, completely hopeless, and had no sense of balance or ball control, so we decided to call him 'Flash'. Jim and the priest realised the problem as well, and we spent the next hour trying to be kind to our guest and not to embarrass him too much. As my memory has it, he stuck around for a few weeks and was actually quite a nice lad, but he wasn't going to be our passport to a professional club and he wasn't going to be our coach. In fact, he wouldn't have got into our team.

Chris and I did eventually get the crack at stardom we had been yearning for, when we were invited to attend for a trial at York City FC – a club which at the time was struggling in the old fourth division. If I'm honest, it wasn't because we had been 'scouted' or anything like that, but rather because I had written to a number of clubs asking for a trial – something one of my 'football annuals' advised was a good way to get noticed in the professional game. Anyway, York was the only club who bothered to reply, so one day after the season had ended, we piled into Chris's dad's car and headed to Bootham Crescent, the home of York City. When we arrived at the ground, we were herded together with all the other 'triallists'. Some were teenagers like us, some were clearly a little bit older, and some were full grown men! The guy in charge separated us into two groups and then started to ask us about where we played, what was our best position, etc. I was ready for this question and had been advised by my 'football annual' to say I could play anywhere! The guy just stared at me like I was wasting his day then repeated his question. I told him I was a left winger and made a mental note not to believe anything I read in 'football annuals' anymore.

In the end, I played on the wing for the 'blue team' and Chris, a fine midfield player, was chosen as a centre forward for the 'red team'. The really good news was that the trial was being played on the actual first team pitch. I experienced one of those nervous breathless feelings as we gathered together in the tunnel and then ran out onto the field. We had a bag of balls, and I grabbed one as we warmed up near one of the goals, and smashed it high into the net I was 15 and had never played in any game where there were nets around the goalposts. What a feeling to see the ball 'hit the back of the net'. I did it again and again until the guy blew his whistle and we got ready to start the game.

I was being marked by one of the 'men', and he was surly and aggressive and not interested in having a chat, as I always liked to do. I decided my best bet was to use my pace and, having received the ball near the touchline, I pushed it past him and ran to regather it. Only I didn't get there, because he grabbed my arm and pulled me back. I shouted out to the ref, appealing for the clear free kick that should be awarded in my favour. But he just told me to shut up and waved play on. I couldn't believe it, and I wasn't surprised at all in the next attack, when my 'friend' raked his studs down my shin, that no free kick was forthcoming. I managed one weak shot that was easily saved, and that was about it for my 90 minutes. Chris didn't fare any better, and as we gathered in the changing rooms after the match, neither of us was surprised when our names were not read out as players they wanted to see again. The guy who had been 'marking' me wasn't in the changing rooms. He had stayed out on the pitch talking to some of the club coaches. Apparently, he was already a full-time professional and York were looking to buy him from Notts County, but just wanted to see him in a match situation. It was hard not to come to the conclusion that we had just been 'used'.

We didn't talk much about the experience as we caught the train home from York, both of us coming to terms with the fact that our hopes and dreams of becoming professional footballers were in tatters. Chris broke the silence as the train pulled into Westgate Station. 'Fucking useless club anyway!' Chris always knew what to say.

It didn't take long before I made my first team debut playing in my favoured position, slightly left of the main striker – a guy called Simon Ives, who was a prolific scorer and certainly a more natural finisher than me. It was a great club to play for, brilliantly administered by a chap called Graham Marshall who, like all great club men, did all the donkey work and did it so well none of us knew just how great his contribution was.

I stayed at the club pretty much 12 years, until I retired at the age of 39. And I only retired then because I accepted the headship at Barlborough and the school worked on Saturdays. I gradually slipped down through the teams, ending up playing for the fourths, but still enjoying my Saturday football and often playing against lads who, just like me, had stayed at their clubs and moved down through the teams as they got older. It was a great league with great camaraderie, and one of the highlights was winning the Senior Division Championship and receiving a winner's medal that stands proudly in my study as I write.

Obviously, playing for the same club for so long meant making lots of friends and acquaintances with the ones who, like me, stayed at the club for a long time. What was quite strange, though, was that while we all played together for Thornes on a Saturday, lots of us also played for other clubs on a Sunday morning in the local Tetley League – a pub league. I played for The New Wheel, the pub in the village of Wrenthorpe where I lived at that time. We played in the third division and were a real mix of good, average, and totally useless players. Good, bad, or hopeless, everyone loved playing and we all enjoyed it, especially having a good few pints after the match, followed by a lengthy sleep on Sunday afternoon. I also found that, given the much lower standard of football in the lower reaches of a pub league, I got a shed-load of goals.

It's interesting today when professionals talk about the different levels in the game that even in the amateur leagues there can be huge differences, for instance, in goal scoring. If you took one of my all-time favourite Leeds players, Jermaine Beckford. He scored at will in League One, and yet when he made the step up to the Premiership with Everton, he was by no means as prolific. Obviously, the reason was that the quality of players he came up against was much higher. I had the same problem even at my low level. I found that on a Sunday morning I would score freely, while on the Saturday I would be lucky if I got a goal every three, such was the difference in standard.

Despite playing at the lower level on a Sunday, I always loved it when we were drawn against a team from the top division in a cup match. This would give me the chance to take on better defenders who had usually come into the game expecting an easy ride. I loved showing them up and taking them on, and while we usually ended up losing the matches, I often found myself on the score sheet. I especially loved it when we played one of the top Sunday teams who had lads from Thornesians in their teams. I really loved the opportunity to try and 'put one over them' in these games, and I remember being given a real hard time one Saturday after a Thornes match by a few of my 'teammates' who we were playing the next day in a cup game. 'We're going to get you,' they chided. 'We're going to do you!' I couldn't wait. There were at least four of my first team colleagues lined up against me, but we had strengthened by bringing my brother Andrew over (he was legitimately signed on) to bolster our midfield. It was one of those games you always remember, and I can still feel the more than cold welcome I was given when I reached the changing rooms; they were determined to unnerve me.

In the end, the match was decided by one goal, and I scored it! I can see it now. The ball was cleared to the edge of the penalty area, roughly in line with the right-hand post. It came perfectly to me, dropping gently from the sky towards me. I let the ball bounce, and as it reared up, I volleyed it up in the air. I hit it perfectly and watched as the ball soared upwards and then dipped down viciously, before entering the net just under the bar and close to the right-hand post. They tried everything they knew to get back into the game. In fact, they battered us, but they couldn't score and we hung on for one of the wins I most remember from my sporting career, scoring one of the best goals I ever scored, and against some of my best friends. The Tetleys tasted very good afterwards.

And I guess that's why I had this little bit of doubt about the game this afternoon. Those ex-Leeds players had much to prove and everything to gain; it was their chance to show all of us just what they could do. I left early and headed the short distance up to Barnsdale Bar - one of the many places it is alleged Robin Hood used to hang around - crossed the

A1 and picked up the road to Barnsley. Like most away grounds I visit, I have worked out the best place to park, and usually you have to get there early to make sure you get a space. I stopped, picked up a Sunday paper and a sandwich, and headed on to Barnsley. The parking space is situated in a little park on the right-hand side of the road, about a 15-minute walk from the ground. There is no charge and it's easy to get away after the match has finished. I am in luck, as there is just one space left, so I take it gratefully and hole up for half hour or so, listening to the radio and reading the paper.

A little later, heading up to the ground, I check the team, which is unchanged, with the exception of Shackleton coming in to replace Forshaw. Not sure what's wrong with him but it's a shame as he has made a good start to the season. I like Shackleton; he's very quick and I think has a big future at the club. We will see. I hate the organisation at Oakwell. You take a right turn up from the road and there is a clear walkway to the 'away' end, which is also used as a car park. But for some reason, both before and after the game this is always shut to fans, which means you have to walk around the whole ground to get to the turnstiles.

I stop and get a programme and walk on to where the police are massed together, looking angry as usual. It's always fairly chaotic getting into the ground – a little bit like the organisation at Bristol, and I wouldn't ever be surprised to hear of accidents or injuries at these venues. Once through the searches, once clear of the undefined queues, you head under the stand into not much more than a corridor, where everyone is again rammed together. Some are trying to buy drinks, some pushing their way towards the toilets, and some like me trying to find the right entrance to get to my seat. Again, I have a good view, and it's right behind the goal. The Barnsley club have in fact created a free zone between the fans, so hopefully there will be less hostility and we can all get on with enjoying the game.

We start well and Bamford, breaking free, draws a good save from Collins in the Barnsley goal. It's not all one-way, though, and Wilks – looking sharp – has a good shot well saved by Casilla before Mowatt cleverly plays Thomas in, only for Casilla to again save well with his feet. Already Barnsley have created more in a half than Swansea did in the whole 90 minutes last week. I am quite nervous, given the number of times we have left this place on the wrong end of a beating. We need a goal to settle things down, and when Shackleton plays Bamford in down the left, it looks as if we must score if the forward crosses the ball. But instead he shoots from a tight angle and the keeper saves easily. We miss further chances before half-time, when Hernandez blazes over and Harrison unbelievably hits the post when it seems easier to score from a Phillips corner. Barnsley haven't gone away, and Wilks flashes a shot across the face of the goal before the teams go in level at the interval.

Costa is brought on in place of Harrison for the second half, and after a great throw out from Casilla and good work by Alioski, he crosses superbly from the left for the on-rushing Bamford to score. It's a great goal, well constructed and well finished, only... it's disallowed for offside, presumably against Costa. I must admit I usually check out the linesman if I think there is a problem, just to be reassured that the goal is given and I can celebrate. I didn't see any reason to check this one, so the decision must have been tight or wrong. Barnsley, still in the game, respond again and Wilks turns Cooper and races away, only for Casilla to deny him. From the ensuing corner, Halme misses a free header, cannoning the ball into one of his own players and allowing Casilla to pick up the loose ball. Then, when a draw seems the most likely outcome, in the 84th minute we score. And it's Nketiah, on for Bamford, who smashes in a Phillips free kick from close range. It's a vital goal and one we desperately needed to make sure we take home the three points.

But Barnsley still won't go away, and Halme has the chance to equalise with a free header from a corner, which thankfully he powers over the bar. Yet another chance from a corner; dead balls seem to be becoming an increasing problem, and surely opposing managers will have noticed the confusion that spreads across our defence when put under pressure in this way. The game is thankfully over in the 89th minute when Halme fouls Nketiah and Klich calmly rolls the penalty into the net. It's a big win, and I can enjoy Sunday night and the week ahead. But in truth, Barnsley gave us a scare, and we couldn't have complained if they had taken a point. Both sides had big chances that they squandered.

The points take us back above Swansea, to top the table on goal difference, but there is nothing in the table yet, with Birmingham in eighth place only three points behind us. Barnsley stay in the relegation places which, after this performance, seems harsh. The question will be whether they can raise themselves to this level every week, or if it was just a matter of a few players having something to prove.

When I left the stadium, I managed to turn right and go the quick way through the 'no through way route'. No-one was manning the gate at the top, so I got right down to the bottom gate before I was challenged. I started to limp heavily, which wasn't difficult as I was experiencing a lot of pain in my right knee and was due to have a cortisone injection the following week. I pleaded with the gateman, saying I couldn't walk all the way back and round the ground. He didn't look sympathetic, and I was about to start to cry loudly when his supervisor opened the gate and let me slip through.

Driving home, I went through the game, as usual looking for pluses and negatives. We had made a lot of chances, but then so had they. Casilla had one of his better games and made some good saves, and Costa continued to remind us that he had the ability, however fleetingly it appeared. It was, in the end, a good three points and I was looking forward to the Derby game at ER already, especially as James was coming home for it. Before then, though, there was more family business to deal with, as we were looking after Margie while Mike and Lou were at a friend's wedding... in America!

We hadn't seen them since Calella a few weeks ago, and now they had flown off to the States on Friday morning, leaving their precious daughter and our granddaughter with us for the long weekend. We were very worried about how she would settle. After all, she was only 18 months old and hadn't exactly seen a lot of us in her little life so far. But we needn't have worried. She was brilliant, and apart from expecting one of us to stay in the room until she had gone to sleep – just as she had done in Spain – she was no trouble at all.

On the Friday we took her to meet Andy's mum, and I decided afterwards to take her to ER; she was old enough to get the passion! We had some pictures taken at Billy's statue and then went in the souvenir shop, where she nicked a blue club dinosaur and ran off round the store, laughing and roaring at her new friend. Given the state of my knee, it was hard to keep up with her, and by the time I caught her she had upset a display of footballs that were rolling around by the counter. She appeared to think this great fun, and after I'd put them all back in place, she did it again as I was buying the dinosaur!

We sent the picture of me, Margie, and Billy, to Mike in New York State, and later I found out he had sent it on to his friends, no doubt quietly proud of the fact that they had only been gone a few hours and his dad had already taken his little girl to ER.

Over the next few days I worked hard at teaching her to say new words like 'Grandpa' and other things. And Andy taught her to dance to Elton John's hit *I'm Going to Love Me Again*. We worked hard at building towers with the coloured bricks, and all the time I returned to teaching her the words that really mattered. At first, she seemed to 'get it' and repeated my promptings almost absentmindedly as she focused on building her tower, but then a few minutes later it had gone, and she'd either forgotten or had just got bored with my teachings. Mike and Lou returned on the Monday evening, and it was great to see them and catch up with all their news about the trip and the wedding. We sat in the garden watching Margie happily running around, and it wasn't just her mum and dad who were surprised and thrilled when, out of the blue, she started to beat her chest and shout out loudly, 'Leeds, Leeds, Leeds!'

CHAPTER 10

NEEDLES, STITCHES AND LECTURES

Leeds United…1; Derby County…1
Saturday, 21ˢᵗ September

Mike, Lou, and Margie – the new super fan – are heading for a well deserved holiday in our place in Calella, and it's an early start for us as they have a morning flight to Girona from Manchester. I hate the journey across the Pennines and especially the bit around 'Mancland', where there seems to be a general plan to stop all traffic with a succession of roadworks and night closures. I have become very familiar with the carnage of these 'smart motorway' developments. I mean what 'smart' brain came up with the idea of turning the hard shoulder into an extra driving lane?

I absolutely realise that there are huge pressure points on our motorway system with the enormous and ever-growing amount of traffic and these key transport routes having to carry vehicles of all shapes and sizes around the country. But really! 'How do we solve the problem?' Yep, let's remove the hard shoulder, where it's relatively safe to stop if you break down, and replace it with an extra lane where, if you are unlucky enough to have a car failure, it's highly likely a great big artic is going to drive into the back of you. I think it is an almost incomprehensible decision to have been taken. It's also the case that in order to make these 'smart' lanes work, most motorways in the country have at some point experienced overnight closures, which are not always well publicised. This means you can suddenly find yourself queuing for miles, only to be pushed into one lane and syphoned off the motorway to follow some diversionary route that sends you careering around the countryside at the dead of night. I do realise some of this work is essential, but please, can we have a safer system? And can we have better publicity and more warning, so we can plan our routes or even decide to stay at home?

I once travelled from our caravan in Ashwell up to a night match at Hillsborough, and after the game found myself almost immediately heading back south and towards a closure. Fortunately, with Ashwell's geographical position, I would probably have crossed to the A1 at Worksop anyway, but I noticed that the M1 had further closures up around Northampton, so I was pretty pleased that my journey didn't involve travelling anywhere too far south on the M1 that night. I wasn't back safely yet, though, and as I moved south on the A1, it wasn't long before the warning lights flashed up to tell me that motorway was also closed at the A14 for the massive upgrade that was taking place around that part of the world.

Once again having some local knowledge, I was able to reroute either to Royston via lots of country roads, or heading up to the M11 and coming off at Duxford. I chose the former route and eventually got back to the caravan in the early hours. Of course, I was lucky. Had I been trying to get to London that night, with both the A1 and the M1 shut, I would have been better off turning round and going home. I am pretty certain any lorry drivers or other football fans heading home from away matches will know exactly the frustrations I was feeling. In terms of motorway works, planning and development, the powers-that-be definitely need to 'smarten up' considerably, especially from the safety point of view.

Today, though, we are lucky; the overnight closures are now all open and we're ahead of the morning Manchester 'rush hour'. I am pretty much able to drive up and drop them off right outside the airport departure building, so we have a hurried hug and a thanks, and best wishes and see you soon, then I 'm off and finding my way back to the M62. We have a busy few weeks ahead, with trips to the doctor's, another caravan visit to Ashwell, ahead of Oliver and Lucy's birthdays. And, following a flying visit to London for the Charlton game, we will be heading back to Calella for a week's holiday. The joys of retirement.

The visit to the doctor's is for me to have a cortisone injection in my right knee, which has been causing me pain and discomfort for some time. I have had trouble with both knees, I guess as a result of too many games of football and too much jogging on roads and other hard surfaces. I had an operation on the left leg a few years ago, but the surgeon said there was no point doing the same on the right leg as the deterioration was too far gone. I had, though, had a cortisone jab in my left knee which had worked really well, and meant that while I couldn't play five-a-sides or go running, I could move around quite freely and I could work out on the cross trainer and bicycle. Like most men, I am a total wimp when it comes to going to the doctor's, but Dr Vega at my local practice was excellent and, importantly, had the ability to put me at ease when discussing various treatments. She was also Spanish, and I wondered what life journey had brought her from Spain to Pontefract.

Loads of people had told me that having such injections was incredibly painful, and being of cowardly disposition I was looking for any opportunity to cancel the visit the first time I was due to have the injection. Andy, aware of this weakness, refused to let me get away with missing the appointment, and called me lots of far from complimentary names about my general lack of balls.

I have to say, when I got there I employed some excellent tactics to make the procedure go as well as possible. I refused to look at the doctor as she prepared the needle, and stared straight up at the ceiling, so not only couldn't I see the doctor but I couldn't see the nurse who was assisting her. I also talked continuously, telling them both a long joke about a nun and a turf accountant. I folded my arms and just kept going, aware that Dr Vega was approaching from my left. I would be telling fibs if I said I didn't feel anything, because obviously I did. But while there was a nipping feeling that seemed to go on for quite a while, I certainly wasn't feeling crippling pain. So, when the doctor said, 'That's it', and I hadn't even got to the punchline of my story, I was very pleasantly relieved. I was also really pleased that the jab seemed to work and the pain in my leg eased considerably, allowing me to walk with much greater freedom.

It was this positive result and the fact that I had been able to survive the whole experience that led me to making the appointment to have the same procedure. This time, though, it was in my right knee, which as I explained had been uncomfortable for some time. So it was that I found myself lying on the patient's bed, reprising my previously successful tactic of telling jokes, and staring at the ceiling as Dr Vega prepared the injection and began to move closer. But, by crikey, it hurt this time! The pain was instant and seemed to get worse as the needle slipped deeper into my knee. I swore in mid-joke and spent the next few minutes apologising, but now I understood what everyone had meant about cortisone injections; this one hurt an awful lot. I just hope it works as well as the last one did.

Unbelievably, having survived this experience, I am now heading to the dentist for a check-up. How could I have arranged such back-to-back appointments, and on a Friday as well? So, I survived the dentist, but it wasn't my finest hour. I wriggled and moaned while he clumsily stabbed around in my mouth, making the cortisone experience fade from my memory pretty fast as I felt like a fish squirming on the end of a fisherman's line. I'm not sure who was most relieved when at last the appointment came to an end – me or the dentist. Either way, it seemed neither of us was in much of a hurry to schedule another appointment. He nodded his head and shut his door; I limped out of the building as fast as I could go. Friday had not started well, but Andy was kind and sympathetic when I got home from my self-inflicted battering, and James was due into Doncaster later on, so at last the weekend was beginning to look a bit brighter.

James is in good form and we have a lovely evening catching up and enjoying a few beers. We try and keep the chat away from football, but inevitably it strays to tomorrow and our meeting with Derby – our chance to gain some small payback for the disastrous night in May when we self-imploded in the second leg of the play-off game. I hobble off to bed with a nagging pain in my right knee and my mouth, and a nagging thought about tomorrow and Derby.

It's a beautiful day, really warm and sunny, and Andy and I enjoy a cup of tea sitting in the garden while we wait for James to stir. It's always the same when he's home. We wait for him to get up after a well-deserved lie-in, and then have the big discussion: a 'full English' or fish and chips at PJ's? It's not too big a decision today as it's a lunchtime kick-off, so we won't make PJ's this time, but there will be plenty of visits through the season. And anyway, what's not to like about a full English in the sunshine?

It's James's first home game of the season, so we are off early to get a quick beer before kick-off. Damien is away on holiday, so we go and get the team news and a can of John Smiths at the centenary place, before we have to separate for the match. Unfortunately, James couldn't get a seat in the Kop, so he has one for the east stand, which I take so he can go and say hello to his old friends. It's actually quite a good view, just the south stand side of the halfway line and far enough up to get a sense of what is happening on the far touchline. Actually, there isn't much happening over there as the away fans have not travelled in numbers, probably selling only about a half of their ticket allocation. It makes that horrible loss in May somehow even more painful, knowing we lost to a club with such feeble support.

Despite Nketiah's goal at Barnsley last week, he is once again on the bench, and Bielsa names the same side that started at Oakwell, with Shackleton again deputising for Forshaw. The bench is looking stronger, with Douglas, Baradi, Costa , Nketiah, and the youngster Gotts bringing an all-round look of strength in case of injuries. Messlier continues as deputy to Casilla who, despite my own misgivings, I must say played well at Barnsley. I am sure Derby will not have forgotten the huge helping hand he gave them last May, when the Spaniard literally provided them with a lifeline back into the tie.

Derby are much changed from that night in May, with only the keeper Roos, Keough, Holmes, Malone, and Marriott – the main beneficiary of Casilla's inexplicable charge out of his area – returning to ER. Lampard, of course, has used the Derby outfit as a stepping stone back to Chelsea, and along with Derby's best players from last season, the on-loan trio of Wilson, Mount, and Tomori, is not here to face the music following his provocative and ridiculously premature celebrations at the end of

157

the game. Keough is, though, and the Leeds crowd give him a noisy and unfriendly welcome, focusing for some reason on the Derby defender's less than rugged looks.

The bright midday sun is streaming into my face as the game kicks off, and we attack instantly, pushing Derby back and forcing them to make mistakes and give the ball away. They look as if they are running in treacle, and from one clearance their keeper Roos plays the ball straight to Hernandez, whose cross is somehow missed by Bamford when it appears easier to score. Undaunted, Leeds pour forward and Dallas sets Hernandez free down the right, only for the Spain international's cross from the byeline to be hit straight at the keeper by Harrison.

We are creating so much space, putting on so much pressure, that a goal simply has to come, and finally it does on the twentieth minute. Phillips hits a long free kick to the far post and Bamford, stretching, does well to pull the ball back across the area for Dallas to shoot first time, hitting the ball into the ground and striking the keeper with his effort. It then deflects onto the hapless Lowe and into the net. It was perhaps a fortuitous goal, but it was more than well deserved. Up to this point, Derby had offered nothing and looked a team who might even have to face a relegation battle, such was their listless and almost casual performance. Leeds should have doubled their score when Bamford brilliantly controlled one of Alioski's favoured cross-field passes, only to unaccountably lob the ball high over the bar when surely, having done the hard work, it would have been easier just to roll the ball past the advancing Roos. Incredibly and worryingly, it is only 1-0 at half-time, but really it is hard to see any result other than a home win. As play resumes, there is a moment when Huddlestone, the experienced Derby man, is standing next to Shackleton and the size difference both in height and bulk makes it look as if the Derby man could be Shackleton's dad. And just like a father and son, the younger man seems to be running rings round the older one. Leeds start where they left off and Dallas, in such good form this season and playing so many different roles, crosses from the right only for Bamford to deflect the ball onto the post and away to safety. Derby then manage their first shot of the game when Waghorn hits a ball high and wide after 55 minutes.

It's a really poor effort and quite comforting, given the fact we seem to be having one of those afternoons when we can't convert the chances our super football has created.

Then Bamford, as ever working hard, makes a cross-field run and bursts through some half-hearted challenges into the penalty area where he is brought down. At last, the chance to seal the three points, and I feel certain we will double our lead, given how coolly Klich despatched the penalty at Barnsley last week. Today, he is cool again, sending the keeper totally the wrong way before rolling the ball agonisingly wide of the left-hand post. It was a big miss and changed the game. Not that Derby played any better or created any chances; they didn't have a go at us like Barnsley had last week. It was more that we just seemed to freeze and lose all confidence.

You could sense it in the crowd. It was almost as if they knew what was coming, and the sense of nervousness was heightened when Casilla came out to claim a hopeful high punt into his area and, under no pressure at all, completely missed the ball, his arms flapping around like some child playing 'catch' with his dad on a beach. He claimed a foul, as all keepers do, but the truth is there wasn't a Derby player anywhere near him. Then heading into injury time, Phillips, our best player, unaccountably sliced a simple clearance for a corner, and by now we have all worked out that dead balls are our Achilles heel. You could almost feel the crowd hold their breath as Derby took the corner. After Forest and Swansea, surely not another killing goal from a dead ball denying us the three points we should have wrapped up along time ago? This time, though, we managed to clear the ball and I checked my watch once again. We were into four minutes of injury time. 'Just get hold of the frigging thing and take it to the corner' was the general consensus of those around me. But we didn't. And in the second minute of injury time, Derby decided to play their best football of the match, no doubt inspired by the groans and moans of some 35,000 Leeds fans whistling and praying for the final whistle.

They broke down the right-hand side and, as the ball came across, Paterson – on as substitute – controlled the ball. Finding his route to goal blocked, he rolled it to his left, where another sub Martin fired a smart right foot shot across Casilla and into the corner of the net. Unbelievable.

For all our super football and clear dominance, yet again a combination of poor defending and missed chances has left us throwing points away. And although this game is a draw, it most certainly feels like a defeat. There is still time for us to be denied a clear penalty when Costa is blocked off in the area, but the feeling of despair has already set in. And when the final whistle blows, there is a faint sound of booing echoing round the ground. I understand the feeling. Everyone is just so frustrated, and even angry, to find another home game ruined when we should have won easily. Make no mistake, this was a very poor Derby side, and if I was Bielsa I would be really cross with the team for the way they let panic flood through them in the last 20 minutes or so, draining them of the confidence to just play the game out.

Poor James. He had been so looking forward to seeing the team win then enjoying a perfect Saturday, celebrating with a few beers in the garden ahead of catching the rest of the results on Soccer Saturday. Poor Andy, too. She will have been watching on Sky and no doubt thinking, *Oh bugger, another weekend down the drain!* It doesn't really lift the mood, but the results later that day don't do us too much damage: Swansea draw at Bristol; Fulham also draw at Wednesday; while Charlton, next up for us, lose away to lowly Wigan. And maybe that's at least a crumb of comfort, as it does look at last that their bubble is beginning to burst.

So, at the end of the day we remain on top of the table on equal points with the Swans, but WBA can close the gap to one point if they beat Huddersfield tomorrow. (They do, winning 4-2.) Now there are just three points covering the top seven places, and I know it's a pointless exercise to do this but really we should have at least seven more than our current total; seven points we have thrown away in games against Forest, Swansea, and Derby. We need to put five past Charlton next week and really blast out a message to the rest of the league.

As for Derby. Well, if their manager Phillip Cocu didn't know he had a problem, he certainly would do a few days later, when Keough was injured in a car crash after the Derby squad had enjoyed a day of team bonding. If I was a Derby fan, I would have been wondering on what planet the person was who decreed that this bunch of players deserved a day off, following such a gutless performance at Elland Road. It isn't just Derby, obviously, but it's this kind of behaviour that gives footballers such a bad reputation and undoes all the excellent work so many do in their local communities, visiting hospitals and schools.

If things don't change, they may find themselves in a relegation scrap before we meet them again at Pride Park on the second last weekend of the season. How great would that be, to celebrate our promotion at Derby on the day they got relegated? Now that would be something, and I suspect the celebrations would go on and on and on, as the Derby faithful filed out of the ground. That really would be payback for last May; just a shame that Lampard and Keough wouldn't be there to witness it.

I didn't have long to lick my wounds, because we were up early on the Sunday and heading down to Ashwell with the caravan, getting ready to celebrate Oliver and Lucy's birthdays. It was a good journey with very few lorries blocking up the A1, as they can do on busier weekdays. And now that we have learnt a bit more about modern caravanning, we quickly get everything set up on our arrival, sharing out the jobs, and having a target of Sunday lunch at the Three Tuns, a pub in the village, before 3pm.

Caravans have come a long way in terms of design, comfort, and technology, since those days we drove the battered Monza round the motorways of Europe. Before Mike moved to Eire, we decided that with children living in Bishops Stortford and St Albans it would be easier to have the caravan to visit them from, as a kind of home base in the south. So we started to shop around the various dealers and eventually bought an almost-new Coachman Pastiche 520. It was just perfect for our needs and would mean we had the freedom to travel around the country in our own home on wheels. Given that it had been nearly 25 years since we had owned a caravan, we were back to being absolute beginners – and how. Andrew had also bought a caravan in the last few years, and he was quick to tell me to video the chap who tells you how the thing works, before you head off into the great unknown. And it certainly was the unknown. It is, of course, always easy when you know what you're doing, but less so when you haven't got a clue. And it's a serious business driving a caravan round the country.

We watched in awe as loads of elderly caravaners seemed to arrive, unpack, set up, and be enjoying a beer or a glass of wine minutes later, while we were still trying to park and push and pull our blessed thing into position so it was in line with the bloody little marker post the caravan club sites insist it should be. So frustrated at my inability to line up the caravan in this fashion, and weak with the effort of trying to push it around the site, I once solved the problem by simply pulling up the frigging post and moving that instead of the 'van'! Once parked, the questions come thick and fast. How does the heating system work? What the hell did they tell us to do with the onboard water system, and why was it so important? How do you turn the fridge on? Why isn't the electricity working when it's clearly plugged in? What about the gas? Where on earth do you start?

Fortunately, on most sites you can find people who are more than happy to lend a hand, and often these willing helpers will be able to tell you the complete technical specifications of your caravan and the subtle changes that have been made between models in 2017 and 2019. I've lost count of the beers I have tossed in the direction of these invaluable 'anoraks' and 'techies'. Andrew had been dead right about the video, but gradually we came to terms with the workings of our new home on wheels and realised just how brilliantly comfortable it really was. Great cooker, working off electricity or gas, brilliant fridge, getting our drinks colder than the ones at home, and a central heating system that would keep us warm as toast, even in the middle of winter. It had everything: comfortable beds, a separate bathroom with shower, great wardrobe space, and a radio disc player. I even took my Sky box and hooked up to Sky Sports with a mobile satellite disc positioned somewhat precariously outside the front window. No doubt you could live comfortably in one of these and, once understood, it was a great buy.

Andy once came back from reception saying she had seen a guy moving his caravan with no hands, just pointing some kind of handgun at it. It was a motor mover, and while it was a bit costly to have it fitted, it is an absolutely vital piece of kit. No more pushing, no more trying to stop the bloody thing rolling away. Now we could just press a few buttons and the thing can move itself! So, now we know how the thing works, it starts to come into its own, and without three small children to have to look after and share the space, it's really quite luxurious. Andy has bought some nice lamps and candles to 'pretty' things up, so really it's a bit like having a mobile hotel room to travel with. Crucially, it helps us see the kids and, as I have mentioned earlier, it means we all get a bit of space as well.

Oliver's birthday is on Wednesday, 25 September, and amazingly Lucy has her special day on the 26th. They are both lovely kids and, just like with Margie, we have tried hard to make sure they know us and feel comfortable when we are around them. This hasn't been a problem with Oliver, as we looked after him every Monday and Tuesday for a year when Katherine went back to work after her maternity leave. It worked well, especially as Nick didn't start work on Mondays till after 10.30, so we didn't leave home till sevenish on Monday mornings then we would be home for 7pm most Tuesdays evenings, and earlier if the boys were playing! It also didn't interfere with our trips off; with them both being teachers, we got a break fairly regularly.

Nick is a great guy and a lovely dad, but unfortunately, he's a Spurs fan. For some reason I never really took to the London clubs, though I always try and show an interest when Nick chats about Spurs. I never liked it when the 'Cockney's' came up to ER in the sixties; they often seemed threatening, brash and loud with their 'skinheads,' squeaky, funny accents, their Doc Martins and blue Crombie coats and their jeans halfway up their shins, held up by cheap braces. It was as if they came from another land. And worse still, they always seemed to bring trouble; they always seemed brash and loud with their 'skinheads', squeaky, funny accents, their Doc Martins and blue Crombie coats, and their jeans halfway up their shins, held up by cheap braces. Years later, I found the same dislike surface in school fixtures when playing against some schools from North London. The 'skinheads' were long gone, now replaced with overzealous and loud, pushy parents, often shouting out criticisms of the referees, their own children and others, and by implication, the coaching of their own teachers. We actually suspended netball fixtures with one of the schools whose parents clearly couldn't accept the regular beatings we gave them, and whose attitudes made our fixtures an unpleasant way to spend a Saturday morning. I've often been asked by colleagues if I would intervene and warn visiting parents about their, shall we say 'over excessive and over exuberant levels of support'. I even wrote some guidelines with a headteacher colleague for circulation to all Independent Prep Schools, giving guidance about what was acceptable behaviour on the touchline.

Of course, some schools don't help the problem by officiating poorly and favouring the home side in a quite ridiculous fashion. I have been at some school fixtures where even Inter Milan would not get a point! These sad teachers really don't help matters and, worse, they set a terrible example of 'cheating' to the players in their teams. Some of my own colleagues went completely in the other direction and seemed to almost deliberately favour the visitors. One former colleague once blew the whistle just as a fine shot from one of our players was entering the net that would have sent us into the final of a cup competition. I could have killed him, and I wasn't alone. It was the other extreme, and in its own way just as damaging. Why on earth can't school teachers just have a feel for the game and ref it without fear or favour, encouraging the children to play the game fairly, and setting the right kind of example? I suppose some of them are a bit like some of the professional refs, just a little too keen to be noticed.

Anyway, Oliver doesn't know any of this, and hopefully by the time he gets to play inter-school fixtures the standards of behaviour by parents and teachers will have improved. With both his mum and dad keen on sport and highly competitive, he will have good educators – and educators of the right substance. Hopefully, by then he will have also worked out which football team to support, and while I am sure he will have Leeds and Spurs scarves and memorabilia around the place, if the day came when they played each other I'm pretty certain he will have to support the team his mother was brought up to love... if he wants Father Christmas to bring any more Playmobil, that is.

On the day of their wedding, I was able to start my father of the bride speech by asking Nick to put his hand over Katherine's hand, and then

I tied their hands together using a Leeds scarf as the binding. They both looked slightly anxious about what I was doing but smiled when I announced to them and all the other guests that this would in fact be the last time Nick would have the upper hand in the relationship. I was also brilliantly able to make reference to the fact that earlier that year Leeds had actually knocked Spurs out of the cup at ER, with goals by McCormack and Varney.

I take Andy over to Kath's on the Wednesday morning, as I have to drive back north to attend a governors' meeting in York later on in the day. I can join in Oliver's birthday celebrations for a while and share the tea party for Lucy when I get back on Thursday. Oliver is so excited to show us his presents. He is a 'real little boy', as you used to be allowed to say, and spends hours in his make-believe world playing with his cars and toys. Sometimes I join in with him and he loves to play 'cops and robbers' and to get me to hide the 'criminals' so he can get all his police vehicles out to hunt them down. We call the worst one 'Malcolm'; he has robbed McDonalds and eaten 40 burgers and drunk 50 glasses of Pepsi. We have a lot of laughter about how fat he must be and what noises he will make, but Oliver's pursuit is deadly serious. He tells me Malcolm is so bad that when he eventually catches him and puts him in prison, he might not let him go home to his mummy until after tea. So lovely; such innocence.

The drive north goes well, and I have time to have a bath before, 'booted and suited', I head to York for the governors' meeting. I am one of the few governors who don't have a direct link with either York or the school, and I think that such neutrality is a good thing as so often local governors can find themselves compromised by friendships and too much local gossip. That said, having worked with, and on, so many governing bodies over the years, this board – brilliantly led by the chairman – is incredibly dedicated and hard-working, and genuinely seeks to support the Head and his senior team in providing the safest and best quality of education possible for the children in the school.

The whole world of education and the lifetime I spent in it as teacher, head, advisor, inspector, and governor, is for another time, but I look forward to writing that story, which inevitably will have some links with the Mighty Whites. Indeed, I was once honoured to be invited by IAPS, the organisation that represents the leading Prep schools in the country, to give a presentation to all the newly-appointed heads as part of their support and induction programme. I felt strongly about this, having seen so many former colleagues come to grief, mainly through a lack of experience and support. It's a tough, hard job, and in some way not unlike a football manager's existence (obviously without the cash rewards of the big clubs!). You have so many people to interact with, so many to serve, so many to support and hopefully inspire, to provide the best kind of education for the young people in the school. But it can be very lonely. And of course, just like it's easy for us all to pick the strongest England football team sitting in a pub, likewise it's easy to run a school from the staffroom.

So, I came up with a 'presentation' designed to hopefully help protect the 'new heads' and give them some strategies to keep them sane and ahead of the game. One of the key messages I hoped to pass was to make sure you kept something – a hobby or a favourite pastime; anything really that could afford you a complete break from the constant pressure of leading a school. It was a lesson I had learnt way back in 1986 when I was appointed to St. Joseph's, and I decided to stop playing football at the age of 32 for fear that an injury could mean a long-term absence from the job.

In those days, local authority advisors used to visit us regularly to see how we were settling into the job. It's a job, incidentally, that there is no real preparation for. Basically, you can be the most brilliant mind, the best class teacher in the world, but if you can't hack the pressure, if you can't manage people, you simply won't survive. Still more similarities with football and the paucity of fantastic players who go on to become successful managers.

My advisor at the time was quite an elderly lady who was coming up to retirement. She was an experienced former head and now worked as a senior advisor for the authority. She understood the job and she could, as the footballers like to say, 'put her medals on the table'. We had a useful chat, at the end of which she invited me to attend a residential conference for all new heads at the wonderful Woolley Hall College, which was beautifully situated in lovely countryside, funnily enough near Barnsley. It was a centre for educational development run as a consortium by, I think, the Wakefield, Leeds, and Kirklees authorities, and sadly ultimately was to become a victim of the Conservative policies to give more control of funds to schools by diverting them away from LEAs.

Anyway, we had spent a good hour going through some of the problems I had encountered and how I had tried to solve them. It was a really useful meeting, and as I walked with her to her car, she suddenly turned and asked me if I had given up anything I loved doing because I thought it inappropriate for a head to be involved with. I think she mentioned pub darts teams or squash, or something I can't really remember now, but I told her about stopping playing football and she told me I should reconsider my decision. Her point was all around the importance of having a total break from the job and following other pursuits, rather than just spending every moment worrying about school things.

Today, of course, it would be all about mental health issues, but back then it was called stress and there was less fuss or support offered. But whatever it was, I realised just how much I had missed playing football, and particularly the camaraderie and banter of enjoying the company of my friends. I decided there and then to play again and found myself involved in two games the following weekend. It was such brilliant advice, and without being one of those cloying creeps that spent their time toadying around advisors and their like, I decided that when I saw her at the conference I would let her know just how important and helpful her advice had been for me.

So, I played that Sunday morning before the two-day conference started, with supper and drinks later that afternoon. I played well and scored with a flicked header, following my favoured near-post run quite early in the game. The conditions were dreadful, and heavy rain was making the already muddy pitch almost unplayable when I set off on a dribble down the left-hand side of the pitch. A guy came in with a clumsy challenge, but I managed to push the ball past him and got my shot away. The effort went wide, and as I was jogging back to the halfway line to await the goal kick, I realised my foot was hurting. When I looked down, I could see my sock was torn around the ankle where he had caught me, but there wasn't any blood so I played on for a bit longer until the aching in my ankle made me pull up again. This time, I asked for treatment, and our manager, secretary, physio and kitman rolled into one person came running on with his bucket of water and sponge. When we took my boot off and tore what was left of my sock away, all we could see was a gash, but there was so much mud in it there was no blood. He started to sponge away the mud with his bucket of freezing water, and it didn't take long before an awful lot of blood came pumping out of the wound.

It was before the days of mobile phones, and the injury certainly didn't warrant anyone running to a local house and ringing for an ambulance, but I did need hospital treatment. I knew it would mean a few stitches, but more importantly, I wanted to make sure the wound was clean. Our kitman said he would take me to the hospital, but as it was a home game I asked him to take me home so Andy could take me up to Pinderfields and be around to take me home when I had been cleaned up. I was aware I had to be up at Woolley for 4pm, and I wanted to make sure I had everything packed and got there on time.

So that's what we did, and after the inevitable wait in A&E, I did sense minor football injuries were seen as self-inflicted. I was eventually seen to and able to make my point about my fears of getting infection in the wound from all the mud and rubbish stuck in it. When the nurse enthusiastically started scrubbing at the injury with a brush, I instantly regretted making the comment, but half an hour later and with six stitches inserted, pulling the skin around my ankle back together, I was on my way home. Andy drove me up to Woolley and helped me into reception. I couldn't put my left foot down or get a shoe on, so I hobbled around with the use of a crutch provided by the hospital, with my toes peeking out of a thick bandage, heavily discoloured with antiseptic stuff all around the ankle.

And that's when my friendly advisor tapped me on the shoulder, and as I turned round to look at her, she said with a broad smile, 'Ah Adrian, well done. Well done indeed!'

The lady in question duly retired later that year, and in truth we didn't have much further contact, but she taught me so much in that first visit, and now all these years later I was passing on her brilliant advice to around 50 'new heads'. Each of them was bursting with ideas to develop their own vision of how they could make their school outstandingly different, each brimming full of the confidence gained from being appointed, and each as yet completely untried. Some of them just like I was, maybe a little unsure of the challenges ahead and keen to learn from those who had earned the right to be listened to; those who could give nuggets of wisdom; those who could help make a difference. They are the ones who, in my experience, will succeed and go onto be excellent heads. Those that don't seek advice, who can't learn to sift the good ideas from the bad, are usually the ones that fail. Mike helped put my presentation together, taking the ideas from my mind and bits of paper and putting them together on my laptop with pictures and key words to support the major points I wanted to get across to the group. When it came to the section about not giving up something you had enjoyed doing before, and making sure you do something that gives you and your family a complete break from the pressures of school life, I used a picture of Jermaine Beckford celebrating his winning goal against Man U in the wonderful cup victory at Old Trafford, and briefly explained my passion for all thing Leeds. Don't give up on something like football that you love, don't give up on anything, any hobby that takes your mind off the job and reduces the stress in your life, I opined.

The point was simple and understood, with many of the group admitting already to having changed something in their life that they previously enjoyed, in order to spend more time in preparation for the job. The presentation seemed to be well received and later, checking through the comments and grades they had been asked to give me for the relevance content and style of presentation, I was pleased to find they had given me high marks, accompanied by some really positive comments. It made me feel pretty confident about mingling with them for pre-dinner drinks later on that evening. I wasn't expecting any criticism, that is until one of them said, 'I don't get the point of your presentation. To me, it simply doesn't make any sense!' Everyone within earshot went very quiet and I was left with no alternative but to ask him what it was that he disagreed with. 'Well,' he said quietly, 'on what f***ing planet could anyone say that following Leeds United could be any kind of stress release!' I look forward, as I have said, to telling the story of a lifetime in education in a future publication.

For now, the governors' meeting goes well, and once I have put all my papers away I enjoy being at home for the night, have a few beers, and catch up with Sky Sports News before having an early night and heading back first thing, in time to make Lucy's birthday celebrations. Lucy is two today and has already learned to speak in a language all of her own, punctuated with odd recognisable words like 'Mummy, Daddy, and ice cream'! She is great fun and not unlike how her mother used to be as a toddler, if perhaps a little louder! She has an infectious smile and likes to laugh, so from my experience, with those attributes she is likely to go far in life. Katherine has got her a new birthday outfit and she looks lovely and enjoys being centre stage as Nick's parents, Jane and John, join us all in a rousing chorus of 'Happy Birthday'. Lucy sings along with gusto and enthusiastically blows out the candles on her cake. Her words for Andy and me are 'Nana and Popa' and she happily shares out some of her birthday cake with us. It's a great day, and Oliver clearly enjoys it, too, as he has managed two birthday parties in two days.

We head back to the caravan and later enjoy a pub meal and a few drinks in the village before having an early night ahead of our return to Yorkshire. It's a quick turnaround before I travel back to London on the Saturday morning for a meet-up with James and hopefully an important three points in the game with early leaders, but now faltering, Charlton Athletic.

CHAPTER 11

CHARLTON, WHATSAPPS, OLD BOYS AND A RETURN TO SPAIN

Charlton Athletic…1; Leeds United…0
Saturday, 28th September

By the time we get home, we are already planning our next trip, and this time it's back to Spain and our apartment in Calella. Mike and Lou left there yesterday and we have to go and get the place set up for winter, putting all the outside furniture away and generally tidying up, knowing that no-one will be living there now until the New Year. The kids are all brilliant with the place. They all think of it as their home and all of them always leave it looking fantastic. They also maintain the house rule of leaving at least six beers and a bottle of Sauvignon blanc in the fridge. We will be joined during the week by James, who is attending a friend's wedding a few miles away at Castel Emporda, at the weekend. We know this beautiful wedding venue very well, and actually stayed there when Mike was at university in Barcelona, taking over three suites for me and Andy, Mike and James, and one on her own for Lou. Obviously, we got a ridiculous deal to go and stay at a top-class hotel only a few miles away from our Spanish home. In fact, it was closing for winter the next day, hence the cheap deal, but we had a brilliant time and it made such an impression on Lou, as in fact did the whole area, that a few years later she and Mike got married at the place.

It was one of those venues that it's best not to share with too many people, as we certainly didn't want to have our beautiful coastal village flooded by Brits anytime soon. But the hotel had become such a successful wedding venue that it had featured in one of those top European wedding venues pull-outs in the *Sunday Times* or *Telegraph,* or one of those types of paper. And that's where James's friends had seen it. As we had a family friendship going back years, Andy and Lou were helpful in explaining how everything worked and trying to do their best to support the 'happy couple-to-be' so to speak. James will fly in at the weekend and we have planned to go to La Blava, our favourite restaurant in the village, and enjoy one of the best steaks I have ever eaten.

The trip to Spain was pretty unavoidable, what with the wedding and the tidy-up, but unfortunately it does mean missing one of the top games of the season, with WBA at home and under the lights one to really savour. It certainly would be if it was anything like last year's encounter when we played one of our best games of the season, completely outclassing the Albion 4-0, with ER absolutely rocking. I will also miss our trip to old friends Millwall, a club who have become a bit of a bogey team for us in recent years. I can't say I like the experience of going to the Den. We never seem to get a big enough ticket allocation, and because of their fans' awful reputation the policing is always quite severe. It's terrible when you are made to feel like a criminal on the streets of your own country.

Last time we were there, James and I met with one of his friends and his dad in a pub in the London Bridge area, and when we were saying our goodbyes we got herded into a long line of Leeds fans being marched up to the station. There was nothing to do but be swept along with them, straight through the station, straight onto the platform, straight onto the train, with 'We are Leeds, we are Leeds, we are Leeds' echoing throughout the streets of London like an invading army taking control.

If I am honest, until last May's dreadful defeat to Derby, one of my most painful football memories was our League One play-off defeat to Millwall at ER in May 2009. Having lost the first leg in London, an absolutely bouncing ER was primed for the victory that would take us to Wembley, and hopefully from there back into the Championship. Alas, it wasn't to be. Jermaine unusually missed a penalty and, despite a Bechio goal following a brilliant run and cross by Parker, it was the visitors who scored the all-important goal through Djimi Abdou after 74 minutes. I remember the complete sense of desolation as I left the ground and contemplated a long journey south and, far worse, yet another season in League One, and yet another summer holiday in ruin. It was only the 14th May, and now there would the rest of that month and all of June and July before we would have a chance to put things right, while yet another long season in the lower leagues stretched out ahead of us. Gutted.

I guess all football fans handle the ups and downs of supporting their club in very different ways, but I bet few become so anxious that they simply can't bear watching or listening or even hearing updates on games while they are actually being played. My nephew Ben is just such a fan. A total expert on anything to do with the club, really supportive of all the players, even Casilla, and hugely active on social media, Ben is a complete Leeds nut... except he simply can't stand the stress of knowing what is happening when a game is being played. Having circulated the latest team news and any other bits of information to all on our family WhatsApp group, aptly named 'Fcoff', he imposes what he calls his 'Benny blackout'!

He just shuts down, walks the dogs, goes jogging, reads, does anything but listen to updates of our games. Then at 5pm he turns on the telly and finds out what has happened during the afternoon, then he catches up with the zillions of WhatsApp messages which have been sent between us, and which effectively tell the story of the game with such intelligent and articulate comments such as:

'Shit.' This means we are losing.
'Fuck.' Oh dear, it's 2-0 to the opposition.
'Yeeeeeessssss!' We have scored!
'OMG, come onnnnn!' This means we have equalised.
'Yyyywnbhffysnejxn!' This means we have gone in front!
'Fucking get innnnn!' This means we have won.

I must admit there have been times, as I mentioned earlier, like the World Cup final when I have, like Ben, simply found it too unbearable to sit at home and watch. And there have been many games I've seen live when I have had my head in my hands and my heart in my mouth, but I have usually always managed to stay and see out the game, often thinking that the opponents would score if I dare to leave the stadium. Football fans and their superstitions: from Ben not watching, to always wearing the same shirt, always following the same routine when on a winning streak, never washing your scarf, never doing anything that might upset the sporting gods. Hopefully, the WhatsApp group will be able to have a special celebration night in May when we are promoted at last back to where we absolutely belong, in the Premiership. Ben will be involved that night, for sure!

It's throwing it down with rain as Andy drops me off outside ER very early on the Saturday morning of the Charlton match. I have decided to take the club coach down to London: A) because The Valley is a fairly difficult place to get to and park in; and B) and much more importantly, so I can have a few beers with James, hopefully before and after the game. The coaches are usually operated by 'Fourways' and, as mentioned, the beauty is you can just relax and forget about pretty much everything until you are dropped off, usually very close to the ground. It's a really good deal in terms of cost as well, as even though I don't look anything like old enough, I qualify for a concession on my ticket. This is so good that rather than face a long journey back on the coach, I use my rail card and book a cheap single back from Kings Cross to Doncaster for later on the Saturday night.

I've got my survival pack with me – sandwiches, water, newspaper, notepad, and radio, as there is some World Cup rugby on during the journey. The coaches are just about comfortable enough, especially if you haven't got to share, and today I am in luck and have a double seat to myself. I settle down to read and listen to the radio, beginning to take more interest in the rugby from Japan as the hosts are giving the fancied Irish a real challenge. According to the Irish commentator, the Japanese are really throwing the ball around and trying to play attacking rugby. I hope they are rewarded for their positivity but doubt they will be able to see it through as the Irish are wily campaigners with an experienced and battle-hardened team. It doesn't look like it at half-time with the Irish ahead 9-12, but in an amazing second half Japan score a converted try through Fukuoka and seal a famous and thrilling victory 19-12, really igniting the World Cup and showing what a top class sport Rugby Union can be when played properly and with a spirit of adventure.

The coach drops us off on a main road about five minutes' walk from the ground, so I'm glad I don't have to find it after the match. James is outside the ground, hoping to buy a ticket for the 'away end' before kick-off. It's always a frustration, and I think he feels more relaxed about trying to canvass people when I am not around. It's also harder for him today, as usually he can go along all the visiting coaches as they park up near the away fans' stand, whereas today the coaches have all had to park away from the ground. It's still quite early but the pubs are rammed and eventually, having walked some distance to find one, it's clear it's for 'home' fans only. He is like a man with a mission, charging on ahead, determined to get a beer before kick-off, and eventually I have to tell him that my knee is killing me and I can't keep up. The bloody injection is taking its time to work, is all I can think to say. We eventually find a petrol station quite near the ground and he buys some cans of larger that we drink sitting on a grass verge at the side of the road.

Eventually we walk back up to the ground and he tells me to go in while he hunts around the visiting fans to try and buy a ticket. I go in past the stewards and am searched by a very charming lady who tells me she hopes I enjoy the game. When I say that's impressive coming from someone employed by Charlton, she tells me she's a Chelsea fan, so I tell her I hate Chelsea almost as much as Man U. She just smiles and I'm through and into the ground, which is a bit old school despite its recent upgrade. I am at the far side, so walk past the bars and around the back, and then down into my seat. Once again, it's well placed halfway up and slightly to the right of the goal.

The team news isn't so good. Ayling is still missing, as he has been from the start, but Dallas has been in superb form replacing him at right back. The big loss is Hernandez, who has picked up an injury; he is replaced by Costa, and it's clearly his chance to force himself into the team. Forshaw is back on the bench and so, too, is Roberts, who has suffered so much with injuries since he joined the club. I really like the look of Roberts and think he can become a big player for us if he can steer clear of more injury problems. I can still see the shot he hit against the post against Sheffield Utd at ER last season. I think if that had gone in we would have beaten them to second place and been promoted.

I haven't heard from James, so I assume he hasn't got a ticket and has gone into the Charlton end where he has been before, so he is legitimately on their computer database. Then, as the game kicks off, he turns up. Making his way through the throngs of fans to a seat right next to me, we have a big hug and a high five. The good news is that he got a ticket at the last minute and at face value from a bloke whose mate took sick.

We settle down to enjoy the game and start brightly when, after a neat one-two between Shackleton and Klich, the Polish international plays Bamford through on the left and Shackleton, who has made an unbelievable run through the middle, just fails to convert the centre forward's cross, leaving a Charlton defender to almost turn the ball into his own net. From the resulting corner, Ben White nearly prods the ball home, only to be denied by Phillips in the Charlton goal. Just like last week against Derby, it's all Leeds, and Alioski finds Bamford with a good ball, only for the number nine to head disappointingly down and wide of the goal.

Charlton have offered little, and following their defeat at lowly Wigan last weekend they look there for the taking, yet here we are again – total domination and nothing to show for it. Then the clever Welshman Williams plays a good ball down the right-hand touchline and Bonne, their centre forward, forces a corner off the covering Ben White. It's pretty much their first attack of the match, but from the corner the centre half Lockyer heads the ball on goal. It's straight at Casilla's midrift and an easy save to make, but unaccountably the keeper tries to fist the ball clear, only succeeding in sending it straight into Bonne's back, then having to watch the ball bounce back slowly past him and trickle into the net.

It's a truly terrible goal to concede, and for a while we look a little shaken, but Costa fires a good chance over before the interval and Bielsa seems unusually bullish with his half-time substitutions, bringing on Nketiah for Alioski and Forshaw for Shackleton. For the first time we will see how Bamford and Nketiah play together. The answer is not so great, and Bamford is replaced by Roberts after 69 minutes. We huff and puff and do go close when Darren Pratley almost puts through his own goal and Nketiah scuffs a shot across goal. Deep into the game, from a Phillips corner, the ball deflects to Forshaw who hits the ball goalwards only to see the keeper and one of his defenders clear the ball to safety.

Another loss and our first on the road. We haven't played as well as we can, but we've created enough to have won two games; we have over 70% possession and win 13 corners. Charlton manage just two corners and three shots in the 90 minutes, and yet score the only goal. It's so frustrating to lose in this fashion, and especially in the way we conceded the goal. Yet more confusion from a corner and yet more fingers being pointed at our Spanish keeper. Worse, following Fulham's win over Wigan and Forest's victory at Stoke last night, WBA win at QPR this afternoon to go top of the table, one point ahead of Swansea who could only draw with Reading. We slip to fourth in the table, only two points off the top, but also only two away from tenth. We are beginning, despite all our attractive play, to throw points away; it's just so bloody typical of Leeds.

We stop the post-match inquisition when the Charlton manager Lee Bowyer tentatively walks towards the massed ranks of Leeds fans. He gets a fabulous reception, with the travelling hordes chanting out his name as they did with such passion in the early noughties.

We queue for what seems ages to get a train into London, and the day has turned cold and grey to match our mood. In defeat the cold seems to attack my knee, which is feeling incredibly sore at the moment. Some

Chelsea fans go past the station on a train heading in the other direction and get a less than friendly abusive chant directed at them. It makes everyone laugh and soon we are all rammed together, listening to various chants and tall stories loudly told by Yorkshire voices heading into the capital for a night of fun.

James and I use his local knowledge and head to a great pub, the 'Old Thameside Inn', situated right on the Thames with a large outside terrace. I'm delighted to get here, as he has raced through markets and side streets, head down, and determined to get to the pub as soon as possible. I have limped behind him, a bit like the disabled Dustin Hoffman character lamely chasing after Jon Voight, the stud, in the superb film *Midnight Cowboy*! The pub is situated right next to the *Golden Hind* on the Southbank; it's a full-sized replica of the one in which Sir Francis Drake circumnavigated the world in 1577, and while James goes to get some beers in I sit and try and imagine the ship battling through huge seas a long way from home. It's almost unbelievable that he could have done that in something as small as this and with no engine power.

We sit quietly sipping our Guinness, talking about anything but football as we try to forget the disappointment of the defeat. We only have an hour or so before I have to catch the train back to Yorkshire, and we are making the effort to talk, knowing we would probably both prefer to be silent at the moment as we replay the missed opportunities of earlier in the day. I would normally have stayed and enjoyed a night out in London, but having just got back from our caravanning trip and with a flight to Girona on Monday, it seemed better not to prepare for that trip with a raging hangover.

A couple of lads come and sit on the bench seat next to us. They look about James's age and it soon becomes obvious they are Charlton fans and have, like us, been to the match. But as we listen to them chat animatedly about their afternoon out, it becomes apparent that their beer tastes significantly better than ours! We introduce ourselves and, in the way that 'real' football fans do, have a really good chat about the match and then move onto wider football issues and who will go up this

LEEDS UNITED: IT'S MORE THAN JUST A GAME!

year. They very kindly suggest that they think we will be promoted and, like us, see WBA and Fulham as teams that have a real chance. Interestingly, none of us think Swansea will be involved, but there are mentions for Bristol City and Brentford who incredibly, despite selling on their best players, have kept a high profile in the division. No-one mentions Forest either, but they seem a mean team to me, and they have Grabben up front who gets a lot of goals at Championship level.

The conversation changes and the beer flows. The lads had both gone to university in Leeds, and suddenly they and James are into the student scene in that city, and talking about favoured pubs, clubs, and eateries. I decide it's probably time to head to Kings Cross, and as I can't keep up with James and he is clearly enjoying himself, I make my farewells, tell James I'll see him in Girona next week, and head to the underground. To be honest, I am knackered and looking forward to getting home. I just hope I get to the train before the urge to pee leaves me dashing round looking for a quiet lamppost, because it's absolutely impossible trying to find a loo in London. And even if you do, you have to have the right change. What bollocks!

We are flying to Girona from Leeds Bradford and know the set-up well, as we use it so frequently with flights to Spain, and obviously to Dublin to see Mike and family. It's a small airport but handily placed for us, taking just about an hour if the traffic isn't heavy on the A1. We cut across from Wetherby, where so many of the players live, to Harewood and Pool and then up the hill to the airport. Parking is pretty easy, and 'Long Stay' is cheap and has a regular bus service to the main building. It's one of those that reads your registration as you enter, though. And – this is only at Leeds, in our experience – it never lets you out when you try to leave. This has become one of my pet hates, like Piers Morgan or the BBC News; it's just irritating, and frustrating, and wrong.

The flight is scheduled for 7.30pm, which means a late arrival in Girona, but hopefully if Marc is waiting with the hire car, we should be home having a beer on the terrace before midnight. Leeds Bradford is always trying to promote itself as a developing hub and the 'Yorkshire airport', and there are some other positives for it other than its handy distance to home. In our experience, the staff who man the departure area and who check boarding cards and security are much more amenable than in most airports we use, particularly Stansted. This is true of arrivals back into the country, where you are still greeted by humans who check passports rather than those ridiculous machines that hardly ever work. A negative for Leeds is the quite tight space, and the fact that shops and food outlets close before the last flights and are not always open before the first early morning flights. I simply don't understand how you can claim to be an airport serving the people of Yorkshire and then close down while travellers are still waiting for their flights. I realise that this is not just Leeds Bradford, but it's where I am now and it's another frustration of the travelling experience.

As it turns out, our flight is delayed, but only by half an hour. So, by the time we land, it's after eleven and fortunately Marc, who runs the car leasing agency we use, is waiting as we come out of arrivals. We exchange the usual pleasantries as he takes us to the car park, and I sign the papers and familiarise myself with the vehicle I'll be driving. As there is only the two of us, we always ask for the smallest, cheapest car, but often we get fairly new ones and this is a quite roomy Fiat. We pay a bit more than you see some hire car agencies advertise, but there are none of the hidden extras or ridiculously high add-on charges. There are no lengthy queues to sign papers, only to join another lengthy queue. And literally 20 minutes after disembarking, we are on the road home.

Marc tells us where to leave the car when we leave and wishes us a pleasant holiday. I notice from my rear window mirror that he is watching us as we drive away, which makes me smile, because we are both remembering the day I got confused by the exit barrier system and drove into the side of a wall as I realised I was trying to exit through the entry gate. While this was hugely embarrassing on my part, it was most helpful in proving to us that our insurance cover was more than adequate.

The apartment looks great, as it always does, and Mike and Lou have done a fine job tidying and cleaning after their visit. They have left some lovely notes for us, and importantly there are 'bubbles and beers' chilling in the fridge. We always try and unpack and have a sweep round before we settle for a beer, and while Andy busies herself unpacking her stuff, I check the television is working ok and then set up the satellite system. It's always a bit of a faff transporting the Sky box, especially with all the increased security, but it's well worth the hassle when I tune it in and Sky Sports News flashes up. The box we bought in Spain is also up and running, so now we have BBC, ITV, Channel Four, etc. It's time for a beer, and as it's way past midnight we settle down with the sandwiches we bought from Pret A Manger before the shop shut in Leeds. The ham and cheese sandwich is excellent and, washed down with a cold San Miguel while watching the moon light up the sea, it's almost the perfect meal. We have quite a few drinks and eventually turn in just before 2am. It's always the same when we come back to Calella; we forget just how fantastic it is and look forward to spending a couple of weeks in one place.

Leeds United…1; West Brom…0
Tuesday, 1st October

I can't believe I'm not at ER tonight. It's such a big game against one of our biggest threats to promotion. But there is nothing I can do about it, with the wedding, James's visit, and the need to put all the summer stuff away. It's one of the judgements all football fans, or at least those who follow their team home and away, have to make: when to fit in family events, weddings, holidays, etc, and how they can be managed around the unfolding fixture list. So while this is a big miss, as is the trip to Millwall which would take me back to London, the planning has to ultimately fit the circumstances and has to be clinical. There will always be matches missed, but the trick is to make the damage as limited as possible.

In this case, there is no way round missing the Albion match, so I just have to live with it, but the experience of actually going to The Den isn't great, even if the trip to London definitely is. And anyway, James will be in Spain, so we wouldn't have been able to meet up, which is half the fun for games in the capital. Another plus for planning the trip at this time is that there is yet another international break scheduled for the weekend after the Millwall game, which means we don't play again until the Birmingham match on 19th October. So there are at least some positives around international breaks.

During the day Sky Sports News runs a breaking story that the FA are looking into an allegation of racial discrimination made by Casilla to Jonathan Leko, the Charlton player. Both clubs acknowledge the investigation, with Charlton saying they will offer support to Leko, and Leeds that they would be 'working with the FA during the investigation'. It sounds quite worrying for the Spanish goalkeeper, and if it's true Leeds will have to take serious action against him, given their quite proper and really strong stance on 'kick it out'.

It's interesting team news ahead of the game, with Hernandez still missing and Forshaw once again injured. On the plus side, Ayling returns to the bench along with Douglas, Nketiah, Roberts, Beradi, and the almost forgotten Clarke. Miazek is the substitute keeper, and with the news about Casilla he might have a role to play when the investigation is completed. Albion are at strength and have both Charlie Austin and Zohore, fine attackers and goal scorers, on the bench. They also have an old school pupil of mine, Jonathon Bond, on the bench as a replacement keeper. He's a good lad, bright and personable, and I'm pretty certain would have carved out a successful career following university if he hadn't made it as a professional. He was a good footballer, too, and didn't play in goal when he was at the Prep school, even though he was already being coached by Watford.

We used to have a football coaching session for the school on Saturday mornings, and while we were waiting for all the kids to arrive and get themselves ready, I would often join in passing and doing 'keepie-uppies' before the sessions got underway. Once, when Jonathan was fielding shots from his friends, I got his attention and took a free kick from wide on the left. I just happened to hit it sweetly and it bent and arced over his head and into the net. I set off on a victory run, just like the teacher famously did in the film *Kes*. The parents looked gobsmacked.

I used to receive reports from Watford on Jonathan's progress, written by his coaches, and I have to say I was pretty impressed with them and the way they catered and cared for such a young man. I used to chat with him about the comments and guidance in the reports, and joke with him that I would be expecting a ticket when he played against Leeds some time in the future. I followed his progress as he moved through the senior school, and as he was only a year younger than James, I often saw him at sporting fixtures. But inevitably, as kids grow up, you do lose contact with them, so I was very surprised to get a letter from him a few years later. Basically, it was an invite from him to attend an upcoming fixture with Leeds at Vicarage Rd, Watford. Jonathan wouldn't be playing, but he had just signed on schoolboy forms. I wrote back to him thanking him for remembering me and wishing him well in his developing career. I duly received two courtesy tickets with his name printed on each of them. What a super gesture from a super young man! He didn't forget his promise and I didn't forget my manners, writing to thank him and not over-celebrating when Rob Hulse netted our winner in the game.

Now Jonathan was at ER and I was a thousand or so miles away in Spain, eagerly awaiting kick-off. We played well from the start and pushed Albion back without creating any clear-cut chances. The atmosphere was buzzing, but strangely the Albion had only brought quite a small travelling fan base – just under a thousand, which for such a game, even if it was midweek, even if it was on television, was a poor effort. There is no doubt if the game had been played at the Hawthorns, the 'away fans' allocation would have sold out.

Leeds suffered a blow when the captain Cooper had to leave the field after only 34 minutes, and was replaced by the popular but occasionally wild Baradi who had covered for him successfully a few times already this season. The loss didn't seem to affect our momentum and we took the lead shortly afterwards, in the 38th minute. It was a well worked goal with Klich, wide out right, passing to Costa, who in turn played it to Shackleton, who found Harrison on the left flank. The winger then cut in looking to shoot on goal, only to find his way through blocked, so he played the ball wide left to find Alioski, who had made a lung-bursting run up to the edge of the area. The little North Macedonian fired in a left-footed cross shot which caught a slight but important deflection off Kyle Bartley and flew into the bottom corner of the net. Pandemonium at ER as the crowd erupted; pandemonium in Spain as I set off on a victory run round the flat once again, unfortunately knocking a bottle of San Miguel as I went. Not a popular move.

We almost doubled our lead before half-time when Bamford prodded another Alioski shot from almost point blank range straight at Johnstone in the Albion goal, but the keeper showed incredible reflexes to deny Costa from the rebound, sticking out a foot to divert the ball wide. We could have had a penalty, too, when a strong shot from Dallas clearly struck Bartley's hand. Still, as I mopped up the spilt beer at half-time, I reflected on a good performance against by far the best team we have played against. Hopefully, we could finish them off in the second half and not squander points, as we had already done three times at home this season.

Unfortunately, Shackleton is injured and doesn't appear for the second half, which seriously weakens our midfield. The more attacking Roberts comes on against his old club, but the game has changed, and for the first time this season we struggle to contain the visitors' attacks. Pereira, their classy number ten, starts to cause some havoc and hits a shot – not dissimilar to the one Alioski scored from – narrowly wide of the post. Then the same player curls a free kick narrowly past a post with Casilla rooted to the spot.

We are beginning to hang on, and Bielsa shows his balls by withdrawing the ineffectual Roberts from the game, replacing him with Ayling, which allows the versatile Dallas to move into midfield and limit the damage Albion are causing. Pereira wriggles free again and this time Casilla saves well, diving to his right. Leeds finish on the ascendancy, with Costa and Harrison forcing good saves from Johnstone and easing the pressure on the defence. In the end, we are praying for the final whistle, everyone so aware of those dreadful goals we conceded so late on against Swansea and Derby. When it comes, the feeling is fantastic and I see Andy breathe a sigh of relief, knowing that this is not going to be another night ruined by football.

We should have won the match in the first half, but there is no denying the fact that if WBA had taken points from us, they would have been well deserved – unlike those of the previous teams mentioned. They actually had more possession than us, which is something that very rarely happens, and they are clearly going to be a threat to us in the promotion race. The other results around the country mean that we go back to the top of the table ahead of Albion and Forest by a point, and two ahead of Fulham who smashed Reading 1-4. Swansea and Charlton play tomorrow, so tonight we can celebrate, and I can enjoy staying up late watching replays of all the goals in the evening's matches. Life is good, but we do seem to be picking up one or two injuries, and with Hernandez, Cooper, Forshaw, and Shackleton all missing at the end of tonight's game, it will be interesting to see what kind of a team we put out at Millwall at the weekend.

It's always great to enjoy a few lazy days in Spain between matches, especially when we have won. Andy loves to walk, and there are some truly beautiful walks to enjoy, both coastal and inland. Over the next few days we try both, walking inland to Ermadus through the forest, and taking the stunning coastal path from Golfet, our local beach, through Calella and onto Llfranc, the next village along, with its little harbour with the bar on the top which is such a brilliant place to enjoy a few cold beers before the journey back.

My knee is really playing up, and it looks now as if the injection hasn't worked like the last one did. Sometimes in the night when I turn over in my sleep, I must twist it and I wake myself up with the pain, yelping like some distressed dog. I guess I will need to call Dr Vega when we get back, though it usually takes three weeks at least to get an appointment. I can tell it's frustrating for Andy seeing this wimp limping on behind her, so I keep doing the exercises the physio gave me and find I can keep going. Bizarrely, while it is really sore going downhill, I seem to be able to almost run uphill. Anyway, we usually walk for anything between one and two hours, and if the sun is out – and so far this week it has been – when we get home neither of us can resist a really cold beer in the garden, looking out over the sea before we have lunch. It is absolutely my favourite bar in the world.

The days race past and before we know it it's Friday and I'm on the way back to Girona to pick up James. He lands on time at 11.20 and we are home for just after midday. Andy has made a tuna pasta salad, but before we enjoy it he is ready for a beer or two, and as before neither of us needs our arms twisting. We have a really nice, relaxed catch-up and he is on top form. In fact, we can't keep up with him, and aware that we are out for dinner tonight, I call time for Andy and I. Having eaten, it's siesta time. Usually when it's warm Andy will mess in the garden for a bit and then fall asleep on the outside sofa, as it falls into the shade. I tend to catch up with Sky Sports News and then go and read on the bed, which usually means I am asleep within minutes.

Today is no different, and when I come round at about 5pm I can see James sound asleep on the sofa and Andy out in the garden pulling up some weeds. I go back to the bedroom and lie down with the big windows open and just look at the sea and luxuriate. Later, we head to La Blava and stop off at the St Roc for a pre-dinner drink on the way, before strolling down the hill into the village. It's October, so the throngs of tourists have gone and everywhere looks completely chilled.

The restaurant is really a big house set right by the sea and underneath the arches that I guess were initially built to keep the fishermen cool into the days before aircon. The restaurant opened a few years ago and is owned by Sergio, whose parents own the house. He was brought up in it before turning the lower part of the building into a restaurant. It's a classy place, and we always try to book the same table upstairs and next to the window. We have been going since it opened and have always hit it off with Sergio and Oscar, his manager. I don't know quite why, but they have always fallen over themselves when I turn up there, saying 'Mr Taylor this, Mr Taylor that'. Some people crave that type of recognition, but it makes me feel a little embarrassed. I just wonder who they think I am! Anyway, it's a cracking restaurant, and we have a fantastic meal and are incredibly well looked after. James gets some pictures and is keen for another drink on the way home. It's probably a 25-minute walk and all uphill, finishing with those 127 steps from the bottom road to the entrance to the apartments. It's one of the reasons in the summer, despite the alcohol, that we always lose weight. And tonight, even in October and at one in the morning. I am wet through by the time we have our nightcap on the house terrace.

It's been a lovely evening, and as we say goodnight James is calling for a morning wake-up to watch England's Rugby World Cup game against Argentina. I don't like to think how much we have had to drink, but I know it's going to mean, for a man of my age, several trips to the loo through the night. I don't know how too much drink and being in a different surrounding affects other people, but often when I am in a really deep sleep and wake up, at first I'm not exactly certain where I am.

Once, on arriving in the flat, I realised I needed the loo but, obviously still asleep, I couldn't find the door. Andy woke to find me walking by the wall with my hands out, trying to find the door to the ensuite. Eventually, having succeeded in this, I carried on feeling my way along the walls till I ended up by the bathroom sink, above which is a light encased in a kind of glass ball. She watched as I carefully unscrewed this light fitting and laid it carefully on the floor. I then proceeded to use the loo and then go back to bed. When Andy told me in the morning what I had done, I literally had no memory of it, but there lying on the floor in the bathroom was the evidence of it. Strange bed, quite a few drinks, deep sleep, and the potential to cause damage to self and property. It wasn't that long ago that I managed to do both, when staying at Mike's in his St Alban's days, ahead of a drive down to Spain on my own while Andy was working. Lou was away on business, so Mike and I went out for dinner, had a few drinks, a good chat, and a few glasses of red as a nightcap. It had been a lovely evening and I pretty much went straight to sleep. I do remember vaguely realising I had missed my step on the staircase, and I launched out with my hands outstretched to try and break my fall. I seemed to be falling for quite a while before I came to a stop at the bottom of the stairs. I had managed to get down the first three, make a left turn, and then fall down the rest, taking framed photos and paintings with me as I presumably tried to grab hold of some kind of safety net.

I remember Mike looking extremely worried, asking me if I was ok. When I replied that I was, he went to make us a cup of tea (obviously), while I rather stupidly went back up the stairs to bed. The next thing I was aware of was being manhandled down the stairs fixed to a stretcher, with a neck brace making everything feel uncomfortable, and a paramedic talking to me. Apparently, when I had gone back upstairs, I had collapsed and Mike, whose nerves must have been shredded, called for an ambulance. I must have started to come round pretty quickly, because I do remember laughing as they tried to get the stretcher down the stairs, telling them that I knew a much quicker way of getting down. There was a lot of concern shown by Mike's neighbours, as you would expect when a 'blue light' ambulance appears next to your house in the middle of the night. They were really kind to him, telling him they would secure the house and look after Diego the cat.

Mike came in the ambulance with me and the paramedic, and while they were talking I was much relieved to see I could wiggle my toes and move my legs. I remember the paramedic telling Mike I was repeating myself a lot, which was apparently a worrying sign of concussion. But Mike responded, 'No, Dad is always repeating himself!' Thanks, son. I ended up being thoroughly checked over, MRI scans, chest X-rays, the lot, which I was very pleased about, though I was still in quite a bit of discomfort with the neck brace that they had put on me. I told Mike not to contact Andy or Katherine, who I was due to see enroute that day. I wanted to make sure I had the all clear first, but he was worried and had already rung them so they were both on their way to Watford General, which is where the ambulance had taken me. Someone else on the way to see me was the Spanish doctor who was in charge of me. He was bringing the good news that I hadn't sustained any serious injuries and I could go home. I was doubly pleased with this news, because as well as knowing I hadn't bashed myself up on the fall, I felt reassured that if they had found anything sinister on any of their tests they would surely have to tell me.

They wanted the bed and they wanted me out, and I was more than happy to oblige, so once they had removed the neck brace I stood up and... fell over. Eventually, leaning on Mike, I managed to walk a few steps, and after a few minutes I could move a little more freely. I don't know how or where they came from, but I seemed to have some clothes on and in great discomfort, managed to limp out of the A&E ward and head for the exit.

I found myself in the car park, waiting for Katherine to pick us up. As I waited, I realised we were very close to Vicarage Rd, and I had some fleeting memories of matches I had seen there. And then Katherine flew into the car park and they bundled me in and took me back to Mike's. Thankfully, I had escaped serious injury, and I now know that falling downstairs could have been potentially fatal. I was a lucky boy, even if I did feel a bit battered and bruised. None of us knew it at the time, but the next time we would be in that hospital would be in a couple of years' time when Mike and Lou's first born, Margie, arrived in the world.

Millwall...2; Leeds United...1
Saturday, 5th October

Having enjoyed a great night last evening, James would be heading off to his wedding later today and Andy was keen to make sure he looked really smart, ironing his shirt and brushing down his suit. James showered and took some breakfast but was more interested in watching the England rugby match. He, much more than me, is a fan of the game, but obviously it's England and we want them to win and go as far as possible in the World Cup. It will be a big ask for them, as the way things look – if everything goes to form – they will end up playing Australia, New Zealand, and South Africa.

But today it's Argentina and we have no problems seeing them off, especially once they have a player sent off for a high tackle on Farrell. The game finishes 39-10, and it will be some time before the tournament gets exciting, other than when the hosts play. It's a little like the soccer World Cup; there are some fairly meaningless matches that end up with the strongest countries giving their reserves a run out and still finish with cricket scores. The final is scheduled for 2nd November, which seems a lifetime away.

Andy takes a few pictures of James in his wedding attire before we leave for the hotel; he looks really smart, and very fit and well. He's going to meet old friends, so he will have a good time and we hug as we say goodbye, not exactly sure when we will meet up again. Though he is talking about coming up for the QPR game in November. I get back in time for a bit of lunch and then settle down in front of 'Soccer Saturday', with fingers crossed for another three points after the hard-won match against WBA. It's time we started to play with more consistency and saw off some of the teams we have dominated yet dropped points to.

Millwall fans have been shocked by the resignation in midweek of their manager of four years, club legend Neil Harris, so surely this is our chance to take advantage. Our team news, though, is not good, with Cooper and Shackleton – injured in midweek – joining Forshaw and Hernandez on the sick list. I hate it when I miss a game, and it's worse still when I can't watch it on television. This afternoon I am in the hands of Jeff and the crew to keep me posted on developments at the Den. And it's not good. Millwall are awarded a penalty, and Baradi is sent off as a result of the decision. I don't see pictures of the incident until later that night, but it's a terrible decision by the referee, with Bradshaw, the Lions forward, diving to the ground after allegedly having his legs clipped by Baradi, as the Leeds man tried to avoid him running across his path. Bradshaw looks around to the ref, and I can't work out if he thinks he's going to be booked for diving or is hoping to get the penalty.

To me, the ref makes three mistakes in the same decision: first, it's not a penalty; second, even if it was, it's clearly not a red card; and third, Bradshaw should have been booked for his rather obvious dive. Wallace scores easily from the spot and we find ourselves under pressure. Then Jeff tells us, There's been another goal at Millwall, but which way's it gone?' And of course, that moment of hope is smashed when we're told Bradshaw has scored again. Two-nil down, and a man down, things don't look good as the players troop off for half-time, some clearly angry about the penalty and also about what looked a possible penalty at the other end waved away by referee Linington.

Things get better when right from the kick-off we pull a goal back, with Alioski once again making a great blindside run to fire home Harrison's cross. We huff and puff, have the lion's share of the game even with ten men, but we can't score and end up giving the ball away too easily and putting ourselves under more pressure. It's another defeat and another bad loss. Though poor refereeing has not helped, we really should be beating teams like Millwall if we are going to be serious promotion contenders. Things don't go well for us elsewhere, as Albion and Forest, who are definitely becoming a threat, both win and Fulham and Charlton draw with each other. We find ourselves slipping to fifth in the table, two points off the top but only four points clear of twelfth-placed Birmingham, who are next up at ER after another of these interminable international breaks.

CHAPTER 12

BILLY!

Leeds United…1; Birmingham City…0
Saturday, 19th October

It always takes a few days to get over a defeat, and as we walk around the beautiful pathways of Calella, I try mentally to put the loss into context, while Andy bubbles on about houses and gardens and changes on the horizon. We are obviously missing Hernandez badly, and with Forshaw and Cooper also absent, the side is definitely weakened. Clearly the sending off of Baradi didn't help matters either, but we were a bit sloppy at Millwall and gave the ball away more than usual. We need to be more clinical in front of goal, and while Bamford is the one who takes most of the criticism, he's not alone. Harrison, Costa, Forshaw, and Klich could do better with the chances they have had.

At the other end, Cooper missing a few matches has caused problems and Ayling's lengthy absence hasn't helped, though Dallas deputising has been a revelation as an attacking right back. Ben White has been excellent at centre half, and you have to wonder how good the Brighton defence must be if they can afford to let a player of his quality go out on loan. Alioski, as always, is a fizz of action and has had some good assists and scored vital goals as well, making up for the occasional defensive slip-up.

And then there's Casilla, who remains an enigma. He is capable of making some decent saves but also can gift goals away, as he did at Charlton, and sometimes look like a kid playing ball on the beach as when hopelessly missing the cross against Derby. I wonder who it was who watched him before he was signed and made him allegedly one of the highest paid players in the club. Probably the same person who advised us to buy the hopeless Wiedwald, who lasted a season and had to be dropped twice, so poor was his keeping. I guess at some point Radrizzani has to carry out some kind of appraisal on the effectiveness of our recruitment programme, and while we seem to have brought in some exciting young talent, we have also spent good money on distinctly average players. For me, the jury is out on people like Victor Orta, who are involved in the transfer and recruitment programme.

Maybe in the mini-break Bielsa will focus on finishing and defending set pieces, particularly corners where as a spectator I always hold my breath until the ball is safely brought clear of the penalty area. So, if I am doing this on the terraces, it must be pretty certain that every manager in the league has worked out how to put pressure on us defensively. I know if I were playing Leeds, I would take every opportunity to put the ball high into our box, and not just corners but long throws and basically pub football punts in the air. I am fairly sure the tactic, however basic, would reap reward. I don't know the exact number of corners we have conceded this season – not many – but the number of goals we have lost from such positions, or as a direct consequence, is ridiculous in comparison to the number we have scored from the literally hundreds of corners we have won. I am eventually aware that Andy is still talking to me. So, certain that Marcelo will be on to sorting out the problems in the coming days, I put it all to the back of my mind. Hopefully the injury list will reduce in the next week or so, and Pablo and Coops will be back for Birmingham.

We really enjoy the next few days in Spain. The weather is beautiful and the apartments, while not totally empty, are quiet, as is the village of Calella and the nearby town of Palafrugel. So, we have all the perks of what attracts the tourists from all over Europe, without actually having the tourists from all over Europe present. We eat well, enjoy probably too many beers in the sun and, despite my aching knee, walk miles and miles. Some of these walked miles are on the golf course at Gualta, which I play regularly when we are over in Spain. It's just a par three course, but it's really pretty and very well maintained. Nowadays, I usually play on my own, but for years before he was old enough to stay at home back in England on his own, James was my regular partner.

I always book to play around 13.30 which, while it is the hottest part of the day, usually means the course will be fairly quiet. I hate getting caught up in queuing, watching players as average or worse than me warming up like Tiger Woods, or some flash git showing off to his girlfriend. And I will know I'm truly getting old when I take about half an hour over shot selection on a hole that's no more than 120 metres. Over the long summer holiday my play and scoring always gets better, and I try to play the course overall at one over par, which pleasingly I manage to do again this week. I have lost all memory of the thousands of bad shots I have played over the years, but there are some that stay in the memory. Once, when playing with James at a time when we were still well matched (he's now a very good golfer), I played a shot bang at the hole and for a moment as it bounced and rolled towards the flag, we thought for just a second it was going to be a hole in one. It finished a few inches from the cup and we high-fived each other on the tee to celebrate a great shot and a very near miss.

Then James played his shot, and just like mine it went straight at the pin and rolled tantalisingly a few inches past the hole. We fell over laughing and set off to claim our birdies. James took photos of the balls lying so close to the flag and, having played out, we confidently marched off to the next tee, which involved a short walk across the car park. Just at that time, Andy and James's girlfriend of the time arrived at the club to meet us for drinks when we had finished the round. We couldn't help but shout out and tell them how well we'd just played the last hole. As they put thumbs up and watched as I played my next shot, I felt a growing sense of pressure. This was not misplaced, as I fired the ball high and wide and straight into the middle of a lake. James, next up and clearly out of sympathy, did exactly the same. The girls looked away with just a glimmer of a smile on their faces.

It wasn't long before we were going through the usual tidy-up procedures at the flat and heading back to Yorkshire. It was a fairly straightforward trip, and we were soon going through the ridiculous hassle of trying to exit 'long stay' parking at Leeds (what is wrong with them?), and heading over to the A1 and home.

Over in Japan there have been terrible storms, which have caused huge damage and destruction and led to sadly many people losing their lives. With such loss, it seems awful to talk about sport, but the nation very much wants to honour those who have perished and wants the tournament to carry on. This decision means England don't play their final group match against the French, because of a dangerous forecast. And anyway, they have already qualified for the quarter finals to play the Australians next weekend.

We, of course, play Birmingham, and it's celebration time as the club is more or less one hundred years old to the very day. There are fireworks and an impressive display put on in the east stand, wishing the club a happy 100. There is also a parade of former players, though in reality it's a fairly understated gathering of old footballers wandering rather aimlessly to the halfway line and chatting in little groups. All the usual suspects are there: Norman, Eddie, Gordon, Wilko chatting to David O'Leary, and I was pleased to see Rod Wallace, a real hero of mine from the championship-winning team of the early 90's. Paul Reaney is there, too, looking slim and fit enough to still be playing.

Of course, there are those who played major roles in the club's history who sadly can't be there. Gary Speed, such a key member of that title-winning midfield of Strachan, McAllister, Speed, and Batty, and who died so tragically at such a young age. The great John Charles, who my dad said was one of the greatest players he had ever seen both in attack and defence, and whose sale to Juventus financed the building of the west stand which proudly bears his name. Don Revie himself, of course; the man who led the club to so much success over the years and who changed the colour of our shirts to all-white as a tribute to the great Real Madrid, and who set us the challenge of achieving similar greatness – and then ensured we did. And of course, Billy – for me the greatest player ever to pull on that white shirt in my time supporting the club, and one of the true greats of his generation.

I remember being with the kids at the first home game after his sad passing at the age of 54 in early December 1997. It's the only time I've ever welled up in a football ground, and tears rolled down my cheeks as we observed the minute's silence for this legend of the club. You often see pictures on Sky of fans in tears at matches because of a bad loss or relegation or something, but much as I 've suffered more than enough of this pain over the years, I've never found myself in tears before. Anger, yes; cursing, of course; and deep depression and despondency, naturally; but never tears. Until then, until that day for Billy. Looking back, I guess the tears were twofold, really. Obviously for Billy and his untimely passing, but also for me and the loss of someone who was such a huge part of my youth.

Of course, there were some fantastic players in that great sixties team, but Billy was always the leader, always the one who you could rely on to pull something extra out of the bag. He was the heartbeat and the spirit of the club. And now he had gone, and I felt his loss. For the first time, someone had passed away who wasn't a close friend or a family member, and I found myself selfishly grieving for my lost youth and so many happy memories. Sometimes when we are chatting at matches, some of the friends I sit near ask me about that great team: What were they like to watch? How good was Clarke or Giles? Was Bremner really the best? What player would he be like today? I always answer that he would be priceless and say the best way to describe him would be as a mixture of Roy Keane and Steven Gerrard. As tough and uncompromising as Keane, a natural leader and fighter, and as talented as Gerrard, with the ability to unlock defences and score vital and often breathtaking goals.

It's amazing to look at the list of important goals Billy scored and, just like Gerrard, often in the biggest of games. He scored the winning goal in three FA Cup semi-finals, against Manchester United twice and Wolves, and he also scored our equaliser in the 1965 Cup Final against Liverpool. It's interesting to read the quote of the great John Arlott, who wrote following Bremner's winner in the third FA Cup replay against Man U in 1970, 'Idealistic managers would select Best for their teams but the "realists" to a man would have Bremner.' He scored other big goals in big games, too. The fantastic goal he got when he smashed in a brilliant equaliser from outside of the area in our European Cup semi-final game with Celtic, played out before a record crowd in Glasgow. And a few years later, he scored a vital goal against Barcelona in the same competition, which helped us to the ill-fated European Cup Final match against Bayern, when it has to be said again the competition was rightly just for champions.

He also scored in the first leg of the Fairs Cup semi-final against Liverpool at Anfield in 1971, which helped us to defeat the Reds as we went on to win the trophy for the second time. And as mentioned earlier, it was Billy (who else?) that scored the goal that dragged us back into that heart-breaking loss at Wolverhampton that cost us the double in 1972. By the time he had played his last game for us in 1976, he had scored an amazing 115 goals in 772 games. With most of those appearance being played at the very highest level, it was a simply astounding record. I have two favourite Bremner goals and they sum up his class and 'never say die' spirit. The first came in October 1967 against Chelsea, the side that had so unfairly robbed of us of our place in the 1967 cup final, when the referee unaccountably ruled out Lorimer's brilliant free kick equaliser. There was no love lost between the teams, and the rivalry would become even more intense in future years.

Chelsea were the London dandies and darlings of the press, the Beatles of the football world, while we were seen as 'Dirty Leeds', the team the press loved to hate, the Rolling Stones of the football world. The thing was, just as the Beatles could more than look after themselves after their tough apprenticeship in Hamburg, and the Stones could write some great music, so Chelsea could, with players like 'Chopper' Harris in the team, go head-to-head with the best of them. And of course, Leeds with Bremner, Giles, and Gray, could play some breathtaking and creative football.

There was a shock for Chelsea before the game, with the surprise resignation of their manager – the colourful Tommy Docherty. And if Chelsea were going to miss him in the weeks to come, then Leeds were going to miss Billy, who had been suspended for 28 days after being sent off against Fulham. He was determined to go out on a high, as Leeds thumped the visitors 7-0, with seven different players getting on the scoresheet. Billy was directly involved in five of them, and scored an absolutely sensational flying overhead kick from the left of the penalty area, to finish off the rout. It remains my favourite goal of all time, such was the athleticism, technique, and skill involved.

So, if the first of my favourite Bremner goals was a piece of sublime skill, the second was anything but, as he forced the ball over for a scruffy but important winning goal against Standard Liege in a Fairs Cup second leg fixture, played on a misty night in October 1968. It was a brilliant game, and yet strangely there were only 24,000 in the ground to see it. Perhaps it was because this was only the first round of the competition and we were probably expecting an easy win, given we had got a 0-0 draw in the first leg.

The game began in a highly unusual fashion, when both clubs came onto the pitch wearing all-white kits. It was surely gamesmanship by the Belgian team, as the visitors are always the club that should change kit. Whatever the reasoning, the plan clearly worked, as the kick-off was delayed until Leeds eventually came out wearing an all-blue kit to sarcastic chants of 'Chelsea, Chelsea', and were very quickly two goals down. We fought back in the second half, of course, and as the game looked to be lost, Lorimer's cross from the right was superbly headed home by the marauding Charlton, pushed up to the attack for just such an opportunity. Lorimer further reduced the deficit with a long-range free kick, and as time began to run out and the fog descended, Billy somehow, almost on the line, forced home a headed flick on from a Lorimer corner. It was right in front of me, standing on the Kop, and the crowd went mental – but not as crazy as Billy, who was actually standing in the net, kicking the ball, and hugging his colleagues. I can still see him in my mind's eye, standing there looking at us, clenched fists pointing up to the misty skies, and sharing the celebration with us.

He was the leader, the captain, but more... he was one of us. He understood what the club meant to us and he shared our pain and our joy. He knew that the club filled the lives of so many fans, taking them out of the drudgery of a boring job and providing an escape from the worries of everyday life, and in my case helping me forget just for a few hours the real fear of failure in my exams. Which is why I was one of the small crowd that witnessed this amazing game when I should have been at home revising.

There will never be another Billy. He was of his time and he was a unique talent. But, and I really feel this, although they are completely different individuals and players, Kalvin Phillips has that indefinable quality, that special something, that could make him one of the Leeds greats. And if not the captain of the club – though surely that will come – then certainly the true spirit of it for many years to come. If, of course, we are promoted.

We lost both games to Birmingham last season, and after the defeat at Millwall it's quite a nervy crowd that settles down to watch the match after all the centenary celebrations have finished. Cooper is again injured, but thankfully Baradi can play after his ridiculous sending off has quite rightly been overturned. Hernandez is again absent, and there is no doubt we have missed his skill and creativity, though Costa continues to suggest he could still prove to be an excellent long-term replacement for the Spain international.

Nketiah remains on the bench, but following his hat-trick in the U-21 international, he must surely now be making a strong claim to start ahead of Bamford who, despite his excellent team play and hard work, is beginning to misfire in front of goal. For Birmingham, the much talked about youngster Jude Bellingham starts the game, so it will be interesting to see if he is the 'new Trevor Francis'. Leeds attack from the start, and Alioski tests Camp in the Birmingham goal with a shot from the edge of the area that the keeper seems to make a bit of a meal of, fumbling the ball away to safety. Then Klich wins the ball in midfield, plays a one-two with Harrison, before playing the ball through to Bamford, whose left foot shot on the run slides agonisingly wide of the far post.

Bamford is involved again, chasing onto a brilliant long ball by Harrison. Realising he is being played away from the goal, he manufactures a superb back pass to leave Costa through on goal. The winger's shot hits a Birmingham defender full in the chest before falling to Dallas, who fires a strong effort on goal which is well saved by Camp. Birmingham haven't offered much as an attacking outfit, but they have worked hard to limit our chances and we go into the interval all-square. Bielsa makes the substitution a lot of the fans have been clamouring for, replacing Bamford with Nketiah for the second half. I must admit I am not too sure about this debate. What I have seen of Nketiah makes me think he is not as good as Bamford at hold-up, defensive, and support play, but he certainly seems to be a more natural finisher. It will be interesting to see how he leads the line now he has a good half to impress. He almost wins us a penalty when he is brought down right on the edge of the penalty area by Harley Dean, the Birmingham skipper. Alioski blasts the free kick just wide of the far post from wide out on the right.

Birmingham remind us they are still in the game and have some potent attackers, when Vilalba hits a fine shot from distance that whistles just past Casilla's right-hand post. Then Gimenez goes down in the penalty area in a challenge involving Ayling and White, but fortunately nothing is given. On the terraces, we are beginning to get a bit nervous, and noisily urge the team forward. It's interesting how Birmingham have started to come into the game as an attacking force in this half. Is it because we are tiring? Or is it because Nketiah is not doing the work that makes Bamford such an effective team player?

We need a goal, and fortunately on 65 minutes it comes. Harrison picks up a sloppy pass from the centre half and drives towards the penalty area. With defenders scrambling across to block his way, he slips the ball right to Phillips who has raced forward in support. The Leeds man shoots straight at Camp, who seems to dive over the ball as he falls to save it and can only deflect it high into the roof of the net. On this day of all days, when our minds have been full of memories from the past, it just had to be Phillips – the Leeds-born boy – that put us in front, and with such an important goal.

The visitors are far from finished, though, and the youngster Bellingham is allowed to run through the centre of the pitch before firing a rising shot at distance, straight at Casilla. The keeper, under no pressure, repeats the mistake he made at Charlton by fisting the ball away. It could have gone anywhere, but fortunately it flies to safety. Encouraged, 'the blues' attack again and Jutkiewicz, who likes to score against us, hits a shot which this time Casilla gathers safely. We need a second goal and should score again when Harrison's clever pass sends Alioski scampering towards Camp on his left-hand post. The wing back does the right thing by chipping the ball over the on-rushing keeper, but unfortunately there is too much height on the ball and it clears the bar.

It's beginning to be head-in-hands time, and we are all aware of the number of points we have lost late on in games at ER. We desperately need to hang on; we desperately need this win. But Birmingham are still there and from a cross on the right Pedersen, leaning back, heads just wide of the goal. We need to hear the final whistle and seem to be under real pressure, giving the ball away badly on occasion, just as we had done at times at Millwall last time out. At last the final whistle sounds and we can relax, knowing we have been in a real tussle against a hard working but not great visiting side. What matters today is we have got the points, even though we have played much better and lost at home this season. Birmingham, in the end, had more shots on goal than we did, which doesn't happen very often at ER. As I am leaving, I'm happy to be thinking that I can relax at least until Tuesday and the trip to Preston. I look forward to sinking a few beers, watching all the highlights on Quest, and buying the Sunday papers.

Suddenly, I am aware of quite a big disturbance in the away fans' area. There are a lot of stewards getting involved and police, too, which is really unusual for today's football, and everything seems to be kicking off. I wonder if this could be a planned attack, as Brum have brought almost two thousand fans to the match, just a few less than Forest who so far have brought the biggest travelling support to the ground. I mean, Birmingham don't really attract big crowds to their home games, getting into the low twenty thousands at best, so I just think it's unusual there are so many here this afternoon.

I limp back up the hill to Beeston, checking the results as I go. Albion have won again at 'Boro, who are slipping down the table, but Fulham have surprisingly lost at lowly Stoke, and Charlton have picked up another three points, while Swansea could only manage a draw at Barnsley. Forest play tomorrow at Wigan – a game I expect them to win. We are, for the moment, back in the promotion places, two points behind WBA and only three points ahead of Bristol in ninth. Things are really tight, and we really did need the points today. On the other side of the world in Japan, England beat the Australians (and their ridiculously aggressive manager Michael Cheka) quite comfortably 40-16, so will play the All Blacks next week in the semi-final. Meanwhile, I am going to enjoy my beer tonight despite my stupid leg, which is really playing up. I'm back to see the doctor next week to see if there is a solution. But not before I travel to Preston for another big game on Tuesday. We are only two points ahead of them so it's another must win, or certainly it's a no lose, as we seek to go on a winning run and put some distance between us and the other clubs in the top six. We will have played 14 games after we play at Sheffield Wednesday next Saturday, almost a third of the season and still no daylight between us and WBA and the rest.

CHAPTER 13

AWAY DAYS, TURNING JAPANESE, KILLJOYS AND THE VOTE

Preston North End...1; Leeds United...1
Tuesday, 22nd October

It's a big week for Leeds, as we visit two of the clubs – Preston and Sheffield Wednesday –who, like us, are challenging at the top of the table. Two tough away fixtures and certainly matches we can ill afford to lose, though Wigan showed how competitive the league has become by defeating the in-form Forest on Sunday. I decide to go on the club coaches to Preston for a couple of reasons, but mainly because of the almost constant closures and delays on the motorway system on the red rose side of the Pennines. If there is a closure late at night on the way home, I can leave it to the coach driver to sort out, rather than get lost following poorly set-up diversion routes. Another reason is that having been to Preston a few times, the traffic near the ground can be horrendous after the game. And usually the police, wanting to get rid of the visiting fans as soon as possible, often hold all the traffic up to allow the coaches to leave pretty quickly and with a police escort. Also, being a good old Yorkshire man, it's pretty cheap on the coaches, especially with my concession.

Leeds are one of the clubs that operate concessions at 60 – or they did six years ago when I bought James's seat as a season ticket holder when he finished university in Leeds to return south, and I retired from headship to head north. Shortly after I had paid for my ticket, I got a phone call from the club explaining that I had paid the full price for my season ticket and was in fact due a concession. Being an honest broker, I explained to them that the concession was in fact for my son, a student, who had now returned south and that I obviously was paying the full price. There was a silence at the end of the phone for a few seconds before, with great tact and diplomacy, the lady at the other end of the line explained that the concession was actually for me. We both laughed at the misunderstanding – her, no doubt with some relief; me, with teeth slightly clenched. I didn't care, anyway. I got a cheap ticket and I didn't feel anything like an old man, so there, pah!

So I found myself on the coach with my usual survival kit and made some notes about previous games with Preston. It had been quite a good hunting ground for us to visit over the years, famously with the play-off semi-final win there, and also last year when Bamford got a second half brace to earn vital points as we fought for automatic promotion. Usually the coaches at PNE try to park at the stadium perimeter near the away end, but tonight it seems only those coaches with disabled passengers can park right next to the ground. Instead, we drive slightly past the stadium and are told to disembark on a road near a park and across the road from the ground. We are told the coaches will all be parked up here after the match, but it all seems very unclear, and the driver can't tell us where he will be parked later. I cross the road to the ground and bump into the lads I sit next to at ER, and we chat about team selection and the usual stuff before we go our separate ways. I need chips! It turns out the side is the same one that played Birmingham, so still no Hernandez or Cooper, and there is no doubt that we have missed them both for obviously different reasons.

It's a new old ground, if you follow me, and actually from the outside looks to be impressively modern. It's less so inside, but again I have a great view, about halfway up and behind the goals. I am realising, probably very slowly, that I keep sitting next to or very near the same people, who all look, shall we say, to be of a similar age. I can't say for certain and I certainly can't be bothered to find out, but it looks to me as if the club puts all its older fans in roughly the same place. Anyway, it doesn't matter a jot as I have, or should I say we have, a fantastic view. The match itself is one of those slow burners that ultimately finished with a bang; one of those games where you know you should win, but in the end are almost happy with a point. Almost. We again dominate pretty much throughout, and Bamford has several chances either side of half-time to equal his scoring feat of last year here. Alioski, Harrison, and Ben White all have chances without being able to capitalise on them, and then in the 74th minute, having hardly threatened in the whole game, Preston score out of nothing.

Their substitute Maguire finds himself in acres of space wide on the right, with Alioski stranded in attack and Baradi out of position. The winger takes the ball on and then, with White desperately trying to cover, crosses from the right for the unmarked Barkhuizen to score easily. It's a hammer blow and one I couldn't really see coming.

Bielsa replaces Bamford with Nketiah in the 77th minute, and with just three minutes remaining, the youngster grabs an equaliser, scoring with a looping header from Harrison's cross. We try desperately hard in the last few minutes to fashion a winner, and you can see Preston are really hanging on. In injury time, a free kick from Phillips is only cleared to Costa, who turns into the area and passes to the substitute Roberts, who is about to control the ball when his legs are taken from beneath him by a Preston defender. It's a clear penalty but referee Kevin Friend, standing almost in front of the incident, waves play on. And seconds later he blows the final whistle, only to be immediately surrounded by frustrated Leeds players.

A game we should have won easily became a game it looked as if we were going to lose. And as the minutes ticked away at one down, we would certainly have taken a draw. Yet with a last-gasp penalty award we could have taken all three points. So frustrating, so disappointing, but in the end it's an away point against a side who would have gone above us in the table had they held on to win 1-0. I head back to the road where I had last seen the coach and am amazed to see the entire street is full of coaches that will transport Leeds fans back home to all points of the country. On a wet midweek night in the North West, it's another reminder of just how big this club is. I wander past loads of them before seeing the distinctive 'Fourways' sign written in red along the length of the bus.

Once safely back in my seat, I check what has happened in the other games played out this evening. WBA have dropped home points, only drawing with struggling Barnsley, and Swansea have been thumped at home by Brentford 0-3. It looks like the 'Bees' are beginning to get their act together and they are one of the teams, along with Fulham, who have the talent to be a threat.

Another club who have quietly put themselves into contention is Sheffield Wednesday, who have beaten Stoke tonight to go third, one point behind us and three off the top. If results go their way, they could be on top of the table on Saturday night, but first of all they will have to beat us at Hillsborough. Three months into the season, only four points separate the top six, so it's all to play for. And there is no doubt that Saturday will be another nail-biter against one of our chief challengers. It's also, of course, a Yorkshire derby.

The coach starts to move and pretty soon we are in a line of buses being given a police motorbike escort through the streets of Preston. There is something quite exhilarating about seeing banks of traffic held at bay by police cars to let these outriders, with blue lights flashing, lead this travelling army to safety and the long road home. When I get home, I watch Sky show all the goals from the Championship. We definitely got caught out badly on the Preston goal, and Nketiah got up incredibly high to score the equaliser. As for the penalty appeal? Well, it still looked 'stonewall' to me.

I'm up early this morning after my late night in Preston, and head to see the doctor and hope she can come up with a solution to my painful knee. As ever, she is pleasant and puts me at ease, so I feel I can chat to her without appearing to be a wimp. One obvious option is to have a knee replacement, but friends have told me to avoid this solution until I am really struggling. The problem is I don't know if I am really struggling and I don't know what the degrees of pain are. I only know one knee hurts more than the other, but both have had the same treatment. I wonder if I should have a repeat injection in the right knee – maybe that's the answer. But the doctor suggests physio to tighten up the muscles and tendons around the knee and this seems a good idea.

So we have a chat about how this works and make some appointments to see someone that works at the practice.

The weather at the moment is absolutely awful and depressing, with dark skies and heavy rain falling it seems all the time. As I head back to the car, I see lots of people 'Lowry-like' scurrying along with heads down into the driving rain, trying to keep umbrellas from ripping inside out. At home, the beck at the end of the garden has risen almost level to the grass, and while it doesn't seriously threaten to flood, it's an indicator of just how much rain is falling. Sadly, there is serious flooding across the country and particularly in Yorkshire, and not too far away in Doncaster, the River Don has flooded, causing huge damage and destruction in places like Bentley and Fishlake. The news teams descend like vultures, ever keen to bring film and pictures into our homes of distraught people with their houses wrecked and their businesses destroyed. As ever with the media, they will be seeking to lay blame somewhere, be it the local council, the water authority, or the government. Anyone, as long as they can hit their target, get their victim. So sad.

Sheffield Wednesday...0; Leeds United...0
Saturday, 26th October

It's wet and murky, almost a typical autumn day, the kind I remember as a child when we dragged along bits of broken branches and built our bonfires in readiness for firework night. I wonder if there will be fireworks at Hillsborough later. It's a lunchtime kick-off and once again it's on Sky, but this time there is serious competition for sporting viewers. In Japan, England are taking on the might of New Zealand in the semi-final of the Rugby World Cup, and the game kicks off early on Saturday morning and doesn't finish until an hour or so before kick-off at Hillsborough. Although I can find the Union game frustrating, there is no doubt that this is a mouth-watering clash between two greats of the game and England certainly must be in with a chance, which hasn't always been the case in games against the All Blacks.

I decide I can manage to watch the first half of the rugby before setting off to Sheffield, which is a fairly easy run on the A1, M18, and M1 back north to Meadowhall, and then following signs into Hillsborough. First half on the telly at home, second in the car listening to the radio. I wish England always played rugby like this. From the start, they were thrillingly dominant, playing at a tempo that clearly surprised New Zealand, and it was no surprise when Tuilagi dived over from close range after a superb move. They thought they had scored again after 25 minutes, only for the TMO to harshly, in my opinion, rule out another 'try' by Underhill. England notched some penalties before half-time, with Ford kicking for the injured Farrell. It's not often the All Blacks are kept scoreless in a half of rugby.

It was time for me to set off for the match, and I found listening to the game on the radio hugely frustrating. The main commentator was quite animated, but his words kept being interrupted by his co-commentators – former players shouting over-excitedly in the background. The problem with all this is that they can see the pictures and you can't, and you need to have them painted for you with words. By shouting over the top of the main voice, the ex-players made it impossible to understand what was happening and where, so what you felt must surely be a try was in fact a break on the halfway line. I turned the radio onto the music channels, because they kept raising and then dashing my hopes and I just wanted us to finish them off. Eventually, England did the job and ultimately beat the All Blacks 19-7, and actually the victory was much more comprehensive than the score suggests. Young, the scrum half, had what appeared to be a brilliant try chalked off again by the TMO, and England literally handed the All Blacks their only try with a terrible throw from a line-out near our line, which we sent directly to them.

So, another World Cup final beckons, against the Welsh or South Africans, and there is no doubt on this form England will be favourites. It could be one of those days next week, one of those truly memorable occasions that stay in the mind forever, like Geoff Hurst's goal or Johnny Wilkinson's drop goal (why has he not been knighted when others far less worthy have?). Saturday is going to be quite a game.

I park as always on the hill heading up away from the stadium and pointing back to the Meadowhall shopping centre and the M1. It's been a filthy journey and I have had to drive through some seriously flooded roads enroute. The wet conditions could make for an interesting game, with the ball skimming off the wet turf and players slipping into tackles. I walk down to the ground, and rather than turn left and walking the long way round to the Leppings Lane end where the away fans are housed, I go right, past the Wednesday souvenir shop, and then turn left down a street that looks straight off the set of *Coronation Street* and which comes out near the entrance for visiting fans. Just up from this is a fish and chip shop on the right, and I head there as I am starving. Having been before, I know they are excellent. I am in the shop queuing when the police march a gang of about 50 young Leeds fans past us, their hands aloft, screaming out 'We are Leeds' as they go. They are quite threatening, and I wonder who it is they are trying to intimidate, given that they are pretty much surrounded by other Leeds fans.

I wander down to the entrance and can't help think about the awful Hillsborough tragedy that happened right here. Even today, all these years later, you can see the problems for crowd control. With the road so close to the stadium, there is so little space for fans to congregate and queue. I decide to avoid the throngs outside and go into the ground early, find my seat, and read the programme. One of the policemen standing by the turnstile says he'll look after my chips while I am being searched. It's great to have some banter with the coppers on duty. I have seen so many good ones up and down the country, but there are also so many who just make you feel like lowlife. I guess it's all down to training and education, or maybe it's just that some people are miserable sods.

Once again, I have a great view and now I am on nodding terms with quite a few of the travelling fans. I smile and wave at some I recognise, and take a couple of pictures of, the players warming up as the crowd begins to grow. I've been to Wednesday loads of times over the years but remember two games particularly. The first one was a Boxing Day clash in 1967 which we won 1-0, and later that night the Beatles' *Magical Mystery Tour* film premiered on television. I remember Mum and Dad saying it was rubbish, and I must admit at the time I was struggling not to agree with them. There was some really great music, though, as there always was with the Beatles.

The second game was when we thumped them 6-1 on our way to becoming champions in 1992, and Gordon Watson the Wednesday player made himself famous for a ridiculous dive that earned Wednesday a penalty – the only way they would have scored that day. I was also here when, a few years ago, Wednesday got their own back and beat us 6-0... so less said. Today is a top-of-the-table clash, and as we play early one, of the two sides could be top of the division at the end of the game. Wednesday have Kieran Westwood back in goal, who seems to save his best performances for games against us. I have seen him make some breath-taking saves in recent years and I had hoped he would be missing, as he had been in Wednesday's midweek game. The irritating but dangerous Forestieri is on the bench, and there is no doubt he has the talent to cause us, or any club, real damage when he is on his game. They have Fletcher and Nuhiu up front, and I have always thought the former to be a very underrated player. I also like Barry Bannan, who had a brief stint with us, and who I think is a classy, hard working midfielder.

We are unchanged from the Preston game, which means Nketiah's late strike that night does not earn him a starting place, despite the fact Bamford hasn't scored for eight games. Sadly, there is no Hernandez again nor Cooper, though the club captain is named on the bench so can't be far away from full fitness. The game starts in atrocious conditions and there are lots of empty seats in the Wednesday areas of the ground, which must be disappointing for the home club, given their lofty position. The away end is full, as always, with over four-and-a-half thousand Leeds fans packing the Leppings Lane end.

Wednesday have the first serious attack with the excellent Reach breaking free down the right, tracked all the way by Ben White who times his block superbly as the Wednesday man tries to cross into the danger area. Then a Sheffield attack is repelled when the ball is headed clear only to fall to Palmer on the edge of the area. He hits a fine shot towards goal, only to see Casilla diving to his left make an equally fine save. Leeds hit back and when White finds himself wide on the left, he cleverly moves into the penalty area and is bearing in on goal when the forward Nuhiu seems to pull him back and clumsily run into him. It looks a clear penalty, but just as in midweek the referee waves our appeals away. Nuhiu is then almost immediately involved at the other end, playing a neat one-two with Fletcher before the Scot shoots well, forcing an outstanding, flying fingertip save from Casilla. The keeper is having one of his best games and I am hoping that maybe hard work on the training ground is helping to make him a more effective presence in goal. Just before half-time I think we have scored, when Harrison plays a delightful cross off the side of his foot and finds Bamford at the far post. The centre forward heads the ball back across the goal, wrong-footing Westwood, but somehow the keeper manages to twist in the air and get a hand to the ball and tip it just round the post. It's a brilliant save, and while some around me are moaning that Bamford has missed again, I think it's more a wonderful save than a bad miss. Whatever, it doesn't reprieve Bamford, and he is replaced at half-time by Nketiah, who gets another big chance to claim his starting place.

The game continues as in the first half, with both sides going close. First, Phillips curls a shot narrowly past the right-hand post before Fox, cutting in from the left, sets up Fletcher. His side-foot effort hits the bar and then, luckily for us, the rebound hits Casilla and bounces away for a corner. Not to be outdone, Leeds respond, and Nketiah shows his class, leaving the Wednesday defence flat-footed as he skips by them and sets up Harrison, whose goal-bound effort is kicked off the line by Fox. Leeds almost snatch the three points when Alioski leaps brilliantly to head a Phillips cross against the post and to safety.

The game finishes goalless, and in truth it would have been harsh on either side to have lost. As far as I am concerned, I'm happy with the point, and in fact we have played two tough away games against top four teams, and missing key players, yet remained unbeaten. Later that afternoon, Albion draw at home to Charlton, who are still picking up useful points, and Preston beat their near-neighbours Blackburn to go into second. After 14 matches, we are just two points off the top and two points off seventh-placed QPR, who have a game in hand at home to Brentford on Monday. If QPR win, it means they will come to Elland Rd next week a point ahead of us. The games are coming thick and fast, and they are not getting any easier.

Driving home from Sheffield, I think again of the points we have thrown away this season and how far ahead of the others we could have been already, if only we had taken the chances at one end and not been so sloppy and panicky at the other. Then I realise what a futile exercise this is when I think the West Brom fans will be looking back on a week when they have drawn two home games and missed the opportunity to put a gap between themselves and the others.

It's looking like a quiet week ahead, with no governors' stuff and no trips away planned or visitors due home, though James has said he might try and get up for the QPR game. I have my first physio session, and while the young lady is very bright and personable, I do worry about her judgement. This is mainly because she tells me that by the end of the course of treatment she will have me running. Now I know this is going to be a problem because a consultant, having taken an MRI scan, has told me there's no real fluid around the knee and it is effectively bone-on-bone. He specifically told me not to run and pointed me towards cycling, cross-trainers, walking, and swimming. My own doctor, having seen these notes and other X-rays, confirms this course of action, so I doubt if I am going to be running another half marathon anytime soon. Nonetheless, she gives me some useful exercises which hopefully will ease the pain and let me walk a little more freely.

Then on Thursday, before the QPR game, we get a WhatsApp from my nephew Josh, Andrew's youngest who is living in Sydney. He has got two spare tickets for Saturday's Rugby World Cup final and is selling them on at face value if anyone in the family fancies heading to Japan for the weekend! Apparently, two of his work colleagues are New Zealanders and they can't be arsed to go to Japan now their team have been knocked out. They offer the tickets to Josh, who snaps them up knowing that if none of us can go, he will be able to sell them on and probably cover all his costs for the trip. For a minute or two I think this could be a fantastic trip, and to watch us win the World Cup and enjoy a 'lads' weekend' would be really something to savour. Andrew is in, and then before I can say 'yea or nay', so is James! So, he won't be needing a ticket for QPR, and I won't be going to the World Cup final.

Actually, I'm quite pleased with the outcome. James will really enjoy the party and get into the rugby, and while I'd love to be there for the 'session' and the game, it's a long way to travel for a weekend. And of course, there's another big clash at ER coming up on Saturday. It's funny reading the text messages between them as Josh, Andrew, and James make their way to Tokyo. Josh is the first to arrive, flying in from Sydney, which is good as he has been the main organiser and has sorted out all the accommodation. Andrew is next, a good 12 hours ahead of James, who had to complete his day at work before flying through the night on Thursday. It's a bit like trying to keep up with those 'magnificent men in their flying machines', but as we wake up on Friday morning, James is nearing the end of his journey. Pictures begin to arrive through the day as the boys start to sample the night life of Japan and mingle with the locals and a hotchpotch of rugby fans from all over the world. James texts Mike to say he has met some guys from Dublin, and he's arranged to meet them on Christmas Eve when he will be over there staying with Mike, Lou, and Margie.

The actual final proved to be such a massive disappointment – from an English point of view. Sadly, for James, Andrew, and Josh, and the thousands of other travelling fans who turned the stadium at Yokohama into a sea of white, the red rose never really got going. From the first minutes when Kyle Sinckler was knocked out in an accidental collision, England were struggling, and try as they might they just couldn't break out of the stranglehold South Africa imposed on them. The truth is they were well beaten by a side playing wholeheartedly to their traditional strengths, and though Farrell had a kick which, if it had been successful, would have closed the gap to 15-12 in the second half, there was only ever going to be one winner of this game.

The Springboks squeezed the life out of us, and long before they scored two late tries – one looking to be aided by a fairly obvious forward pass

– England were a beaten team. It hurt, obviously. No-one wants to lose a World Cup final, but it was nowhere like the gut-wrenching depression that followed the play-off defeat against Derby. My sister Janet, who lived just outside Durban for over 30 years and had been a regular at the Natal Sharks games with her husband Steve, posted a picture of herself grinning broadly in her Springbok jersey. I smiled wryly and hoped she hadn't sent it to the boys out in Japan. They must have been truly gutted as they made their way from the stadium.

All that excitement, the journey, the preparations, and the fun the night before, as expectant fans gathered to have the party of a lifetime. All shattered by a crushing defeat on the field where the dreams lie in tatters. It doesn't matter the sport or the competition, if you are a passionate fan there is nothing quite as bad as losing in the biggest of fixtures. It's a complete lack of sportsmanship, of course, when ten minutes after the end of the FA Cup final all the visiting fans have left. Proper sports fans would stay and congratulate the victors on their lap of honour, as we teach the kids to do at school. Fight as hard as you can, but when the game is over shake hands and be friends. That's how it should be, but when the team you follow through thick and thin, all around the country, at all hours, lose in a big game, I am afraid all you want to do is skulk out and get home. To the victors the spoils. So, they put a brave face on it and made heroes of themselves in a karaoke bar later, posting pictures of themselves dancing and singing through the night, which made me smile as I headed to ER and an important date with QPR.

Leeds United…2; QPR…0
Saturday, 2nd November

I have time to get to PJ's and realise that with all the excitement of the rugby, or should I say lack of it, I haven't eaten all morning. I absolutely devour the fish and chips and think that if I were on Death Row and choosing my last meal on this earth, then this dish I was rapidly consuming would have to be on the shortlist. Spaghetti Bolognese, perhaps, or beans and cheese on toast, moussaka, a really good steak, or a Sunday roast? I ponder the choices for a while and then tune into Radio Leeds for the team news. Cooper is back and so, too, at last is Pablo, named on the bench along with, among others, the keeper Meslier, Baradi, and the almost forgotten Clarke. Roberts is also in the starting 11, after coming on as a sub at Preston and again at Wednesday.

The big team news is that there is no Nketiah, who is unwell and apparently needed hospital treatment during the week. It's tough on the Arsenal loanee, who it appears was due to be named in the team for today's game, as Bamford's goal drought continues. I catch up with Damien and Rick, and we have a moan about the rugby and also the increasingly limited space in the centenary building, as the club hands over more and more areas to corporate packages. There is quite a bit of chat about Nketiah and a fair bit of disappointment in some quarters that he can't start today. I think even those, like me, who think Bamford is the better option for the team, are beginning to feel the forward would benefit from a rest. If only he could get that elusive goal.

We start the game well and Klich, running free into the penalty area, misses a glorious chance, volleying over from Ayling's cross. Dallas curls a shot narrowly wide and then Klich, winning the ball in his own half, spots Bamford running free and plays him through with a beautiful pass. The centre forward is forced wide but rounds the keeper and is about to score when the covering Rangers defender, Wallace, makes a superb tackle. Then with halftime approaching, we score, deservedly taking the lead when Roberts finishes well with his right foot, almost passing the ball into the net after Harrison had checked back in from the left. One of the things I always enjoy doing in a match is keeping an eye on the opposition's key players, providing they are not too influential, and the Rangers number ten Eze looks a real talent with the ability to hold the ball, dribble, and fashion defence-splitting passes. He seems to me in the classic tradition of Rangers players of old, like Marsh and Bowles, full of confidence and skill, and he will definitely be one to watch – and I suspect not just here this afternoon. He goes close to setting up an equaliser when he finds Wells on the right, whose cross is almost turned in by Hugill.

Roberts, no doubt buoyed by his goal, is having an impressive afternoon and Bamford arrives just too late to turn a fine cross into the goal. Roberts again finds space on the edge of the area and this time his fine cross is headed home by Bamford, diving in at the far post. At last the forward has ended his barren run and it's a fine goal. …Only it's not, as the linesman has raised his flag for offside. It must be the narrowest of margins and it's so frustrating for Bamford and the rest of us, who are very well aware that QPR are not out of this game yet. And just to prove the point, Kane crosses from the right only for Hugill to completely miss the chance. But it's a warning, if we needed it.

Why do they always seem to do this to us? Why can't we just turn our domination into goals so we can enjoy the closing stages of a game, instead of expecting the worst every time the opposition get the ball? It's head-in-hands time as we go into the last ten minutes, and then we are put out of our misery as Harrison makes sure of the victory. He cuts in from the left, getting a lucky deflection from a defender that puts him clean through, and curls the ball past the helpless Kelly in goal. The ground erupts in celebration and relief, and the players celebrate knowing the points are ours. We can enjoy the last six minutes or so. Except not everyone does, as quite a few fans head for the exits. I simply don't get this. Why come to a match and leave before the end? Sometimes at matches, it seems people are pushing past us to go and get food or drink, go to the loo, God knows where else. What are they doing and why the chuff have they bothered to come? It drives me crackers, and especially when the 'fuckwits' stand on my freezing toes.

It's a big win and takes us back to the top of the table on goal difference from Swansea, who have won at Wigan, and a point clear of WBA, who play on Monday at Stoke. After 15 games of the season, just three points separate the top six. I pause at the top of the stairs as I climb back up the hill to Beeston and take a selfie that shows the Leeds city centre skyline lit up behind me. It's a replica picture of one we took after we beat Sheffield Wed last season, with me, Andrew, Mike, and Ben, all smiling happily into the camera. I post it on our WhatsApp group with a message for the boys in Japan: 'At least we got one big win today.'

We are now unbeaten in our last four games, winning the two at home, and drawing two difficult games away from home. We have dominated most of the teams we have played against, with perhaps the exception of West Brom, and we have made lots of chances in every fixture. Up front we seem to have options, with Nketiah and Roberts both capable of pushing Bamford for the starting berth. But there is no denying that we should have scored an awful lot more goals than we have. Defensively we have been strong, despite losing Cooper for a few games and having the unpredictable Casilla in goal.

To me, we seem to have a favourable run of fixtures, starting with Blackburn at home next week, and running through to the game with Fulham just before Christmas. It's surely time to put a good run together and help us break away from the chasing pack. And this is exactly what we do, beating Blackburn at home 2-1 before grinding out wins away to Luton and Reading, with key late goals in each match, Bamford forcing the unlucky Luton defender Pearson to deflect into his own net, and Harrison finishing a sweeping move with a fine far-post header. Luton is a new experience for me, visiting the ground for the first time – and it's quite a shock. Fortunately, I have decided to go down on the coach, and as we reach the town centre I wonder where exactly the ground is. The coach seems to get beached up one of those *Coronation Street* types of road, and there's much fussing and waving of hands by club stewards as we sit looking out of the window and wonder how on earth we actually get out of the fix we are in. The road seems to be blocked ahead of us and there's absolutely no chance of reversing. With cars parked outside the little terraced houses, it seems we are well and truly stuck.

Then we are told to get off, and as we mill about on the road, I realise that the actual entrance to the ground is just ahead of us on the left-hand side. It's bizarre; an arched opening between two houses, with a flat or apartment above the arch! I've never seen anything like this before, and now I know how to get in, I wander off to find some food. At the top of the road, what I thought was a dead end is actually just a temporary roadblock made by the police to manage matchday and local traffic. There's a little car park across this road, opposite a bit of a club shop, and while I'm taking a few photos the police 'blue light' the Leeds team coach into the car park. Quite a few fans gather, and we watch the players disembark; they seem as disoriented as we are as they stumble off the bus and take in the surroundings. They must have felt they had gone back to their 'pub league' days, walking through the car park, crossing the road, and finally disappearing into the changing rooms.

They obviously recovered enough to take a vital three points, though Luton missed an absolutely glorious chance to equalise in the last play of the game, when Potts headed wide with the goal at his mercy. I must admit I was looking forward to getting out of this depressing place, and the rain pouring down did nothing to make the surroundings any more appealing. The ground looked as if it was falling down, and with plans to build a new stadium I'm pretty certain this old one won't be missed. I bet the residents in *Coronation Street* can't wait for the club to go, if they have to put up with this every Saturday. As we file out of the ground, I see Vic and Julie waiting by the gate, and we have a quick catch up about the game and the trip to Reading coming up on Tuesday. The coach is parked right outside the ground, along with lots more, all parked heading the wrong way down a one-way street. The police wait until the coaches are ready to move and then set us off in a great line, with motorbike outriders providing our escort, whizzing ahead and stopping traffic at various junctions in the town centre. We speed along behind them, going on the wrong side of the road and through red lights, until eventually we are free of this grubby town and heading up to the welcoming sign of the M1 North.

It's a good journey home, and once I've checked all the results, I go online and read about the information for 'away' fans heading to Reading and the Madejski Stadium. This, for those who know it, is a completely different experience for travelling fans than the trip to Luton. The Madejski is one of those modern stadiums built near shopping centres and eateries, and off a main route into the town centre. It's one of my least favourite grounds, with little or no atmosphere generated by the home fans and poor car parking facilities around the ground. The very best way to travel is by coach, and with the police as always holding up traffic, the buses can quickly be away and onto the nearby motorway network.

Unfortunately for me I am driving, and despite having a degree of local knowledge (my sister-in-law lives in the town), there is no easy way out and the queuing goes on and on. I guess this is ok for the locals, but it's a disaster if you're driving back to the north, and especially with the frigging motorway closures and diversions to deal with. Significantly, with the good run of results continuing, the victory over the 'R's' sees us go back to the top of the table a point ahead of West Brom, who have a game in hand, and now five points clear of Fulham who are up to third. Once free of the traffic, I think of the game coming up at the weekend against Jonathan Woodgate's Middlesbrough team, who are struggling under 'Woody' – a former hugely talented centre back and really popular player at ER. Katherine used to keep an extensive scrapbook about everything Leeds in her teens, and Woodgate was her favourite pin up. I like him, and hope he will be successful in management – just not next Saturday.

Leeds United...4; Middlesbrough...0
Saturday, 30th November

Nketiah, recovered from illness, is back on the bench for this game against our Yorkshire rivals from the North East. Looking at the team for today, it's probably now just about our strongest eleven, though Forshaw, Roberts, and Alioski would no doubt all come under consideration such has been there contribution so far, and Baradi has been a fairly reliable replacement for Cooper particularly. In recent times, games between the two clubs have been fairly close and quite feisty, due mainly to our fans' dislike of the 'Boro centre back Ayala, who cheated a penalty out of us a few years ago, and our former manager Gary Monk, who rightly or wrongly is viewed as someone who deserted us.

One game that wasn't so close was our hammering a couple of seasons ago at the Riverside when Patrick Bamford, our misfiring centre forward, only went and scored a hat trick against us. We could do with one of those today as we strive to keep the unbeaten run going. And it is Bamford who puts us ahead, scoring with a falling header from a Hernandez cross. We go two up when Klich hits a deflected shot past Pears in the 'Boro goal, and 2-0 becomes 3-0 when Costa, cutting in from the right, bundles past a few half-hearted challenges and smashes the ball into the net. Poor 'Boro are getting battered and we look back to our best, moving the ball with pace and creativity, pulling the defence out of position and opening gaps up all over the park. Harrison and Bamford both go close before Klich scores the goal of the game, curling a right-foot shot wide of Pears from the edge of the area.

It's a comprehensive win, and as we file happily out of ER, it's now eight games since we lost at Millwall and we remain top, a point ahead of WBA who have a game in hand. I go over our upcoming fixtures as I limp (still hurting despite the physio) up the hill to Beeston. Huddersfield away up next, followed by Hull and Cardiff at home, before my favourite away trip of the season down to Craven Cottage and our meeting with Fulham. The Huddersfield game always brings back loads of memories of games in the past, and of great players like Trevor Cherry and Frank Worthington, who played with distinction for both clubs. I used to love the atmosphere at the old Leeds Rd ground, and it was one of the first grounds I ever visited when Dad took me one Saturday afternoon to see Town play Newcastle. I don't know why he did this, as it was usually Trinity games he took me to, and I have no real memory of the game except for a player called Coddington, who took the most enormous run-up before scoring for Town with a penalty.

We used to live in Flockton, a village between Wakefield and Huddersfield, and I knew lots of people who supported 'The Terriers'. Another connection was the occasional game I played in the 'Heavy Woollen League' for Steve my brother in law's team, the wonderfully named Gomersall Mills AFC. I signed for them along with Chris, so that we had a team to play for when we were home from college. It meant we could turn out, if they were short of regulars, in quite a few games at the start of the season, over Christmas, and of course in the closing games of the year when councils were keen to turn areas of greenery from football pitches to cricket fields and matches were played in the evenings to ensure the season finished on time.

One such match remains in my memory as one of the most enjoyable I have ever played in, and Steve and I reminisce about it often when we are enjoying family chats about great days in the past. It was a game in somewhere near Mirfield, on a council pitch just off the Huddersfield road. It was an evening kick-off, just a few games from the end of the season, and our opponents, I can't remember their name, would be crowned champions if they won the match. We, on the other hand, had endured a miserable season and were struggling along at the bottom of the table, needing points to ensure our survival. It was one of those games where Chris and I could play, as a number of the team could not finish work in time to get to the ground for an early evening kick-off and we were back home from college.

Unusually for one of our matches, as we ran out of the changing rooms, we noticed quite a crowd beginning to gather on the touchline. It was fairly obvious, given the number of girlfriends, wives, partners, and friends all dressed up in their finery, that our opponents were going to hit the town after the game, to celebrate winning the title. Their over-confidence was a much greater stimulus for us to up our performance than our manager's (wonderfully named Alf Ramsey) usual team talk: 'Now listen, lads, spread out and keep it tight!' Quite simply, they underestimated us. Steve, strong and determined, marshalled the defence and Chris relished his role in midfield, spraying passes all over the pitch. I played my favourite free role up front, enjoying pulling their central defenders all over the place. And in goal, Charlie 'the flying pig' showed unusual athleticism by on occasion actually getting airborne and thwarting their attack time after time. As the game progressed and it was clear we were not going to simply lie down and give in, the crowd on the touchline became increasingly agitated and began to heckle the ref and shout not particularly pleasant comments at us.

We won the game in the end quite easily, something like 5-2, and I managed to score a couple – one of which remains a favourite, when I scissor-kicked a volley from the edge of the area past a stranded keeper. As we left the field to more insults, there were shouts that we had played 'ringers', but if the club ever made a complaint, they would have found that all our players were properly signed up. In the end, it was us that celebrated avoiding relegation, and going to the pub buzzing with the feeling of victory. Charlie, supping his fifth pint, profoundly suggested that he thought we could make a push for the title next season, and while none of us actually agreed with him, we did kind of nod our heads in recognition of the keeper's comments. Such is the beauty of sport when sometimes, against all the odds, the underdogs come through and triumph. In my playing days, I played in league and cup winning teams, I came up against Spurs, QPR, and Fulham, and got a bronze medal in the British Colleges football tournament. They were all achievements I felt hugely proud of, but none of them felt quite as good as the beers we shared that April night in a pub near Huddersfield, celebrating our defeat of the 'nearly Champions'.

Such thoughts filled my head as I drove towards the new John Smith's stadium where Town now played their matches, not far from the old ground. I wonder if we can keep the unbeaten run going and claim our sixth win on the bounce against our near-neighbours. And we do, with fine goals from Alioski – a wonderful volley from the edge of the area – and Hernandez scoring with a stooping header after a super cross from Harrison. Town battled hard and had their chances, Casilla showing his unpredictability with a couple of world class saves from Mounie and Grant, balanced out by another reckless charge out of his area that left an easy chance for Grant to score. Fortunately for us, the forward missed. So we keep the run going and we also stay on top of the table, again by just a point from WBA who have the game in hand, but we are now eight points clear of Fulham in third, who have lost at home to Bristol City.

The game against Hull isn't the most free-flowing, and missing Cooper again we don't look as solid at the back as when he plays, nor is Baradi as effective as his captain at playing the ball out of defence. Hull always carry a threat with Bowen, who scored winning goals here last season, and Grosciki – both dangerous forwards raiding down the wings and supplying the rangy Eaves, who our fans dub 'as a shit Andy

Carrol' owing to his physical similarity to the West Ham player. In fact, it's quite a tense game, and Casilla does well to thwart Eaves before finally we take the points with an own goal from de Wijs and a fine finish by Alioski, following up on a Bamford shot that rebounded off the post, and scoring from the narrowest of angles. It's another nervy night and a big win, and we do seem to be playing like a team who just know they can dig out a result. More importantly, the result puts us 11 points clear of Fulham and Bristol City in third and fourth place, with Albion, as always, our constant companions at the top.

We need to make a 'Christmas visit' to see Mike and Lou, who is now heavily pregnant with their second child and can't fly to the UK for any family celebrations. The question about which game to miss is easy, as Cardiff are an awful team to watch and one of those sides we often slip up against. They are also now managed by Neil Harris, the ex-Millwall man – another team that always seems to do well against us. To be honest, there are lots of similarities between the two clubs, and both of them hate us anyway. It's not a game I would be looking forward to, and in terms of games there is no way I am going to miss the trip to the capital for the Fulham match.

We don't fly to Dublin until the day of the Cardiff match, and enjoy our Christmas party night with the Parkinsons at the Wentbridge House Hotel. It's just about the only place we can get a good meal in nice surroundings, and we always get a table in the bar part of the bistro. We have probably done this about once a month for the six years or so we have been retired, and usually the evening ends with all of us quite merry, having had a laugh catching up on family stuff and what's happening with the Spanish connection.

Tonight is no different, and we are all well-oiled before the taxi arrives to take us back home. Given the enjoyable evening and the alcoholic haze we find ourselves in, we chatter animatedly on the journey back before clambering out of the taxi and letting ourselves in. It's then I remember that after weeks and weeks of politicking, today has been a general election and tonight is the results show.

One of the beauties of retirement is that on such nights, or things like the golf Masters, you can stay up half the night watching telly and not worry about getting up the next morning. Tonight is just such a night, and both of us are keen to stay up. The country has been through utter turmoil since the Brexit vote, and whatever your own view on this hugely divisive topic, it has given the press and media far too many opportunities to undermine the country with their frustratingly negative style of journalism. This is not a story of politics, but it's impossible not to have been dragged into the debate one way or another, as for the last few weeks we have been bombarded with party broadcasts, leaders' debates, and news specials. It seems that the TV channels are trying to turn a serious event into some kind of reality television show, and it's disappointing to think they haven't quite worked out that we actually have minds of our own and are quite capable of making our own decisions.

In my lifetime I have voted Labour, Conservative, and Lib Dem, always casting my vote based on my own circumstances and the position of the country at the time. I have always tried to use my vote wisely and have always tried to read deeper into issues than the sensational press and biased news channels would give us credit for. I think that perhaps the narrow education of life and life experiences of those who produce the news channels has misled them into thinking they know what the country is feeling. Or maybe they think they can just tell us how to vote, given the huge platform they have to influence us through programmes like the six o'clock news.

I think this was best illustrated by the Brexit vote which clearly took the 'Londoncentric' media by utter surprise, and led to the resignation of David Cameron, and eventually Theresa May. Now after years of discussion and debate, people's marches, and that ridiculous man hijacking every newscast from the green outside Westminster with his booming voice, we were at last going to get some resolution. Only we weren't... because the Labour Party and the Lib Dems conspired to hand the election to Boris Johnson and the Conservatives. They did this by adopting completely unbelievably stupid positions, with the Lib Dems showing scant regard for democracy by claiming they wouldn't leave the EU whatever the people said, and the Labour Party not having a position at all about the biggest issue the country had faced in 50 years.

What was achieved was an end to all the 'People's vote' debate, because what was very clear was that if he won, Johnson was leaving the EU as quickly as possible, so at last there was an opportunity to resolve this oh-so-divisive issue. It was more than clear that if you didn't want to leave the EU, whatever you did with your vote you most certainly shouldn't vote Conservative. The fact that Johnson won the biggest election victory since the 1930s rather put an end to all the huff and puff of the Brexit issue. It pretty much ended the career of Jeremy Corbyn as well, who announced his going at some time during the night, and going in abject defeat too, having managed to even lose his 'Northern heartland,' who were angry and betrayed by his increasingly wacky politics and outlandish policies.

We watched through the night, listening to various politicians laying blame or claiming victory, and it was funny to watch BBC presenter Huw Edwards – or 'the undertaker' as we call him (he seems to relish bad news and emphasises this with a curled lip on his Mr. Angry face, which we find quite funny) – struggling to come to terms with the Tory landslide. I am no member of the Conservative party and there is much I disagree with in their planning and policy making, but at least they had a plan, at least they had a policy, and they stuck to it. For me, what matters most in our country is that we maintain our democracy and the right to vote as we see fit, and that we respect the votes and views of those who disagree with us and don't try to bully those who don't.

Hopefully, the Labour Party and the Lib Dems will sort themselves out, so that the next time we have an election there will at least be a democratic choice worth making, and not the mess – in part created by the news media – that we were faced with this time.

CHAPTER 14

DUBLIN, LONDON, XMAS IN SUSSEX, (A CRAZY GAME IN BIRMINGHAM), BARCA AND ANGRY LETTERS!

Leeds United…3; Cardiff City…3
Saturday, 14th December

Mike was waiting for us as we got through passport control in Dublin, after we'd walked almost half the distance from Leeds just getting from the stand we were dropped off at to this meeting spot. It was great to see him, and we chatted all things family as we headed through the tunnel on the quick way into the city. We were on the early flight from Dublin, so we were enjoying toast and tea with Lou back at the house in Sandymount before half past eight. Margie was in great form and we went through all the silly sounds and games we played with her, including running on the circular route round the house, and of course shouting out 'Leeds, Leeds, Leeds' that Grandpa had taught her. It's great to be with them all for the first time since September, and we have a lovely walk down the beach and into the bustling village of Sandymount.

Margie plays with the football on the little green there and does that peculiar stare thing when she comes face-to-face with another toddler, a bit like two gunslingers in a western movie sizing each other up and waiting for the first sign of a move. Eventually she decides enough is enough and picks the ball up and runs to us, slightly tempted if truth be told by the sight of a chocolate ice cream. She hasn't many words yet, but she knows her chocolate! We have a lovely morning, and for the first time since the Millwall game settle down in front of the TV to watch *Soccer Saturday* with Jeff and the team. Given our early start, we left home at 4am, Andy decides to go up and have a rest and Lou does, too, with Margie having her afternoon nap. It leaves Mike and me free to talk football and our chances for this afternoon's game.

I tell him of my unease about this one and he shares my concern. Then again, Leeds fans are not known for their over-confidence. We are still missing Cooper, but otherwise we are at strength, with Nketiah again on the bench and joined by the unlucky Alioski, who is such a good attacking option at full back. But despite scoring crucial goals against Huddersfield and Hull in recent weeks, he can't dislodge Dallas, who has been in such good form this season. We settle down for news from ER and we don't have long to wait before Jeff announces 'and there's been a goal at Elland Road' followed by that second or so when you're just not sure who has scored. But then, as they switch to the reporter at the ground, the huge celebrations let us know we are in front by a goal from Helder Costa settling all the nerves in the home stadium. Mike and I leap in the air shouting before Lou sends us a text reminder that Margie is asleep!

We share a silent celebration a couple of minutes later as we score again, with the reporter at the ground describing what sounds like an excellent finish by Bamford from a Dallas cross. This gets me thinking that maybe I was wrong to miss this one after all, and the atmosphere in the ground sounds fantastic. It gets even better in the 52nd minute when Bamford scores our third from the penalty spot. Surely another three points in the bag? And as Margie wakes and we are distracted from the telly playing with her, I do my arithmetic and work out there is just 38 minutes to go. Our family chat is interrupted a few minutes later when Jeff tells us of another goal, but it's not game over at 4-0. Instead it's a lifeline for Cardiff, thanks to a Lee Tomlin goal after what is described as a poor punched clearance from Casilla. With thirty minutes and a two-goal lead, surely we can hold out? But then with time running down and just eight minutes left, Cardiff score again this time through Morrison. I suddenly get an attack of anxiety and find, just like Ben, I can't bear listening any more. I decide to go for a bath and hope by the time I have finished we will have the three points and we can get on with enjoying the weekend. I am still running the water when I hear

Mike shout, 'Dad.' I wrongly think we have scored and that the points are ours, but in fact he is shouting to tell me that Morrison, who has just scored for Cardiff, has been sent off for a wild challenge on Nketiah.

I lie in the bath waiting for the loud shout from downstairs that would be confirmation of our victory. How slowly does time go when you want it to race away? And then I hear the shout, but it's muffled and it's a swear word. I frigging knew it, and I guess every Leeds fan in the world would have predicted it; Cardiff have scored their equaliser through Glatzel, their substitute. I stay in the bath for some time, trying to come to terms with our loss before I realise it's not a loss after all. It just feels like one.

On reflection, the unbeaten run continues, and it's now 11 games since our loss at Millwall. It turns out we could even have won the game in the last seconds, had White been able to turn the ball in after it was pushed clear following a Nketiah header. So, what went wrong? And did the fact that Cardiff scored twice following Bamford's substitution point the finger at the work of Nketiah in defensive areas of the pitch? We have to sort it out. There's also the question what to do with Casilla in goal – brilliant saves at Huddersfield and Wednesday, but a real howler letting Cardiff back into the game. It seems to me that when the transfer window opens we need to recruit a top keeper and a proven goalscorer if we want to ensure we gain the promotion which we threw away last year.

The good news as we head to the Cottage next week is that we find ourselves 12 points clear of Fulham who have lost again today at Brentford, and ten points clear of Preston, who we meet next, at home on Boxing Day. If we win those games, we could be out of sight of third by the time we head to the Hawthorns for our top-of-the-table clash with WBA on New Year's Day. It will be another nail-biter as the Baggies have opened up a two-point lead over us in recent games. So, after a run of 11 games unbeaten, we now find ourselves playing four top six sides in the next five fixtures, and Birmingham – the other one – is a team who always save their best for us at St. Andrews. It will be interesting to see where we are by the time Sheffield Wednesday arrive at ER on 11th January.

Aware that the bath is going cold, I leave worries about promotion behind, get dressed, and head downstairs to meet the family. Andy is already changed and ready for her evening out. We are going to see Michael Buble at the Dublin Arena – a belated birthday present from Mike and Lou. I like some of Buble's music, especially when he sings the more modern up-tempo records like *Beautiful Day, Some Kind of Wonderful,* and *Just Haven't Met You Yet.* I am less of a fan when he covers some of Sinatra's and Elvis's stuff; I mean there are just some songs you leave alone. It's a really lively crowd and Dublin is clearly in the mood to party. Buble doesn't let them down. He is brilliant from the start and the concert flashes past, the time melting away so quickly, unlike this afternoon when it seemed to go on strike. Before we know it, we are out on the streets of Dublin on a real high and I can't stop singing *It Goes to Show You Never Can Tell,* the old Chuck Berry song which he covered brilliantly. It's been a really excellent show and without doubt one of the most entertaining we have seen... and we have seen a lot of the greats over the years.

Mike texts, as we walk roughly in the direction of Sandymount, and comes and picks us up to drive the last few miles home. We stay up quite late, enjoying a few glasses of wine and a catch-up, and I feel really happy and relaxed as my head hits the pillow. It has been a long time since we woke up at three-thirty this morning and headed to Leeds Bradford airport, and that fateful flickering thought reminds me that all is not completely happy in my world as I lie waiting for sleep. Fucking Cardiff!

We have a lovely few days with the Dublin Crew, and it's great to share some time with Mike and Lou and see how Margie is growing up so rapidly. We are due to stay in a hotel for the last night of our visit, and we want to look around Dublin again and do a bit of shopping which Andy enjoys while I listen to the talents of the street musicians on Grafton Street. There are some great pubs in this area, and Mike joins us for a quick Guinness after work before taking us to a lovely bar in the Westbury Hotel where he spoils his mum with 'bubbles'.

It has been lovely to spend a little time with him before we leave, and it's not going to be too long before Andy tastes champagne again, as Katherine and James have plans for a birthday breakfast for her at the 'Ned' in London, before the girls enjoy a day in the shops and James and I head to the Cottage and the big match with Fulham. We literally get home on Thursday and set off to Kath and Nick's first thing Friday morning.

Fulham...2; Leeds United...1
Saturday, 21st December

So, first thing Friday morning, we head back down on the A1 to Bishops Stortford; the car knows the journey well and we make good progress. The kids are pleased to see us, and after a quick chat and a cup of tea, Kath and Nick slip away to enjoy their Christmas present to each other – a night in London staying in a hotel, meeting up with old friends and going out to dinner. They have earned a night off, as any parents of young children will understand. The plan is for Nick to head back to Stortford the next morning, while Andy and I will catch the train into London to meet Katherine and James for a late breakfast/ early lunch. Nick's mum Jane will hold the fort until Nick gets back to look after the children.

The youngsters behave brilliantly in their parents' absence. In fact, just like their cousin Margie when Mike and Lou went off to America, they hardly mention them at all. I think this is a tribute to the parents and to us, in that the kids are clearly relaxed and at ease in our company because both sets of parents have made it clear that we are family, so as far as the children are concerned no problem.

We go out to the park and the children's play area and call in at the supermarket for some goodies and a paper. Oliver plays with his Playmobil toys and his police and criminal game, which I get roped into playing with him. While Lucy and Andy mess with Play-Doh and preparing a make-believe dinner to serve to us. At bedtime, Andy quickly has Lucy ready for her cot and she goes to sleep without any problem. I read to Oliver, and we have a chat about the day and how bad Malcolm the serious and constant criminal has been again. He chuckles to himself when he remembers the game, and I promise to play again tomorrow and say goodnight, turning the light down as Katherine has shown us. Sitting downstairs, collapsed into the sofas, we are enjoying a well-earned drink after a day on the go, which obviously didn't include an afternoon siesta. We can hear Oliver chatting to himself when suddenly he starts calling out 'Poppa', the name they have given me. He's not distressed or shouting, so we just leave him, thinking he will soon fall off to sleep. But he doesn't. He just continues quietly calling my name.

Andy pops up to see what it is, and he tells her, 'Poppa didn't close the door.' Which is true, as I always left the door slightly ajar when our kids were growing up, so they could see the landing light. Later, Katherine explains he always has the door shut, and he's such a creature of habit and routine that he can't settle unless things are done just right. I wonder why he didn't just get out of bed and shut the door himself, but she smiled and said he would never dare get out of bed until she or Nick went to get him.

They both sleep well, and it's not long before Jane arrives to relieve us and we head into London to meet Kath and James. We all meet up in Threadneedle Street by the Bank of England, and James walks us round to the Ned, the club he has joined for its gym facilities and bars and restaurants. It's very nice and plush, and the sitting areas and bars are busy and lively. It's a great start to the day and not unlike the 'buzz' of the Westbury and our drinks with Mike just 48 hours or so ago.

After James gives us the tour, we go upstairs to the restaurant, which has fairly stunning views of London, and I am sitting looking out to Big Ben and the Parliament buildings. James and I have a few beers while Andy and Kath enjoy their bubbles before we have a lovely meal, and then it's time for us to head off up to Fulham and the girls can relax and just enjoy their day kicking around the capital. We arrange to meet somewhere after the game but decide to text later to work the venue out, depending on where the girls have got to. As we head to the underground, James shows me a picture someone has sent to his mobile. It's of a boat sailing down the Thames and it's completely covered by Leeds flags and banners. The boys are back in town. We have had some great nights at Fulham in the last few years, though they have been built around having a good laugh and a few beers with Mike, James, and friends, rather than any positive results. The Cottage has not been a great hunting ground recently.

Today is the first Saturday afternoon game by the Thames that I can remember for quite a while. In one sense that's good, as we can actually avoid the puddles and muddy areas around the grassy parkland on the way from Putney Bridge to the ground. There are loads of Leeds fans around, but not as many as usual. The ground developments have limited the so-called 'neutral end' where so many Leeds fans bought tickets for at recent matches. James is hopeful again of being able to get a ticket for the 'away' end and he has tried a few pubs as we walked up from the station, without success. As always, he prefers me out of the way while he canvasses the crowd. I get a programme and go and find my seat to check the team news.

Cooper, who has missed quite a few games over the season so far, is back in the centre of defence, with Baradi dropping to the bench along with Alioski and Nketiah. It's a strong side, and after the disappointing surrender of a three-goal lead against Cardiff last week we need to impose ourselves from the start against a Fulham side who have lost back-to-back games. If we win today, we will go 15 points clear of Fulham. Only we don't win. We lose our first game since our last visit to London and the defeat at Millwall. And again, the opposition are given a helping hand by the referee awarding the home team a very dubious penalty. James arrives as the teams come out, buying his ticket at face value from a Leeds fan, already half cut, who has decided to find a Thameside pub to finish off the job completely. Seeing him coming into the row and pushing his way along to join me is, as it turns out, the highlight of the game. In our first attack Costa shoots straight at their keeper Rodak. It was a good chance set up by good team play but Hernandez, involved from the start, is down injured and takes no further part in the game, with Alioski coming onto replace him. It's a bad loss and the way he left the field suggests it could be a hamstring injury, which could mean he might be absent for some time. Not good news when we are embarking on such a tough run of fixtures. Then comes the penalty. As Mitrovic heads a deep cross back into the danger area, referee Robinson adjudges Ben White has pushed Reid, the Fulham forward, in the back. I didn't see the incident, but James did and he thinks it's a pen. TV later shows it isn't, but Mitrovic scores with a shot that Casilla gets a good hand to but can't keep out.

Leeds respond as they always do, and Harrison sets up good chances for Dallas and Klich, with Rodak kicking away from Dallas, and Klich hitting the post. Then Phillips crosses to Bamford, who brings the ball down well but shoots straight at the keeper. There's a lovely moment at half-time when Fulham induct one of their 'old boys' into their Hall of Fame, and it's one of our great old boys, too – Allan Clarke. The tannoy system, which is almost inaudible, extols Clarkie's time at Fulham and his great contribution to the club in his short time there, before being sold to Leicester and then obviously to us. A club official marches Allan down the main touchline and towards the goal, where the most vociferous Fulham fans are housed. He waves and acknowledges the warm applause and then the official marches him back down the line towards the tunnel, which at the Cottage is situated in the corner of the ground by the famous building that gives the ground its name. As they are nearing the end of their walk, Allan veers away from his minder and walks towards the Leeds fans, crammed in behind the goal, and for several minutes he is given a fabulous reception. Smiling and clapping, he can be in no doubt as he wanders away just what a legend he remains in the eyes of those who support the club. Looking round me, I guess there would have been a lot of those present today who would have witnessed his brilliance over the years, and of course that wonderful flying header that clinched our first ever FA Cup final when we defeated Arsenal in 1972.

Nketiah comes on for Costa at the interval, and as the game restarts he breaks clear on the right and shoots across Rodak, who can only push the ball out to the incoming Bamford and the centre forward fires the ball into the empty net from close range. We are back level and deservedly so, and I can only see one winner now the way we have been dominating the game. But Fulham, to their credit, don't lie down and from a corner (what else?) they retake the lead. The ball isn't cleared and falls to Onomah who, faced with half the Leeds defence, does just about the only thing he can do and smashes it goalwards. He gets lucky, misses all the defenders, and hits the net. We try so hard to get back level, with Phillips and Alioski going close before Mitrovic, of all people, clears off the line. It's our first loss in 11, and it's a bad one. I get so cross with the frustration of it all, screaming at the ref for his incompetence and the Fulham players for their time-wasting. James calms me down and we troop off, miserable and fed up, into the wet early evening.

When we've played here before, we usually go into a hotel the other side of the bridge for a few beers after the game, as the pubs are just so rammed. We head there again, but for some bizarre reason their pumps have bust and all they have is alcohol-free beer and soft drinks. We head off looking for a pub, but there are bouncers on the doors keeping people out, and coppers everywhere urging people to get to the stations.

The girls are in some bar near Liverpool St, which is miles away, and as James just lives down the road from Putney in Wandsworth, he decides to go home. I give him a hug and head off to meet them. Unlike us, the girls have had a great day, and they're both in lively moods when I finally arrive. Katherine has a pint of Guinness waiting for me and I absolutely devour it. I take my time with the second, and while the girls chatter, I see the results come through on the telly. Despite the loss, the damage isn't as great as it could have been. Preston draw, Forest lose, and Albion are held at home by the improving Brentford. West Brom extend their lead over us to three points, but we still have a nine-point lead over Fulham, now up to third on the same points as Preston. Behind us, eight clubs are separated by just four points!

We head back to Yorkshire the next day to finish off Christmas preparations, before driving down to Sussex and Christmas with Andrew, Ben, Janet, and Steve. It has been good to see all the children and grandchildren in the build-up to the feast, and it will be good to spend some time with my brother and sister and enjoy remembering 'Christmases past' with them and Andy, Steve and Ben. It will, though, be the first Christmas Andrew has spent in England since the so, so sad passing of his wife Trish, our friend and sister-in-law of many years.

Just two years ago, we all gathered in Yorkshire to celebrate Christmas together, little knowing that within a few short months she would pass away in a Marseilles hospital, ending her and Andrew's idyllic retirement in France – the country she had loved all her life. She was a wonderfully unique character and, like all of us, had her strengths and weaknesses. There were times over the years we would have disagreements, and I can still see her face as we argued – a mixture of shock and disbelief at our falling out, before tears would well in her eyes and she would leap forward, put her arms around me, and tell me she loved me. All the family gathered for her memorial service and I can't remember a funeral or service which captured the love and spirit of a person better than that service did for Trish. A few months later, as that first emotional Christmas without her approached, Andrew and Ben flew to Australia to spend the festive holidays with Josh, their youngest, and Emily his partner. We saw the fabulous pictures of Andrew and his boys trying to come to terms with their loss and together trying to move forward, as Josh put together a wonderful holiday for his father and brother. I had travelled back from France with Andrew when he realised it was time to return to England, try to sort out his affairs, and work out just how he could begin to piece together his life again and try to move forward. As he talked, I remembered so many times in his childhood when I had looked after him, so many of the fun times we had enjoyed growing up together. And I realised I probably hadn't spent as much time alone with him since I left the family home and got married. I also realised how proud I was of him and the way he was dealing with the horrible situation he found himself in, trying to put others first, his boys and Tricia's sisters, Caroline and Georgie, leading his family in their grief. My little brother was all grown up but I still wanted to put my arms around him.

I have always loved Christmas and now, sitting in Andrew's local, chatting with my two siblings, reminds me of some of the great days we enjoyed growing up as children in Wakefield including that first time I went with Dad to ER on Boxing Day 1964. Despite the feelings of panic and desertion I felt when he pushed me down to the front 'for a better view', the feeling of excitement that I experienced has never left me. It was not just going to the game that was fantastic, that Christmas just about everything was perfect.

What a time to be ten! For me, it was a special age: no longer quite believing in Father Christmas, but not yet having lost the magic of the occasion; buzzing with the anticipation of teenage life, but not yet challenged by the 'growing pains' of the teenage years; no exams; no spots; no fights; no broken hearts;, just a fantastic feeling of warmth and security, open fires, Christmas tree lights, and special treats and goodies, such as orange and lemon slices covered in sugar, the oh-so-nice but sickly chocolate oranges, and a range of nuts so hard I could never manage to crack them open.

Andrew was pretty much a constant companion, and while I was expected to look after him, play with him, and read him to sleep at night, he also provided great spirited, and on occasion, violent opposition in a variety of competitive games. Our favourites were balloon football and rugby, boxing (Andrew once floored Dad with an illegal low blow), and of course Subbuteo which we played constantly, even buying a couple of floodlights to make things even more realistic.

I loved playing those games with my brother and enjoyed the fun of it all, but I also had a fantastic friendship with my sister, by then 13 and enjoying her teenage life, especially fashion, music, and as I have already mentioned the Beatles. While Janet was growing up, she was still very much part of the family and would help me out with pop information as I tried to widen the scope of my newly-created newspaper (produced on my new Petite typewriter) to more than just articles about United and Trinity, and the Subbuteo results.

What a Christmas! Family fun, the Yuletide festivities, and a train set that filled mine and Andrew's bedroom, such was the size and scale of the model railway Dad had bought. I knew instinctively that sadly I was leaving the days of Father Christmas behind, but now there was something else that was filling my mind and taking the place of those wonderful childhood memories. The Beatles and Leeds United, two new experiences that Christmas, and ones that I just knew would stay with me for the rest of my life. It was such a wonderful time, and now all these years later we are sitting in The Cat, in a sleepy West Sussex village, remembering all these things and other family stories that are well worth revisiting. It doesn't take long before Andrew mentions the 'takeaway' incident, and we both look at Steve and laugh at the memory of the evening he and Janet had a bit of a falling-out and Andrew and I were the beneficiaries!

Often on Saturday nights, Mum and Dad would go out somewhere and Andrew and I would keep each other company, playing football in the garden or Subbuteo, or watching television. Janet and Steve would usually be out, coming back in with some supper to watch *Parkinson* or a late night film. This didn't always go down so well with Andrew and I, as we would normally be watching *Match of the Day* when they came in. Steve, six or seven years older than me, would show his love and affection for us with his usual 'go play in the traffic' line, which on this occasion was his way of saying it's time for bed.

That particular night, though, we could hear the two of them having some kind of argument as they approached the house, and this continued as they put their takeaway in the oven to warm it up. Suddenly the argument got hotter and Janet pulled off her engagement ring and threw it at Steve, pushed past him, and ran upstairs to her bedroom, slamming the door behind her. Andrew and I ran back into the lounge and pretended nothing had happened, but then we heard the front door shut and we tiptoed out to see Steve get in his car and race off. What to do? Andrew bravely crept up the stairs to check things out and came down to confirm Janet's light was out. We peered through the curtains, but there was no sign of Steve. And that's when we realised this was not such a disaster after all. We could go back and watch the end of *Match of the Day* and... it smelt very much like there was a fish supper in the oven.

I can remember we froze when we heard the door bell ring, followed by plaintive shouts of 'Janet', then we could hear the little pebbles hitting her bedroom window as Steve tried to get her attention. It was like a scene from Shakespeare and, unfortunately for us, Romeo had returned. We heard her bedroom door open and her feet on the staircase as she came down to open the door. We heard the 'Sorrys' and the kisses as they made up, then we heard him utter those fateful words... not 'I love you, Janet' but 'Let's go and eat those chips!' Andrew looked at me and I looked back at him and we just legged it into the garden, staying outside until thankfully we saw the headlights of Dad's car light up the garage door and knew we were safe. Now, sitting in the pub on Christmas Eve, we can laugh about it, though I notice that Steve's laugh is more of a grimace as he pushes his glass towards me and tells me 'to get them in'!

We have a lovely Christmas Day and we all seem to fall asleep at the same time, watching some television programme after consuming far too much food and drink. I realise I am totally out of it and make my apologies and turn in. We have an early start in the morning in order to get back to Yorkshire in time for me to drop Andy off and get to ER for our teatime clash with Preston.

Leeds United... 1; Preston North End... 1
Thursday, 26th December

On the long journey home, we chat family and upcoming trips and just the general stuff that we have to do when we come out of the New Year celebrations. We are hosting a return gathering for Janet, Steve, and Andrew on New Year's Eve before heading back to Spain, where Andy particularly loves the Spanish celebration of 'Kings'. This is when the Spanish remember the arrival of the three kings at the stable, following the birth of Jesus, and not surprisingly it usually means lots of presents for the kids and firework displays for all the family. Born on November 5th and told by her father that all the fireworks on that day are in her honour to mark the day of her birth, it's hardly surprising that she looks forward to such displays. The one in Llafranc and Calella is particularly enchanting, and we always gather with hundreds of others to watch the sailing boats carry the three kings round the headland, lit up by fairy lights and fireworks, and on their way to the harbour to deliver presents to the children.

I can't help my mind drifting to matters of football as Andy snoozes on the way up the M1. This afternoon is yet another big game against top six opposition, and yet another one that we need to win to maintain the distance between us and third place. I know I'm not alone among Leeds fans who don't really care about winning the title; what we all want is promotion. It seems crazy after our recent run of 11 games unbeaten to be worrying about our form, but in recent years we have started off the season really well, only to stumble and fall away after Christmas. Surely with Bielsa in charge, and with the painful memories of last year still just under the surface, we can't let it happen again this year. I definitely need to be more positive. If we can beat Preston and Wednesday at home and get some points from the away games at Birmingham and West Brom, we are heading towards a group of fixtures which should be more than winnable. I should have known it just never works out that way for Leeds. We never do things the easy way; we always have our ups and downs.

In the run-up to Christmas, we played 11 games finishing with the draw against Cardiff, winning eight and drawing two, and gaining 27 points from a possible 33, giving us at one point a 12-point advantage over third place. After and including the defeat at Fulham, we played ten games up to our draw with Brentford, winning only two, losing five, and drawing three, for a total of just nine points from a possible 30.

Against Preston, we found ourselves up against a side prepared to work incredibly hard to knock us out of our stride. This was perfectly illustrated by Maguire's tackle on Klich which allowed him to drive the ball forward before it came to Browne and he fired past Casilla, who seemed rooted to his line like a Subbuteo goalkeeper. We came back into the game, of course, and Alioski hit the post before Rudd made great saves from Alioski again and a Nketiah header.

It looked for all the world as if we were going to suffer back-to-back defeats until, in the last minute, Ayling brought down Harrison's deep cross at the far post and set up Dallas, whose shot on goal deflected off a Preston defender and flew past Rudd into the net.

The point kept us still three points behind WBA, who could only manage to draw at Barnsley, but Brentford narrowed the gap between us and third to eight points, when their fine form continued with a 3-1 win over Swansea. Fulham slipped up against struggling Luton, only managing a 3-3 draw, and it does seem amazing just how teams seem to raise themselves for the challenge of playing against us only to lose the following game. This kind of reaction shows itself again when we head to St Andrew's to face a Birmingham side in the lower half of the table and only eight points clear of the relegation places.

Birmingham City...4; Leeds United...5
Sunday, 29th December

I decide to get the coach to the Midlands, as Birmingham's ground is notoriously difficult to get away from after the match, situated between main roads and not far from a busy route into the town that football traffic seems to have to queue for hours to access. I don't like St Andrew's, as I've mentioned earlier; their fans are quite surly, and James and I have had worrying incidents twice when attending matches there.

On one occasion, James was hit by a coin thrown randomly at Leeds fans as we were being held from leaving the stadium while police dispersed the home fans. Another time, we were walking back to the car which was parked in a city centre car park, and we passed a pub festooned with Birmingham colours. As we walked past the entrance, a group of Brummie fans leaving the pub started to follow us down the street, which suddenly seemed to get very dark and deserted. We kept going, heads down, as they taunted us, and I found it hard not to start running. But eventually we turned right into the car park and the gang behind us just kept going. James and I hadn't spoken while we had been walking, but as soon as we had reached the safety of the car we

240

both breathed a massive sigh of relief and admitted we thought we were going to be attacked. Catching the club coaches was a much safer option, guaranteeing safety in numbers and usually a high police presence all around us. It was the same today as we rolled into the away coach parking area right next to the visiting fans' entry turnstiles. As we started to disembark, we were told the coaches would be moving during the game, and we would find them easily after the match. Apparently, this had been a police decision, prompted by the disturbances that happened with the Birmingham fans at ER earlier in the season. A number of them had just been in court and some had been jailed, so clearly the police didn't want any repeat of the troubles. I was not happy, however, that no-one could tell me exactly where the coaches would be.

But what a fantastic game; one of the greatest I have ever witnessed. Not because of the quality of play, because our defending was hopeless and Casilla had a nightmare, but due to the sheer level of entertainment. There was a lot of chat among the crowd with Nketiah in the side in place of Bamford. Some were saying Bamford was injured, others that he had been dropped. Sadly, we were still without the injured Hernandez, but Roberts was back on the bench to give cover up front and in the attacking midfield role. Alioski continued at wing back to allow the versatile Dallas to cover in midfield.

I have been to this ground lots of times and am yet to see us win, but we get off to a great start with Costa running onto Harrison's pass to score a fine goal in the 15th minute. Then we double the score when Alioski tees up Harrison to score with a deflected shot. It's a great start and after quite a depressing Christmas on the football front, I am looking forward to us at last getting an easy victory, and one that doesn't leave us biting our nails and holding our heads in our hands praying for the final whistle. Typically, we concede just six minutes later, with the 16-year-old Bellingham finding himself unmarked in the penalty area and stroking the ball confidently past Casilla.

Birmingham are level on 61 minutes, when a corner from the left is headed back into the area and Casilla, under pressure from Bellingham, can only push the ball in the direction of Jutkiewicz who nods the ball past him for the equaliser. It's a real blow, and the Birmingham fans celebrate loudly and hit us with the old 'Leeds are falling apart again' chant. Leeds fight back and a few minutes later Ayling charges into the area on the right-hand side and sends a great half volley past Trueman in the Birmingham goal. Surely now we can see the game out against a team who, after all, are not having the greatest of seasons? But no, back come Birmingham to level through Bela, who heads in a free kick at the near post with poor old Casilla seemingly clutching at thin air as he runs out to try and claim the ball. Again, Leeds respond, and again it's Ayling who is heavily involved when he drives forward, exchanges passes with Harrison, and then chips the ball into the area for Dallas to hook the ball high into the net from close range.

Dallas scores in the 84th minute, but as the game goes into injury time, the home team attacks down the right and a long cross goes over everyone and finds Jutkiewicz sliding in at the far post to bring the game level yet again. Now, I am usually quite a pessimistic kind of fan when we concede late goals and often fear the worst – and it usually happens as well. But for some reason, I really don't know why, I just feel deep inside that we will score again even as the game goes deep into added time.

And when Roberts – on for Nketiah – wins a dubious corner, I am sure we will score. But the 'Blues' clear the ball and the chance seems gone. I can see the ref checking his watch as Baradi of all people intercepts a clearance and pushes the ball forward for Costa, who slips in the ever-willing Ayling. With a goal and an assist to his name already, the full back hits the ball across the area and as Harrison races in to finish, Harding, the Birmingham defender, steers the ball wide of his keeper and into the net. The travelling fans explode with joy and the Leeds players celebrate ecstatically in front of us. This time, there is absolutely no way back, and the referee brings to an end one of the most extraordinary games I have ever seen.

As they always do, after shaking hands with their opponents, the players walk towards the Leeds hordes gathered behind the goal. The fans are still jumping with the excitement of such a fantastic game, and the players are laughing and joking and clapping us. Then they go into a huddle, with Cooper and Phillips prominent. It shows how much it means to them and it shows how much they are together – except, as the huddle breaks, Casilla is nowhere to be seen.

I don't think there can be a better feeling than winning away from home in the very last minute, and we leave the ground loudly proclaiming the fact that 'We are top of the league', as Albion have lost, surprisingly, at home to Middlesbrough 0-2 earlier in the day. It's then I wonder about the coaches and where they will be, but I needn't have worried, as the stewards send us through an entrance I have never left through before, and the coaches are all lined up on a pleasant-ish side street, surrounded by police on motorbikes. I get on the 'Fourways' bus and go right to the back, where I have the whole of the back seat to myself. Looking out of the window, I watch all the police activity as they stop all the traffic moving and give us our own private escort out of the city. I sit there looking down the centre of the bus with a massive smile on my face, feeling like Dustin Hoffman in *The Graduate* when he snatches his girlfriend from her own wedding ceremony and legs it out of the church to get on the first bus possible.

What a feeling. What a day. 'We're Leeds United. We're top of the league!' Heading home, I can't help feeling that the players huddle was a real statement of intent and a sign of their determination to get the job done. I somehow feel it's going to be alright and there isn't going to be the implosion of last year. And with that thought, I park football happily away for a couple of days to enjoy bringing in the New Year with the family, knowing that I will have to miss the top-of-the-table clash with WBA on New Year's Day. To be fair, Andy would have told me to go, but we will be hosting my family and they will be leaving the next day. And of course, the Albion game is an evening kick-off and on telly, and as we will be flying to Spain the next day anyway, it just seems a match too far.

West Brom…1; Leeds United…1
Wednesday, 1st January

So, I stayed at home and watched it on Sky, aware that I couldn't jump around and curse as much as I would normally do, given the circumstances. I really hate watching football when, with great respect, the others watching are not really interested. I remember once at school during one of the World Cups, the games were shown live in the early morning. Some bright spark came up with the idea of showing 'breakfast games' in the school dining room where kids could come in early to watch the games before school life kicked in.

The particular attraction was the match between England and Brazil, the one where Ronaldinho (one of my favourite all-time players) scored with a centre-cum-cross that floated over David Seaman's head. I tried to establish the fact that if you came into the room, then you had to sit down and watch the game quietly. No chance. I don't know which group was the most irritating: the kids being silly, or the teachers showing off to them. I could usually put up with some of the staff's desperate need for popularity, and it's not particularly difficult to make ten-year-old kids laugh and think you're cool, but I mean this is football. F**k off!

The Albion match was one of those we could have lost in the first half but should have won in the second, so I guess a draw was a fair result in the end. Nketiah started up front for the second game in succession, with Bamford returning to the bench. But by far the biggest news is that the young Arsenal forward has had his loan cancelled, and this will be his last appearance for the club. This is a real blow for us. While I was never completely certain that he could lead the line as well as Bamford, there is no doubt he was a more natural finisher, and a really important option to have on the bench. Unfortunately, being on the bench seems to be the problem for both Nketiah and Arsenal, and both have decided he needs more 'game time'. There are rumours that Bristol City are keen to take him to Ashton Gate, but for tonight at least he starts for us. In fact, the side is the same one that took the field in that incredible game at Birmingham.

We concede after 75 seconds, and it's the usual problem. Albion swing in a corner, Casilla flaps at the ball and sends it straight to a West Brom player, the ball ping-pongs around, before Bartley heads it back into the danger area for Ajayi to stick out a leg and send the ball into the net. Harrison makes a brilliantly athletic effort to clear the ball, but sadly for us it has already crossed the line. WBA definitely have the best of the half and should have gone into the break two up when Phillips broke clear only to send a weak shot into Casilla's legs. Bamford replaces Nketiah at half-time and Douglas comes on for Alioski, and immediately the game changes. We start to take control and equalise seven minutes into the half when Harrison crosses for Bamford, who has made a great run across the penalty area, to head goalwards. The ball is going wide until it strikes Ajayi on the shoulder and deflects into the net. After that, we pretty much dominate the game, and we miss a great chance to claim the three points when Bamford shoots from a wide angle, with Harrison and Klich running into the penalty area unmarked and screaming for the pass.

There is no doubt, though, the centre forward's appearance has changed the game in our favour and that for all his inconsistency in front of goal, his presence is vital to the way the team perform. We desperately need to bring in an experienced player who is a regular scorer at this level to replace Nketiah as back-up to Bamford, and before the transfer window closes. I really think that Roberts can do this, but again the forward, having come on as a sub at Birmingham a couple of days ago, is missing from the squad. I have thought for a long time we should go for Dwight Gayle – a regular scorer in the Championship, who is kicking his heels at Newcastle.

Amazingly, given our run of six points out of the last 15, we remain top of the league on goal difference from Albion, and still nine points clear of Brentford and Forest, in third. Fulham, having raised themselves to beat us, lose at home to Reading.

It's time for us to head to Spain, which means I will miss the trip to the Emirates Stadium and our FA Cup clash with Arsenal. We booked the flights before the cup draw was made, and I was praying it wouldn't be an away trip to Anfield or Old Trafford and the chance to take a big scalp in a frenzied atmosphere. But Arsenal don't do frenzied atmospheres any more, with even their own fans referring to the ground as 'The Library'. I've been a couple of times and enjoyed the trips to London more than the trips to the ground. I was there when Snodgrass scored a penalty right in front of us and we went on to earn a replay at ER. And I was also there the night Thierry Henry returned to the club and chose that moment to score a great goal that deservedly won the game and knocked us out of the cup a few years later.

I pray if we ever redevelop ER, we will do it by redeveloping the current stadium so we don't lose the atmosphere that I have loved all my life, as seems to have happened at so many clubs who have built modern soulless stadiums, and particularly Arsenal. Actually, we have enjoyed some of our best days against Arsenal in cup competitions, winning the League Cup in 1968, and of course the FA Cup in 1972. Tonight I settle down to watch the match in front of my telly in Spain, and for some reason my mind goes back to watching the brilliant game we played out with the Gunners' when they came to ER near the end of the season in 1999, needing to beat us to stay in the title hunt with Man Utd.

It was a night match under the lights, and because of work commitments (I had pretty much just started my new job down there in Berkhamsted) I was unable to travel north to watch the game live. For some reason, our Sky system wasn't working, so I took Katherine and Mike with me and we walked down the canal to 'The Boat' – a pub where I knew they would be showing the match on their big screen. It really was a fantastic match, with both sides going full out for the win and lots of close shaves and near-misses, none worse than Ian Harte's first half penalty miss. Arsenal threw themselves forward as the game came to its climax, desperate for the win that would keep their title hopes alive, but Leeds broke down the left and Harry Kewell's deep cross was brilliantly headed home by Jimmy Floyd Hasselbaink diving in at the far post.

We just exploded into the air shouting 'Yes' and hugging each other, and then we realised the pub was almost silent except for us raucous Northerners loudly celebrating. We didn't know it at the time, but 'The Boat' was an Arsenal pub and there were a lot of disgruntled punters in there just realising they had blown their chances of winning the league. We got the feeling it was probably time to go. I never liked the pub anyway.

Tonight, we play brilliantly from the start, making Arsenal look slow and clumsy. Bielsa has made a number of changes, and one sees the debut of Meslier in goal. The young Frenchman has a fine game, looking confident and self-assured and particularly adept at passing the ball accurately to his colleagues. Robbie Gotts, the highly rated youngster, also made his debut and played well, unfortunately failing to convert a good chance that would have made him a real hero with the travelling hordes. We had 15 shots in the first half, and went close on a number of occasions, with Bamford hitting the bar and Harrison and Alioski going close.

Arsenal were better in the second half, and Nelson scored what proved to be the winner with a scuffed effort in the 55th minute. We were well worth a draw and would have won the game if we had managed to convert our chances in the first half. Arsenal were poor and Lacazette, their excellent forward, should have been sent off for kicking Baradi, but unbelievably VAR decided against the red card. This was our first experience of the 'video referee' and I wonder how he could sit there and watch a blatant and petulant kick and ignore it. One thing is for sure, if it had been Baradi on Lacazette, the Leeds player would have been sent off. For me watching in Spain, it's the perfect result. We have shown the country and the Premiership just what a fabulous brand of football we can play, and we have also reminded the nation what passionate fans look and sound like, by bringing some kind of atmosphere to 'The Library'! We can now concentrate on the league and the far more important goal of winning promotion so we can entertain the Premiership on a weekly basis. And so after a lovely break, some wonderful meals eaten in our cosy Spanish escape, with fairy lights and a blazing fire, a few nights out with the Parkies, and of course the fireworks on Kings, it's time to head home and get the New Year underway with a big game against Sheffield Wednesday.

Leeds United...0; Sheffield Wednesday...2
Saturday, 11th January

Here we go again. Another must-win game against tough opponents from South Yorkshire. Hernandez, thank goodness, returns to the bench and Alioski steps down at left back, replaced by Douglas. With Neketiah gone and Roberts injured, our need for another forward is very obvious, and it's to be hoped that Bamford stays clear of injury while we pursue our number one target, Che Adams from Southampton. Jack Clarke has also gone – recalled by Spurs and sent back out on loan immediately to QPR, our next opponents. I fear for Clarke who, as previously mentioned, hasn't played well since that collapse at the Riverside last Spring. I do hope he is ok.

After our impressive display at the Emirates and a strong second half in the game at West Brom, I am really hopeful we can get three points and keep the pressure on the closing pack. Basically, we batter what looks to me like a poor Wednesday team, who have lost their last three games and who are now going to miss their leading scorer Fletcher up front, out for some ten weeks with injury.

It seems to me Wednesday are there for the taking, and yet so many chances to score and none taken. Harrison side-footing wide when surely he had to score; Bamford striking the post and having a goal chalked off for offside; chance after chance goes begging. So I suppose no-one in the ground is the least bit surprised when Wednesday take the lead through Murphy in the 87th minute, the winger being well set up by the substitute Nuhiu. I am right behind the line of the shot and there is no way he should score, as Casilla has the near post covered, but the ball blasts past him, leaving the Spanish keeper clutching thin air yet again. I am absolutely furious and full of frustration, and it hardly registers that Wednesday score again through Nuhiu in injury time.

It's a game that shows up our weaknesses for all to see. Firstly, we have a suspect keeper, capable of making some decent saves, but as our former striker Jimmy Floyd Hasselbaink said on Sky after the West Brom game, one whose judgement is poor and who makes his 'defence nervous'. Secondly, we have a centre forward who, hard as he tries –

and he really does work hard and very effectively out of the box – simply misses too high a ratio of the chances created inside it. For all our brilliant play, we are in danger of failing again, just like last season. And the critical weaknesses then still remain today; they have not been remedied. I am so fed up about this and our lack of success in the transfer market that I end up writing a couple of days later to Angus Kinnear, the club's chief executive, about it. Once I have cooled down, of course.

I learnt as a headteacher never to respond in anger. So, often my response to a parental letter of complaint would change from the original:

Dear Mrs So and So,
I am sorry that you feel our games staff are incompetent fools for putting your son Henry in the C team. I do realise that his coach for his Sunday league team – I understand that's Henry's uncle – thinks he's another Gareth Bale, but the problem is if I insist he is put in the first team as you request, then clearly I have to disappoint another child and family. As I refuse to be bullied by someone who can't even be arsed to make sure he has the right kit on games day, I am afraid to tell you that I will not be putting Henry in the first team, basically because he is frigging useless, and secondly, a bit like you, he is a loud-mouthed little shit only interested in himself.
Yours…

To:
Dear Mrs So and So,
I write to thank you for your letter about football team selection and the concerns you express about Henry's placement in the C team. I would be very happy to discuss this matter further with you should you wish to make an appointment, blah blah blah…
Yours…

So I think the email I sent to Angus was fair and restrained. I reprint it below:

Dear Angus,

I feel I must contact you following the match against Sheffield Wednesday on Saturday. I have followed Leeds since 1964 and as they say, I have seen some 'ups and downs'! My concern now is not the past but rather the 'now' and the immediate future. In the last few years, Mr Radrizzani, you, and the team, have done a fantastic job in resurrecting the club's fortunes. Marcelo Bielsa has taken a group of underachieving players and made them play some fabulous football. I and many other fans believe we are on the brink of another golden age. However, it is clear that everything hinges on gaining promotion this year. In this, I mean that should we not do so, we lose our best player Kalvin Phillips, and probably our manager as well. I realise you and Andrea will be more aware of this than anyone, so I just wanted to offer my support at this time, and also make an observation that again you will be well aware of. In my opinion, there is a clear need to recruit a proven Championship goalscorer. Patrick Bamford has worked hard and is much improved in all areas, except the most important, i.e. converting chances. I hope your pursuit of such a player is successful asap. The other area of massive concern is the goalkeeping problem. If you are an opposing manager, it's not difficult to see how many goals we concede from set-pieces, and what tactics to pursue. Our weaknesses in these key areas cost us promotion last year, and my fear is that this is likely to happen again if decisive action is not taken. I hope you see this as a positive contribution from someone who has loved the club for 55 years. I know the pressures of leadership, but sometimes decisive action has to be taken and I hope you will make the funds available to solve these problems. Any investment will come back in huge profit if this great club returns to the Premiership. I do hope you will have the opportunity to read my thoughts.

Best wishes,
Adrian

Well, I thought, *there's no point bleating on the terraces. Tell it like it is and go to the top.* I don't know if Angus Kinnear ever read the email but I do know he didn't respond to it. Maybe it got lost in reception, which is where I sent it, asking them to forward it to the Chief

Executive. Maybe he just chucked it in the bin. Actually, and this is true, James once met Andrea Radrizzani on a train from London to Leeds and they had a brief chat about how things were going, and James took a few pictures of himself with Andrea. I got the pictures developed and one framed for my study ahead of the hoped-for promotion of last season. I decided, God knows why, that our owner might like a memento of the day he met James, so took a copy into the main reception at the ground – the one with the flashy entrance and club badge prominently displayed high above it. And I asked the lady behind the desk if she could give it to Mr Radrizzani. I swear, and this is the gospel truth, she said, 'Who?'

I couldn't believe it. So, I took the photo out of the envelope and showed her who her boss was. No recognition; absolutely zero! I asked her to take a good look so that if she saw him coming through the main door of the club she could spring impressively to attention and say, 'Morning, Mr Radrizzani.' I have to say, while on the topic of administration, the staff who manage the ticket office are totally brilliant and always helpful and respectful, even when they are explaining that in fact you are being given a concession 'cos you're an old git!

CHAPTER 15

DEFEAT IN LONDON, DESPAIR AND MEMORIES AT FOREST AND THE BEGINNINGS OF RECOVERY

So, having got things off my chest, I watch to see what activity happens in the transfer window. And while there are lots of players mentioned, there is nothing of substance, except what appears to be our dogged pursuit of Che Adams. I only hope it doesn't turn into another fiasco like our attempt to buy Dan James from Swansea did last year, when the young man had passed his medical and even had his photo taken in a Leeds shirt, before Swansea pulled the plug on the deal. James later signed for Manchester United.

Queens Park Rangers…1; Leeds United…0
Saturday, 18th January

We head to QPR and then entertain Millwall and Wigan at ER before the 'transfer window' closes. Games we should, and indeed desperately need to win. We are back to strength for the clash in West London, though our bench looks decidedly lightweight now that Nketiah and Clarke have left and Baradi and Roberts are out injured. It's a poor game, in truth, not helped by my nursing a serious hangover after a brilliant night out with James and his flatmate Kieran, which finished in the early hours with us drinking far too much red wine in their flat. When I woke up, I was surprised to see the blinds on his bedroom window all askew, which they hadn't been when I turned in a few hours earlier. I can only assume I had gone looking for the loo, and in my deep sleep had mistaken the window for the door. Now there's one thing falling down a few stairs, as I had done at Mike's, but James lived on the sixth floor of a block of flats. Fortunately, the window was locked so I couldn't escape and try and kill myself. As I came round, I realised I would have to develop some kind of survival strategy for nights in strange rooms when I have had too much to drink.

James managed to get a ticket from a tout standing on the corner just across from the tube station. He had to pay over the odds, and we checked the ticket closely against the one I had received from the club. It was definitely genuine and once again 'sold on' by a fan who was stopping the true supporters getting tickets for away games. We were both quite angry about it really, and we felt even worse when we found ourselves in front of a group of lads purporting to be supporting Leeds but who spent the game trying to make cheap laughs among themselves about how rubbish we were. They seemed to be targeting Cooper, along with Bamford and Costa. They were all about late twenties and early thirties, and they were certainly the type who would be holding down white-collar jobs, probably in the capital. They weren't in the slightest bit funny.

We put up with it for so long before eventually turning round and just staring at them. They calmed down a bit but then left about 15 minutes from the end so they could get to their pub ahead of the crowds. I can't believe a group as big as that, who were so obviously just out for a cheap laugh, could be real fans and could have been to the amount of away games that qualified them to get tickets. So just how do they get their hands on them?

In truth, our performance that morning gave the moaners lots of ammunition, and it was a game to quickly forget. Wells scored for Rangers, clearly controlling the ball with his hand before slotting home. We made lots of chances. Bamford firing high over the bar when all he had to do was chip it over Kelly, the advancing keeper, and then worse, missing a penalty, shooting weakly to the keeper's left, allowing him to make a comfortable save. Things couldn't really get any worse, but they did. Hernandez clipped the post with a beautiful free kick, with the keeper stranded, and then Kalvin got sent off. We could see it coming as he lunged forward to wrestle the ball from Cameron. It was a clear red; Phillips knew it, and we knew it, too. Just when we needed him most, we were going to be without one of our key players for three hugely important games. I hugged James goodbye and headed to Kings Cross and my train home.

Amazingly, WBA lose at home to Stoke, so going into yet another frustrating, but now maybe necessary ten-day break before our clash with Millwall, we still lead the 'Baggies' on goal difference, with the chasing pack led by Fulham, now just four points adrift of us. It seems like West Brom and ourselves, for so long seen as certainties for promotion, are beginning to wobble at the same time.

With no game the following weekend, we fly to Dublin on the Monday to help Lou and Mike with childcare. Lou is expecting their second daughter any day, and her mum Anne is unable to travel as she recovers from an operation. It's lovely getting to know Margie again and we enjoy walking round to pick her up from her little nursery setting at lunchtimes. She is great fun and so like Mike to look at.

Lou is doing brilliantly but has to be in huge discomfort with the size of her tummy. It's good to catch up again, and as we have an open ticket, I am hoping my soon-to-be-a-Leeds-fan fourth grandchild will arrive safely on this planet before the Millwall game. And she does. Georgia Anne Taylor is born on Wednesday, 22nd January. Mum and baby are both safe and doing well, and Lou is quickly home to introduce Margie to her little sister. Margs is funny at first and wants to play with Georgia as if she is one of her dolls, which is not particularly advisable. But Mike and Lou are careful to nurture the sibling relationship while at the same time protecting their newborn child. Andy is brilliant as a helper and a much better person than me, selflessly getting up in the night to care for Margie, and trying to give Mike and Lou some much-needed sleep, especially Lou of course, with all the pressure of being a new mum and everything that entails.

We stay for a few days, which helps Mike sort out some of his work before he takes a week's paternity leave. It will be good for them to have some time to bond as a little family, and Andy will be back in a few weeks when I am in London involved in interviews. We seem to be travelling a lot at the moment, and with trips coming up back to

Ashwell in the caravan in early February, out to Italy in March for the international, then to Nice at the beginning of April, it is good to be home for a few days. Especially now I have had time to escape the depression of the defeats to Wednesday and QPR and am quietly confident of taking six points from our upcoming games at home to Millwall and lowly Wigan.

Leeds United...3; Millwall...2
Tuesday, 28th January

It's great to be back at ER and under the lights as well, despite Millwall's upturn in form of late – unbeaten in their last five. I am looking forward to the game tonight, especially as we have at last done some business in the transfer window. We have signed Ian Poveda, an attacking midfielder/winger from Manchester City, and he has quite a CV for one so young, having had spells at Chelsea, Arsenal, and Barcelona, as well as City. He has also played for England at every level from U-16 to U-20, so must have something. So, why have City and all the others let him go?

STOP IT, ADRIAN!

Now is not the time for negatives. Anyway, he's on the bench, so hopefully if all goes well, we will see him later tonight. We have also signed a forward, but it's not as was beginning to seem obvious Che Adams, which is really disappointing as he is such a proven finisher in the Championship. Instead, we have gone for a chap called Jean Kevin Augustin, a French youth international who was signed by RB Leipzig from PSG and then loaned out to Monaco, who are obviously happy to loan him out to us. Slightly worrying, but again a pretty useful pedigree. There is no sign of him tonight, but it's good to see Roberts back on the bench and Shackleton, too.

My pre-match confidence was horribly misplaced, and by half-time we are losing 2-0, with Casilla and a linesman conspiring to give Millwall a potentially match-winning lead. The first goal comes after only four minutes when, after Woods shot over, Hutchinson headed home at the far post – another goal from a corner, and Casilla once again uncertain of how to defend it. The next day there is criticism of the keeper in the press and on the BBC football page. I mention this because I don't want it to be seen that its only me who questions our keeper. Anyway, the visitors double their lead when Alioski brings down Bodvarsson as he charges into the area following a pass from Woods, who clearly took the ball out of play before the penalty award. How is it possible that a linesman and a referee can't see that when 35,000 people can? I hold my head in my hands for the second time that night and we've only played 23 minutes.

I have to say whoever it was at that Heads' conference who made the joke about watching Leeds and stress, was absolutely right. I don't know what to do and seriously think about going home to avoid any more anxiety and upset, but then along comes the second half. And with the crowd going crazy, we play probably one of our best 45-minute periods of the season so far. Bamford scores his first goal since the Fulham game, tapping home after Bialkowski saved brilliantly from Harrison, and this is followed up by an Hernandez strike that deflects in past the helpless keeper.

Millwall are absolutely rocking and so is the crowd as Bamford scores the winner, diving in at the far post to head home. There is still time for Costa to send a deliciously curling shot against the bar and Klich to somehow blaze over an open goal from eight yards after a sensational move that ripped the Lions apart. It's a vital three points, made even better by the news that WBA have lost at Cardiff and Brentford have gone down at home to the dour but dangerous Notts Forest – our next away opponents, who are now in third spot just four points behind us. We lead the table by two, despite our spluttering form in recent weeks, and have the chance to claim another three points at ER at the weekend when we entertain struggling Wigan.

Leeds United…0; Wigan…1
Saturday, 1st February

They say lightning doesn't strike twice, but in this case it bloody well does. What can I say? Last season, Wigan pretty much ended our automatic promotion hopes, winning at ER despite playing most of the match with ten men and giving us a goal start. After the shock of going 2-0 down in midweek against Millwall and then our really excellent play to eventually win the game, I was in no doubt that we would pick up another vital three points this afternoon. This was especially as, following today's game, we faced two of our closest opponents, Forest and Brentford, in tough away fixtures. So, we definitely needed the cushion of a victory today.

As always, we dominated; as always, we created chances. Harrison hit the post and unbelievably missed from almost on the goal-line, and Bamford had two excellent efforts cleared off the line. We threw the kitchen sink at them. We huffed and we puffed, but we just couldn't blow that ball over the line. Somehow Wigan's defence held out. We had 77% possession, 19 shots, and 13 corners, we played with energy and creativity, but we just couldn't find the net. And there was no sign of Augustin, no striking alternative for Bamford, though Roberts did come off the bench to help create a bit more impetus upfront. And while we couldn't score at one end, we contrived to do so at the other. A Williams corner brushed off the back of Hernandez and, unbelievably, Casilla completely missed his push or punch or whatever was in his mind to do, as he watched the ball sail over his head and into the net.

On the terraces at the other end of the ground, I was apoplectic, screaming out in frustration, turning round and sharing the anger and disbelief of my friends. We have been here so many times before, WHY don't we do something about it? It's as if we are sleepwalking towards a cliff edge and simply can't wake up. Bielsa is clearly a genius of a coach and has us playing a brand of football that is fast, exciting, and so pleasing on the eye. How can he not see that we are in danger of throwing it all away because we have a weakness in goal that is beginning to hurt us badly? I simply don't understand how we have not replaced him. Every player, everyone in any working capacity, can have a bad period, and when they do, they are usually taken out of the firing line and offered support and extra training. It's almost reaching the stage where the club are being negligent in their support of Casilla; he needs to be rested for his own good.

Some argue that it must be the threat of punishment in the racial abuse case that is weighing on his mind. But he threw goals away at Ipswich and in the play-off semi-final last season, and they were long before the incident at Charlton. I am so, so fed up. It really does look as if we are 'falling apart again', but the solution is in our own hands and we are being remiss in ignoring it. Sometimes loyalty can be totally misplaced.

Elsewhere, Albion beat struggling Luton, Brentford smash Hull 1-5 at the K Com stadium, Fulham keep the pressure up by beating Huddersfield 3-2 at the Cottage, and Forest – where we head next – slip up, losing 2-1 at Birmingham. After 30 games, just six points separate the top six clubs, and we play three of them in our next three matches. We are still hanging onto a promotion place… but only just. Three points ahead of Fulham and one behind WBA, it's very much still all to play for.

It takes me all the weekend to get over this defeat. I am angry and listless and can't bear reading the papers or watching any of the matches on Sky. I record the highlights of the Wigan game on Quest. and watch the key moments through spread fingers. hoping in some way that it wouldn't hurt as much. But it does. What an awful, awful goal to concede. Fortunately, I have quite a bit of educational work to keep me occupied this week, and as Monday turns to Tuesday I begin to feel a little better. We are heading down to the caravan park at Ashwell to see Katherine, Nick, and the kids, and have a few days away, once I have finished my working commitments on Thursday evening. The Forest game is an early evening kick-off on the Saturday, and the match is on Sky. I feel so anxious at the moment that I don't know if I will travel back north for it as I had planned to do or watch it with Kath at her place. I figured the trip to Forest from Ashwell was a similar distance to Forest from home, so I was happy enough about the journey. And being further south made it easier for me to get to Brentford for the Tuesday night match.

Nottingham Forest…2; Leeds United…0
Saturday, 8th February

In the end, I decide to spend the day with the family, and settle down in front of the telly with a cold beer, some garlic, a prayer mat, and some rosary beads, to watch yet another must-win game. I've never really enjoyed going to the City ground, as there's a lot of animosity between the fans and we don't usually get much of an allocation. We are housed, or rather squeezed, in behind the goal and pushed round to the corner flag, and the Forest fans in the tier above regularly sling abuse – and occasionally more physical objects – as we exchange ritual insults.

The problems, as previously mentioned, are historic, essentially revolving around the miners' strike. Leeds fans perceive the Nottinghamshire Miners broke the strike, hence the chant of 'scabs'; and Brian Clough, well, enough said. It's the same with Derby, though Pride Park always seems to me less threatening than here. Though they do have a drum at Derby, which is so annoying! I've been to Forest a number of times and seen us pick up a few wins along the way – some good wins at that, but perhaps none better than a few years ago when we beat them 0-4, with goals by Snodgrass, Howson, Becchio, and Clayton. It was unusual for us, because we went with a friend, Miles Harrison, the Sky rugby commentator and just an absolutely super man. Miles is a very keen Forest fan and knows a fair bit about Leeds as well, having started his professional career working for the BBC in Leeds. We hit it off straight away with a shared love of sport – obviously football and rugby, and also Miles' passion for all things cricket. And Subbuteo!

Miles was friendly with a chap called Mark Arthur, who at the time was the CEO at the City ground, and we had an invite to the match as his guests, which included dinner before the game and drinks at the end. Mike and I duly turned up, booted and suited, for Miles to drive us up to Nottingham. James, happy to take the lift, turned down the invite to dinner, preferring to stand with the travelling fans behind the goal.

Mark was a real gentleman and an excellent host, and there were a few former players at the dinner – notably, from our point of view, Peter Lorimer, our all-time leading goal scorer. Soon it was time to go up some stairs and into our seats, which were brilliantly situated near the halfway line. I have often wandered if we were an embarrassment to Miles, as Mike and I just couldn't help jumping to our feet when we scored our goals. But it was a great experience and after the match, as we gathered in the dining room for post-match drinks, the Forest group were more than generous towards our performance and so friendly towards us. It was nothing like we had been used to on our previous visits to this ground. Mark, aware that I had brought both my sons to the ground, and having chatted for some time to Mike, suddenly asked me where James was. I told him that I hoped he would be in the car park waiting for us to finish and head back home, to which Mark said I must go and bring him in for a drink. I told him I couldn't because of the dress code; James wasn't wearing a suit, and in fact was wearing his Leeds shirt. No matter, Mark sent his son out to find James and he brought him in and poured him a drink and was really welcoming. That is how I think it's fair to say my youngest became probably the only person ever to be wearing the opposition's club colours in the formal directors lounge of Nottingham Forest AFC.

We wrote to Mark, of course, to thank him for his generosity and friendship, and as it goes in the world of football, later that season Forest came up to ER and put seven past us. Miles also took revenge for his home town club's defeat that night. On a visit to stay with us a few years later, we turned back the clock to our childhood days, and in a very tense game his Forest beat my Leeds 1-0 in a Subbuteo match. I blame my defeat in part on the fact that I couldn't stop laughing at the thought that at any time soon one of the great voices of sports commentary would burst into action describing the move that led to his winning goal, kneeling on my front room carpet and flicking Forest to victory.

We turn up at the City ground hoping to avoid our fourth defeat in five matches – a disastrous run at just the wrong time of the season. Phillips serves the last game of his suspension, and it seems silly, but if we had buried some of the many chances we created against Wigan, we would and should have won the first two. Roberts and Augustin are named on the bench, and with Shackleton and Baradi there as well, it's looking stronger than in recent weeks. We have 70% of the possession, eight corners to their three, and 13 shots to their 14, yet we lose 2-0. In a nutshell, Forest take their chances and we miss ours, though in fairness

Lewis Grabben does miss a chance that he would normally score in his sleep, shooting straight at a prostrate Casilla with the goal at his mercy.

Forest have one or two penalty shouts: one a foul by Cooper I would have given; the other a challenge by Alioski which was a dive by the Forest man. Again, despite the fact that Forest worked their socks off, we are our own worst enemies. Casilla, having saved well from Silva, lets an Ameobi shot squeeze past him on his near post, and Cooper, completely unmarked, heads straight at Samba in the Forest goal, who manages to knock the header up and away just as it seems certain to cross the line. Forest score their second in the fourth minute of injury time, breaking away as Harrison loses the ball in his desperation to play it forward. It's a horrible defeat and the statisticians have a field day. We haven't scored in four of our last five matches and we haven't kept a clean sheet for ten games, having had seven in the previous ten before that. Something is going drastically wrong... and yet... we are still dominating games and creating chances. To be fair to Forest, though, not as many today.

What is interesting is the way their players and management celebrate at the end. It's as if they've won the league and must be an indication of just how valuable our scalp is. We're still obviously the team to beat, even after all our recent defeats. Fulham and Brentford have both won today, so we will go to another incredibly hard game at Brentford on Tuesday level on points with Fulham and just one in front of Forest. If Brentford beat us, they will go ahead of us in the table. We have won just twice since 10th December, at which point we were eleven points clear of Fulham. I apologise to Nick for my anger, bad language, and general miserable demeanour. Being a Spurs fan, he knows exactly how I feel. It's time to head back to the caravan and sink a few drinks, play music, watch a film – anything but football –until the anxiety starts all over again and I will be heading to meet James for a few beers ahead of the game against Brentford. I am feeling punch drunk and deflated. 'Bloody football, bloody Leeds.' I wonder how Marcelo feels? It's time for us to dig in.

Brentford... 1; Leeds United... 1
Tuesday, 11th February

Having pretty much avoided Sky Sports and Sunday newspapers, and tried to immerse myself in playing Oliver's criminal game with his Playmobil characters, I realise there is no hiding from the fates any more and leave Andy at Katherine's while I drive up to Brentford. The satnav tells me to head down the M11 towards London and then pick up the North Circular, but I've been that way before and it takes forever with rush-hour traffic banking up at roundabouts and traffic lights.

So, I go round on the M25 and pick up the M4, which brings me out almost at the ground. I park up on some fairly quiet residential street and head towards the stadium about a 15-minute walk away. James is meeting me for a drink or two before trying, as he has done fairly successfully at Charlton, Fulham, and QPR, to buy a ticket in the away end. I'm not sure about his chances tonight, as Brentford's ground is so small and we only have around 1500 tickets. He texts me the name of a pub in the town, and as I head to meet him, I pass a guy selling tickets. He offers me one in the away end, but when I check it against mine his has the word 'Hospitality' stamped across it. He tells me it's legit but wants £50, which I know James would pay, but I'm worried that maybe there's some snag or that he would have to be wearing a tie or something like we had to do at Forest. Deciding fifty quid is a lot to lose, I press on and meet James in the appointed pub.

We have a nice chat and a couple of beers, and then head back towards the ground. The guy who tried to sell me the hospitality ticket has gone so James, as always, sends me off into the ground while he tries to find one. Once again I have a tremendous view just to the right of goal and right at the front of the upper tier, and keep looking round for James, but all I see are the two lads I sit next to at ER. I go up for a chat until the players come out for kick-off. Sadly, this time James doesn't make it and texts me to say he's watching it in one of the four pubs that mark each corner of the tiny ground. The bouncers let him in because he can show proof of a London address and he watches the game in a Brentford fans' pub. I feel a bit guilty and wish now I'd bought the 'Hospitality' ticket.

We are pretty much back to full strength with Phillips restored to the team following his three-match ban. It's brilliant to see him back on the pitch as we have missed him, particularly at the City ground. Augustin, our new loan striker, is on the bench, as are Baradi, Alioski, and Shackleton, giving us more options than of late. We start well and Harrison dances along the edge of the area, creating a good position for himself before shooting weakly. We look surprisingly confident given our run of poor form, with Phillips imperiously striding through the middle like some modern-day general pulling the strings and organising the troops. Brentford have really only managed one shot, which flew narrowly wide before Cooper, under no real pressure, rolled the ball back to Casilla. He must have played this kind of pass a thousand times before, only this time our troubled keeper, with no opposition player anywhere in sight, simply let the ball roll under his foot and we watched in horror as Benrahma joyfully smashed the loose ball into the empty net. I slump over the edge of the terrace wall and bury my head below it, a bit like Kevin Keegan did when Stan Collymore's late goal beat his Newcastle team. Just a few feet below me, the Brentford players joyously celebrate their good fortune. We have done it again and I can't believe it. Just in case you think I might be being unfair again to our troubled keeper, the BBC were once again hugely critical of his performance in their match report following the game.

I seriously thought about going to find James and just drink my troubles away, such were my frustrations, but I was driving and, well, we were still in the game and only 25 minutes had gone. We recover well, showing real guts and determination, and following a corner Cooper equalises when Brentford's keeper Raya has his own Casilla moment, and our captain is on hand to stab the ball home. We are the better side after that and Costa and Hernandez go close in the second half as we move Brentford around the field, dictating the play and dominating possession. But for all our efforts, the game finishes 1-1.

In some senses that may seem massively disappointing with yet more dropped points, but despite knowing that if Fulham win tomorrow night at the Den they will go above us, and realising that Brentford had all but closed a 16-point deficit on us since December – and of course, recognising yet another goalkeeping error – there was still something about tonight that made me feel a bit more optimistic.

If I had been a Brentford fan, I would have been massively disappointed. Surely Leeds had been there for the taking? They had been given a one-goal start and they couldn't take advantage; it was almost as if we had been hanging over the precipice and simply refused to fall over. I missed James at the end of the game, waiting in the wrong place after my mobile ran out of charge. But speaking to him later, he had survived his night surrounded by Brentford fans, and he too felt we had shown some real determination, picking out the return of Phillips as crucial to our future hopes.

I drove back to the caravan rather than waking everyone up at Katherine's, and I knew I would be able to relax there, have a beer, and watch the highlights. I also knew I could sleep in and not be disturbed by Lucy's smiling face at 5.30 in the morning. It had been an interesting night elsewhere, with Forest being brought back down to earth after their over-the-top celebrations against us last weekend, this time losing at home to Charlton. The more I think about it, we have made a big statement tonight against one of our biggest rivals. Lots of people, including the sporting press and some of our own fans, were writing us off, so now just maybe it's time for us to fight back and for others to feel the pressure. The following night, Fulham draw at Millwall, and WBA win at Reading. With 14 games remaining, the table is looking pretty tight, though it does look as if WBA are beginning to pull away from us all now.

WBA......62
Leeds......56
Fulham....56
Brentford..54
Notts F....54
PNE.......53
Bristol C..53

Leeds United...1; Bristol City...0
Saturday, 15th February

Next up for us now, Bristol City at Elland Rd. The place will be rocking and we will need all the support possible as we try to push the demons away and win yet another massive match. I think a lot about the Bristol game as we say our farewells to Kath and the family and get the caravan tidied and ready for the trip back to Yorkshire. The Robins are in good form, winning five out of their last six games; if they beat us, they will be level on points with us. They are obviously still harbouring hopes of automatic promotion and certainly will be hoping for a play-off place at the very least. They will be a tough test, and worse, they have recently signed Nakhi Wells from Burnley on loan until the end of the season. Wells likes to score against us and has done so since his days at Huddersfield Town. Just a month ago, he got the winner for QPR while on loan there, albeit following a hand ball, so he will definitely be one to watch. I wonder if other football fans do this, mentally going through the opposition, wondering about team selection, working out the possible number of points we should gain in the upcoming fixtures.

I find myself making plans for the end of the season on 2nd May, after the Charlton game. What a celebration it will be if we have been promoted! Where will we all meet up? Or will it be the play-offs? Will I be able to get to Calella as soon as possible and enjoy a summer planning trips to Old Trafford and Stamford Bridge? Or will I be desperately trying to work out the dates of the play-off semi-finals (why don't they publish them earlier?) to see if we can make a flying visit between the semi-finals and the final, which is usually held at Wembley on Bank Holiday Monday. My mind is a maelstrom of thoughts, permutations, and possibilities, and usually in the end I do manage to work out some kind of plan of action, if only... Do other fans do this, or is it just me?

I am so desperate for us to go up, and the pressure is so much greater than last year. There is just so much riding on promotion, and as I said in my unanswered email to Angus Kinnear, if we don't manage, the consequences from a football point of view will be catastrophic. We will almost certainly lose Bielsa and Phillips. I wonder why on earth we didn't try and get Wells, a proven goalscorer at our level, and someone who surely would have scored a hatful for us with the chances we create.

In the end, we beat Bristol with a goal scored by Ayling, who spent some time at the Bristol club, though it didn't stop him celebrating. We actually batter them, making and missing chance after chance, disallowed goals, shots against the bar, brilliant saves by Bentley in the Bristol goal, yet that elusive second goal just wouldn't come. And then there's a moment when Ayling seems to bring down one of their players in the penalty area. I can't tell you how stressed I was in the second it took for the referee to wave away the appeal. Lee Johnson, the Bristol manager, is stressed by the decision, too, jumping up and down in his dugout in a manic fashion that reminded me of Nathan Jones' *Fawlty Towers* impression earlier in the season.

When will this game finish? Why can't we ever seem to have a calm last 20 minutes? Why can't they take care of our nerves, our mental health, for fuck's sake? We absolutely should be out of sight. We have played so well and they have literally offered nothing, nothing.

And then there he is, Wells, bearing down on our goal, having been played clean through by Diedhiou. He is going to score and ruin the weekend. They don't deserve this; we don't deserve this. I can barely look as he cuts in towards the penalty area, and it's as if time is standing still. Ben White is desperately trying to catch the forward, Casilla starts to come out in an attempt to narrow the angle, and then Wells shoots. And for a second, I'm waiting for that deathly moment when the deafening silence is punctuated only by the celebration of a few travelling away fans.

And mercifully, it doesn't happen. Wells' shot skews just wide, hitting the side netting and drifting off to safety. We have won, and the gut-wrenching tension can be released, replaced by the joy of victory and the knowledge that at least for this week we can enjoy the trappings of victory, Saturday night beers, Sunday papers, match highlights. It's a good day for us all round, as our rivals all slip up: WBA drawing with Forest; Brentford dropping points at Birmingham; and brilliantly, Fulham unexpectedly being walloped at home 0-3 by bottom-of-the-table Barnsley.

We are due out for dinner with the Parkies at the bistro at Wentbridge tonight, and I just know the beer is going to flow and we are going to have a great time. Then later, when Andy heads to bed, I will stretch out on the sofa and relive all the highlights, watching Quest into the early hours. Such a massive win.

The tension returns, though, the following Saturday with an almost repeat performance against Reading, whose form has been inconsistent but who have improved under their new manager Mark Bowen. I meet Damien and Rick in the pub up in Beeston we have started going to for our pre-match drinks since the Centenary pavilion has been given over increasingly to corporate 'fans'.

We are all hopeful for another three points and chat a bit about Casilla who is awaiting his punishment, having been found guilty of the racial discrimination charge against the Charlton player Jonathan Leko. It's not something you would want on your record through life, and the club are bound to take a strong line with him, given their commitment to 'Kick it out'.

We enjoy a beer and watch the end of the lunchtime kick-off game between Brentford and Blackburn. It's a 'topsy turvy' kind of match which eventually finishes with Blackburn claiming a draw – another good result for us if we can just take advantage of it. And we do, beating the team from Berkshire 1-0, with a brilliantly taken goal from Hernandez. To be fair, Reading offered more of a threat than Bristol had done, and again it was one of those head-in-hands kind of afternoons where one goal never seemed to be enough. If football were a boxing match, we would win every game we played on points. But just like with the top boxers, we are often prone to a sucker punch and it oh-so-nearly hit us as the game went into added time.

Reading broke down our left flank and the defender Moore found himself in on goal and facing up to Casilla. As we expected the worst and were just waiting for that awful silence – and it would have been silence, as Reading fans don't travel in numbers – waiting for the net to bulge as the ball flew into it... a wonderful thing happened. Casilla, so often criticised, braced himself for the shot and managed to turn the ball away! It was a critical save and, just like the Wells missed shot last week, prevented the opposition gaining an undeserved point. I screamed out with the stress of it all, 'Alexa, tell him it's finished!' as the referee seemed to play endless stoppage time. Another win and another clean sheet, and at the end of it all we have extended our lead over third-placed Fulham back to five points. We are still four behind WBA, but while the title would be nice, the only thing that really matters is promotion.

Middlesbrough…0; Leeds United…1
Tuesday, 18th February

It's Middlesbrough away next, and though it's quite an easy drive up to the Riverside, it's never a pleasant trip as the natives there most definitely don't like us. I always try to get there early, and there is a good place to park just off the dual carriageway and on the road to the ground, if you get there before all the parking spaces have gone. It's just a ten-minute walk up and over the railway tracks and it brings you in right next to the away end. There seems to be a fair amount of chaos as we try to get into the ground, with quite large queues developing by the turnstiles. I simply don't get this when we are visiting a modern stadium, but the crowd are good-natured and joke with the rather harassed-looking stewards. As always, it's the female ones who are the smiliest and keep things calm, unlike many of their male counterparts who strut around like little 'jobsworths', barking out instructions and getting on everyone's nerves.

The team news is not good, with Phillips missing through injury, following his early withdrawal against Reading. He is a big loss, and Bielsa goes with Ben White to cover his key position in the heart of the team. Baradi comes into the defence with, among others, Roberts and Shackleton on the bench.

We win again, and it's another nerve-wracking experience. Their keeper Pears makes some good saves and gets lucky when, just before half-time, Hernandez hits the post. His luck runs out, though, when the ball is worked back to Klich who scores with a fine shot that gives us a 0-1 to take into the interval. 'Boro, in danger of getting sucked into a relegation battle, fight back and almost score when Casilla saves well from a Saville shot, and then Tavernier curls a shot against the bar with Casilla this time well beaten. We continue to dominate the match but it's clear 'Boro offer a threat, and as the clock heads down towards the last few minutes and the lead remains so slender, it's that awful 'squeaky bum' time again. We are all biting our nails and holding our breath as stoppage time approaches.

Then I hear a police announcement over the tannoy saying that Leeds fans will be held back at the end of the game for security reasons. I totally understand why, but it's a stupid decision, aimed at ensuring there is no trouble at the actual ground where, of course, there are loads of police and stewards around to prevent such incidents. All that happens is the visiting fans get increasingly angry. And anyway, those fans from both sides who are intent on trouble won't have their plans disrupted by a ten-minute delay; they will just be waiting for each other somewhere else.

I hate leaving games early and usually like to stay to celebrate or commiserate with the players at the end of the match, but on this occasion – factoring in the time delay and traffic problems that await, and well aware of my shredded nerves – I decide to leave as the game goes into added time, telling the steward on the gate that I have to leave to get to work. He lets me through just as a copper is coming to investigate.

I kind of run and hobble on my silly leg, praying that I won't hear the roar from behind me that will tell me 'Boro have equalised. It doesn't come, and I get back to the car to join the queue of mainly 'Boro fans heading back to the dual carriageway. I am on the way home when the game finishes, ahead of the police embargo, and listen to the radio as the results from other grounds come in: Fulham score in injury time to beat Swansea, but we keep the gap between us to five points; elsewhere Albion keep their four-point lead over us, having beaten Preston the night before.

I mull things over on the journey home. We are now suddenly 12 points clear of Bristol City in seventh place, a team who would have gone level on points with us if they had beaten us at ER just a couple of games ago. What a crazy division this Championship is. How will it all end?

Hull City…0; Leeds United…4
Saturday, 29th February

That's four games unbeaten – three wins on the bounce, and without conceding a goal – and though we have only managed to score three times in that winning run, the goals have been decisive. And suddenly, after the miserable run-up to the Brentford match, we have taken ten points from the last 12. It's Hull City at the KCOM next for us, and they seem to be in freefall, having sold their best players Bowen and Grosciki in the January transfer window. At least one thing is looking likely at the moment and that is we should safely make the play-off places, something we would have seen as a real achievement just a couple of seasons ago. It shows just how far we have come and what has been achieved under Bielsa.

I am down to London in between games for a course, and arrange to meet up with James and Andrew, who is also in the capital, for a few drinks before I get the train home. We always meet in a pub called the 'Founders' right on the Thames and close to Blackfriars station, which is good for both Andrew and me in terms of getting our homeward journey going. It's great to see them, and we meet some of James friends and enjoy a good laugh and quite a few pints of Guinness, before James leaves to go to some works 'do' and Andrew escorts his elder brother to the station as the effects of the drink begin to kick in.

We are both laughing and singing and notice a few people smiling at us as we make our merry way onto the platform. In fact, I think they are laughing with us rather than against us, but either way, they probably don't understand how important this midweek break has been to us, escaping the stress of following Leeds United through the agonies of the last 11 matches of the season, and the long hoped-for dream of a return to the 'Promised Land'.

I've been to the KCOM a few times and it's an easy run for me along the M62 and on to the city. The ground is really close to the town centre and there are loads of car parks, pubs, and eateries, so it's a really good venue both for home and visiting fans. The 'away' fans guide recommends parking in the hospital car park, which is a huge area, but I know there's another smaller one a little further on and to the right. As it turns out, I go past the entrance to the road and end up turning left onto a dead-end road a little further on. It's the perfect place and there are a few street parking places still free, so I park up and follow my usual pre-match routine, bang the radio on, open my sandwiches, and start to read the paper. About an hour before kick-off, I lock up and wander down the street to the main road. There are fans all over the place and a few coppers standing by the entrance to an overpass that leads directly to the ground.

I like the KCOM; it's one of those 'new' grounds that seems to work and, unlike Derby, Bolton, and Reading, it's not surrounded by supermarkets, shops, and eateries. In fact, the approaches are quite rural for a ground so close to the town, and the walkways around the ground are quite wide boulevards. I wonder if this is a deliberate plan, as the 'Tigers' share the ground with Hull RLFC, whose famous old stadium was called the Boulevard. I decide I am being 'anal' and reading too much into all of this and go and get a matchday programme. Chatting to some Hull fans, they do not have high expectations for the afternoon. To be honest, with the sale of Bowen and Grosciki, the club have completely stuffed up their season, and if I supported them, I would have been furious. Whatever cash they made in the short term is surely going to get lost in the debt that will follow with relegation to League One. I think the owners have gambled that they had enough points in the bag to avoid the 'drop', but it's not looking good for them at the moment as they are plummeting towards the relegation places at a rate of knots. So sad for those genuine fans who, not so long ago, were thinking of a top six finish.

It's a lunchtime kick-off, and bright sunshine greets the players as they come out at the start of the match. In terms of team selection, I think we have just about got our best ten outfield players on the pitch and a strong bench, too, with Baradi, Shackleton, Alioski, and Roberts, all named. The biggest selection news is that Illan Meslier, the 19-year-old French goalkeeper, replaces Casilla in goal. The Spanish keeper has at last learnt of his fate over the 'racial abuse' case, and he has been banned for eight matches and given a significant fine. The FA decide the case is won on the grounds 'of reasonable probability', and so far the club don't appear to be appealing the decision. I don't know if Casilla will challenge the verdict through the law courts, but I know he has always denied the allegation against him, and it must be a terrible burden to bear. I mean, who wants to be known as a 'racist'? It must be said it must also have been a pretty horrible time for Jonathan Leko, the Charlton player, who challenged Casilla about his use of words. No-one should ever be insulted because of the colour of their skin, and society in general needs to learn big lessons in this area.

My seat at ER is a row and a few seats along from one of the few black men I have seen at the ground. I think that's a pretty awful indictment of our football supporters' community, and it's not just Leeds that has this problem; it is an issue throughout the country. It's just so sad when black players increasingly represent clubs on the pitch and have since Viv Anderson played for England with great distinction. Barnes, Ince, Walker, Wright, Campbell, Cole, and Sterling; the list is endless. Indeed, our own club was one of the first top flight clubs to play a black player when Albert Johanneson turned out for us in the sixties and became the first black man to play in an FA Cup Final. And as I have said, Lucas Radebe, 'the Chief', became a legend of the club, immortalised as the inspiration behind the naming of the Leeds group, Kaiser Chiefs.

I know that Leeds fans historically have a bad reputation for behaviour, though I have seen little trouble at the games I have attended in recent times, and I have heard some pretty horrid chants about people like Jimmy Saville, both from sections of our own support and those from other clubs. But I can honestly say I haven't heard any chanting of a racist nature for a long time. I also think if anyone started that kind of thing anywhere near my seat and in the hearing of our friend, they would feel a very strong reaction from the rest of us. And in the end, that is how racism will be defeated, when the people, all people, rise up and say, 'Enough is enough.'

As for Casilla, he must do what he thinks right to clear his name if he can. But if guilty, the club have little option but to take the strongest of disciplinary action. Most certainly, if a fan had been found guilty of using the words Casilla allegedly used, they would be banned from the terraces for life, and the club rightly highlights its views on racism in every matchday programme.

Well, if Hull are in freefall, sliding down the table, the last thing they needed was to come up against us in such confident form. From the minute Ayling put us in front, with a shot that deflected wickedly over the Hull keeper Long, there was only going to be one winner. And it was so nearly two just before half-time when Hernandez cut in from the left and unleashed a tremendous shot that cannoned off the bar. We were even better in the second half, playing some beautiful football which simply left the Hull defenders chasing shadows. So, it was no surprise when Costa slipped Hernandez in on the right for the Spaniard to score with an instant cross-shot; he didn't even look up, he just instinctively knew where he was and where the keeper was, and he rolled the ball past him into the empty net. The Hull keeper and captain for the day proceeded to keep his side in the contest, with excellent saves from Costa and Klich, before Harrison beat him from distance only to see his shot crash against the inside of the post.

Hull did try to rally, and from one of their few attacks they managed a shot which struck the outside of the post before flying to safety. Not long afterwards, Harrison, in super form, robbed a Hull player deep in our half and ran free before passing to Roberts, on as a substitute for Bamford, who spread the play wide to Costa. The Portuguese saw his moment and played a super pass across the area to Klich, who simply cushioned the ball into the path of the onrushing Roberts to sweep the ball home. It was a superb team goal. And there was another one to come when Hernandez fed Klich, who chipped the ball into the area and again found Roberts for the forward to brilliantly head back across Long and into the goal. It was a fantastic team performance, and better clubs than Hull would have been destroyed by us today, such was the quality of our play.

I walked happily back to the car, listening to the woes of the home fans as they realised that a proper relegation scrap was staring them right in the face. I got back to the car and was surprised and pleased how quickly I got into the main stream of traffic heading for the M62. Most of the road ahead was controlled by traffic lights, so I couldn't understand why suddenly we weren't moving, even when the lights were showing green. Then all became clear as the police outriders, blue lights flashing, stopped all the traffic and cleared the way for the escort bikes to flash forward, stop, look back, and then start to gesticulate with their arms. And then like some monster train crashing into gear, they came rolling through the road block – five, ten, 20, 30 and more coaches full of Leeds fans, happily celebrating and heading to all parts of the country, safe in the knowledge that the promotion push was well and truly gaining impetus. Four successive wins and not a goal conceded.

I love playing at lunchtime when we have won, because it means I can put my feet up and watch *Soccer Saturday* without too much stress. I suppose it can get a bit troubling when teams we are challenging against seem to be doing well, but as long as we have won it's almost like a free hit, so I am fairly chilled. This afternoon works well for us, because although Fulham win, Brentford drop points at Cardiff, and WBA go and do what we did and amazingly lose at home to battling Wigan. It's a crazy stat, but I hear somewhere that Wigan have won only three away games in a year – at Leeds twice, and West Brom.

Suddenly that six-point lead the Albion had over us after the game at Brentford is down to just one, and we maintain our five-point lead over Fulham, which is effectively six given our better goal difference. What a crazy league this is, and it's Huddersfield up next for us – a side who always raise their game for a trip to their big city neighbours.

We have a busy week before the 'Terriers' come to town. I am back to London for a couple of days, and Andy is flying to Dublin to catch up with Mike, Lou, and the grandchildren. When I was in full time work, I often used to hear retired people say stuff like, 'I don't know how I ever found the time to go to work' – and now I am one of those people, though I have long since dismissed the word 'retired'. For me, it smacks of growing old and giving up on life, and I am most certainly not interested in doing that.

I have long since replaced the 'R' word with the 'O' word... Opportunity. The opportunity and freedom to follow different pursuits, head to new places, enjoy new experiences, and sometimes just to do the stuff you couldn't do when the alarm clock woke you up at 6am every day – like staying up through the night watching Test cricket, or the Masters. I would also include watching American football, but no matter how hard I try, and I've stayed up through the night on a number of occasions, I simply can't get this as any kind of 'sport'. With the exception of the obvious skill of the quarterback, it really just seems to provide a great chance to showcase some fantastic pop music during the interminable breaks for adverts. This week, I 'm meeting up with other colleagues involved in the interview process to appoint a senior member of staff to the school. I also have some training to do, so I am staying at the Leonardo Royal Hotel in St. Paul's, for a couple of nights. This kind of commitment also provides the chance to meet up with James and Andrew again, and we have a lively reunion once the work is done.

I have been involved in loads of different activities and initiatives since 'retiring' as a headteacher, mostly revolving round education, as you would expect. Such 'consultancy' work has proven to be quite varied and interesting, and provided me with not just an opportunity to use my experience to support others, but also a useful top-up to the teachers' pension. Those educational stories are for another time, as are some of the rather bizarre happenings I experienced while interviewing others or being interviewed myself. One of the things I am reasonably proud of is that when applying for jobs in education, I almost always got called for interview, and over my career found I managed to be offered the posts I'd applied for more often than not.

I have only ever applied for two jobs outside of education, and in both cases my application came to naught, but for two very different reasons. I applied for a medical reps job when I had been teaching for about four years, attracted by a bigger salary and a company car. I met a guy in some coffee shop at an initial interview and must have impressed in some way, because he rang me later and invited me to a formal interview at some hotel in Leeds. I chatted the pros and cons through with Andy and also my mum. Andy was fine about it all, seeing it, like me, as an opportunity to develop a new and more financially lucrative career. Mum was not so supportive, worrying that I was giving up on a vocation that was much more important than just a job, and would live to regret it. There must have been something in her words that troubled me, and after a few restless nights I decided to withdraw from the interview. This is not always such an easy thing to do, as I have found on other occasions when involved in the interview process. The problem is the competitive juices start to flow, and in the end proving you are the best person for the job becomes almost more important than the job itself. The second position I applied for came shortly after I had 'retired', and for me it was the perfect opportunity, the job of my dreams, and I spent a long time poring over every detail of the job spec. The job I applied for was as an Assistant Kit Man at Leeds United.

The family thought this was hilarious, especially given my age and dodgy knees. In truth, I could see the 'knees' could be a problem, if part of the interview process involved running, but I actually felt my age – 60 at the time – would be a real plus, indicating a man of experience and one who could be trusted to keep any dressing room gossip totally private. The more I thought about it, the more I convinced myself I was just the man the club were looking for. I can't remember what the salary was, but given my teachers' pension, I would have done it for nothing just to be involved in the world of professional sport and my beloved Leeds United.

I took ages composing my letter of application, trying to highlight any part of my professional experiences that might be relevant. Obviously, the world of headship doesn't easily equate to that of an 'assistant kit man', but surely there were transferable skills: the ability to work independently yet be part of a wider team; organisational skills; tact and diplomacy; bloody hard graft; and accountability. It was made for me. I spent quite a bit of my application highlighting my coaching skills and awards and mentioning my work with adult teams as well as the coaching I'd done in schools. I even mentioned my goal against the 'Leeds former players team' and the fact I'd played against Spurs, QPR, and Fulham, when I was a student. So, here was a mature man with certain proven skills, dependable, trustworthy, hard working, and successful, with some significant achievements in his working career. I read through my letter of application and felt it was just about right and ticked all the boxes we were invited to address in the details of the post provided by the club.

Happy that I would be hearing from the club sometime soon, offering me the chance to expand on my letter with a more formal interview, I clicked on 'send' and off it went, winging its way no doubt to Angus Kinnear's personal 'in tray'. I guess Angus must have been pretty busy, because I never heard another thing about it, not even a 'thanks but no thanks' response. I was devastated and still couldn't quite understand why everyone I related the story to, both friends and family, just started laughing when I explained what I had done and how pissed off I was that I hadn't had any kind of response from the club.

I must admit a little time later I did re-read my letter of application and felt perhaps it was just maybe a tad over the top. My kids told me not to worry about the rejection and made it worse by suggesting at least it would have given the people charged with drawing up the shortlist a good laugh. Not helpful.

A few games later, standing behind the goal at some ground somewhere in the country, I noticed a new figure supporting the players on the field. He was quite young, maybe late twenties to early thirties, and he had a ponytail. He was handing out water bottles and collecting footballs, and as the players finished their warm-ups and headed back to the changing room, they smiled at him and acknowledged his work as he started to collect in discarded cones and footballs. He was obviously one of them, a part of the team, and he probably had no clue or even the slightest bit of interest in the fact that he had my chuffing job.

I travelled back to the north first class on an LNER service. I hadn't done this before, but as the tickets had been booked for me by the school and everyone else in the team travelled that way, I decided the days of saving them all money by getting the cheapest ticket available and using my senior persons' railcard were definitely over. I had always found expenses a tricky area and used to be gobsmacked at Heads' conferences how so many used their 'school debit cards' to buy rounds of drinks for their cronies. I never felt comfortable doing this, preferring to spend my own money and thus get the first round before the full group had assembled. I guess it was down to my days at St. Joseph's, where every penny mattered and there wasn't a budget heading for 'Head's expenses'! Interestingly, the Heads who often seemed to be first to spend their school's money appeared to me to be the ones to have the deepest insecurity issues. Apart from a rather obvious need to be noticed, this was also manifested in the fact that they also seemed to wear a kind of 'Head's uniform', consisting of exactly the same checked sports jacket in a range of autumnal colours, with a checked shirt, garish tie, and either brown, green, or maroon corduroy trousers, depending of course on the colour of said jacket.

I guess we all like to belong at some time in our lives, and I can distinctly remember the days when I had to be seen in my Levi jeans and jackets (and, of course, heading to fixtures in club colours), but I never much wanted to belong to the 'insecure Heads' club, much preferring my individuality and having the confidence to run with it.

We are what we are, and my eldest son Michael has on occasion been ragged in the family for being too 'rah'; he runs with the joke and often plays up to it. But he was in no doubt where he wanted to have his 'stag do', and that's why he and shedloads of his friends – mainly, though not exclusively, having some link to Exeter University and its rugby teams – caught the train from Kings Cross to Leeds one busy Friday night. The tickets had been booked for ages, but as can happen there was some mix-up, and as the train prepared to set off it became apparent that some seats had been double-booked. The man in charge tried to resolve the situation by offering seats in first class to people who found themselves in the same carriage as Mike and his pals, who it must be said were highly charming and great fun. What was lovely, and a real tribute to their humour and friendship, was that a number – it has to be said, all female – turned down the upgrade to enjoy the ride with Mike, now dressed as a giant chicken, and his friends.

James, our youngest, was Mike's appointed best man, and would later perform brilliantly and very humorously in making his best man's speech at the wedding. But he had also arranged much of the 'Stag', using his local knowledge of the city hotspots, picked up while at university in the city. He had also arranged a visit to ER with tickets in the Kop for all the stag group for our game against Huddersfield Town. By the time we got to the match, Mike had shed his giant chicken outfit, replacing it with full Leeds kit, and of course by the time 3pm came round, a number of beers had been sunk. I had met them earlier and was going to spend the day with them, which finished with a double-header rugby international Six Nations games, with the late kick-off being France v England, before I took my leave and they all hit the clubs. I decided not to sit with them, especially as they were much more at home in rugby grounds and spent a lot of the matches doing shuttle runs to the bars and back. I guessed they would pretty soon get bored with singing 'Marching on together' and didn't want my enjoyment of the match being disturbed by their fun and antics. James popped up before kick-off to say hello to his friends and explained what was happening, and why he was sitting further down in the Kop. I could just about see them if I stood on my seat and was happy I wasn't surrounded by them. The chap I sat next to said he'd had a text from one of his mates in the Kop who said, 'There's some' right rah pillocks' in front of me, and one of them is dressed up as a Leeds player.' I pretended I didn't hear him. After the game (we lost 4-1 that day, if memory serves me right), we all headed into Leeds, and during the ensuing hours I realised what a fabulous bunch of blokes these guys were. Intelligent, kind, respectful, charming, and very funny; we had a great time before I bowed out at about 11pm and left them to it.

Leeds United…2; Huddersfield Town…0
Saturday, 7th March

And so back to ER, and the visitors are once again Huddersfield. I'm certainly not expecting a repeat of that 1-4 drubbing today, particularly as we are on such a good run and the performance last week at Hull, especially in the second half, was outstanding. We are again missing Phillips, who has been struggling with injury for a few weeks now, and Baradi comes into the defence to allow Ben White to once again take up the Phillips role. Roberts, after his brace at the KCOM, finds himself back on the bench, along with Douglas, Alioski, and Shackleton. Neither of our January transfer signings are included, which looks like fairly disastrous business in terms of them making the immediate impact we needed to replace Nketiah and, to a lesser extent, Clarke.

The Covid pandemic that started in China in December has now begun to impact on our country, and while none of us there felt the slightest panic or fear, the players themselves showed some acknowledgment of the disease by missing out their traditional pre-match handshake.

It doesn't take the team long to ease our nerves against traditionally difficult opponents who have arrived in good form, having secured back-to-back wins in previous matches. Harrison attacks down the left and swings a long ball across the area for Ayling, running in at pace, to volley in his stride into the top corner. It's a brilliant strike and sets the crowd buzzing, and while Huddersfield work hard, we continue to dominate with Costa and Bamford going close. We eventually seal the win when White forces a brilliant save from the Town keeper and Bamford, quickest to react, runs in to fire home. Harrison then hits the post with a stunning strike, almost the same in every way as the one he executed at Hull last week.

Ayling survived a penalty appeal as Town rallied towards the end, but it would have been a harsh award if given, and the crowd celebrate a fifth win on the trot and a fifth clean sheet. I didn't even get stressed as we approached the final whistle. Just like last week, there was no way we were going to lose this game once we had scored the second goal.

It's a big win for us and results elsewhere make it even better, with Fulham drawing, and WBA also dropping points at Swansea. It means that we have clawed back Albion's six-point lead and head the table by a point – seven points clear of Fulham in third, and 11 clear of Brentford and Forest, in fourth and fifth respectively. And it is then that the Coronavirus smashed into our world, wrecking lives, destroying the economy, and bringing heartache and fear to the country.

CHAPTER 16

BACK TO THE FUTURE, THE SEASON RESUMES AND THE 'BECK' DEVELOPMENT IS FINISHED!

Wednesday, 17th June

It seems a long time now since, on 27th March, with the season halted and the country in lockdown, I wrote my last entry. Much has happened in the intervening period, and it is fair to say that the country has been devastated by the Coronavirus with, as I write, 42,153 deaths relating to the virus being recorded.

With hindsight, it seems amazing that after the win against Huddersfield and with the virus already among us – and against our children's wishes – I was planning how to get to the game in Cardiff and Andy was preparing to do a week's supply teaching. It's symptomatic about how this virus crept up on us, before unleashing its terror, that at first so many, including me, couldn't quite understand what was happening, couldn't quite comprehend the seriousness of the situation we were all in. That would change pretty quickly over the next weeks and months, as the virus took hold, the death toll rose, and the country suffered. Where to start to try and fill in the gaps between that last game at ER and our planned visit on Sunday to play at Cardiff behind closed doors?

This book is not a social history of the period. It's not a political inquisition or a medical investigation; it's a book about supporting a football team, and it's not my place to describe the timeline of the virus and how it wreaked its devastation throughout the country. What I can say is that there will be a time in the future when questions can be asked and hopefully answers given as to just how well we reacted to the threat of the virus, and how well we were led by the government and other politicians charged with the responsibility of supporting our communities.

There will rightly be questions asked about how prepared we were to handle such a pandemic, one that had been widely predicted. There will be questions asked about the lack of personal protection equipment (PPE), particularly for key workers in the NHS, and the time it took to establish widespread and accurate testing for the illness. There are going to be questions asked about the support for care homes and the way in which patients were apparently discharged from hospitals to return to such homes, taking the virus with them.

The government will rightly be challenged and judged on how they handled the pandemic, and so will the opposition parties – one of whom, Labour, elected their new leader Sir Keir Starmer on 4th April. There seemed to me to be a real danger that, despite a pledge from Starmer to work with the government to beat the virus, party politics began to emerge and damage the country even more as the crisis deepened. Perhaps, being an educationalist, one of the areas in which this seemed most pronounced revolved around the proposed reopening of schools and the hysterical reaction of trade unions and opposition parties to such announcements.

It was clear from their response that this was a dangerous, almost cavalier approach, putting the lives of children and teachers at risk. The pressure seemed relentless, but then when the government withdrew the plans, there was a similar outcry about 'U-turns' and the great harm that continued school closures were doing to our children's mental health. It seemed whatever direction the government tried to take, at some stage it would be hijacked by someone somewhere. It was the same with the 'confusion' apparently caused by the changed messaging, as the government began to move towards an easing of lockdown. I mean, can anyone seriously claim they don't understand what 'Stay Alert' means?

As previously mentioned, I have voted at different times for all the main political parties, so I was massively disappointed that at a time when our politicians needed to be coming together to support us all, to look after us, they were as always seeking to undermine each other and cause mistrust and division. There will need to be a time when a proper assessment is made of what was done well – in my view, the daily news conferences, Nightingale hospitals, and the furlough programme; and also what we struggled with – the timing of the lockdown, PPE, and testing – will need to be reviewed, so that as a country we can learn from our mistakes and be more prepared the next time such a horrible illness strikes us.

If the politicians seemed to undermine and cause confusion with mixed messages, this was nothing compared to the media, through the press and particularly the major news stations, BBC, ITV, and Sky. They seemed to broadcast a message of unrelenting gloom and appeared only interested, as always, in undermining the country by constantly attacking government policy. I started to impose my own 'self isolation' from the evening news and found it quite reassuring when a Sky/YouGov poll, published on 23rd April, showed the press and media to be by far the least trusted organisations in the opinion of the public.

I have no feelings for Dominic Cummings and certainly, initially, I felt he should have resigned or be sacked after he left London to take his sick wife and child to Durham to potentially self isolate. That is until I saw the 'press pack' gathered outside his home. How on earth could anyone criticise him for protecting his family from the awful gaggle of humanity camped outside his front door, shouting out, and jostling him and each other to get the best film footage or picture? And incidentally, as highhanded as the media felt about Cumming's actions, taking absolutely no notice of safe distancing guidance. I think he was absolutely right to take his sick family as far away from that awful group as soon as he possibly could. That he chose to drive to Durham and then take his family out for the day on a supposed 'practice drive' was clearly wrong and against the spirit of his own employer's guidance. Cummings should have resigned, but so should some of the editors and news producers who allowed their journalists to behave so horribly.

I honestly feel at the end of this pandemic, when performances are reviewed, if the politicians are quite rightly held to task, then so too should the various news stations and particularly the producers and journalists who promote the style and philosophy they have adopted. They have such an important service to provide in reporting the news openly and without bias, and have such a huge platform, beaming their message into all our homes on such a regular basis. They have very badly let us down and should face some kind of parliamentary enquiry or questioning on the way they have misused their powers to cause such worry and unease, especially among those perhaps unable to see beyond their biased and, at times, ghoulish reporting.

While as a country we struggled to deal with the impact of the virus, we suddenly became embroiled in another huge and emotive issue when, following the callous and horrific murder of George Floyd by a policeman in America, the Black Lives Matter movement launched marches of protest across the UK. These protests highlighted not only the gruesome murder of George Floyd, but also issues of racism and inequality felt by black people across the world.

I have already touched on some of these problems in relation to football, and there is simply no doubt that we as a country need to look into our hearts and minds to come up with a fairer, more inclusive society. In my opinion, we are all created equally, and the colour of our skin should not be a barrier to what we can achieve as people living and working side by side with each other in our communities. Education, as always, must be at the heart of change, and change that is not hijacked by extremists, black or white, on the right or left, who only wish to cause disharmony and chaos.

I honestly believe the death of George Floyd does not have to be in vain, and can be the stimulus needed for us to create the very real change required to make our country a fairer and more equal society, where a person is identified and valued for their spirit, decency, and contribution to the community, rather than by the colour of their skin or their religious beliefs.

As Dr Martin Luther King said in his famous speech, delivered in 1963 in Washington, 'I have a dream that my four little children will one day live in a nation where they will not be judged by the colour of their skin but by the content of their character.'

In terms of sport, as the pandemic raged event after event was postponed: the Euros, the Olympics, the Masters golf, and Wimbledon. The list was endless, and throughout the lockdown many followed the poor example of Karren Brady by trying to use the media to promote their views, almost exclusively dripping with self interest. Brighton's Glen Murray, Aston Villa's Tyrone Mings, and someone high up at Norwich City who reckoned to have once been a season ticket holder at Leeds, all came out calling for the league to be 'voided', or at the very least for there to be no relegation.

Not surprisingly, given that his club are in freefall towards League One, the owner of Hull City also claimed it was not safe to return and that the league should be cancelled, even at a time when other owners like Steve Parish at Crystal Palace said that training at his club was safer than going to the supermarket.

Sky pundits like Gary Neville seemed to be making proclamations about literally everything and anything. And while he often talks good sense, you can very much have too much of a good thing. Others, like Jamie Redknapp – more lightweight than Neville and less cerebral – waded in with his thoughts that there should be no relegation. So, no family connections with West Ham then! And Robbie Savage, writing in the *Daily Mail*, endeared himself to all Leeds fans by suggesting we should be promoted. I think we all started to feel more secure about final conclusions when it became clear the FA wanted the season to be finished on merit, with promotion and relegation. However, it was eventually curtailed.

I must admit my own view was that to 'void' a season after so many games have been played seemed to be rewarding failure and penalising success. So, Liverpool would be denied the title and Norwich, who clearly deserved to be relegated, would be saved, denying Leeds,

WBA, or any other Championship team, their promotion dream. With every day that passed, there seemed to be another view, another opinion, but gradually as the lockdown began to be eased across Europe, a picture began to emerge that was quite positive for all us Leeds fans. The Dutch league finished on 24th April, the season just unaccountably cancelled with no champions and no relegation or promotion. Four days later, the French league also came to an end, but this time PSG were declared champions and there was relegation and promotion, the season being decided on points per game.

The same decision was taken in Scotland, while the Italian, Spanish, and English leagues declared an intent to finish all matches behind closed doors and even, if necessary, at neutral venues. The German Bundesliga restarted on 16th May, and two days later it was confirmed that Celtic would be Champions of the SPFL, with clubs relegated and promoted. The Premier League announced its return from the 17th June and the Championship from 20th of June. It looked like we were back in business and, should there be any reason now that games could not be completed, then it was confirmed PPG would be used to decide final positions. We couldn't have asked for any more and at least now our fate would be in our own hands.

The club throughout, unlike many others, had behaved with great dignity and common sense. And while some fans would have taken promotion by PPG, it was right and proper that the club voted – as they had consistently said they would – to finish the league on the pitch. The lockdown was finally being eased and football at last would be played again, though sadly fans would not be able to watch live games, which would all be played behind closed doors. The idea of games being staged at neutral venues seemed to have quietly disappeared. During the lockdown, the country discovered new heroes almost daily, with the selfless bravery of those working in hospitals and care homes recognised weekly when neighbourhoods came out to clap, play instruments, and generally celebrate and show support for these key workers.

One of those who literally walked the extra mile to show his support was Captain Tom Moore, a 99-year-old former soldier, who decided in the days leading up to his 100 birthday to try and raise a £1000 by walking laps of his garden to raise funds for NHS charities. Tom's spirit, character, and refusal to give in, caught the mood of the country and by the time his challenge was over, as he reached his centenary, he had raised over £30million – an incredible sum, an incredible achievement, and an incredible man. Along the way, Tom also became the oldest man to have a No. 1 single when his version of *You'll Never Walk Alone*, accompanied by Michael Ball, topped the charts. His birthday and his indomitable spirit were honoured by a fly-past by the Royal Air Force and his appointment to the position of Honorary Colonel of the Army Foundation College. He received over 150,000 birthday cards from a grateful public, who recognised in his achievement an almost spiritual link between those dark but ultimately successful days of the Second World War, where the bravery and sacrifice of so many saved the nation, and the present dangerous times. Colonel Tom received his final and most fitting accolade, when on 19th May, his award of a knighthood was announced – an honour that would be conferred on him by the Queen in a special ceremony at Windsor Castle.

Up and down the country, families discovered 'Zoom' was not just a way that businesses could keep in touch, and we regularly chatted with the kids and made silly noises down the line to our grandchildren, who responded in like fashion. We started off with quizzes for a few weeks and then, bored of those, moved to a theme of Desert Island Discs, and had great fun all choosing songs from different genres. At the end of the evening, James would create a new playlist and send them to us all on Spotify. We made some great playlists, including best Tamla, best solo artist, best songs from the films, and so on. Lots of people embarked on fitness regimes and Joe Wicks became regular viewing for millions. I created my own version of the fitness instructor's programme, calling it 'Dancethon', which meant I basically chose loud music like *Satisfaction*, *Addicted to Love*, and *Town Called Malice*, and danced around the living room, running up stairs, and doing standing exercises when I was too knackered to dance. I tried to do this for at least half an hour a couple of times a week, and went cycling as well if the weather was good, which amazingly it was through most of lockdown.

Some people started new projects, trying to learn a new language or a musical instrument, and others threw themselves into gardening and home DIY. Hopeless at DIY, I threw myself into this writing project, catching up with notes I had been making throughout the season and deciding to put them together in this book. Andy on the other hand, who worked so hard throughout the year at developing her excellent Spanish, decided to close all her books and climb over the fence at the back of our garden to try and tidy up the bank of land which led to the beck which divided our land from the farmer's field at the other side.

At first, she was just weeding and digging up loads of old brick and broken fragments of pot and general rubbish. There were already one or two plants that I had put in under sufferance a few years ago, and she managed to find a few bits of limestone that looked really good and placed them round the flowers. Both of our neighbours had removed their fences and let their gardens run straight down to the Beck. They were both former design and technology teachers and had the talent and skill to create stone bankings that made quite a feature of their gardens. I didn't have this ability and knew it, so l let Andy soldier on, occasionally making her a cuppa and admiring her work before running back inside to my writing. Nigel, the neighbour to our left, let Andy know he had seen loads of limestone dumped at one end of a farmer's field, and we made trip after trip, heaving these large stones into the boot of the car and ferrying them back for use in the 'project'.

Gradually, after several weeks of hard work, the banking began to resemble a rockery, and in the evenings when we enjoyed a chat and a drink, we discussed how she could develop the rockery still further. The problem was that for all her hard work, and the fact that the wild and overgrown banking was being turned into an attractive rockery, we just couldn't see or enjoy it because of the blooming fence.

This had always been an issue for me, with Andy keen for me to strim the bank on the other side of the beck, as both our neighbours did. For them, it made perfect sense, as they sat on fine nights with a drink looking out over the beck into the farmer's field and beyond. For me, it was a frigging nightmare, and a real pain doing battle with a temperamental strimmer which was forever cutting out, and wallowing in the muddy waters of the beck with water cascading over the sides of my 'waders' and drowning my feet. And what exactly was the point as we couldn't see anything anyway?

So, it had been a contentious issue between us, but now this new project offered us an opportunity to finally discuss a solution to the problem. We could take the fence down completely – something neither of us was keen to do – or we could put a gate in it and create some kind of access to the rockery so Andy could work more easily than she was able to do at the moment. Eventually, after a couple of weeks mulling things over which gave us the time to ferry even more limestone rocks in, we decided on the gate option and invited Oliver (the builder who had helped us redevelop the house) to see what he could do about access. The beauty of having worked with him over so many years is that we knew his skills and he knew we knew what we wanted, especially Andy, for this was indisputably her project.

I think he came up with a great idea, which was to put some wooden steps down the bank from top to bottom and then put a fairly substantial plank in place to link the bank at our side to the one at the other by the farmer's field. This would allow me quicker access with my strimmer, which at the moment I had to carry half a mile round the village to the nearest beck crossing point – not an easy walk in waders, carrying the blessed strimmer and the oil or juice, or whatever the liquid it guzzled up far too quickly was called.

It also gave Andy another idea – let's call it 'Beck Development phase three', which involved her putting grass seed down on the farmer's side in an attempt to make that side look more like a lawn than the rough land it actually was. This led inexorably to plan four, which involved buying a cheap lawnmower to keep it looking better than a strimmer could do. We were beginning to take over the field, and Andy's rockery was gaining lots of positive comments from the many villagers who wandered down to see what the hell was going on. As I carried on writing and Oliver's work came to fruition, Andy – grateful for once again being able to go to the local garden centre – planted more and more shrubs and flowers, making the rockery look more like a 'Magic Garden.' And then suddenly it was finished – or at least, I thought it was – and so we planned an opening ceremony, with the neighbours sitting on the far bank and admiring Andy's fantastic creation.

But there was still something not quite right, still one last problem to solve, and this time it involved me and my DIY skills. It obviously was not my idea, as I was a fairly reluctant worker on the project and keen not to wreck things. Thus far, I had been employed as a labourer, just lugging great chunks of stone here and there, and I was relatively happy doing this and not being challenged by having to make any technical contribution. The problem revolved around an idea being discussed at length by Andy, Nigel, Oliver, and Mike, our neighbour on the other side. The discussion involved the six-inch drop from the last wooden step into the water, and how the gap could be made: A) safer; and B) more attractive, to fit in with the brilliantly rustic look Oliver had already created.

I listened intently to the debate, slightly in awe of the technical excellence of what was being proposed. And feeling a lot out of my depth, I volunteered to make the tea. When I returned, Nigel had gone, and Andy seemed convinced he was going to help put the plan into action. The plan was essentially to dig all the silt from the bottom of the beck – at least two feet of the stuff – and when the hard rock underneath all this grunge was eventually reached, place very large limestone rocks on the bottom of the beck. This would then provide a level foundation to build up a wall of rock to reach the bottom step that ultimately would allow Andy to cover it in soil and plant trailing flowers to complete the project.

No problems. Except that Andy had clearly misunderstood Nigel, who returned to ask how we were getting on. It was in that moment that I realised, looking at Andy and Nigel and Oliver and Mike, that despite all their technical 'nous' and 'know-how', it was going to be me who would be donning waders and digging all the shit up from the bottom of the beck. I had a fleeting memory of a dead mouse caught in a trap that we had once given a 'Viking burial' to by slinging the trap in the beck because neither of us could face taking the poor thing out of it. I had meant to throw the trap into the field, but it hit the branch of an overhanging tree and dropped straight into the beck roughly where I was standing now listening to all these frigging experts telling me what to do. It would be absolutely my luck to trigger the bloody trap and take my finger off.

I was very unhappy and began to sulk badly, swearing profusely under my breath. Mike leaned forward and gave me a bucket with holes in the bottom with which I could scoop up the muck and rubbish and mouse traps on the bottom of the beck. I stared at him, unable to speak for fear of the words that might shoot out of my mouth.

The water stank as I started on my task, and as I leaned over my face was getting far too close to the surface of the water, which was already filling my waders and swirling around my ankles. Eventually, as the 'advisers' chatted and drank my frigging tea, offering helpful suggestions that I had to bite my lip not to respond to, I hit hard rock. Oliver and Nigel somehow managed to get a huge piece of limestone down to the last step so they could pass it to me to lay the foundation stone. It was so heavy it nearly took me down to the bottom with it, but joyously as it left my freezing fingers it settled at a reasonably level angle, and from thereon it was a fairly easy task to build up the wall in the way that the 'technical support' team had suggested, but more importantly that met with Andy's smile of approval.

It was done. Wet through, covered in muck, freezing, and smelling like a sewer, I smiled the look of someone who was just about to have a tooth extracted and, checking that all was accomplished, brushed past the team and headed back to my writing via a deep, hot, Radox bath.

The drinks party was a great success, and as more and more villagers began to hear of the project and take their daily exercise by walking along the farmer's field to view it, we both realised that by retaining the fence we had also gone a long way to maintaining our privacy. We'd also created a barrier so the grandkids didn't go flying straight down the garden and straight into the beck.

I raised a glass and toasted Andy for her vision and work ethic in creating this wonderful 'Magic Garden,' and couldn't help adding through clenched teeth a toast to the 'technical team' who I just know had had such fun watching me thrashing about in the water, cursing and swearing, and realising just how incompetent, inept, and bloody miserable I was feeling. Chuffing DIY. Chuffing neighbours!

The nation has suffered so much in these lockdown months: families separated from each other; children away from their friends and the important stimulus of education; parents worried about finance, jobs, and security; and of course, the horrific death toll that has affected so many families.

As a football club, Leeds suffered, too, with the untimely deaths of two legends of the club – Norman Hunter and Trevor Cherry. Trevor passed away on 29th April, just a few weeks after Norman, his old teammate. He was signed for the club by Don Revie in 1972, and went onto captain the club and make 486 appearances, scoring 24 goals. My memories of his great times at Leeds are not as clear as the ones I have for Norman, mainly because he joined the club at a time when I was heading away down to London and college. He was playing with Huddersfield, his home town club, during much of my teenage years, when supporting Leeds became a welcome distraction from the worry and implications of exams failure and growing up generally. I obviously watched the team as often as possible during the college years, but I was committed to playing myself, and as my dad said, 'Play for as long as you can. There will be time enough to watch football when you have finished.' And he was dead right. By the time I had left college and started my teaching career, I was playing twice a week and coaching two teams midweek to earn extra money through nightschool. There wasn't that much time left to go to ER. but I followed the team as much as I could in the news and on *Match of the Day* and Yorkshire Television.

I do remember seeing Trevor break through the Manchester City defence, scoring a winning goal in a tense FA Cup game at Elland Road, and of course he will be forever linked with that 'famous' FA

Cup moment when Jim Montgomery saved impossibly from Peter Lorimer following Trevor's initial header. Every time I see that incident, I pray that as the ball comes back off the crossbar Trevor, lying on the floor, will score as he flicks his boot up at the ball. Sadly, he doesn't, but he had some great days in the all-white shirt and probably none better or more important than when he marked Johan Cruyff out of both legs of the European Cup semi-final in 1975. At the time, Cruyff was probably the best player in the world, and the fact that Trevor could keep him quiet for two games reflected hugely on his importance to the team and his own high level playing ability, which was rewarded and recognised by the fact that he made 27 appearances for England. He was just 72 when he died; like so many in this pandemic, far too young to leave this world.

Norman's passing affected me in the same way Billy's had years earlier. It was just like losing a friend, and I wrote the following words about him when I heard of his untimely death at the age of 76 on April 17th, at the very height of this awful pandemic.

Fulham gets a makeover

Andrew James and Josh in Japan

All Mike are we

Mike travels Chicken Class to Leeds !

James and Andrea on the Leeds train

FCOFF WhatsApp Zoom champions

Centenary celebrations

James and Kath at Cardiff

I could have saved it! Great view at Brentford.

James celebrates in Wandsworth

Celebrations in Sussex

FCOFF celebrations in Bishop's Stortford

Kath and Mike enjoy the moment

With the boys at Christmas

CHAPTER 17

NORMAN

17th April, 2020

It's the middle of April and a month into lockdown, and listening to the scientists and health advisers, it seems we are approaching the peak of this awful pandemic. There are constant updates on *Sky Sports News*, including sadly, details of former players who are unwell. Kenny Dalglish and Jimmy Greaves have both been poorly, but thankfully are reported to be recovering.

Then today, a beautiful spring morning, I had been messing with jobs, getting the coal in, trying to get the bloody strimmer to start, etc, and hadn't turned the telly on or checked for messages before sitting down about 11am with a coffee. Then I saw it, a message on WhatsApp from James: 'Poor Norman Hunter. So sad. RIP Norman.'

I immediately felt a sense of loss, even though I had never met Norman, never been nearer to him than being a fan in the stands watching him play. It was exactly the same when Billy Bremner died; I felt as though I had lost a dear friend or family member. I have never been one of those football fans who cry at grounds when things go wrong for their team, however upsetting, and I totally get the pain as with the play-off loss to Derby. After all, these are sporting events.

But when people I have loved very much have died – my mum and dad, my grandpa, and Trish my sister-in-law – I have usually gone somewhere I could be alone and sobbed, privately saying my farewells and remembering special moments I have shared with them. I am sure some psychologists could come up with a reason for my very real sadness for the loss of a man I have never met, but I think I understand my reaction, or at least I think I can explain it. I was, as I have mentioned earlier, just ten when I first saw Leeds on that Boxing Day in 1964, and as I got older into my teens, I would travel to Elland Rd on my own or with Chris. It was a straightforward journey, service bus to Morley and then pick up the Leeds bus, which in those days stopped right outside the old Greyhound Stadium, now the new headquarters of the Leeds Constabulary.

Chris would usually come to the weekend games, but his family expected a greater commitment to his studies than mine did, so I often travelled to those midweek games on my own. I grew up with Billy and the team, and their names still just roll off my tongue: Sprake, Reaney, Cooper, Bremner, Charlton, Hunter, Lorimer, Clarke, Jones, Giles, Gray, Madeley. And though they never knew me and they didn't know it, they helped me through some tricky growing years, particularly my anxiety around a fairly unsuccessful academic school life, and later, in the early seventies, my parents' divorce.

So often in my teens, faced with the option of Latin homework or some revision tests ahead of exams, I took the easy way, put my books down (well, slightly untrue; I never really picked them up!), and headed off to Elland Rd. I knew it was probably the wrong choice, especially as 'O' levels got increasingly closer, and it certainly was a bit stupid to head out on a freezing night to watch some replay against a lower league club. But well, it was my escape from the reality of the failure my laziness was inexorably leading me to.

Leeds United, the Beatles, Paul Simon, Dylan, Tamla Motown, all made life a bit more bearable and helped push all thoughts of my impending day of reckoning to the back of my mind, at least for an hour or two. The really great thing was that they were always there, striding onto the pitch in the fabulous all-white kit, tearing the opposition to shreds, playing such incisive football, led by the genius of Bremner, Giles, and Gray. And so they became my friends, someone to lean on when times were tough, someone to cheer me up, someone to read about, and now someone to write about!

That friendship has never left me. Yes, the players have changed over the years and we have definitely had our good days and bad days, but all these years later I still get the same feeling of excitement, same feeling of escape, getting ready to head to ER which itself has become a good friend. Whatever happens in the end this year, whether we are promoted or not, when the good times eventually return, I pray we won't make the mistake of Arsenal in ruining their spiritual home. Develop Elland Rd, as has been the case over the years, but don't take the soul out of the club.

Which brings me back to Norman, whose spirit and ability will always be revered by Leeds fans wherever they are. The papers today are full of tributes to him, many leading on his 'bites yer legs' legend, his hard man reputation, and his huge importance to the Revie team. My own memories are of his very real ability and his class. He could do pretty much anything: defend obviously, but he could pass the ball well and when he got forward, he had a hell of a shot. He had a style all of his own, slightly stooped but in no way ungainly, and he was along with George Best and Mick Jones one of the few players I tried to model myself on. I was never a defender really, always preferring to play up front, but once playing in a friendly game where I was by far the youngest member of the team, I was pushed into a back four and decided I would be Norman. In my mind, for that match I was him, and I must have impressed as following the game I was invited to join a team from a much higher division! I remember his huge leap of celebration when Allan Clarke scored the goal that won us the cup in 1972, captured brilliantly by a cameraman at the far end of the ground. But for some reason, I remember above all a goal he scored in one of those midweek games I went to when I should have been at home working. The game was an Inter-Cities Fairs Cup match against Hanover on a dark Wednesday night in December 1968. We had already established a first leg lead with a 2-1 win in Germany, so there should have been little danger of defeat. That was reflected in a crowd of only 25,000 or so, as I guess most people were saving their money for Christmas – or probably revising for exams!

We won the game comfortably, eventually running out 5-1 winners, with goals by Lorimer (2), Jack Charlton, and Mike O'Grady. But the first goal, and the one I remember, was scored by Norman. Driving forward from the halfway line, he simply unleashed an incredible left foot, long distance shot that flew into the net at what is now known as the South Stand. It was a brilliant strike and one of the goals I saw which is forever seared into my mind. It will be my lasting memory of Norman the player – hard yes, but hugely talented, an England international, and a linchpin of the Leeds defence for over 700 games.

I have memories of Norman away from the pitch, and even though I never met him I think I know the kind of man he was. When I was a student in the 1970s, I played in the British Colleges football tournament, which was a competition held in the early part of the Easter holiday. It was arranged a little bit on the lines of a World Cup, with group winners ultimately playing out the semi-finals and final, and quite a prestigious event, attracting the best college student football teams in the UK. In keeping with the level of football, the tournament also attracted top class referees, and one of them was David Smith who had refereed our 1972 Cup final win over Arsenal. My own college, St Mary's Twickenham, had played above ourselves to reach and win the third and fourth place final, and it was a double celebration as Leeds were the reigning champions and on their way to a European Cup Final appearance. I was getting showered after the game and looking forward to the presentations and celebrations, when Referee Smith noticed the Leeds beanie I had worn on my way to the showers. He said something like, 'You don't support that lot, do you?'

We had a good chat about what it was like to ref Leeds, and I have to say when I mentioned various players his answers were not exactly full of warmth and admiration. However, when I tentatively mentioned Norman, he changed his mood and simply said, 'Ah Norman, a gentleman.'

Years later, as I prepared to retire from my post of Headteacher at Berkhamsted Prep, I was given a card and gift by the Harrison family. As mentioned earlier when we had travelled with Miles, Mike, and James, to the Forest match, Miles had begun his career in sports broadcasting in Leeds and often covered matches at Elland Rd for Radio Leeds, and he still had a number of friends and contacts in the north. When I opened the wrapping paper, I saw that they had bought me a Leeds shirt, which was lovely. But when I opened it up, written on the front was a message to me:

'To Adrian... Mr Taylor... The Gaffer, best wishes, and signed Norman Hunter 'bites yer legs'!

Today that shirt is framed and hanging in my study, and every time I go in there I will be reminded of Norman, a hugely talented athlete, but more importantly a lovely man and a real gentleman.

CHAPTER 18

THE RESTART, A MIXED BAG, TRAVELLING WITH HEROES AND MODELS

Cardiff City…2; Leeds United…0
Sunday, 21st June

And so, 106 days after we beat Huddersfield Town on 7th March, we are due to play again at Cardiff City – the match I had been planning to go to by coach until first my daughter's text, and then the FA and Government's lockdown, quite rightly put paid to my plans. Football returned to England on 17th June, when Manchester City comfortably beat Arsenal 3-0, and Aston Villa – desperately needing points – drew 0-0 with Sheffield United. Before each game, players from both sides knelt in memory of the appalling murder of George Floyd and showed their recognition and support of the 'Black Lives Matter' campaign. The teams' shirts bore the same slogan in place of the players' own names, as football sought to make its stance against the evil of racism. While Championship clubs didn't have the 'Black Lives Matter' logo on their shirts, they did 'take the knee' along with match officials before the start of each game. A powerful message to the country, given by those who can have such a positive influence on so many.

The game wasn't without controversy, when Sheffield clearly scored, the Villa keeper carrying the ball well over his line after colliding with one of his own players. Apparently, some weird combination of factors rendered the goal-line technology useless and so the goal was not given, even though players on both sides clearly saw the ball had crossed the line. It would have been a crucial win for Sheffield, who were chasing hard to gain one of the Champions League places,

311

and it gave Villa a priceless and undeserved point in their battle against relegation.

Following the game, in interviews about the incident, it was clear the Villa camp's attitude was something like 'we just got lucky!' They had got similarly lucky at Elland Rd last season as we battled with them for promotion and Klich scored, having refused to kick the ball out of play following an injury to a Villa player further up the field. That particular incident caused significant upset, and certainly among the Villa players, who accused Leeds of cheating and unsporting play in not stopping the game, even though the referee had chosen not to do so. I mentioned this incident earlier and had to admit I was one of the crowd urging Klich on towards goal. The Villa players were going down all over the place and causing huge frustration on the terraces with their delaying tactics. For them to take the high ground about fair play and attacking Klich for his unsporting behaviour, seemed ridiculous. In my opinion, the game should have carried on. Surely the ref would have stopped the game himself if he had suspected serious injury?

In the end, Marcelo Bielsa solved the problem and proved himself the ultimate sport by instructing his players to let Villa score when the game restarted. He did this under the pressure of knowing that three points would have been vital to our faltering promotion bid. Even so, Villa still huffed and puffed about the incident after the game. It struck me now, a year or so later, that not many of the Villa players or indeed management team showed any respect to their opponents nor understanding of fair play by accepting their good fortune. And even though they absolutely knew a goal had been scored, they refused to acknowledge it in any way. Surely given the sense of injustice they had felt about the Klich 'goal' and their appeals for fair play and sportsmanship, they had to do something about this Sheffield 'goal', knowing as they did that the goal had been scored. Why didn't Dean Smith or Jack Grealish tell their players to let Sheffield score? Why didn't they live up to the expectations of fair play they insisted Klich should have done? It's amazing how quickly players can forget such incidents and how they can so often let themselves down with apparent double standards. How good would it have been for the game if Dean

Smith had also taken the high ground and followed the behaviour of Marcelo Bielsa? Then I think I would have had a little more respect for the Villa players who called out Mateus Klich that sunny afternoon at ER.

The Championship returned on Saturday, 20th June, and it's worth noting that before a ball was kicked, the positions at the top of the table were as follows:

Leeds United......71
WBA..............70
Fulham...............64
Brentford..........60
Notts Forest.......60
Preston...............56

It's going to be so close and such a nervy finish to the season, with huge celebrations and great heartaches along the way before the season eventually finishes on 22nd July. I had put together my own predictions of how the fixtures would work out and how things would look at the season's end, before we travelled to Hull on the 29th Feb. But at that time I only studied the fixtures of the top five as, to be honest, I didn't really see Preston as realistic challengers for automatic promotion. So, with my own knowledge of the various teams, how they were playing, and who they still had to meet, I came up with my own predicted final table.

WBA...........88
Leeds United..87
Brentford.......81
Notts Forest...79
Fulham.........77

I just gave Albion the title, but only just – maybe trying to be a little too fair to the opponents we were due to play. Perhaps I was worrying that I might be being too over-confident about our chances, and that such over-confidence might come back to bite us. It is Leeds, after all, so I didn't want to upset the footballing gods. For me, Fulham would be the losers, having by far the most difficult run-in on paper of the top five. That said, of course, this is football, and if they beat Brentford at the Cottage and we slip up at Cardiff, a win at ER in the second game back would put the 'Cottagers' only one point behind us! How I hate all this.

That first Saturday afternoon back was quite a bizarre experience, watching matches being played behind closed doors, but I found as I got into the game, I more or less forgot about the crowd or lack of one, and just got into the football. I only saw the last ten minutes of the Fulham v Brentford game, but it was enough for me to realise that as I had predicted way back in February, Brentford were going to cause problems with their attacking menace and mean defence, marshalled of course by Pontus Janssen. They came away from Craven Cottage with a 0-2 victory, and you could tell they were flying and relishing the challenge of reigning in the clubs in front of them. Their next game is away to WBA in a week's time, and the result of that one should be a clear pointer to how nail-biting the end of season race for promotion is going to be. Albion played a local derby against Birmingham later on in the afternoon, though how intense a derby is without fans is difficult to say; perhaps only the players can explain it. Some interesting statistics have come out of Germany, suggesting that home advantage is neutralised with the fans being absent. In that case, and if the stats are right, that should help Birmingham this afternoon and be massive for us tomorrow, as Cardiff has not been a happy hunting ground in recent times, and they don't like us much down there in Wales.

In the end, the 'Blues' played out a goalless draw at the Hawthorns and I found it difficult to watch the last ten minutes, worried every time Albion went forward that they would score – and they very nearly did in the last throes of the game. I decided in added time to go and inspect Andy's 'Magic Garden project' and come back when it was all over. The results couldn't have gone better from a Leeds point of view, with WBA dropping points at home and Fulham missing the chance to close the gap on us to four points. Things got better still as the rest of the results came in, with Sheffield Wednesday scoring in added time to take points from Forest at Hillsborough. It was all set up nicely for us to go to Cardiff, get a big win, and start to pull away from third spot. If we could win tomorrow, we would be ten points clear of Fulham. If. And then, of course, back come the memories of going to the Cottage on the back of blowing points against Cardiff and throwing away the chance of establishing a 12-point lead over the Londoners.

Strange that we should reopen our season with the same sequence of matches that brought to an end our seven-match winning run before Christmas. Was this a sign? We were in the middle of a five-match winning run when the season was halted. Was it all going to unfold again? And there was something else that helped to bring that winning run to an end: Pablo Hernandez was injured in the first minute at Fulham and missing for several games, of which we only won one, that incredible affair at Birmingham. And Pablo, we have already been told, will be missing at Cardiff. The omens, as they say, don't look good. And even my 'predictor' has Cardiff down for a home win.

I spent the hour before kick-off swapping emails with the LUTV support team, trying to access live pictures from Cardiff. I had tried earlier in the week without success, but wasn't too bothered as the game was live on Sky. The club had given season ticket holders various options to overcome the problem of reimbursing fans for the games they would be forced to miss, and I had chosen to forgo any refund in exchange for live streaming through LUTV of all the final nine games. Only I couldn't bloody get it! Well, that's to say I could get into the LUTV website, but even though I had entered my unique code provided by the club, I simply couldn't get the live pictures.

I have to say technology isn't my strong point, and increasingly as I came to the last months of my headship the kids helped me with preparing presentations and the like, as Mike had done with my 'New Heads' course. Looking back, it was something I should have asked for greater training in, but I ended up just getting by, like I did when I was a teenager copying homework on the school bus and praying my lack of knowledge wasn't exposed. Stupid. Really. Stupid of me and stupid of my employer not to offer greater support. As I have said, my thoughts on the world of education and my experiences in it are for another time, but I guess I am not the only older person who the world of technology simply flooded over. In terms of headship, I actually feel I could still do the job with my eyes closed today, and apart from the fact I would be more decisive in dealing with idle colleagues, the only area I believe I would struggle with would be technology. But as the football fans chant 'Time to go, time to go, time to go', whatever your job or chosen occupation it's always important to recognise when it's time to go.

The LUTV support team probably realised this quite early in our frequent exchanges of emails – they don't let you talk to them. Why in today's crazy world can't you ever talk to anyone without having to listen to God knows how many messages, queue for ages listening to awful 'smaltzy' music, and be told constantly that this message is being recorded for training purposes. 'I hope it frigging is. Someone pick up the fucking phone!' Anyway, essentially they were telling me that my laptop was too old and I needed to do this and that and download this and try that, and basically I had to tell them they might as well have been talking in hieroglyphics, the sense it was all making to me. I eventually managed to get the pictures by following their advice to download something called 'Google Chrome', which is apparently a web browser in its own right rather than just using the Google search engine. So there you go.

Tyler Roberts came into the side to replace Hernandez, and apart from him the side was probably at its strongest. The bench looked useful with Baradi, Alioski, and Shackleton joined by the returning Davis, who I think looks a really useful prospect for the future. The obvious weakness is in the lack of an experienced goalkeeper and a back-up striker. And, no matter what should happen in the next few weeks, the club have been negligent in my eyes in not properly strengthening the squad in the January transfer window. Cardiff are at strength, and the fact that Tomlin who played so well at ER is on the bench indicates just how strong they are. They are just one of those teams that you don't like to play. And before the enforced break they were in good form, closing in on the top six.

The players have a minute's silence before the game to honour Norman and Trevor, and also Peter Whittingham, the Cardiff player who died so tragically young. I liked Whittingham. He was a skilful player and I never enjoyed it when he played against us, and often hoped he would be one of those that we managed to bring to the club. Now he was gone, and his passing must have been a reminder to so many of the importance of living life to the full, none of us quite knowing what is lurking round the corner. After the silence the players 'take the knee', as they did in all the games yesterday, before the match starts.

It's as if we have never been away and we start brightly, forcing a number of corners without ever looking particularly threatening. It's odd, but given the number of corners we force during a game, our goals return as a result of them is really quite poor – unlike many of our opponents, who seem to score far too easily against us from far fewer similar situations. Ben White headed over before Vaulks cleared a goal-bound effort away, and with Cardiff struggling to create anything or even hold onto possession, it seemed a goal had to come. Unfortunately, when it did after 35 minutes, it was Cardiff who scored it. Phillips gave the ball away with a careless pass and Hoillett ran at the Leeds defence, who seemed to back off, allowing the player to shoot hard at goal from the edge of the area. I must admit I thought Meslier should save Hoillett's effort; it was powerfully hit but at a good height, and it wasn't going in near the post. But his dive was in vain. We responded as we always do and continued to dominate the match, and when Roberts crossed from the right it seemed Harrison must score, but unfortunately his goal-bound shot hit Bamford and flew to safety.

At this stage I was prowling the front room, running ever nearer the screen if we were getting close to scoring. It's awful not being at the match live, and it's awful screaming, shouting, and cursing when you're watching in your own home. I missed the camaraderie and banter of the terraces, and the shared feelings of joy or despair when a goal was scored. We almost equalised when Bamford headed a Dallas centre back across goal for Roberts to shoot, but Smithies in the Cardiff goal blocked brilliantly. Another chance came and went when Bamford failed to control the ball when put through by Costa, and the centre forward couldn't convert a Phillips pass when it looked as if he must score.

I was still feeling optimistic as the game entered the last 20 minutes; even a draw would be a good result and better than I predicted. Then Cooper sent a defensive free kick, under no pressure, straight to Mendez-Laing, who crossed for substitute Glatzel to score with a firm shot that went in off the post. Cardiff were leading 2-0 and I honestly couldn't remember them creating one threatening move in the whole game. We had been sloppy defensively and poor in front of goal, so typical of Leeds this season. We huffed and puffed for the last 20 minutes or so, but never really looked like scoring, and in the end, it was a bad defeat and a missed opportunity to put distance between us and the chasing pack.

I guess Bielsa summed up the game up perfectly in his after-match comments when he said, 'We could have won, we should have won. We created enough chances to score the necessary goals.'

At least I wasn't faced with the long journey back from the Welsh capital, whether in the car or on the bus. And while I was depressed by the defeat, it wasn't as if we had been outplayed. We had more than contributed to our own downfall and, as Bielsa said, we should have won the match. I suppose the only positive in terms of the table is that after a round of fixtures we still remain seven points clear of Fulham in third. So, while it should have been so much better, the damage was not too great.

I read through the texts from the WhatsApp group, all pretty much saying the same thing: 'we blew it', but some in more colourful language than others – all of them realising, as if we didn't know before, just how massive the game with Fulham would be next Saturday. I had been hoping to try and actually get to watch some of these games, as it struck me that I could use the fact that I was writing a book about the season as a fairly good reason to request some kind of press pass to get into the ground. I searched the information at the front of a home programme to find a suitable email address to forward my request to, and there was in fact only one there which said,

'To contact the club with questions or complaints please email: sloquestioms@leedsunited.com'

So, I did. I also sent my email – very nicely written, I thought – to the ticket office, knowing that the staff there were usually pretty helpful. I sent the email on 11th June and got an automated reply from the ticket office later that day, saying they would respond between four to six working days. I didn't get anything from the 'sloquestions' address, but then I hadn't got anything back when I had applied for the 'assistant kitman' job or written to Angus Kinnear about our desperate need for a new striker and keeper. So, nothing unusual there, I suppose. Quite pleased with my idea, I informed the WhatsApp group what I had done, thinking they would be impressed by my initiative. They obviously were, as later I got this response from Katherine. Referencing Leeds United receiving my email, she wrote:

Bet they are like 'Oh my God, here is this Adrian Taylor again! Who wants to deal with him this time?'

Dear Adrian,
Thank you for your continued interest in LUFC. We are delighted our fans have such broad and varied interests. We are sorry the position of 'ball boy' couldn't be filled by you – sorry, assistant kit man – as we appreciate you have strong skills for this role. With regard to your comments on our future investments, we have taken these into account and perhaps we could have you on a Zoom call in our next 'pow-wow' with all the board of directors. Your opinions will be greatly valued. Finally, we would love to offer you a journalist's pass, however I'm afraid at the current time we have our limit of press and media. Should anything change, we will of course contact you and you will be next in line. Please do not hesitate to contact us in the future if there is anything you would like to make us aware of or offer to contribute to our great football club. We hope to see you back in the stands soon. NOW STOP EMAILING US!!!!!!!!!!!!!!

This made me laugh a lot, and also made me wonder if I was really becoming such a sad old thing that I just sat at home firing off letters and emails about everything that made me slightly unhappy. I'm glad I never told anyone that I wrote to Andrea Radrizzani imploring him not to appoint Aitor Karanka when it was rumoured the ex-Middlesbrough manager was being lined up to come to ER!

Interestingly, as we approach the Fulham game, I still haven't had a response from the 'sloquestions' site. Maybe it doesn't really exist. Maybe they couldn't be arsed. But I did get a helpful response from the team in the ticket office, basically saying that they had forwarded my request to the press officer but that they didn't think there was much hope. I emailed them back thanking them for their help and apologising for involving them, as I knew it wasn't something they would really deal with. There was absolutely no need for them to respond again, but later that same day I received the following:

'Dear Adrian

Thank you for your e mail. You are quite right in saying it is not a ticket office issue. The email was passed on and if you have not heard, then I am guessing that all passes have been issued, sorry. We look forward to seeing a copy of the book.

Take care.
Leeds United Customer Services.'

So, top marks to the Customer Services team for representing the club and themselves in such a helpful and positive fashion, and absolutely nothing but contempt for those at 'sloquestions' who haven't even got the decency to respond. Really, the club does so much good in so many areas, but needs to weed out the weak links that let them down so badly. They need to know that they are providing a service, and that is their job, and they need to know that service matters. It takes me most of Sunday to come to terms with the loss at Cardiff, but I have to get my head round it quicker than usual as Katherine, Nick, and the kids are coming to stay for a few days – and they're coming today, the Monday after the game. We have already built the cot for Lucy, and Oliver will sleep in one of the double beds. Andy is busy planning meals, and I get the lawnmower out to tidy up the garden and get the nice stripe in the lawn that the kids all call 'Wembley'.

The weather is absolutely beautiful and we are looking forward to catching up with them. It's been a long time since they have been to stay with us, and while we are sure Oliver will recognise the house, we are not so certain about Lucy. We manage to get everything done before Kath texts to say they are 20 minutes away, and as Andy potters in the 'Magic Garden,' I sit and drink a coffee in the front, enjoying the sunshine and just chilling. I mess a bit with my phone and look at some of the silly video clips we have of the grandchildren; they are all very different, and all characters in their own right. I have a lovely clip of me and Oliver when he was just a toddler, where he steals my car keys from my knee as I pretend to sleep, and crawls off as fast as he can go, squealing excitedly when he realises I'm awake and crawling after him. I find a clip of Lucy that Katherine took the last time they were here when we are dancing to the Turtles singing *Eleanore* and suddenly become synchronised, twisting and turning in perfect harmony. So funny and such great memories. And right here, where I am sitting waiting and drinking my coffee, is where Margie surprised her daddy by beating her chest and shouting out, 'Leeds, Leeds, Leeds' on their return from America.

The car pulls into the drive and there is great excitement as the children get their bearings, and Oliver is already keen to 'walk the plank' in the Magic Garden. I fist pump Nick, and even though I think it's still not allowed in the ever-changing rules, Kath and I have a big hug as we head into the house. We have a great time in the next few days. The kids enjoy the adventure of being somewhere different for the first time in months, and Kath and Nick enjoy having a bit more adult support as Andy plays with Lucy and I go to war with Oliver's Playmobil stuff. The four of us really enjoy the evenings when, with the kids asleep, we can eat and drink and catch up and have a laugh.

Nick is still involved in Zoom meetings during the day, but he has brought the kids' paddling pool with him, and it's really quite a big one with a little slide incorporated in the middle. It reminds Andy and I of the one we had when we were expecting James nearly 30 years ago, and Kath and Mike splashed around most of the day in the warm summer weather. One difference from those days, though, was that Katherine had bought two quite powerful water guns, and there was absolutely no way Andy and I weren't going to become victims of Oliver and Lucy at some point during the week. In fact, the first water fight was quite tame, and Nick, enjoying his lunch break, took the biggest battering while I sat at the garden table enjoying the fun. Until, that is, Katherine encouraged the kids to splatter their 'Poppa' by blasting me full-on in a surprise attack. Revenge was sweet the next day when, using the old ruse from *Butch Cassidy*, I made everyone stop while I explained the rules, before blasting my unsuspecting daughter and then chasing down Oliver, shouting 'Pow-Pow' until eventually he fell backwards over the side of the pool as I ran off in triumph. Kath later posted a clip of my attack on the family WhatsApp, 'Dad's celebration when he knocks a four-year-old into the water!' That evening we sat outside late into the night and enjoyed a BBQ and some chilled stuff. Nick, a Spurs man, brought the television outside so we could watch his team beat West Ham – a result that pleased us both, because I am still hoping Karren Brady will get her 'comeuppance.' Too soon it was time for them to be heading home, and it was good that Oliver in particular wanted to stay longer. We had had a great week and were looking forward to catching up again soon when Mike and Lou would be over from Dublin for their first holiday since the birth of Georgia and the blessed lockdown. As they drove away, Andy and I settled down for a coffee in the garden, still enjoying the beautiful weather. It was Thursday, and there was a bit of tidying to do ahead of the weekend, but not before we enjoyed our first afternoon siesta for a few days.

Leeds United…3; Fulham…0
Saturday, 27th June

I went on 'Leeds Live' to see if there was anything about Hernandez in Bielsa's news conference and whether Roberts would be fit, as there had been some media chat about a groin injury. The news was good about Tyler. He was fit to play, and as for Pablo, they would see how he reacted to training. I so hoped he would be fit to play or even be on the bench, because he is such an important member of the team. Unusually for us, we were playing at ER on a Saturday afternoon and kicking off at 3pm. We seem to have our fixtures moved so often for television purposes that we have got used to playing at all times of day and night and on every day of the week. However, unusual as this may be, it's definitely not as unusual as playing at ER without any supporters in the ground, and I just wonder how this might affect us.

I guess ER can be a fearsome place to come as a visiting player, and yet personally I would really relish a crowd baying for my blood. I would want to show them how good I was, I'd want to score and run around celebrating in front of them, cupping my hand over my ear to mock the lack of sound. Yes, for me it would be something that would make me raise my game, and far more than say playing at some soulless ground like Reading.

The other side of this argument is when opposition players seem to genuinely freeze when bombarded by the wall of sound that hammers around the ground at ER. I remember seeing the clip of Charlie Nicholas on *Soccer Saturday* when we were playing Bristol Rovers in that must-win League One game. Jeff Stelling turns to Nicholas and says, 'A goal at Elland Rd, Charlie?' to which Nicholas responds, 'It's the crowd, Jeff', insinuating that the noise had in part led to the Bristol keeper throwing the ball straight to Bradley Johnson in the build-up to Jermaine Beckford's famous winning goal.

I have seen us win the First Division title at ER, and I've seen us beat Barcelona and destroy Manchester United 5-1 and Chelsea 7-0. I've seen amazing comebacks like the game against Standard, and the remarkable injury time comeback against Blackburn a couple of years ago. I've watched great players, Bremner, Best, and Cruyff among them, but in all my time I've never witnessed a game where the crowd played such a part in the win than that day in May ten years ago when we clinched promotion on the last day of the season.

What a day it was, and ultimately what a celebration. I remember driving up the M1 and seeing all the cars heading north, flags and scarves flying. It was as if everyone knew this had to be our day and, a bit like this year's title push, it was a 'must go up year'. Not to do so would have been unthinkable and, just like this year, we would lose all our best players. But actually, worse that year, we would finish up still in League One. I listened to some CDs on the drive up, and one song caught my mood, *The Greatest Day* by Take That. Surely if we could do this, it would be the greatest day. I decided there and then, if we won, I would play that record all the way home.

And win we did, in the most nerve-jangling fashion, with Max Gradel getting sent off, and then going 1-0 down when Duffy scored at the start of the second half. I remember feeling totally fraught and almost shaking with anxiety, and then Beckford played the ball to Johnny Howson who fired home a glorious bending shot. I was right behind the flight of the ball, and it was a goal as soon as it left his foot.

A few minutes later, Beckford latched onto a poor clearance from Johnson's cross shot-cum-centre and everyone in the ground absolutely knew he would score, and of course he did, writing his name in the history of the club for the second time, following his match-winning goal against Man U in the FA Cup. I honestly thought I might have heart failure as we played out the remaining 20 minutes or so to the end of the game. I was literally wringing my hands, going through every possible emotion, and checking my watch a million times. It was sheer agony, and the thought of a Bristol equaliser too unimaginable to bear.

When it came, the final whistle was greeted with an explosion of noise, and many shed tears of happiness – or maybe they were just tears of release. I have never seen so many people so delirious at the same time. It was simply a fantastic moment, and I soon became aware of my mobile phone going crazy as friends contacted me to share in the celebration. When I eventually left the ground to head home, I was aware of the fact that I just felt so incredibly happy. I was smiling all over my face and had a brilliant journey back south, with every passing car seemingly full of celebrating Leeds fans. It was just such a party. I played the blessed Take That record as promised, over and over again.

The party continued when I got home, and Kath was there with Andy, with chilled champagne and loads of cold beer, and we relived every moment of the game and watched the highlights on *Sky Sports News*. The boys were both out of the country – Mike somewhere in Spain, where he had been at university, and James in Sydney, where he was on a football scholarship, playing for the university and coaching in a local school. It was early morning in Sydney as we prepared to go to bed, and I just thought I'd try James on Skype on the off chance he was up. He answered almost immediately, and it was obvious he had been celebrating. In fact, he hadn't been to bed, and amazingly had found a place in some casino that was showing the match. He was as drunk on happiness as he was on alcohol, and we had a good laugh talking about our 'Greatest Day!' Let's hope we are celebrating another one very soon; it was such a fantastic feeling.

It remains to be seen how the lack of atmosphere affects the players this afternoon, but certainly both sides will be hugely aware of the importance of the game. Win, and we are ten points clear of Fulham; lose, and they will have reduced the deficit to four. It's all made more interesting by the fact that last night Brentford kept their good form going by beating WBA and have very much pushed themselves into the race for automatic promotion. They are just five points behind us now, and having beaten Fulham and WBA in successive matches, must be in with a real chance of catching ourselves and West Brom. It's becoming hopelessly stressful, and I understood Kath's text suggesting someone please just wake her up when it's all over.

Hernandez was named on the bench and Roberts was fit to continue in his place, so Bielsa played the same team that started at Cardiff. Fulham were at strength, fielding Mitrovic, De Cordova, Reid, and Knockaert up front, supported by our ex-academy player Cairney – someone who seems to take delight in showing how wrong the club was to release him, by always playing well against us and often scoring.

It's clear from the start that both sides were 'up for it', but Fulham seemed over-excited, and a couple of minutes into the game Mitrovic, who had fallen over untouched by White to con a free-kick just a minute earlier, smashed his elbow into the centre half's face several seconds after White had played the ball. It was a cowardly cynical challenge, and one that was so late that neither the referee or linesman saw it. Mitrovic stayed on the pitch, and it would be just our luck if the big centre forward scored the winning goal and then got banned retrospectively.

I realised I was up on my feet and cursing badly, and sat down as Fulham threatened a couple of times through Knockaert, who had started the game in particularly lively fashion. I was on my feet again soon after, as Bamford put us one up in the tenth minute, superbly finishing Costa's excellent pass with a fine side-foot shot from the edge of the area. I went crazy jumping up and down and shouting, and unable to respond to the kids' texts because my hands were shaking so much.

Bamford went close again a few minutes later when he couldn't convert a pass from Harrison, weakly pushing the ball wide under pressure from a defender and the keeper. Fulham were clearly pumped up, and the whole team went chasing after the referee when the ball bounced up off Roberts' thigh to hit his hand as he tried to clear in the penalty area. Knockaert was booked by the ref for the strength of his protests, and it could have been a lot worse for him if his sly stamp on Harrison had been seen by the officials. Fulham continued to dominate, and as half-time approached were clearly the better side, even though we had that crucial one-goal lead. Bielsa changed things at half-time, bringing on Hernandez and Alioski for Costa and Bamford, and there is no doubt the changes worked and altered the flow of the match in our favour.

Roberts moved to centre forward and seemed more mobile and dangerous than Bamford had done, and crucially seemed to hold the ball up better, something that was usually such a strength of Bamford's game. The changes had an almost immediate effect when Phillips sent Roberts away on the right and his excellent cross found Harrison, whose goal-bound shot was deflected just past the post by desperate last-ditch Fulham defending. It wasn't long before we scored the hugely important second goal, and again the substitutes were heavily involved in a speedy break-out from a Fulham corner. Meslier started the move quickly, sending Ayling away to find Klich in midfield, for the Polish international to send Harrison free down the right flank. His pass across the area eluded Roberts and a couple of Fulham defenders, and fell perfectly for Alioski to delay fractionally, sending the keeper and last defender flying across to the left-hand post, before playing the ball calmly and firmly into the right-hand corner of the net.

For me, even as I jump around the front room, it's a great finish. It would have been so easy for him to have just shot straight at the keeper, but he had the nerve to just hold for the second it took him to pick his spot. Even though there was still half an hour to go, you could see it was a killer blow for the Fulham players, and Mitrovic particularly seemed to lose complete interest in the game, waving his arms, dropping his shoulders, and wandering around fairly aimlessly.

Just 15 minutes later, the game was over when Hernandez brilliantly played in Harrison down the left for the winger to score with a shot that went through the keeper's legs. I loved the way that Alioski and Harrison celebrated their goals with the pop-up crowd, and it was clear that the players of both sides knew just how big a victory this was for Leeds. Kebano, the Fulham substitute, summed up the London club's afternoon when he earned a second yellow card for a clumsy challenge on Ayling moments after he had committed almost exactly the same foul on Phillips. In my eyes, Fulham could easily have had three players sent off, and after their bright period of possession in the first half, they had been comprehensively outplayed and outcoached in the second. I had a pint of John Smiths in my hand within seconds of the final whistle. This was going to be a very happy weekend.

Leeds United...1; Luton Town...1
Tuesday, 30th June

If we win tonight, we go six points clear of WBA, and no matter what Brentford do at Reading, we will be at least eight points clear of them in third place. I have felt good all weekend and enjoyed reliving the Fulham game and catching up on my writing. I know all football fans tend to be a bit pessimistic about their team's chances, and of course we at Leeds know better than most not to count our chickens, but surely this time we can't possibly blow it. Or can we?

We've had so many disappointments over the years, and it's frightening to think of what we could and probably should have won but managed somehow to lose. In the Revie years, we won two First Division championships yet finished runners-up five times; we reached four FA Cup finals, but only managed to win one. In the same period, we lost in the finals of the European Cup and the European Cup Winners' Cup, and while we can claim those two games were unfairly influenced by the referees, we still lost. We have had some great days where we played champagne football and tasted sweet success, but we have had far more days where we have had to hang our heads and taste the bitter tears of defeat. Even in our promotion year from League 1 that I mentioned a few pages ago, we only just crawled over the line, having led the table convincingly earlier in the season.

And now, all the pundits are saying we're home and dry, and the race is between WBA and Brentford for the second automatic promotion place. I can honestly say the only Leeds fans they would find agreeing with them are those who don't really understand the club or who are just plain stupid. Luton are coming to ER desperate for points in their bid to stay in the Championship. They've just appointed Nathan Jones, bringing their old manager back from Stoke and making it hard not to start singing, 'Nathan Jones, you've been gone too long'. They have just beaten Swansea at the Liberty and are not coming to ER to lie down; they are coming to fight and scrap and work their socks off, and that's exactly what they do. They beat us up and challenge our mental toughness, daring us to shake off all those deep and hurtful memories that caused such paralysis in the run-in last season.

Bielsa kept faith with the side that started the game against Fulham, meaning Hernandez and Alioski returned to the bench. I was disappointed that he hadn't decided to give Tyler Roberts a start up front in place of Bamford, who hasn't seemed quite to have recovered his excellent form of before the lockdown. As for Luton, they indicated the way they were going to play by leaving their leading scorer Collins on the bench, along with Harry Cornick and Issy Brown, their most creative attacking players. I was watching the match on LUTV, which I had eventually worked out how to download, and pushing all thoughts away of previous painful defeats against supposedly inferior teams. The list is endless: Colchester, Sunderland, Histon, Newport County, and even Wigan last season. I settled down to cheer us to a victory that surely would be ours. A victory that would ensure the eight-point gap to Brentford in third would be maintained following the 'Bees' emphatic 0-3 win at Reading earlier.

We started brightly, with Bamford forcing a corner in the first minute and Roberts and Costa shooting over, without really suggesting we were beginning to dominate. Luton showed their fight and determination, and McManaman was booked for a nasty challenge on Dallas before they forced a corner that Meslier flapped at, a little 'Casilla' like, but which we eventually cleared. A few minutes later, Cooper was left on the ground after a ball was swung into our penalty area. It seemed to me as if one of their players had kneed him in the back, and he certainly looked in no condition to carry on and was replaced by Baradi, who almost let Luton clean through with a clumsy first touch.

Despite the valiant efforts of the legendary Jermaine Beckford – acting as co-commentator – in trying desperately to find positives to our start to the game, we were playing poorly, giving the ball away too easily, and not really playing our dynamic fast brand of football. In some ways, we seemed intimidated by the visitors, who showed their desperation by eventually racking up five yellow cards. Bielsa made changes at the interval, bringing on Alioski for Baradi, sacrificed to allow us to go to a back three.

Harry Cornick came on for Luton and made an immediate impact, scoring with a superb shot across Meslier, having been played in brilliantly by Ryan Tunnecliffe with an Hernandez-style pass. It was a shattering blow, and for a moment the team seemed stunned, but Bielsa put the Spaniard on after the hour, and five minutes later Dallas equalised, slotting the ball coolly past the impressive Sluga in the

Luton goal. He had been played in by Alioski's fabulous pass through the Luton defence, and there was no doubt the North Macedonian international was pushing for a starting place for our visit to Blackburn.

Sluga had been right on his game, making a number of excellent saves as we cranked up the pressure, but he should have been left with no chance when, after tremendous work by Harrison, the winger's cross seemed certain to be headed home by the unmarked Bamford racing into the area. I was already on my feet celebrating our much-needed winner when I realised he had completely missed the ball. In the commentary box, even the normally positive Beckford was momentarily speechless, though later someone came up with the theory that the ball got lost in the floodlights' glare. I mean, come on. Shortly before the end, Costa found himself in a similar position and he too failed to convert the outstanding chance. Up in the commentary box, I bet Beckford must have been thinking he would have had a hat trick tonight. I mean, for fuck's sake, so would I. The final whistle came with no further score, and Luton celebrated their hard work and the point they had come to get with a mass huddle, as our players left the field knowing they had missed a fantastic opportunity to take a giant step towards promotion.

It was just so typical of following Leeds, but these players weren't around when we were blowing our chances in the 60s and 70s, and there was no crowd there transmitting our anxiety. So, what went wrong? How could we have thrown such a golden chance away? Maybe there was something in that 'gypsies' curse that Revie was always banging on about. I could already here the Brentford fans chants of 'Leeds are falling apart again' ringing in my ears as I turned the laptop off and headed to bed, knowing that I would be counting lost points and missed opportunities tonight rather than sheep.

I couldn't find sleep and mulled the game over as I waited to drop off. We had had 75% of the possession, forced 15 corners and had 23 shots on goal, yet managed just one goal. Luton, on the other hand, managed with just 25% possession, forced one corner and had three shots on goal, scoring the same number of goals – one. It doesn't sound like we did a lot wrong, and we missed at least two gilt-edged chances, but there seemed to me something missing. I wondered about the injuries. Both Cooper and Dallas looked in trouble when they left the field, so it will be interesting to see the team Bielsa fields at Blackburn at the weekend. Personally, with only six games remaining, I would find a place for Alioski in the side, possibly instead of Dallas if he's injured, and would definitely start Hernandez however fragile his fitness is. I would also drop Bamford and let Roberts show what he can do leading the line.

Looking at the fixtures ahead, we are going to play some teams as desperate as Luton in the coming weeks. Barnsley had a massive win over our next opponents Blackburn, who will really need to beat us if they are going to maintain a push for the top six. And Stoke, our opponents after that, got thumped 3-0 by Wigan, so they too are going to be fairly desperate for points. It's not going to get any easier and I just wonder if Blackburn and Stoke, having seen what Luton did, are going to emulate their fairly basic and physical style. Surely we didn't get bullied out of the victory this evening? But it's true at every level that when players are expecting to get 'hit', and possibly unfairly, they might just snatch at chances and misplace passes, the fear of injury always at the back of their mind just affecting their normal play. It could have happened to Leeds tonight. I know it happened to me a few times. I remember one team we played regularly had a reputation for being as hard as nails and they most certainly didn't take prisoners. That said, it was rumoured one of their players had spent considerable parts of his youth staying at Her Majesty's pleasure, and for GBH at that. No-one much liked playing them, because you knew you would be in for a tough time and would be verbally, if not physically, abused throughout the match. It was ok playing hard, and I think most amateur footballers are used to the language and banter that goes with the game, but most amateurs have to go to work the next day and can't afford to get seriously injured by some nutcase playing in a Sunday morning game. Chris, now a solicitor, once brought an action against a player who broke the jaw of one of his teammates. The lad was self-employed and was off work for some time; he was married with a new baby, and suddenly found himself off work and with no income. Some people, even in professional sport, argue that it's not 'cricket' to take incidents that happen on the sports fields into the law courts, but I absolutely disagree with them. For me, the 'game' shouldn't protect the thugs and cheats who deliberately go out to harm fellow players, biting and eye-gouging, and deliberately diving in with two-foot tackles. This kind of behaviour has no place in sport, professional or amateur, and those who 'play' in this way shouldn't be protected by the sporting authorities. They should be punished in the courts and then banned 'sine die'.

I played in a number of leagues of varying standards over a period of 20 years and only came across a handful of lads who just went out to intimidate their opponents, to gain a 'hard man reputation' among their mates, like some kind of primary school playground bully. Often, they were sorted out by their own teammates, especially the young hothead variety, but the really dangerous ones were those older types, usually without very much ability, who wore their thuggery like some badge of dishonour. They were the ones who shouldn't have been allowed on a pitch, and the fact that they were meant you very much had to watch out for your personal health and safety.

It wasn't just on the field where you had to have your wits about you, either. I have heard of local league players being threatened off the pitch, and in one case, a player sent off in a local league game drove onto the pitch while the match was continuing and attempted to run over the referee.

The day we played our local rivals, the ones whose player had served time, a number of our players 'cried off.' It wasn't unusual; it was never much fun playing against them. To be fair, they did have some good players and I knew one or two of them from my 'Mecca days', so I figured I had some kind of protection if things got out of hand.

We actually played quite well and going into the last few minutes we were still on level terms when a ball fell free just outside their area. I knew I would have the pace to reach it first and from the corner of my eye I saw him, the hard man, chasing back to try and clear the ball. I was about a yard in front of him and, as I controlled the ball and ran into the area, he lunged in behind me, sending me literally flying off the pitch. I don't know if the ref had heard the story of the guy with the car, but he seemed to take an age to point to the penalty spot. It was such an obvious decision that none of the opposition even bothered to appeal.

I was our penalty taker and, as I picked myself up and got hold of the ball, I walked past the culprit, who started to walk with me. For a second, I actually thought he was going to apologise to me, but he didn't. He just said, 'If you score this, I'll break your fucking leg!' I remember thinking, *Oh shit!*, and wondered what to do. Then I remembered there were only a few minutes to go. I could hug the touchline, or feign injury. I could even start to cry! I always take the same shot at a penalty. I am left-footed so I side-foot the ball towards the left-hand post. I think it helps to know exactly what you are going to do, and I never look at the goalie or take notice of anyone else. It seems to work, because I honestly can't remember missing one, though I'm sure I probably did. I didn't miss this one, though, sending the ball low into the left-hand corner of the goal.

I spent the last few minutes of the game wandering rather aimlessly out on the left-hand touchline, a long way from my 'friend.' And when the final whistle blew, I legged it pretty quickly to the safety of the dressing rooms. We had been playing at home and, having won and having scored, I was looking forward to my pint in the local afterwards. I was queuing up at the bar when, to my horror, he appeared at my side. 'You owe me a pint,' he said. 'It was never a fecking penalty.' 'Absolutely not,' I replied, and bought him a beer. Strangely enough, and for whatever odd reason in his head, I never had a problem with him again.

As for Leeds, they are going to have to 'man up' and go to Blackburn, work their socks off, and show everyone that they mean business and they're not going to blow it again. Before I eventually fall asleep, I decide we should definitely bring back Hernandez and Alioski, and play Roberts up front in place of Bamford. In the days after the game as always, I kept mulling over the missed chances and team selection, looking at our upcoming fixtures and those of WBA, and Brentford, and trying to work out where we could pick up points and they could drop them. Albion played at Sheffield Wednesday the night after the

Luton game, and the Owls had picked up some useful results since their return, drawing with Forest and winning at Bristol City, who seemed to have imploded since they lost to us in February.

With Albion stumbling a little, I had hopes that they would drop points again at Hillsborough, but they returned to winning ways with a bang, winning 0-3 and returning to just a point behind us. Forest also kept up their challenge, sneaking a 1-0 home win against struggling Bristol. There is something about Forest that worries me. They are still involved in the chase for automatic and, as they say, are going 'under the radar'. I don't think that they will make it, but they are well organised, strong defensively, and have Joe Lolly and Lewis Grabben up front, who can always change a game with their goals. I get side-tracked again thinking why we couldn't have signed up a decent striker to compete with Bamford and turn some of the many chances we create into goals.

I love Bielsa and he has made us play some beautiful football, but when he explains in post-match interviews that we have created more chances than the opposition, I simply don't get that he hasn't knocked Radrizzani 's door down to get the final piece of the jigsaw – a goal scorer – and start turning those chances into goals and points.

The weather has turned bad and last week's beautiful sunshine has been replaced by leaden grey skies full of rain. I push on with the book, starting to edit the first few pages as Andy busies herself getting ready to welcome Mike and Lou on Saturday. I want to cut the grass – both the gardens, and the extended one across 'Andrea's bridge' – but it's far too wet. There is loads of football on the telly as the Premiership and Championship seek to finish the season, and I do watch some of it, but to be honest I'm not really interested in the Prem, though I'm pleased that Liverpool have been able to win the title on the field rather than by PPG or any other such solution. I'd love to see WHU relegated, for reasons already mentioned, but unfortunately, they beat Chelsea 3-2 and now look safe. I do like the look of their forward Antonio, though, and would love to see him in a white shirt.

It being the first week of July, the Wimbledon tennis should be on television and Andy particularly loves watching some of the thrilling matches the tournament can throw up. But of course, it isn't on telly because of the virus. I must admit I can't see why the singles couldn't be played behind closed doors, but anyway decisions have to be made, and I guess this one had to be taken early before anyone really knew what the future held. The BBC has decided to put on some of the great matches from the past, but with the football season restarting I haven't bothered to watch any of the programmes.

Whenever I hear the word 'Wimbledon', my first thought is always about football anyway, ever since that famous FA Cup tie between Leeds and the 'Dons' in January 1975. We were champions of England and on our way to the European Cup final in Paris later in the year. I was a student in Twickenham and in the middle of a teaching practice in Staines, and Wimbledon were a non-league team who had knocked out first division Burnley in the third round. I decided to go home for the weekend and go to ER for the match. It would be full, of course, because this was in the days when the cup really did mean something.

I caught the train up in Kings Cross and found myself sitting next to an old man and opposite quite an attractive girl. The old man started talking to us as the train left the station. He told the girl he thought she must be a model or an actress and, turning to me, he suggested I was probably a pop star or a footballer. It must have been because he had caught sight of my *Shoot* magazine, which I still enjoyed reading even though I was almost 21. I decided to go and look for the buffet car and left them to their chat. As I moved through the carriages, I noticed a group of young men all sitting together in quite a large group, laughing and joking and looking as if they were enjoying themselves. It was the Wimbledon team en route to Leeds and their fourth-round cup tie.

I started to chat to some of them and they were really friendly and happy to talk. I told them I was going to the match tomorrow and also all about what I was doing at college and about the football I was playing. I had actually played against some of the teams they came up against. like Southall and Walthamstow Avenue. and we had quite a laugh talking about their prospects at ER tomorrow. I must have been chatting to them for about half an hour before returning to my own seat and taking with me a paper with all the team's autographs and a personal message written to me from them with best wishes in my career. What a top set of guys.

The old man had left the train when I returned to my seat, so there was just me and the pretty girl sitting in the four seats separated by a table. We started to chat, and I noticed as she took some mints out of her bag that she had an NUS card in her wallet. So, she wasn't a model or an actress, she was a student, just like me. But that's not what she told me when I asked her what she did. When I asked her, she did indeed tell me that she was a model trying to break into acting. This made me laugh inwardly, and remember once when I had met Andy off the Manchester train to be told she had been invited for a weekend away with a guy who reckoned he was a world class snooker player. Andy, being Andy, told him that she was Princess Anne and left him to himself.

A few weeks later when we were watching some sports programme on television, she suddenly blurted out, 'That's him! That's the guy who invited me to spend the weekend with him!' It was Alex Higgins!

Meanwhile, back on the train, the chat with the 'model' was going very smoothly and, getting into the swing of the conversation, she asked me what I did. I told her (and I still can't believe I said this) that I was a professional high diver, adding that I travelled the world diving in such places as Acapulco, just like Elvis did in that film. She was clearly impressed. We continued chatting to each other in our make-believe world until it was time for me to leave the train at Wakefield. We had been getting along famously, and even though I had told her about Andy and she had talked of a boyfriend, she scribbled her address on my cigarette packet, and I could tell – as you just can – that she was quite interested in me. We had pretty much been flirting in an imaginary world since I had returned to my seat after chatting with the Wimbledon boys. What a journey, what great days.

I was at a packed ER the next afternoon to see my new friends perform heroically in the cup tie. It was a game that literally changed the life of Dickie Guy in the Wimbledon goal, who capped an incredible performance by saving a Peter Lorimer penalty, and then in the very last seconds dived to save at Giles' feet, after the inside forward had been played clean through by Duncan McKenzie. Standing right behind Guy in the Kop throughout the second half, I was almost praying that he and his colleagues would hold out for the draw their efforts and courage deserved, obviously thinking they could have their moment of fame, earn some money in the replay, and we could go on to win the cup.

In fact, the replay couldn't be played at Plough Lane because of poor weather, and the match was switched to Selhurst Park where an incredible 45,000 people turned out to watch Leeds scrape through 0-1, when a Giles shot was deflected past Guy. We had done it, but we didn't get to Wembley that year, losing to Ipswich in the sixth round, after three replays! For the first replay, there had been over 50,000 at Elland Rd – amazing attendances, and indicative of the club's fantastic support and pulling power, which remains to this day.

I always kept my eye out for Wimbledon after meeting the team, and noticed that Dickie Guy maintained his links with the club, celebrating their FA Cup final success over hot favourites Liverpool, when Dave Beasant saved a penalty of his own as the 'Dons' held out for a famous victory. Dickie was an outspoken critic of the club's proposed relocation to Milton Keynes (which fan wouldn't have been?) and became the club president in 2000. I took my autographs back into the school in Staines on my return south, and my street cred – already high as a Northerner and a Leeds fan to boot – went through the roof, as the kids huddled round to hear the story of how I met the country's cup heroes.

A few weeks after this memorable train ride, I was sitting in the college bar when a visiting sports team came in for a post-match beer or two. One of my housemates knew the opposing team's skipper, and he came over to join me and introduce his friend. He was a nice guy and very chatty, and I smiled as he introduced me to his girlfriend. It was my model friend, who looked decidedly uneasy in a kind of 'for Christ's sake, don't say anything' kind of way! I told her it was nice to meet her and then paused before adding, 'It's strange, you look exactly like a girl I saw in the paper the other day. You're not a model, are you?' I left before the discussion could turn to Elvis films.

CHAPTER 19

A BIG WELCOME TO THE DUBLIN CREW
AND A HUGE WIN AT BLACKBURN

Blackburn Rovers…1; Leeds United…3
Saturday, 4th July

Oh, the permutations! I spent the next few days after the Luton game recovering from the disappointment of dropped points and, along with Andy, getting the house ready for the visit of Mike, Lou, Margie, and Georgie. We built cots, changed sheets, cut the garden both sides of the beck, and generally tried to have everything as welcoming as could be for their Saturday arrival. I was up early writing and thinking, picking teams, and planning a route through the last six games. In the end, there was only the simple fact that if we won all our games, we would be home and dry and be promoted. But we are Leeds, and we don't do it the easy way. Ever!

They arrive about 2.15pm D Day minus 45. And even as we hug and greet one another, Mike is in the house checking out my laptop and the live match stream from LUTV. It's great to see them all, and although Mike and Lou look tired after the long journey from Dublin, they know it's the first day of a fortnight's well deserved holiday following lockdown and the birth of Georgie in January. Margie is all excited, and it's lovely that she recognises us, due mainly I think to the regular FaceTimes we have done since March. She goes through all the tricks making her funny sounds, playing peek-a-boo, and finishing with the 'Leeds, Leeds, Leeds' chant I taught her when she was last here in September.

Lou knows that kick-off is nigh, and she and Mike decide to leave most of their stuff in the car, only unpacking essentials for the moment. We drink tea, but Mike – quite rightly following the long drive from Holyhead and it being the first day of his holiday – has a beer. I decide against beer just yet but make a mental note to check there are sufficient John Smith's cooling in the fridge to hopefully celebrate with around 5pm. The team news is mixed: Cooper is back in the heart of the defence, but neither Costa nor Dallas is in the squad, their places being taken by Alioski and Douglas. Hernandez is once again named on the bench, along with Baradi and Shackleton, but there isn't an attacker there and we really have to pray that Bamford and Roberts stay fit. Blackburn are also injury-hit, particularly missing the dangerous Bradley Dack – a player I would like to see us show some interest in. They have also left Stewart Downing on the bench, which I am quite pleased about.

We score early when Klich robs Travis and plays a simple pass forward to the onrushing Bamford, who beats Walton from the edge of the area with a finish not dissimilar to his goal against Fulham. Watching the replay, it's possible Klich has fouled the Blackburn player, but maybe it's too close to call and the goal is given. Thank goodness there is no VAR. It's a brilliant start, but with so much activity in the house, it's hard for Mike and me to concentrate on the game, particularly Mike, as he has 'Daddy duties' to attend to. That said, we seem to be at sixes and sevens at the back, and Rothwell plays a beautiful pass to Gallagher that goes right through the spine of our team. The big centre forward finds himself clean through and one-on-one with Meslier, and as he shoots, I am just waiting for the net to billow... but it doesn't. Gallagher unaccountably shoots wide and we escape, for now. Minutes later, Meslier sends a clearance straight to a Blackburn player, and the keeper has to dive bravely at Armstrong's feet to stop a goal. Then Holtby, played through by Gallagher, shoots against the post and as Harrison runs across our own area, he loses control for Holtby to score. Only he doesn't. Fortunately for us, the ref gives a free kick for a push on Harrison. We are living dangerously and both teams seem to have thrown caution to the wind, attacking freely from all areas. Bamford turns neatly on a loose ball and sends a shot against the left-hand post before Walton saves well from Ayling, who diverts a Douglas corner goalwards. Blackburn make a mess of the clearance and Harrison is brought down on the edge of the area. Phillips takes the free-kick and scores brilliantly with a curling shot high into the top corner of the goal.

Two-nil.

But no time to relax. Margie comes in and wants to jump on me and play games. I need to concentrate on the match and I am worried that I might lose the plot and start screaming and cursing at the television. I don't want to frighten them, especially as Margie is clearly enjoying seeing 'Ampa', as she seems to call both me and Andy. Georgie also is beginning to smile as she lies in her pod watching the action.

We reach half-time with our lead intact, and I suddenly realise I can't bear to watch any more. I need to focus and concentrate; I need to curse and jump up and down; I need to throw things and let off steam. So, I do something I haven't done for probably 50 years and decide I can't watch any more. Instead, I suggest to Andy we take Margie for a walk and that's what we do, staying out until five past five, when I know the game will be finished. It's now I can begin to understand why Ben does his 'Benny blackout' thing, though I must admit not watching any of the games seems to be a little extreme. Still, 'whatever gets you through the night', as John Lennon said. The positive about not knowing until after the event and then turning on and finding out, is that you only take one hit rather than suffering the death of a thousand cuts.

We come back from our walk along by the beck side and cross over from the farmer's side of the bank, walking along the plank towards the house, and then I see Mike gesticulating by the French windows. He's showing the score by putting up his fingers, but his left hand is partially obscured, and it looks as if it's 3-3. My heart sinks and I shout out at him, 'Three all?' and then experience floods of relief as he comes out and tells me that we won 1-3. A huge victory which restores our six-point (really five) lead over Brentford. We lead WBA, too, but they play Hull tomorrow and must be favourites to win, even though Hull scored that last-minute victory over 'Boro.'

I see Andy exchange knowing smiles with Lou. It means our celebration dinner of their homecoming will go with a swing, and it does, as we sip champagne to 'wet baby Georgia's head' and have a really good catch-up about all that has been happening since our last visit to Dublin in January. Later, the girls turn in and Mike and I watch the EFL highlights on Quest that I had taped earlier. It's great to be able to watch the highlights and slow things down to watch key moments again, and even greater to watch knowing that we have won. We enjoy a nightcap watching the programme, before both of us fall asleep as we struggle to keep focused on *Match of the Day*. It's been a long day, especially for Mike and Lou, and even though they have travelled and have the two little ones, I had been up earlier than them, writing up my notes and praying for three points. So I was knackered, too!

The matches are coming thick and fast now, and the joy of Saturday's win is soon forgotten as WBA duly beat Hull on Sunday, though the Tigers made them fight for their 4-2 victory. Swansea also won, beating Sheffield Wednesday, though I'm not quite sure how the Owls messed it up, having been so dominant in the early stages. So, Swansea are also back in the scrap for the play-off places.

On the Tuesday, we wander round a neighbouring village and Margie plays on the swings and slides. We also visit our local, The Shoulder of Mutton, where we haven't been since the end of February. It's been 'done up' and looks good. It's a totally brilliant 'proper' pub that encourages chat and friendship and puts on the best free bar snacks ever on a Sunday lunchtime and Friday evening. Lots of pickle, cheese, pork pie, and wedges – totally yum! I think we are reaching the stage of the season where I need to go back to the idea of a diary to help record results and the jockeying for positions. Just over two weeks and it will all be over... Unless, that is, we find ourselves in the dreaded play-offs.

Tuesday 7th July

Lots of big games today, and I have my fingers crossed that Lee Bowyer will do us a favour and take a point from Brentford, who are chasing us and West Brom down, and looking a real threat. What's amazing about all this tension and the quick turnaround between games is the number of teams who seem to have 'blown it' but suddenly find themselves back in contention. Fulham are one of them and, having lost back-to-back games against Brentford and ourselves, they have dragged themselves back into the fight for automatic promotion. They scored an injury-time winner against lowly Birmingham at the weekend, and then today won at Forest. It's now a four-horse race and no-one can afford to be the team that slips up; there is so little time to recover.

Blackburn show how good our win was on Saturday when they go to in-form Cardiff and twice come from behind to win 2-3. This is good news, as it means Derby are still in touch with the race for play-off spots, so they still have everything to play for at WBA tomorrow evening.

Mike and family head to Wakefield this afternoon to visit Andy's mum, 'Great Nana', and after an early night last night we are looking forward to another champagne dinner (why not?) this evening before they leave on Wednesday to visit Lou's mum Anne, in St. Albans. It's been great to see them and be able to get to know Margie again and see how much Georgia has grown into her smile since that first day in Dublin when we were there to celebrate her birth.

Brentford and Charlton is the evening kick-off and starts while Mike and Lou are still settling the children. Forest v Fulham was the televised game earlier, so we get the first news of the match from Griffin Park from Jeff and the panel, and what news it is! Charlton have taken an early lead through their forward Bonne, who got the winner against us at the Valley. I share the good news with Mike as he comes back downstairs and get a few WhatsApps from the group encouraging the Charlton team to 'park the bus', which they happily do. They want the points just as much as we want them to get them!

We pour our drinks and I make a few discreet visits to the study to get a quick score update. It's good news; Charlton still lead and it's half-time. I decide to turn the television off and just go back to the results at the end of the game as we are having a really relaxed and happy evening and I don't want to put a damper on it. When we finish eating, we pour a nightcap and soon Lou is ready to turn in. As everybody starts to say goodnight, I go and turn the telly back on, and have that awful half-second of panic as my eyes struggle to take in all the information in front of them. Bugger! They have won! I had been praying somehow they'd get at least a point, but Benrahma scored with a penalty after 75 minutes, and Pinnock headed the winner from a corner in the 85th minute. They are now just three points behind us and suddenly that relief and optimism that filled us on Saturday has all but drained away. 'It's still in our hands,' Mike comments, but he's fooling no-one and his words just mumble into nothing as both of us realise we are in a real fight now and simply can't afford to drop points against Stoke. We turn the telly off, and with Lou in bed, Mike, Andy, and I sit drinking red wine and chatting through to the early hours, thankfully taking my mind off the unfolding drama in the Championship.

Wednesday, 8th July

It doesn't seem a minute since they arrived, but Mike and family leave us at lunchtime, heading south. We will meet up with them next Monday, so it's not an emotional farewell, just more a case of a 'see you later'. I guess as you get older you forget how much energy you need looking after toddlers, but as they leave I head to the village shop in Darrington, a few miles down the road, and buy some bread and a paper. Within 30 minutes of their departure, we are eating toast and drinking tea; five minutes after that, we are reading the paper... and a few seconds later, we are both asleep!

Later, as we come round and realise it is still raining, I write some more notes and then settle down to see if Derby can take points from the Albion at the Hawthorns. But despite the fact they can go level with Cardiff in sixth place, they never look like causing any kind of upset. They are understrength, missing Lawrence and Waghorn – both serving suspensions – but they never really give it a go, preferring to play possession football and often passing back to their keeper rather than humping the ball into the penalty area – a tactic which had brought them their totally undeserved equaliser against Forest last week.

Thankfully, I am not a Derby fan, and wouldn't want to be either, but if I was, I would have been hopping mad with their performance at WBA. They played with a total absence of ambition, and deservedly lost 2-0. I seriously hope they are on their game against Brentford on Saturday. We desperately need them to be and so do they, as defeat should end all hope they have of reaching the play-offs. One interesting result I note before I crawl off to bed is that Preston have won at Hillsborough, and just like Fulham who seemed completely out of things a few games ago, they are suddenly right back in the scrap for the play-off places. Having been up late with Mike last night, it's an early bed, and once more before sleep comes I run through the fixture lists in my head. WBA's win puts them back on top of the table, two points clear of us, with Brentford just three points away in third. We have to make our game in hand work; we have to put the pressure back on Brentford; we have to win tomorrow. We simply have to!

Thursday, 9th July: 5.15am

I am awake, and I lie there knowing something is wrong but not sure as I come round just what it is. And then I remember the results and the table, and I feel depressed. It's still raining – I can hear it beating against the window – it's been raining for days. I slip out of bed, grabbing the shorts and jumper I'd left lying on the rather nice bedroom chair Andy bought from Laura Ashley before it shut down. I had slept fitfully, like I usually do when we have to be up early to get to an airport or travel to look after the grandkids. Only we don't have to be up; we're not going anywhere today. Downstairs it's quiet, and the early morning light is a wall of unrelenting grey, reflecting my mood. Today is another 'D Day' and there are going to be another four more like this before the season ends on the 22nd July, just thirteen days away. We need ten points from a possible 15 to be certain of promotion, 2/3rds, 66%, three wins and a draw. We can even afford to lose one of these 'D Day' games and still have promotion in our own hands. Just ten points. I find myself writing these notes longhand rather than typing on my iPad. It seems my thoughts just fly out of my head almost without thinking, filling the empty pages with words and thoughts, so frenziedly written that, later on, I find them almost impossible to read. There is a Beatles song that comes into my head as I write, and which perfectly fits my mood and the day dawning outside.

'Words are flowing out like endless rain into a paper cup
They slither while they pass, they slip across the Universe
Pools of sorrow, waves of joy, are drifting through my open mind
Possessing and caressing me.'

Genius.

I am caught up completely in this race for promotion, gripped by the uncertainty of it all. Lifted so high by the 'waves of joy' experienced after the relief and release of our win over Blackburn, and dragged right down by the 'pools of sorrow', knowing that if we lose tonight we are effectively two points clear of Brentford. Two points that just 16 days ago was a lifesaving ten, given their point for a better goal difference.

I think back to last night and WBA's win over a toothless Derby side. They seemed to have so many options up front, with three forwards fighting for the starting berth and two excellent championship players, Grosciki and Robinson, recruited in the transfer window to bolster their promotion push. What on earth were we doing during the 'window', desperate for another striker, desperate for an experienced keeper, desperate for the additions that to my mind would have made promotion a near certainty, rather than having to live through this blackness and frustration? I know the tables and the remaining fixtures for most clubs, and I know all the permutations. They are branded into my mind, filling my thoughts with anxiety and foreboding. We have been here before.

Last night, just to make things worse, Swansea beat Birmingham 1-3. It's a win that puts them right back into the play-off race, just a point behind their Welsh rivals Cardiff, and means they will be completely 'up for it' for our game against them at the Liberty this weekend. There are so many clubs involved in so many huge games in the Championship at every level: the race to avoid relegation; the race for the play-offs, and of course, the race for automatic promotion. Almost every game means something. And almost every 'fan' will know that their mood is completely dictated by not just the fortunes of their own team, but also by the progress, or lack of it, of those around them.

The highs and lows, the raw emotion of following a football team, mean we are every bit as 'possessed and caressed' by the fates as John Lennon was.

CHAPTER 20

JACK, THE FAMILY GATHERS,
THE TENSION MOUNTS,
PROMOTION AT LAST

Leeds United…5; Stoke City…0
Thursday, 9th July

Having made an early and rather listless start to the day, I realise that Andy's sympathies for her distracted husband are unlikely to last until kick-off time, so I suggest we should get out of the house and head for the shopping centre near York. We are heading down to Ashwell with the caravan on Sunday to get ready for the family reunion on Monday, when we are all gathering at the rather large and very attractive house Mike and Lou have rented for the second week of their holiday.

I need some smarter casual clothes for the trip, basically a polo shirt or two as for some reason I've lost one of mine and the other has lost all its colour through overuse since the lockdown. Andy is happy to get out of the house, so we set off mid-morning and, as it's still throwing it down and we are under no time pressure, I decide to go the long way round on the minor roads rather than pick up the A1/A64 route. I haven't been in a shopping centre since probably Christmas and am really impressed by the organisation of the centre in terms of its recognition of the continuing dangers of the Coronavirus. As we enter the buildings there are several handwash areas and clear signage about the way of travel and social distancing. Perhaps more impressive, given the ridiculous behaviour of those that headed to the beaches of Bournemouth and Brighton recently, is the common sense and respect of the shoppers who happily follow the 'rules' and enjoy the experience of being out and about again in what is a really well maintained centre.

There are loads of shops here, but I know exactly what I want and Andy isn't really in a shopping mood and knows she is better off without me skulking behind her when she is. We wonder round to the 'Polo' shop and I quickly choose a couple of shirts, one pink, one white. Fortunately, because I hate changing rooms, I am dressed for as easy a change as possible, wearing shorts, a t-shirt and jumper, so I can try the new stuff on as easily as possible. It's a good job as when I have made my selections, I realise the 'changing rooms' are in fact closed. Given what I am wearing, I just take my jumper off and try one of the shirts for size, putting it on over my t-shirt. They fit no problem, and as Andy has a quick look round, I head towards the payment tills and she joins me, having chosen a nice collar shirt she has seen. Job done.

We take our time walking round the centre in the general direction of the entrance we came through. We would normally, after such a trip, go and find a pub to have some lunch, but the ones we like are still shut so instead we go into a coffee shop and get some cheese and ham croissants, which are really tasty. As we sit there eating, looking out at the shoppers wandering past, I notice a few are wearing Leeds shirts and I wonder if they are feeling the pain like me. It's just a few hours to another 'D Day' and our home fixture with Stoke City. It seems a long time since that gloriously hot August afternoon that I stood outside the Stoke ground looking up at the statue of Gordon Banks and getting ready to watch what turned out to be one of our best performances of the season. We could do with another one this afternoon, we really could.

The WhatsApp group is full of nervous chatter, and Ben has already said he is heading out on a long walk, only returning when he is certain the game is over. Katherine is watching with one eye on the telly while she gets the kids ready for bed, and then she will base herself in one room while Nick watches Spurs in another. A 'Carling' wife if ever there was one! James is home in Wandsworth and able to watch the Sky coverage, while Mike has discovered Anne, his mother-in-law, doesn't have Sky and is in a panic about how to watch the game. I consider for a moment whether to record the match and just enjoy a meal and our usual early evening routine, checking the score at the end so I can watch it 'as live' knowing we have won, or just delete it if we haven't. In the end, though, I can't help sitting down five or so minutes before the game kicks off and deciding to watch the start to see how we are going to play and how confident we look.

Dallas and Costa, who has just signed permanently, are both back in the team, with Alioski and Douglas back on the bench. They are joined there once again by Hernandez, still apparently struggling with a hamstring problem. I think the use of Pablo has been really good, as Roberts has worked hard in the first half and Hernandez has come on in the second, where his vision, creativity, and sheer class has been able to change most of the games he has appeared in.

Stoke have had a dreadful season given the players at their disposal, and while results have improved under Michael O'Neil, they still find themselves in real relegation trouble. They will need to get something from this match, so I'm expecting a really tough challenge. It seems, on paper at least, that they have better players than Luton, who made things so difficult for us last week. Joe Allen is out on long-term injury, which must have been a huge blow for O'Neil who achieved so much with a small pool of players during his tenure as coach of Northern Ireland, getting the very best out of some lower division players, including our own Stuart Dallas.

I'm glad to see Ince is on the bench, as he always seems to do well against us, probably because our chant about him and his dad winds him up so much. Nick Powell is a danger, though, and on their day Vokes up front and Butland in goal can do well. Let's just hope today is not their day. Stoke actually start quite positively, and after Butland saves well from Roberts in the first seconds, they slowly play their way into the game, chasing us down and making it difficult for us to get into our usual pattern of play. Gradually we begin to create openings, with our pace and movement beginning to pull the Stoke back five out of position. Bamford in space runs into the penalty area to clip the ball goalwards as Butland races out to close him down. The ball seems to take a slight deflection off the keeper, which helps the covering Stoke defender to clear off the line, but only straight into the path of Tyler

Roberts. I am already jumping from my seat to celebrate what surely must be the opening goal, but Robert's goalbound shot is blocked by the desperate dive of Danny Batth. And it looks as if Stoke will survive until half-time and go some way to ramping up the anxiety on our players, just as Luton did, by disciplined defence and the chance for quick counterattacks.

Then as they play out a few minutes' added time, Costa breaks through the Stoke lines with a diagonal run towards the left-hand corner of the penalty area. The ref plays an excellent advantage as a Stoke player pulled on his shirt, and well done, ref, because if he hadn't we wouldn't have won the penalty that comes when Tommy Smith stupidly scythes down Costa as he runs away from the goal. I can't imagine how angry his manager will have been at such a reckless challenge, made at a time when the visitors had almost achieved their first objective of getting to half-time without conceding. Who will take the penalty? We have not been very good from the few penalties we have been awarded, with Bamford, Klich, and even Hernandez, all guilty of damaging misses from the spot, which just this season have cost us two points against Derby and at least one at QPR. It seems ages before eventually Klich puts the ball on the spot, and I find myself standing by the study door, half in and half out, hardly daring to look. But Klich has no such fears and calmly sends Butland the wrong way before coolly passing the ball into the net.

It's a massive goal, and I shout and shout with the momentary release of tension. Such an important time to score as well, but still 45 minutes to go. I wish it could finish now; I'd just take the three points and move on. But such is life. If I had been able to do that, I would have missed one of our best performances since that sunny day in Stoke all those months ago. We are simply brilliant in the second half, blowing Stoke away with the power, pace, and precision of our football. Costa scores the second, played in beautifully by Dallas, though just for a moment it looks as though the chance has gone as he seems to turn back into the defenders before righting himself and toe-poking the ball home into the right-hand corner. It is a finish I used loads of times playing five-a-side football, and it's amazing the power you can get striking the ball with

350

your toecap – and the accuracy, too. I had no doubt he would score and a great way for him to celebrate his new contract.

The third follows soon after. We force a corner on the left and Hernandez, on as a second-half substitute, switches the play and follows his pass by running unmarked across the width of the penalty area. Amazingly, he isn't tracked by a defender – our best player just allowed the freedom of the most dangerous part of the pitch. Unbelievable. Kalvin Phillips knows where he is, though, and slides the ball through for Hernandez to attack the byeline before picking out Liam Cooper, who scores with a right foot shot that goes in off the post. A brilliant team goal, and there is more to come as Stoke disintegrate under the pressure. Ayling sends Costa away down the right-hand flank and the Portuguese looks up before passing across the area and Bamford shows real class, letting the ball run under his foot to the onrushing Hernandez, who curls the ball superbly past Butland from the edge of the area. Breathtaking stuff against a team who should have been fighting for their lives but who had long since given up the ghost. FOUR-NIL. And for once, no nail-biting, heart-stopping last few minutes to negotiate. FOUR FRIGGING NIL!

There is even time for a fifth and it is Bamford who scores it, fastening on to a superb long diagonal pass from Ayling and slowing his pace to ensure he is balanced enough to send a shot scudding past Butland and into the net, off the right-hand post. What a fantastic performance and, as the Sky commentator said, it actually flattered Stoke.

They had been awful in the second half, with some senior players following the example of Tommy Smith by letting the club down, behaving and playing like raw, inexperienced juniors. I don't care about Stoke, but their fans do and they deserved better than this, just like Derby's fans deserved better in their club's meek surrender at WBA. At least Charlton showed some fight at Brentford; it's always better to go down scrapping. Fans usually forgive anything if the players show fight and determination. Show some spirit, for God's sake. Andy poured some drinks, and after the football finished I think she sensed my mood and need to watch over all the key parts of the game again, So, after a glass or two, she decided to turn in and leave me to my celebrations and writing. I didn't do any writing, after all; just had a few beers and checked the league table out (we are back on top, a point ahead of WBA, and have restored the six-point – but really five-point – lead over Brentford in third).

I watched a bit of the Villa/Man U game, but after our match and style of play it all seemed a bit dull. I did see the award of a penalty to Manchester, which was given even after a VAR check, and I wonder how hopeless the people who sit in judgement are when they make such obviously wrong decisions, even with the benefit of slow motion replays. I am certainly no Villa fan, but really how bad was the decision? And earlier there was another one when Harry Kane was clearly fouled in the penalty area by a desperately clumsy Bournemouth player, only for VAR to rule out the penalty award. I am basically a big fan of VAR, and there seems no reason to me why it shouldn't work as well as it does in rugby league, but it doesn't. So, like in rugby union, it must be down to the incompetence of match officials. As I have argued before, it's time to make the job as attractive to former players as possible, in the same way that coaching is, for example, and then reward them properly for using their understanding of the game along with making them pass the most stringent of physical, mental, and obviously rules-of-the-game tests.

In the end, I pour another John Smith's and settle down to watch the whole of our second half again. We were brilliant, and as Andy said when I was saying we could have scored eight, 'Just shut up and enjoy it.' I did. Just seven points needed from four games to play. Crikey! We can even afford to lose one.

Friday, 10th July

With the games coming thick and fast, there is some discussion on our family WhatsApp about whether it is better to play first and get your match over with, or play second – as we seem destined to do now until the end of the season. Mike thinks it's a bonus for Brentford, as the team chasing the top two, to get their points on the board. And certainly that's the way it has been playing out, such has been the form of the men from West London. On the other hand, if they slip up, then we know – playing later – exactly what we must do. So, who exactly is under the most pressure?

I think the truth is that, certainly since the resumption, it is the top two who have been most under attack, and who have had to deal with the pressure of being 'chased' down, especially by an in-form Brentford side. This weekend, all the top sides have potentially tough games and all are away from home. Brentford visit a Derby team who, if they are serious about reaching the play-offs, have simply got to play with more ambition than they did in their meek surrender to WBA in midweek. The Albion themselves go to Blackburn – a side whose top six ambitions were seriously damaged by our 1-3 win there, but who recovered in midweek to defeat a strong Cardiff outfit on the Welsh club's home ground. As for us, we head to South Wales again and a battle with an in-form Swansea at the Liberty Stadium, a ground where we have had some disappointing results in recent times.

Andy drives to Wakefield this morning to see her mum, and I busy myself with getting stuff ready for our caravan outing down to Ashwell on Sunday. The Caravan Club have text to ask us not to arrive at the site before 1pm, rather than the usual 12. It's all about the 'virus' and giving the management team time to prepare the facilities between departures and arrivals. I completely get this, but with the game in Wales due to kick off at 1.30, it means we will struggle to get onto a pitch and get the caravan up and running before kick-off. I reckon if all goes to plan and I arrive about 12.40, they should let me on the site and we should get first pick of the pitches, get the jobs done, and be just about ready to stress about whether I will be able to pick up the signal from LUTV before the match starts. It will be touch and go, but at least I have a plan.

Later that day there are some interesting results from the Championship. Luton beat Huddersfield 0-2, which I think is a surprise after Town's win at Birmingham, and Fulham drag themselves right back into contention for automatic promotion with a 2-0 win over top six-chasing Cardiff. It's very clear now there are four again, and the question will be just whose nerve will hold out: the two leaders, Leeds and Albion; or the two chasers, Brentford and Fulham. Just 12 days to the end of the season; 12 days until we will all know our destiny.

Saturday, 11th July

For once it's not raining, and I have work to do, with both the garden and the 'new lawn' development on the banks of the beck needing cutting. This 'lockdown' development has seriously added to the gardening workload, but now we have opened up the access to the Magic Garden, even I can see the benefits. So, it makes all my effort worthwhile and Andy just loves pottering and adding more plants and colour to the project she created. While I am linking up three different extension cables to stretch from the house across the garden over the fence and across the beck, in order to get the lawnmower plugged in, Andy goes up to the caravan with some clothes and electrical stuff, like the television and iPods, so that we're not bogged down with jobs in the morning.

I was due to go into the beck with Mike and Nigel to clear a load of pond weed out of the water from a little further down from our houses and which is affecting the flow of the water. This 'fun' activity is, thankfully, cancelled as: A) the water level is too high, following all the rain of recent days; and B) Mike wants to watch the Derby v Brentford game, which is being shown at lunchtime. I wasn't sure about this one and know I have jobs to do with the car once Andy is back, like checking tyre pressures, and maybe getting it washed as well. In the end, I tune into the match from Derby just before half-time, with the score at 1-1. This would be a great result for us, and on my own predictor I have all three of the top teams due to draw their games this afternoon.

Andy walks in almost just as the half-time whistle blows, and we have a sandwich and a cup of tea before I nip for a quick bath to get rid of the smell of my stinking beck waders. I am listening to 5Live while I clean myself up, but there's no update on the score from Pride Park – or whatever the ground at Derby is called now. This is good news. Except there is a shock waiting as I go into the study to check the score. It's only just the start of the second half, and already Brentford have retaken the lead through Benrahma, courtesy of a dreadful mistake by the Derby keeper. Benrahma does it again a few minutes later, with a brilliant curling shot into the top corner to seal yet another three points for the team from West London.

Derby are again hopeless, passing the ball square and back with seemingly no urgency to attack or to try and save the game. Rooney is getting caught a lot in possession, and it does look as if this might be a season too far for him as a starting player. I am praying for him to get a free kick on the edge of the area, but Derby only seem interested in passing the ball to each other in non-threatening areas. I hope they are as passive and lacking in creativity and desire when they play us in a week or so, but I bet they come out fighting against old enemies.

The three points send Brentford back just three points behind us, and they can rest up now as the pressure switches to West Brom later on in the afternoon, and ourselves tomorrow. I settle down to watch *Soccer Saturday* with Jeff Stelling, but I don't like the fact that the game from Blackburn is being followed in the studio by Paul Merson and you can hear him shouting and making comments. For some reason, I don't like this; I'd rather just be told the score or see it come up on the screen. Anyway, it's clear from Merson's comments that WBA are well in charge, and it's not long before he and Albion have a goal to celebrate, scored by Krovinovic just before half-time, though it sounds from the commentary that Albion have squandered a number of chances. Sensing a comfortable win for WBA, I decide to go to sort the car out and hope that Blackburn can fashion some of the chances that they did against us last week. I keep the car radio off so I can't follow the scores, and I'm not interested in listening to the commentary of the Premiership match as I go about my business. But once the jobs are done, I dare to press the switch on button. And it's great news.

The commentary match is interrupted to go to Blackburn, where the home side have just equalised through Rothwell, the substitute who had played so well against us. There were still 25 minutes or so to go, so I switch off again, go and check the tyres, and then drive the long way home as slowly as I can. Eventually I have to check the score, and find the game is in added time and the teams are still level. 'Come on, for goodness sake finish,' I say to myself – and then it does, and Albion have dropped two points. This must be a big blow to them, especially as they were so dominant in the first half. They have Fulham next, and the Londoners know that they must win at the Hawthorns if they are to have any hope of finishing in the top two. The thought crosses my mind that just maybe we should hope for Albion to drop points, as we still have a slender lead in the goal difference stakes.

Elsewhere, Preston draw with Forest, so will still be just about in contention for the play-offs when they play at Brentford next. And at the bottom, none of the clubs in danger can fashion a victory, so all still have much to play for, even Barnsley who are next up at ER… but not before our tough encounter with Swansea tomorrow. There is plenty to think about as I climb into bed, but by far the biggest and saddest news linked to Leeds United today is the announcement of the passing of Jack Charlton at the age of 85.

Following the loss of Norman Hunter and Trevor Cherry in this lockdown, it's yet another day of sadness for the club and its fans, especially the older ones like myself who have clear memories of the great sixties team. The press and media coverage of Jack's passing is huge, with tributes paid to his life not just by the great of football, but also by the Prime Minister, the Leader of the Opposition, and the President of Ireland. Such glowing comments reflected so well on Jack the person – the character loved equally in Leeds and Ireland: uncompromising, driven, funny, and successful, an immense man who lived his life in the way he was brought up, with honesty, occasional bloody-mindedness, and very real talent. His life skills allowed him to be successful in many different walks of life. Obviously as a footballer and a hugely successful manager at both club and international level, but also in the world of television media, where he was an incisive and at times humorous contributor to a variety of sports programmes. He developed a successful career as an after dinner speaker, too, and I saw him once at Maidenhead Rugby Club of all places, where my brother-in-law was a player at the time.

He was very funny and wove his speech around three players he had special memories of playing with and against – Billy Bremner, Nobby Stiles, and Bobby Moore. I can't remember all of the stories, but one of being scared of Stiles coming to 'get him' and another when he was telling Moore to kick the ball out of the ground before the English skipper sent Geoff Hurst through to score his hat-trick goal with a stunning through ball, were very well received. I went to chat with him after he had finished speaking, and got his autograph on a souvenir mini rugby ball, which is right in front of me as I write.

The ink is a little faded now along with maybe some of my memories, but not all of them. Jack, like Norman, was a part of my youth, the constant part of my life that let me escape the worries of school and exams, and just for 90 minutes or so immerse myself in another world of high emotions and the shared dreams of what it was like to be a fan of Leeds United. His nickname was 'the giraffe' because of the length of his neck, and possibly also his tall, leggy appearance. His running style was more of a flustered gallop than a smooth measured sprint, and he could appear ungainly and anything but a balanced athlete. But if any of that description were true, and if anyone decided that such a player couldn't be a threat or make a significant contribution, they would have been very wrong. Very wrong indeed.

Jack could play, and so well that even before his great success began at Leeds in the early sixties, football managers of the stature of Matt Busby and Bill Shankly were interested in signing him. Their delay in making formal approaches allowed Don Revie, newly installed as manager, to get Charlton 'on board' for his plans for the development of the club. Jack had been at Leeds since 1953 and had developed a bit of a reputation as an outspoken member of the dressing room. That he was 'savvy' enough to understand what Revie was planning helped forge an important relationship between the two men that would have hugely beneficial outcomes for the club.

Revie knew that Jack could play and that he could be a cornerstone of the successful club he was planning to deliver. He just needed to know that Jack wanted to share the dream. And for both men's futures, thank goodness he did. As a footballer, Jack won every domestic honour playing for Leeds. He also won European honours with the club, winning the old Fairs Cup, and of course, playing for England in 1966 he was immortalised when he was part of the team that won the World Cup. In addition, he was voted 'Footballer of the Year' in 1967, and in a Leeds career of 762 appearances he scored 95 goals. If you add the six goals Jack scored for England in his 35 appearances, that's over 100 first class goals. Not a bad return for an ungainly centre half. He was famous for the little 'black book' in which he said he had the names of two players he would willingly kick into the stands if he got the opportunity. But in truth, he wasn't a dirty player and was only sent off once in his career, when reacting to an off-the-ball attack by a Valencia player.

He was also famous for the tactic he and Revie came up with of him standing by the near post when waiting for a corner. There were lots of people who didn't like this, arguing it was unfair on the goalkeeper, but it didn't break the rules and Charlton scored goals for Leeds and England using this move. Strangely, the match I remember Jack playing in most vividly was his testimonial game against Celtic in May 1973, just a couple of days after that awful FA Cup loss to Sunderland. Jack didn't play in the cup final, having been injured in our semi-final victory over Wolves at Maine Rd. It was a day we left the ground celebrating what we thought were going to be back-to-back FA Cup victories, when we heard the news that Sunderland – a Division Two (Championship)) club in those days – had beaten Arsenal in the other semi-final. The pain of being a Leeds fan.

The game against Celtic was obviously a friendly, but both teams went full-on for the victory in a kind of unofficial 'battle of Britain'. I remember the ground was rammed and there were thousands of Celtic fans adding to the atmosphere. It was a little reminiscent of our Fairs Cup match with Rangers, when over 50,000 squeezed into ER to watch us knock out the Glasgow club on the way to winning our first

European trophy. That night, I had started out in the 'Scratching Shed' and had almost been pushed round into the East stand, such was the pressure of the crowd. I remember listening to a very drunken female Rangers fan trying to explain, with the use of God knows how many numerous expletives to a policeman, that her 'F**king' husband had left her and she had no 'F**king money', and didn't know how to get 'F**king home', as he patiently escorted her from the ground.

While the testimonial match lacked the prize of a European trophy, it didn't lack a competitive edge, and you only need to look at the names of the goal scorers to understand the quality of player on show that night. Leeds lost in the end 3-4, with Clarke (2) and Bremner scoring for us, and Johnstone (2), Lennox, and Dalglish on target for the Celts. It was a fantastic match played in a great atmosphere, though sadly Big Jack could only manage a cameo appearance before being forced off after 20 minutes or so. He came back on at the end, and it was that moment that provided the vivid memory I still have today as Jack ran round the Elland Rd ground, waving and clapping the fans he had entertained throughout his career, and ended up throwing himself into the arms of Don Revie – the man who had almost certainly reignited his career. It was an emotional moment for both men and one that had been forged by a mutual respect over many years. There was just something about that embrace that made a big impression on a young 19-year-old watching on from what is now known as 'The Revie' stand. Rest in peace, Jack.

Swansea City...0; Leeds United...1
Sunday, 12th July

Sometimes being busy is the biggest antidote to having a stressed mind, and for me hitching up the caravan and driving it 150 miles or so is perfect, in that it actually doubles the stress level and leaves precious little time for any positive or negative thought. Today is no exception and aiming to get to the site in time for a 1.30 kick-off doesn't help matters. Neither does the fact that we haven't been in the 'van' since February and the visit to Brentford, and I've forgotten how everything works!

When we get up to the storage base, we quickly get the legs down and I stand with the motor mover, which brilliantly helps move the caravan into position, avoiding all the pulling and pushing that used to be the case. Only, nothing happens. The frigging caravan refuses to move even one centimetre, even when I shout abuse at it, and Andy has to warn me there are other caravanners in the vicinity. I push the buttons harder, but still nothing, and then I realise I haven't fixed the connecting piece of equipment which allows the whole thing to operate successfully. Stupid me.

Eventually we are ready to hook up, and for some reason this relatively easy operation takes much longer than usual, with the hook seemingly unwilling to connect to the ball on the car. Andy clearly gets frustrated by my uselessness and bad language, but fortunately before sparks fly the damn thing falls into place and we are ready to roll. It's a journey we know so well, and on a Sunday the traffic is much lighter with, especially for a caravan driver, far fewer lorries to worry about. We are making good time and, having been told not to arrive before 1pm, we pull into the Peterborough Services and get a sandwich and some milk for a cuppa later. With the roadworks around the A14 nearing completion, we can go one of two ways: either coming off the A14 heading to Royston, or staying on the A1 to Baldock and picking up the A505. We decide on the latter and approach the caravan site at Ashwell at about 12.45, just as I had planned, hoping to be there just a few minutes ahead of the queue.

I was wrong. The queue was in front of me, and the checking-in process seemed to be taking an age, particularly as one woman was fussing around so much, I was almost ready to let the handbrake slip momentarily. Every time I thought she'd finished, she took a few steps and then spun on her heels and went back for more. The reception people were far too kind and civil to her, answering her every query with patience and understanding, while I watched as the clock face moved round to five past one, 25 minutes to kick-off. 'Shut the fuck up!' Once we had gone through the arrival process, we set off to drive around the site, checking where there were spaces and hoping we could get one that got the evening sun, as we knew some of the pitches went very quickly into the shade. We were in luck and got probably the best pitch on the site in terms of the light.

Once unhooked and legs down, we busied ourselves with various jobs, Andy working in the caravan sorting clothes and foodstuffs, and me working outside setting up the water systems, toilets, and electricity. By the time the basic stuff had been achieved and some beers were in the fridge freezer, it was already 1.40 and the game at the Liberty was ten minutes old. Nick had advised me about buying a new iPad and reckoned I should be able to pick up the internet on it and access Sky Sports and LUFC. The match was on the Leeds channel, and I nervously signed in to await the score. It was still 0-0.

We were pretty much at strength, with Roberts continuing to start ahead of Hernandez, while Swansea also looked strong and had the Liverpool loanee Brewster, a regular goalscorer, playing up front. I found it difficult to concentrate on the game as Andy was working around me, and in fairness I knew there were things I needed to be doing. The signal from Swansea helped my decision-making as I kept losing the pictures, so I got on with setting up the television and tuning it all in. I kept going back to the game and saw one great chance for Bamford, who placed his shot too close to the keeper Woodman. I kept with it until half-time, with the picture frustratingly coming and going, and then went back to my chores.

It was a lovely day, and though we were quite close to Katherine's, we were not meeting up with anyone until tomorrow. So, we could put our feet up and enjoy a few chilled beers in the sunshine if... if only we could get a result at Swansea. A draw wouldn't be a disaster, especially after WBA's slip-up at Blackburn. I kept my eyes on the time and tuned in again, only to see Meslier make a good save from a strong Gallagher shot. Not good for the nerves. And then Hernandez, on at the break, passed to Harrison, whose volleyed cross bounced up perfectly for the incoming Bamford to surely head home. I was up in the air, only to sit down with a thump as Bamford placed his header again just too close to the keeper, who gratefully made the save. F**k!

361

It looked as if we were going to be held, but with time almost running out, in the 89th minute Ayling made another lung-bursting run down the right and pulled the ball back to Hernandez, who seemed to be well covered but somehow swivelled and turned and fired a shot into the net off the far post. Watching replays, it was the only place he could possibly have put the ball and score, and he did it to perfection. Commentating on LUTV, Bryn Law caught the mood brilliantly as he screamed, 'Gol-gol-gol-gooooool!' down his microphone. Andy raced into the caravan to shut me up, half delighted that we'd scored and half aware that I'd woken up a slumbering Sunday afternoon group of 'happy campers' with my 'gol-gol-gol' celebrations.

I couldn't believe it. I'd started the afternoon hoping for at least a draw, but secretly worried that Swansea might inflict their second defeat of the season on us, especially as I'd been so disparaging about their performance at ER earlier in the season when they scored an undeserved last-minute winner. Now it was our turn to steal the game in the last seconds, and how good did it feel! Except, of course, the game hadn't finished and there was still time for Swansea to pull a goal back.

I think I saw a sign saying five minutes' added time but I can't remember exactly. I was too excited, too nervous, talking gibberish, and wringing my hands. I realised I couldn't bear to watch these closing minutes – the three points, if we could hold on, were going to be massive. I prop the iPad up against the telly and realise my hands are shaking so much I can't get it to settle. So, I put it back on the sofa and set off to walk round the perimeter of the site, which I reckon should take about five minutes to do.

I couldn't help thinking of all those West Brom and Brentford fans watching on their televisions and listening on their radios, praying we would drop points. I know how they will be feeling when someone like Jeff Stelling says, 'And late drama at the Liberty!' You just wait for that split second, knowing you are going to feel elated or crushed. They will all feel crushed if this goes our way, experiencing that awful hit-below-the-belt feeling. I reckon I've been walking a good seven minutes, so

I brave going back to the caravan – and they are still playing! What the frig is going on? Why are they still playing?

I heard Bryn Law saying, 'No-one really knows how much longer there is to go' and then realised there had been an injury to the Swansea keeper, and that is why the game was still being played out. And then suddenly the whistle blows and we have won! You could tell in the players' reactions, the way they celebrated Hernandez's goal, the way they rejoiced at the final whistle, that this was a huge win. And it was. I couldn't believe it, and sat down to listen to the closing headlines on LUTV. This kind of thing doesn't happen to us Leeds fans, does it? We are so used to our dreams being shattered at the last hurdle; so used to the pain of defeat. Yet suddenly we are three points clear of West Brom and have kept Brentford at a six-point distance. The players seem to be handling the pressure better than the fans; the players seem determined to win the prize this time.

How good does the world seem when your team has won? We sit outside the caravan in the late afternoon sun, drinking cold beer, and know we can completely enjoy the next few days until our next match at home to Barnsley on Thursday. Before then, WBA and Brentford have tough matches against Fulham and Preston respectively. Fulham, if they can beat Albion, are still in the hunt for automatic promotion.

It's time for the others to feel the pressure, but I definitely sense that we have taken a massive step towards promotion today, and the others will think so, too. They will all have been praying that Swansea could cause us some problems and take some points from us, but we held firm and won the kind of match that, frankly, last season we would have lost. I don't know if Swansea will recover. I don't know if they will make it to the play-off places, but I do know revenge is sweet and that their manager Steve Cooper didn't bother to talk about any plans they had worked out to beat us this time, having got so lucky at ER. That defeat on the last day of August still rankled with me as much as the dropped points against Derby in our following home game. We had righted one wrong today, and in a few days' time hopefully we could go to Derby and right another and some. But first, there is a family reunion and then another huge game against a plucky Barnsley team, who I am sad to see are still in very big relegation trouble. Andy suddenly asks me 'if I'm listening' but I haven't a clue what she is talking about.

Leeds United...1; Barnsley...0
Thursday, 16th July

A lazy start to the day and a trip into the village to buy a paper, followed by a nice read in the sunshine. It seems now that the sporting press have decided we are going up, and certainly that's the view of friends who are 'non Leeds fans' and who have been texting since the win over Swansea. I have to say, after the pain of last year, I won't be convinced until it's actually happened... if it happens. None of us wants to be the one who 'spooks' things by being over-confident. There isn't a proper Leeds fan in the world who doesn't know what I mean. We have a great reunion – the first time we have been with all three children together since Mike and Lou's leaving do ahead of their move to Dublin 18 months ago. They have rented a big house in a village not far from Royston, with a plan to have a base so they can entertain family and friends during the week.

Nick is looking after the kids, so we won't see him until later in the week, but Katherine arrives with James just a minute or two after Andy and me, and we are quickly catching up, drinking champagne, and playing football with Margie in the big garden. It's great just to sit and listen to all the jokes and enjoy the moment. It won't be long before we will all be heading in different directions, and probably not be together again like this until Christmas. The weather spoils itself just as James is finishing the BBQ, and as the rain begins to fall we move inside to eat and carry on the chat. With the children asleep, the time just flies and eventually we turn in a little after 1am. In the seconds it takes me to fall asleep, I think briefly how good it would be if we could all be together the day we were promoted. Then, cross with myself for being too positive, I fall deeply asleep.

The next day is definitely the 'morning after', and while we can hear the kids downstairs, we don't rush to get up. I go through some of the texts about the Swansea game and look at the league table again for the thousandth time. It dawns on me that if we beat Barnsley on Thursday, and WBA or Brentford have a bad week, we could actually be promoted before we go to our old friends at Derby. That said, if we lose at home to the 'Tykes', they could both be ahead of us before the match at Pride Park. The problem with the Championship is it's just too competitive. Realising that all this plotting and planning is a hopeless activity, I am about to get up when I notice Katherine has changed the picture image for our family WhatsApp. She has replaced a lovely picture of us all at Mike's leaving do with a picture of me taken yesterday when I was playing with Margie in the garden, pretending I was angry when she splashed me with water from the paddling pool.

The more I shouted and protested at her splashing me, the more she laughed and splashed. At some point, Katherine got a picture of this game which made me look vaguely like a gorilla! This she found hugely funny, and later when we were having a drink and the kids were asleep, she posted a picture of an actual gorilla next to the photo she had taken of me. Katherine found this likeness so funny she actually had tears rolling down her cheeks, and while the joke was clearly on me, it was great to see the kids enjoying themselves, laughing and rolling about like those robots in the Cadbury's Smash advert. Nonetheless, I must make a point of telling her the old pic was the better one!

We head off mid-morning, with Mike dropping James off at Royston station and then following us to the shopping outlet off the A505. It's time for us to get some food and then head back to the site for a lazy afternoon. For Mike, it's time to replenish stocks and get ready to welcome the other side of the family. We won't be seeing the Dublin Crew again until Friday when we are all meeting at Katherine's for afternoon tea. It sounds very civilised, though I doubt it will be, with the kids on the go and already calls for the paddling pool and watergun fights!

I am worried about the Barnsley game and keep pouring caution on some of the WhatsApp texts – a couple of which seem to think this is going to be three points in the bag. I suppose the win at Swansea has given everyone a real confidence, especially coming after the super performance against Stoke City. But if you just take 'each game as it comes', then I can't forget how well Barnsley played in our first game at Oakwell back in September. They were so unlucky that day, creating as many chances as we did and playing really quite clever football. It can't just have been me who left Oakwell that day thinking that late goals from Nketiah and Klich (pen) made the final score a touch flattering.

It's not just Leeds fans who are anxious, of course, and the way the fixtures are staggered means that almost every day there is a match that has a bearing on promotion or relegation. And having beaten the pressure of playing last again this weekend, as well as defeating Swansea, it's now West Brom's turn to test their mettle. And it's a really tough challenge they face against a Fulham side who have clawed their way back into contention for automatic promotion. For them, this is simply a must-win match, and it couldn't be a worse fixture for Albion who dropped points at Blackburn last Saturday.

I see a little of the game, popping in every now and then, really just to keep an eye on the score, as we are having our evening drinks and catch up while the drama is being played out at the Hawthorns. Really, we need a Fulham win or a drawn game, to heap more pressure on WBA and to ease some of our burden ahead of the game on Thursday. From what I can see, Fulham start well and Hegazi makes a crucial goal-line clearance to stop the Londoners taking the lead, but for all both sides' efforts it's still goalless at half-time. And if that score remains and we can beat Barnsley, then we will be five points clear of 'Brom, who will be only one point clear of Brentford if they beat Preston tomorrow, of course. If, if, if, if! In the end, I don't go back into the caravan until the match has finished, preferring to have a stress-free chat about potential trips to Calella, so I only find out later that the game finished all-square – a result probably neither side wanted. For Fulham, the result almost certainly means their automatic promotion push is just about over, while Albion find themselves still two points behind us with only two games left to play, and we have a game in hand. But at least for the Baggies, they still have matters just about in their own hands.

The next night is just the same: more football, more games that matter, and this time it's Brentford's turn to play catch-up against a Preston team who seem to blow hot and cold at all the wrong times. They must be a frustrating team to support, getting themselves in really good positions and then losing silly games to frustrate and deny them what seemed to be, until recently, a certain top six finish. It's just possible that if Preston can win tonight, they might yet reach the play-off places but they have given themselves a mountain to climb. And the mountain gets very much steeper when Ollie Watkins scores in the fourth minute – a goal that, for all Preston's hard work and occasional chances, proves to be the match winner. The result pretty much extinguishes PNE's chances of the play-offs, but critically moves Brentford just a point behind West Brom. And of course, their goal difference is very much better, should Albion slip up again. The Baggies have now picked up just two points out of the last six – absolutely the wrong time to have a 'wobble'.

We are due to have a bit of a gathering at Katherine's on match day, when Andrew and Ben are driving up from Sussex for lunch. We haven't seen them for ages because of 'lockdown', though like many families we have had our weekly Zoom link-ups.

Katherine has some tutoring to do in the early afternoon, but we all meet at 'hers' at about half-ten for coffee and her truly remarkable strawberry cream cake. Inevitably, the conversation turns to tonight's game and I voice my concerns about Barnsley and the dangers I think they pose. As ever, Ben is the voice of calm and reason, reassuring us that 'Barnsley are bottom for a reason' and pointing out that their influential creative player Simoes is missing through injury. I do get all this but I'm still worried. And anyway, if Ben is so confident about success ,why is it he always goes into 'blackout' when the games are actually being played? And also, Luton were bottom of the table when we played them, weren't they? And another thing, Phillips is missing. And …… Well maybe this time I'll just join Ben.

We have a great catch-up, and when Kath goes 'tutoring' we go round to 'Rosyleas' and have a really nice lunch sitting outside in the sunshine. And later, as Andrew and Ben get ready to leave, I decide it will be better for us to drive back to the caravan to watch the match rather than go back to Kath and Nick's. It's a teatime kick-off and the kids will be having tea and then getting ready for bed, so it will be difficult to focus on the match without appearing to be rude and neglect 'Poppa' duties. With the sun out, we should be able to enjoy a few chilled drinks sitting outside chatting about non-football things before the game actually gets underway. And that's just what we do, enjoying the early evening sun and planning for further trips and 'away days'.

As the minutes tick away to kick-off time, I realise this pleasant chat must come to an end and be replaced by the tension and anxiety of another 'must win' game. I never really bother watching all the pre-match chat, as I know how we're doing and I know the strengths and weaknesses of the opposition , I don't mind watching the 'review' after it's all over, but obviously only if we win! Team news is not good – not good at all – though in truth we knew in advance that Kalvin would be missing, after injuring his knee at Swansea. It's a big blow and, worse, he's out for the rest of the 'season'. He will be such a loss as for me, he literally holds the team together, protecting the back four and providing the ball for the offensive players. He has missed games before through injury and suspension, and we have managed to cope, most recently just before the lockdown when he missed the wins against 'Boro, Hull, and Huddersfield, but the team never quite seem as balanced when he is absent.

Baradi comes into the team and once again Roberts starts, with Hernandez, after his brilliance in recent games, waiting on the bench. The thought crosses my mind that if we do make it, if we actually get promoted, using him from the bench in the last third of the game could be a brilliant option and really help us change a match. He is 35 and still our most talented and creative player.

Barnsley really need to get points from this game, possibly even more than us, as bizarrely we can afford to lose and still hold our destiny in our own hands. They pick an attacking team with Brown, Woodrow, and Chaplin all starting, and being supplied by Alex Mowatt, our 'old boy' and a skilful passer of the ball, if a little lacking in pace. I'm sure that must have been a part of the reason we released him a few years ago.

They start as if they mean business and when Dallas gets caught, Styles and Woodrow play Brown into the area. He's running away from goal and there's a second where he should shoot left-footed, but fortunately he doesn't, electing to switch to his favoured right foot and in the end firing an aimless shot-come-cross across the goal. It's a warning, though, and as they continue to attack Styles has a shot deflected away for a corner from which Mads Andersen, in a central position, unbelievably sends a powerful header just wide of the post. He surely had to score, and I can imagine all the Barnsley fans – along with the West Brom and Brentford supporters – holding their heads in anguish at such a missed opportunity. And then seconds later, we score. Klich passes a superb ball through the defence to Bamford breaking into the area down the right, and though his first shot is blocked, he manages to pull the ball back into the danger area just as it's about to roll out of play, and it cannons off the defender Solibauer and into the net.

Watching on television and without the reaction of the crowd, I find there's just a fraction of a second where you need a double-take to reassure yourself the goal has been scored. Just for a moment, I am scared it has gone out of play before Bamford pulled it back across the area, but it didn't and the goal is rightly awarded. I sit in more drained relief than jubilation and as Barnsley continue to look dangerous, I realise that much as I am missing my 'live' football, this is a game I certainly wouldn't be enjoying if I were at ER. It would be one of those where I held my breath as the opponents broke forward, just waiting to see the ball hit the net and experience that awful silence before a tiny section of the ground broke out into riotous joy and told me that our visitors had scored.

The score remains one-nil until half-time and Hernandez once again comes on for the second half replacing Tyler Roberts, who has had a quiet game so far. In fairness, most of the team have. Barnsley also make a change, bringing on Thomas for our ex-defender Halme, in what is clearly an attacking move. Barnsley are going for it and

Chaplin, cutting in from the left-hand side, fires a shot narrowly wide of the post. This game is getting out of hand and it's a far from enjoyable watch. It's looking worse when Ayling gets trapped 'Leeds-like' by three Barnsley attackers in a central position just outside the area, and they bear in on goal. It's a three-on-one and they are going to surely get a well-deserved equaliser, except amazingly, they don't when Styles elects to shoot – and shoot wide. What was he thinking, when he could have played Chaplin clean through on his left? It's such a let-off, but we are definitely being bettered by these plucky and inventive 'Tykes'. How could they have ended up at the bottom of the table playing they way they have done in two games against us?

We look completely unbalanced, and worse, Costa is off following a strong challenge by Mowatt, and replaced by Alioski. Harrison is taken off, too, as Bielsa tries to stem the tide, bringing the highly rated Struijk on to stiffen the midfield. But the chances keep coming, and Solibauer misses the opportunity to score for both sides when he sends a free header straight at Meslier.

Andy joins me inside the caravan and gets the situation straight away, feeling the tension, and seeing with her own eyes how the players are struggling against a determined opponent. I wonder what the effect would be if we were all in the ground. Would the support be deafening, urging us on to complete the victory as it was when we came back against Millwall? Or would it be like the match after that, when the crowd's anxiety might have transmitted to the players and contributed to our defeat by Wigan?

We needed a second goal, and it almost came when we broke out down the left and Alioski curled a superb pass around the back of the Barnsley defence. At last, this was the chance to finish the game and Bamford, unmarked, swept the ball goalwards only for Walton to stick out his boot at the last second and make a brilliant save. My nerves were just about shredded, and with four minutes left on the clock, I went for a quick walk round the site, figuring this tactic had worked in the Swansea game. And it worked again! When I got back, the game was over and the television screen still read 1-0. We had held on for the win, and even spurned another chance when Dallas cut in from the right.

What a sport football is, and what a fantastic competition the Championship is. I am almost breathless with the release of tension and the gradual realisation that, having somehow taken another three points we are now needing just one more from our remaining games against Derby and Charlton to ensure promotion, no matter what WBA and Brentford do. For the first time, I am beginning to believe that at last this is going to happen, that after 16 long years we are finally going to return to the Premiership. Surely now not even Leeds can blow it? Surely this time, after all the pain, after all those bitter play-off defeats and last-minute implosions, we are going to earn our chance to celebrate?

The sun is just going down and I sink quite a few quick celebratory pints of John Smith's. Andy, too, is happy and enjoying her wine with the growing realisation that this time her summer holiday is not going to be ruined by the result of a football match. I can still remember her waiting for James and me when we got back from ER after the Derby defeat, powerless to come up with any words of comfort, struggling to think of anything positive she could do to make things better, and eventually deciding just to go outside and water the plants, leaving her husband and youngest son to their misery and silence. I had been on the terraces when we played Bristol Rovers, and lived through the agony of needing to win that game to ensure promotion. I really don't want to go through that again and pray that we get something at Derby so we don't have to face a Charlton side fighting for survival, as Barnsley had been this evening. Poor old Barnsley. I feel for them and hope they manage to pull out of the bottom three, though with games against Forest and Brentford to come, it's not looking too hopeful for them. As I lie in bed counting points, it strikes me that if WBA slip up again at Huddersfield – and they are under real pressure now, having drawn their last two – or if, as seems unlikely, Brentford slip up at Stoke, we could actually be promoted before we even play Derby. My God, how close are we now! This thought is shared by the family, and though sadly, James will be at work, the rest of us are due to meet at Katherine's tomorrow afternoon for a BBQ and to have a last get-together before Mike and Lou head back to Dublin and we set off to Yorkshire on Saturday morning. Katherine wonders in a WhatsApp message if we should buy in champagne just in case our old friends Huddersfield can take a point off WBA. For once, no-one sends a scornful comment. We really are that close now. Just one point – or maybe none at all!

Friday, 17th July

We are all due to meet at Kath and Nick's at around three, so it's a lazy start to the day and actually quite a painful one. I don't know what I have done, but I went to bed absolutely fine and woke up unable to walk with the pain in my right knee. It's been getting worse, but doing the stuff the physio gave me and cycling has kept me fairly mobile. Today it's real pain and not just a dull ache. I guess I must have twisted it in some way as I turned over in my sleep, but given that I can hardly walk, I decided to ring the surgery and try and get to see Dr Vega. I haven't been to the surgery since that last visit when she gave me the cortisone jab, and I realise that with the pandemic, surgeries will have had to prioritise, but at the end of the day I am fairly desperate for some kind of advice, even if it's just to go to A&E.

I got outside by keeping my right leg straight as I negotiated the two steps, and then fell into the recliner, again keeping the leg straight. I found that if I got in a certain position, I could bend it, and I tried to warm the joint up by swinging the leg to and fro. This seemed fine as I did it, but the minute I stopped everything stiffened up again, and if I stood up and started a normal walking action, I was in real pain. What a silly thing the body is! Before my knee got this bad, I found that I could literally run up steps no problem, but try and walk down a steep hill and, wow, the discomfort. Anyway, I got through to the surgery, listened to their advice about Coronavirus, and then joined the queue for appointments. I was told I was eighth in the queue; it was 10.20am.

Over the next 25 minutes, I gradually moved up to number two, and as I waited I watched the caravan site come to life with people wandering around and doing their morning chores. Somewhere, not far away, someone was cooking bacon. Andy gave me a cup of tea and suddenly it was my turn. I was number one. The receptionist was, it has to be said, very pleasant. I explained my problem and that I wanted to book an appointment with Dr Vega, and specifically for her to administer a cortisone shot during the appointment. I wanted it this way, because the standard waiting time to see the doctor was usually about three weeks. I figured I couldn't wait three weeks and then find myself waiting again after the visit, so it was better to let her know what needed to be done so she could get on with it.

Anyway, and I'm sure I heard this correctly, the receptionist told me they weren't yet doing 'face-to-face' appointments, and they definitely weren't doing injections. The thought crossed my mind that they could have given this information as a recorded message at the start of the call, as they did about the virus, thus saving me a 25-minute wait. I tried to explain as tactfully as I could that this wasn't really helpful and I assumed that I would just have to go to A&E. The receptionist rallied and told me I could have a phone consultation with Dr Vega, which sounded a little more hopeful. At least I could get to speak to someone I trusted and try and establish what my options were.

I wanted to try another injection, but I had increasingly come to the realisation that I might have to have a knee replacement. This was something I'd been advised by friends to try and avoid doing for as long as possible. The good news was that I would only have to wait six days for a telephone chat, which gave me time to hopefully find the knee improves and, if not, well at least I'd have time to prepare my questions which ultimately might lead to me having to stump up a shedload of money to get some pain relief as soon as possible. I have read somewhere that there is a massive backlog of people waiting for knee and hip replacements, but I have just had enough of limping around in, at best, pretty constant discomfort.

Andy has driven into the village to get a paper and some bread so we can have a sandwich and sit and enjoy the sunshine for a bit before we head to Katherine's. As always, the football section is dominated by the Premiership – a little like the football phone-in programmes on the radio. I know we're desperate to get back to the Premiership, but how much excitement is missed by the lack of coverage of the lower leagues? I guess it means these programmes and articles are aimed at the 'passing fan' who dips into the game to follow the clubs most likely to win trophies, 'the glory hunters' who know little or nothing about football. The type who latch onto clubs like Manchester United, driving the prices up while they're winning and keeping the real supporters away because they simply can't afford to attend. I have to say, Leeds have so far been brilliant in this respect, keeping season tickets frozen for existing holders, even though next season we might be watching Liverpool and Chelsea rather than Wigan and Luton.

Today, the back pages are full of the FA Cup semi-finals between Arsenal and Man City, and Chelsea and Man Utd. I am not sure which of these clubs I want to lose most, or perhaps to make things easier, which of the four I'd like to see win the trophy. Probably, if pushed, Man City, but only because it does seem that over the years they have had a loyal fan base who have endured the fall into the lower leagues and yet stayed with the club to enjoy the glory days they are experiencing now. I've mentioned earlier my sadness at the way the modern game has devalued the Cup, especially with the ridiculous decision to play the semi-finals at Wembley. I must admit, as a player I was never really bothered about cup matches, often not knowing which cup competition it was, whether it was an 'open' cup, or just a cup for teams in our league. I always preferred playing league games where, as regulars, we had some idea of the importance of the game and the quality of the opposition. In all my years of playing, I can only remember two cup matches I played in and for very different reasons.

I know a little about the first because I still have the winner's medal. It was called the 'Kingston Wednesday League', the cup was named the 'Charity Cup', and I won it playing for St. Mary's in 1974/75. Obviously, the game was played at a neutral venue, and I remember that the pitch was really flat and green. I remember the weather was good, which makes sense, as the cup finals usually came at the end of the season. And I remember the match was played after I'd done well in the British Colleges tournament, played over the Easter holiday. There were a lot of students at the ground to support us, and we were playing in a new kit of all-blue shirts and white shorts, rather than our traditional blue and white stripes kit. I had broken into the college first team, mainly playing on the left wing, but as the year turned and the older students left, I moved into a more central role and actually enjoyed stuff like holding the ball up and bringing others into the game. I wasn't the tallest, but I could time my jumps and usually won at least 50 per cent of my aerial duels. I also scored my fair share of goals but never, as I have said, thought of myself as a natural goal-scorer, though I had finished up as our leading scorer in the tournament, which was clearly a much higher standard than this. So I went into the game full of confidence.

Our opponents were obviously older and physically stronger than us, and probably thinking of themselves as favourites to beat a bunch of students, especially as we had run into problems finishing our league fixtures because so many of our players were away from the area during holiday periods. As I was playing up front, I knew I would probably take a battering from the centre halves, but I was in my 'Joe Jordan' phase and relished the challenge. I knew if I could get the ball on the ground, we had too much ability and pace for them. And so it proved to be.

I can't remember the final score, and I know I didn't score and was subbed in the last few minutes, but I do know we won because, as I say, I have the medal in front of me. It was the only cup winner's medal I managed, and it sits alongside the Championship Trophy won with Old Thornesians in 1986/7 and the third-place medal from the British Colleges in 1975 in pride of place on my library shelves, gathering dust along with the fading memories. Funny then, that I have much clearer memories of the other cup game I actually remember playing in. This time, the standard was lower and it wasn't a final, but it was a game that mattered a lot to me. The trophy we were playing for was the league division three cup of our local Sunday pub league. It was a semi-final and we had home advantage. We were playing against one of the top sides in the division but at least they were in our division, so we had some kind of chance.

I was coming to the end of my time with the club and I was desperate to win something with them. We weren't very good in terms of our league position, but we had some reasonable players and everyone tried their best, and I had so enjoyed the fun of playing with this team over the years. It wouldn't be the highest standard and it wouldn't mean much in terms of some of the other trophies I've just mentioned, but it would mean an awful lot to me to put some kind of trophy from this pub league on my library shelves.

I could tell I was up for it, as it took me a few minutes to get my breathing sorted out – a normal occurrence when I was playing in a big match. Our opponents attacked from the start and played with the confidence of promotion challengers, but crucially they didn't score in those early minutes. We gradually came into the game and enjoyed more possession, not that we kept it for very long; we never played much controlled football, being a lot more comfortable with hit-and-hope style of tactics.

From one of our charges upfield, we forced a corner, and as usual I took up my position at the back of the penalty area, ready to run towards the near post and try and get ahead of the defenders. I have to say I got a lot of goals in this league following this move, mainly because a lot of our opponents couldn't move very easily, or were probably too hungover from the night before to be bothered marking me properly. I can still see the ball coming towards me. It was hit hard but without any height, and as I outstripped the defence and ran beyond the near post, I hit it with my weaker right foot and it literally flew into the net. I was so chuffed to have scored that goal and celebrated loudly shouting out 'Yes!' and encouraging my teammates to 'Come on' as I ran back to the halfway line. And we worked and worked, and still they couldn't break us down. I ran past the ref and asked him how long there was to go and he told me five minutes. I clapped loudly again, shouting for extra effort, knowing we were so close to pulling off a surprise result, which at the very worst would lead to getting a loser's medal and a cup final appearance. And then they scored an equalising goal with almost the last kick of the match. We were gutted, falling to the ground in disappointment, and knackered with all the effort we had put into protecting our lead.

The match went into extra time, but we all knew our chance had gone, and our opponents eventually ran out 2-1 winners. When the final whistle went, I was so down and disappointed. It wasn't the greatest game, and to be fair, it wasn't by a long way the best standard I played in, but I had so wanted to get some kind of trophy playing with these lads and this team. I suppose I did get something to keep as a memento of those days, winning the club's player of the year award a few weeks later, but I would have swapped it for a cup final appearance.

We got to Katherine's at almost the same time as Mike and Lou, and Nick had done great work repairing the big paddling pool. The weather had stayed fair, and it wasn't long before the children were in costumes and splashing around. Katherine encouraged the use of spray guns and pretty soon there was a very big water fight with excited children blasting any adult silly enough to cross them. Kath ganged up on her brother, who fairly soon was totally saturated and determined to get his own back with surprise attacks on Nick, Oliver, and Kath. It was great fun to see them all having such fun and for the children, particularly Lucy and Margie, to get to know each other. I loved the way at first they just stared at each other like gunslingers before one of them splashed out and the other followed, and then they both just started laughing. A thought flashed into my mind that whoever writes Peppa Pig might have got their idea for finishing every programme with Peppa and co falling over laughing, from moments such as these. I felt a bit of a spoilsport not joining in, but my leg hurt so much that I just sat with it stretched out in front of me, hoping no-one would fall over it. Soon it would be time for the Huddersfield v West Brom game to kick off, but I stayed outside eating cake and sandwiches rather than going inside to watch it.

To be honest, I didn't expect Town to get anything from the game, especially following their woeful performance against Luton. And anyway, if we couldn't get one point in two games, we didn't deserve to go up, did we? But Michael had other ideas and started to mess with his phone trying to find what odds he could get on Leeds actually not going up! In his eyes, winning a substantial amount of money might in some ways ease the pain of throwing away yet another certain promotion. I have to admit, the thought had crossed my mind once or twice, but I wasn't really a betting man, having only placed two bets at a 'bookies' in my life.

The first was in 1979, when for some reason I got it into my head that the Arsenal v Man Utd Cup final would finish 2-2, so I put £1 on that score at 25/1 at the local bookies. In those days, 25 quid was a lot of money, and I was fairly fed up when Arsenal led 2-0 at half-time. But then in the 86th minute, one of our old boys Gordon McQueen pulled a goal back, and two minutes later, Sammy McIlroy dribbled past a couple of players to score a dramatic last-gasp equaliser. I was up and off running into the village to claim my winnings and enjoy a celebratory pint at the pub, which was handily situated right next door. I put my winning slip on the desk and was stunned when the cashier refused to pay out. Unfortunately for me, as I had travelled the few hundred yards round to the bookies, Alan Sunderland had unbelievably headed in an injury-time winner for the Gunners! The match has become known as 'the five-minute final' but for me it will always be the day I lost out on 25 quid.

The only other time I placed a bet again involved Man U, when they played Barcelona in the Champions League final, also at Wembley in 2011. Barca were probably the best team in the world at that time and in a way were our 'second' club, given our home in Catalonia and Mike had been a regular visitor to the Nou Camp when he spent a year at university in the city. For some reason, I had dreamt that Barca would win the game 3-1 and as I walked home from work, I passed a bookies on the High Street which had a whole load of 'bets' about the game posted in its window.

I stopped briefly to check out the information and saw that Barca to win 3-1 was at 12/1, so I went inside and put a fiver on and headed home. When I got in, I told James what I'd done and about the dream, etc, and he suddenly got quite animated and decided he was going to place a bet on the game, too – something he was far more used to doing than me.

When he came back, I asked him what score he had put his money on and was surprised to hear him say 3-1 to Barca. I was just about to tell him that was daft as I had the same bet and we had a better chance of earning some money if he had chosen a different score, when he added 'and Pedro to score the first goal'. This was fairly long odds as Pedro, gifted a player as he undoubtedly was. did not really qualify as a regular goal scorer. being more often involved with 'assists' than actually getting on the scoresheet.

Nonetheless, as we settled down to watch the game, we knew that if Pedro did indeed score first and Barca did win 3-1, we would win just over £700 between us. At first, Manchester held their own and tried to deny Barca the space to play their normal passing game, but gradually the Catalans began to impose their style, and we were on our feet when Pedro flashed a shot just wide and then Van der Sar saved well from David Villa. Xavi was dictating the course of the game, and in the 27th minute he played in Pedro, who wrong-footed the United keeper with a simple finish. We would have cheered the goal anyway, but this time there were extra celebrations, and when Rooney equalised before half-time the bet was still very much on.

Things got better when Messi, in brilliant form, shot past Van der Sar in the 54th minute, and we held our breath as Barca continued to dominate and Fabio cleared off the line from an Alves shot. And then in the 69th minute, Villa curled a fine shot past the United keeper and we were like Barcelona – almost there. Except there were still 20-odd nervous minutes to go. Andy, not much bothered about football other than Leeds, came in to watch the last few minutes of the game. Initially unaware of the bet, she soon picked up the tension as we told her about it and was dancing round the room with the rest of us when the final whistle blew. Two visits to the bookies, one loss and one very big win, but whatever information Mike found out about his negative Leeds bet, it seemed to be forgotten as we sat in the sun and watched the children play in the paddling pool.

And then as we chatted about other things, Katherine charged out of the house doing an impression of an aeroplane and raced down the garden shouting out 'Huddersfield' at the top of her voice. Town had scored, and we rushed inside to see the replay of the goal. I couldn't believe it! They were winning after only three minutes. If the score stayed like this, we would be promoted today… in less than two hours. But there's a long way to go, so we head back outside and play with the kids, who are all now more interested in ice cream than splash guns and football matches. I am trying to work out what to do: it's our last night and pretty soon the kids will need to go to bed; Mike and Lou leave for Dublin tomorrow, so they will need to pack; and I'm thinking to head back to the caravan and watch bits of the match there, while enjoying a few beers in the setting sun. So I tell Kath we will make a move at half-time, which I think Nick and Lou seem to think is an idea, given the kids are approaching normal bedtime. But Kath is adamant when she says, 'You can't go now and then find we could all have been together when we are promoted!' So we decide to stay, and I go in to watch the last minutes before half-time, only to watch WBA equalise following a free kick taken by Pereira, which the keeper can only scoop out to O'Shea who scores with a stooping header. There are appeals from Huddersfield that there has been an offside in the build-up, and the replays suggest they have a case, but the goal is given.

Albion go close again even before half-time, and there seems to me little doubt that they will now go onto win the game. At this stage, I am unbelievably calm and still don't expect that we will have to do anything else but to get a point from either our travels to Derby, or worse, wait until our final match against Charlton next week.

In fact, WBA don't offer much as we settle down to watch the second half. Their only danger comes from Pereira, and they suddenly look an old team with Livermore and Phillips already replaced, and Robson-Kanu and Charlie Austin between them showing little goal threat. Then in the 82nd minute, they at last fashion an opening following a neat interchange between Pereira and Robinson, which leaves the sub through on goal. We hold our breath, as he's usually a strong finisher, but with the goal at his mercy he hits his shot into the ground and it's easily saved by Lossl in the Town goal. I reckon now there are probably about 12 or 13 minutes between us and a return to the Premier League, and for the first time in the afternoon start to get nervous as 'Brom continue to push forward.

And as we continue to check our watches and the game goes into the 84th minute, Town's hard-working midfielder O'Brien picks up the ball near the halfway line and starts to run forward. Krovinovic sees the danger and attempts to block him, but he shrugs him off and the ref, right behind them, plays an excellent advantage. I can see there's a real chance here as the West Brom defence retreats, and the Town sub Smith-Rowe can see it too, charging on ahead and splitting the defence with Sawyer letting him go and Ajayi running to cover the advancing O'Brien. Smith-Rowe points where he wants the ball played and O'Brien delivers the perfect pass, allowing the striker to control the ball instantly with his right foot before shooting with his left across the keeper and into the left-hand corner of the net.

Cue EXPLOSION!!!!!!! We are all on our feet, the pain in the knee momentarily forgotten, as we shout and scream and punch the air, hugging one another and chanting 'Na-na-na-na-na-na, Leeds are going up going up, Leeds are going up!'

We calm down a little when we realise the kids look terrified and sit down to watch the last few minutes of the game. There is no way Albion are going to score twice, even with six minutes of injury time. Suddenly, after weeks and months of anxiety, after 16 bloody years of trying, after driving thousands of miles at all times of day and night to grounds like Yeovil, Swindon, and Walsall, we are going back to the promised land, to Old Trafford, Stamford Bridge, and whatever the new Spurs ground is called. The final whistle sounds at last and is followed by more shouting and dancing. 'Don't you know, pump it up, Leeds are going up!' A sign flashes up in the top corner of the TV screen. It reads: 'Leeds are promoted to the Premier League.'

We have done it!

At last!!!!

Kath had the champagne on ice, and we toast the success with more hugs and songs, and then start taking pictures of our celebrations. Mike is wearing his Leeds shirt, and I can't believe I left mine back at the caravan. They all have their scarves out and the pom-pom hats Lou sourced from Ireland. This is unreal, as are the number of text messages coming in from friends old and new. I can hardly believe what has happened. My phone is dancing to the sweet tune of success.

I catch a picture of Slaven Bilic shaking hands with the Cowley brothers, who have just about made sure Huddersfield don't slide from the Premiership to League One in a season. I like Bilic and think, win or lose, he is always fair, obviously supporting his own team but not blind to the play of the opposition. Albion have gone head-to-head with us all season and had a real chance to pull away from us around early February when we lost at Forest. Now they know that if Brentford win at Stoke tomorrow, automatic promotion will no longer be in their own hands, but will have been torn from their grasp with just one game left to play. I can't imagine how Bilic feels. I've never been a manager, but I absolutely feel the pain of their supporters who, like us, must have thought they were heading back to the Premier league. It's going to be a nervous 24 hours until Brentford play and they absolutely must be fearing the worst and, just like us last year, go into the play-offs having thrown automatic promotion away.

I know exactly how they are feeling. But as for us, we are flying, promoted for the first time in ten years, and with every chance now of being promoted as champions – something that hasn't happened since 1991, the year James was born, and that's very nearly 29 years ago. After the champagne and the hugs and high-fives, it's time to get the kids to bed and to head for home. We are all elated and full of smiles, and suddenly realise now we are heading in separate directions and have no idea when we will all meet again. Certainly, for the whole family, it will probably be Christmas, but hopefully Katherine will come up to Womersley in August, and James should also be home at some point soon. It's a bit more uncertain with Mike and Lou, because Eire is still imposing a two-week self-isolation period, so we will have to wait and see what happens there. We are also hoping to head to

Calella in late August, probably for a month, before coming back in late September for Oliver and Lucy's birthdays. And, of course, the anticipated start of the new season, and hopefully the chance to watch some live football again.

We head back to the caravan and stop in at the Marks and Sparks food centre to buy some Indian food that we can heat up in the microwave. With all the celebrations, the sun has long gone down, but we still sit outside and have a lovely chat about the family and what a great few days it has been, and of course the football and the incredible happenings since we have been away. The brilliant late win at Swansea, the nervy three points against Barnsley, and then the news tonight from Huddersfield that we are promoted. I can still see Smith-Rowe pointing for the pass, still see him cushion the ball with his right foot, still see him pass the ball home with his left. Perfect! No counting points tonight or looking at fixtures and who needs a win (just about everyone in this league!), just a deep, happy sleep... that is, always assuming my bloody leg will let me, of course!

Saturday, 18th July

I wake up and realise I am still smiling, though the next couple of hours will challenge that. Trying to pack up the caravan and drive back to Yorkshire with a gammy leg is not something I am looking forward to. Before then, we can enjoy a Saturday lie-in, a few cups of tea, and plan the next trip away – a conversation we always enjoy. My knee is really stiff and painful, and I find it difficult to move with any freedom, so try to avoid activities which involve me having to flex the knee. Somehow, between us we get the jobs done, and about an hour after getting up we are hooked up and ready to go, leaving the site at about 10.20. With any luck we will be home, with the caravan securely parked up before 1.30.

With the excitement of last night, I've almost forgotten that Brentford play Stoke at lunchtime in a pretty much must-win game for both of them. If we hadn't already been promoted, I would have been praying for a Stoke win, but as it is, I don't really care. Except that I do, because if Brentford drop points, then we are not just promoted but promoted as champions.

It's an easy journey once I have got the knee bent, very few clusters of lorries, and just a few tiresome car drivers who I have to pull out and overtake. We get back to the caravan storage place about 1pm, which is pretty good going, manage to get unhooked fairly easily, and after a blip with the 'motor mover' we are fairly quickly dropping the keys off with Mark, the owner, and heading home.

We always follow the same routine when we get back. Andy opens up and I start emptying the car, clothes on the staircase, bags to the back door, kettle on. It's only been six days, and while it's been a momentous six days for Leeds, in terms of the house everything is fine and there isn't too much mail either. My leg is seriously aching after this little burst of activity, and I think Andy has recognised this, and tells me to go and lie down while she makes a sandwich. I don't argue, and without thinking put Sky Sports on to find Stoke are leading Brentford 1-0 with only about ten minutes to go. This time last week, I would probably have turned it off and spent ten minutes saying 'Hail Mary's' praying for the score to remain the same, but with promotion assured I try and get comfortable and watch the last few minutes.

Brentford miss two good chances to level and have a possible penalty claim turned down before the referee blows his whistle, and in so doing robs Brentford, after seven wins on the bounce since football returned, the chance to go second above WBA. Amazing how pressure kicks in and affects performance. Until today, Brentford were 'just having a go', threatening the top three with the freedom of their play and the quality of their football. Then suddenly, when the chance for automatic promotion stares them in the face and the pressure for the first time falls on them, they can't take the opportunity.

The ref's whistle also means that a misfiring and under-achieving Stoke City side are at last safe from the threat of relegation, and I'm really pleased for Michael Hughes their manager, who has done a good job since his appointment and who I think handled his clear anger and frustration following our 5-0 win the other week with great dignity and restraint. The whistle also means that now we are...

CHAMPIONS!

It's so difficult to think that just a few days ago I was anxiously pacing around a caravan site unable to watch the closing seconds of games against Swansea and Barnsley, so aware that we could still be overtaken by WBA and Brentford, so gripped with nerves. And now we are CHAMPIONS, and it's so long since we have been able to use that title. There was obviously the promotion under Simon Grayson in 2010, but before that it was 1991 and Howard Wilkinson's title-winning side. 29 long years. As James said, it's never happened in his lifetime, so now it's time to enjoy the moment and to celebrate.

Pictures start to emerge from ER of the players toasting their success after WBA's loss to Huddersfield. They must have had a feeling, because they had all gone there to watch the match. Bielsa and his team were there, too, as well as a few thousand fans who had turned up just to be near the club in its moment of triumph. And they got their reward when the players came out onto a balcony and joined with them, all punching the air, singing the songs, and celebrating an oh-too-rare moment together.

We were celebrating too with Zoom calls and champagne and lots of John Smiths. And I knew at last I would be able to watch the final few episodes of the Amazon series *Take us Home*, which is a documentary of the last ultimately disappointing season. I couldn't bear to watch that Derby play-off semi-final defeat again; the one that ruined yet another summer. It had been in my mind from the minute I had seen the fixture lists last June how absolutely brilliant it would be to win promotion at Derby, especially if they were being relegated or given a points deduction. And at least part of that was going to happen. They were even going to have to give us a guard of honour!

The only sadness, and I felt it today more than at any other time, was that we wouldn't be there to share in the moment, to sing our songs to celebrate our championship. After all those years, summed up in the absolute desolation that followed that play-off exit, now it was our time, and I for one couldn't think of a more deserving opponent than Derby to have to clap us out onto the field.

Not everyone agreed, and one Derby fan showed their general lack of class by phoning the 5Live radio talk-in to say how we were not fit to have a 'guard of honour', that we were unworthy, and a disgrace to football. 'The most dishonourable club in the entirety of football!' he said, and added that he wanted to take the moral high ground on behalf of football.

What an absolute pillock!

And the funny thing was that he was talking about Derby frigging County, for f's sake. This club of Brian Clough, with an owner who was investigated (and eventually cleared) for breaking financial rules, and who, along with their former manager, over-celebrated their play-off win with such a lack of style that they couldn't recover in time to mount a successful attempt to beat Villa in the play-off final. A club that effectively sacked its captain following a boozy outing, as he was left seriously injured and apparently unconscious in a car, and two of his teammates were charged with drink-driving. And that's not forgetting some of their fans who generate an atmosphere by banging a drum and can't sell their 'away ticket allocation' this year at ER, yet allegedly qualify for a Wembley final ticket by dint of attending just one home match.

So yep, Derby County AFC, a club that takes the moral high ground, a perfect example to us all of how to care for those who have given lengthy service when they find themselves in need of support. In my view, 'people in glass houses shouldn't throw stones' and Derby County along with the kind of fan that rang the '5 Live' radio programme should do well to remember that.

So gutted we can't be there to share our joy with them.

386

Derby County...1; Leeds United...3
Sunday, 17th July

How good to be two games from the end of the season and no last-minute worries, no biting of nails, hiding behind sofas, or walking round caravan sites. For the first time in many years, we are home and hosed, have taken the main prize and can enjoy the season unwind, watching how it finally ends, who stays up and who goes down. Barnsley had a sensational last-gasp win against Forest earlier in the day and can still just about save themselves, but it's going to be massive for them, as their last game is away to Brentford who are now in last chance saloon in terms of automatic places.

I think I want Albion to go up because I like Slaven Bilic, who always seems to be fair whether in victory or defeat. That said, the away trip to the Midlands isn't as attractive as heading to London, and Brentford will be housed in their new ground built very close to Griffin Park. Maybe Brentford will make it through the play-offs, but who else will be there? Fulham, certainly another good away trip, and Forest or Cardiff, both clubs who don't very much like us for reasons already explained. In terms of relegation, I really hope Barnsley can save themselves, and I'd like Lee Bowyer to stay up at Charlton, though they have to come to ER in their final game. Sadly, Hull look certainties for the drop, and while I feel for their fans, the club's owners will have brought relegation on themselves after letting such vital players leave in the January window. Luton are scrapping away and Nathan Jones, having failed miserably at Stoke, seems to have reinvigorated the team and they are picking up points that might yet save them. So strange how some managers just 'fit' a club.

I feel for Wigan, who have been hit with a 12-point penalty and whose good recent form might not be enough to pull them clear of danger. I know how they feel, as we got hit with a 15-point punishment back in the Ken Bates' days. Wigan's chances look less hopeful, having conceded an added-time goal at Charlton yesterday that cost them two vital points. After all this, there is still a threat of points deduction hanging over Sheffield Wednesday and Derby. And while unfortunately that might not be enough to relegate Derby, it would certainly put Wednesday in big trouble.

In the end, the Derby players showed more style than Joe, the fan who rang 5Live, and they clapped us onto the field, though the youngster Sibley showed his immaturity by very slowly bringing his hands together as if trying to make some point – no doubt to losers like Joe. Bielsa made lots of changes for the match, with Baradi, Poveda, Struijk, and Douglas coming into the team, along with an unexpected recall for Casilla, which I have to say surprises me especially in the current climate of promoting 'Black Lives Matter'. I realise when someone has served their punishment there must be a chance of redemption, but I honestly feel the club has caused itself a problem which might come to hurt them in the future. I have absolutely no doubt if a fan had said what Casilla allegedly did, then they would have been banned for life.

Hernandez is picked to start the game, and without doubt he is the most skilful and creative player on the field, looking fitter and more influential than Rooney, who really only seems to be a danger from dead-ball situations now. He just plays the ball largely backwards and sideways ,as Derby have been doing inexplicably in this last run of games, completely giving up on the chance of snatching a play-off place with a kind of 'safety first' attitude, lacking in bravery and passion.

I don't know how much preparation went into this game, coming as it did in the midst of our title celebrations, but however hungover the players may have felt they still looked sharper than Derby, and Alioski and Shackleton caught Bogle on the edge of the area before Roberts shot over. Poveda had a 'goal' rightly disallowed when he overran a breakaway down the left and came back from an offside position to curl the ball past Roos in the Derby goal. Derby seemed to surprise themselves by taking the lead in the 54th minute when, despite several opportunities to clear, we allowed Chris Martin the chance to swing a leg and send a deflected shot past Casilla.

The Derby players' reaction to the goal seemed to sum up his side's attitude, as he turned away without any kind of celebration, as if he almost couldn't be bothered. Surely worrying symptoms for times to come when the new season gets underway.

The goal seems to wake us from our slumbers, and almost immediately we are level when Hernandez plays the ball wide to Poveda and then runs forward to collect the winger's cross. At first it looks as if he wants to hit a first-time volley, but at the last minute he alters his position and, faced by Rooney, sends a weakish shot toward goal. The ball strikes Davies and rebounds back to the Spaniard. Sitting at home, I absolutely know he will score. It's as if the situation is created for his skills, better even than being given a penalty, and he fires the ball into the net, curling his shot just inside the right-hand post. Rooney, who had been in front of Hernandez before the first shot, doesn't attempt to interfere with the second, and has the best view of the goal in the ground as he stands motionless and watches the trajectory of the ball. As it hits the net, he drops his head and looks at the ground. Just about the perfect reaction to the goal from a Derby perspective!

After this, we take control of the game and it's no surprise when Ayling, on as a substitute following Baradi's injury, feeds Roberts for the striker to spin on the ball and send a lovely pass through the heart of the Derby defence for Shackleton, who finishes superbly with a right-foot shot and scores his first goal for the club. Derby offer little, although Casilla did make a good block from Knight when the Derby player found himself clear through after Ayling's slip. We score again before the end, with the help of Clarke the Derby defender, who slices a super curling cross from Alioski into his own net while trying to clear the ball. It's a very comfortable win over lacklustre opponents who are clearly ready for a holiday and, it seems, a much-needed clear-out, which might possibly include the manager. Whatever his excellent qualities as a player, he seems unable to inspire any passion into his team. And so just a week after that brilliant but nail-biting victory at Swansea – where, had we lost, we would have been level on points with WBA and only three ahead of Brentford – we find ourselves eight points clear of 'Brom and nine ahead of Brentford, and we are Champions of the EFL. What a difference a week makes.

CHAPTER 21

'CHAMPIONS'

Leeds United…4; Charlton Athletic…0
Wednesday, 22nd July

The players celebrated long and hard on the pitch after the victory over Derby, and watching at home you couldn't help but get the feeling that this was a kind of payback for last May. Such a shame that we couldn't be in the crowd to share the moment with them after all our travails and travels over the season. Mateuz Klich tried to represent us, though, clambering over seats and singing and clapping from the empty stands as his teammates drank champagne and celebrated on the pitch.

High up in the seats reserved for visiting dignitaries, Andreas Radrizzani smiled as he looked on, no doubt enjoying this moment of success after all his hard work. Close by, Victor Orta rather made a fool of himself and the club by imitating the 'Spygate' actions and laughing like a miscreant schoolkid at his own sad sense of humour. This kind of stuff would be ok from teenagers or even fans intent on causing more enmity between the clubs, but from a senior employee of Leeds, well, to my eyes it simply lacked class.

Derby had done this in spades last May, shown themselves up and let themselves down, and ultimately won nothing. This was our chance to prove ourselves better than them, to show respect to our opponent and the competition we had just become champions of. We really didn't need Victor Orta letting us down. That said, celebrations of our success continued all over the world wherever Leeds fans gathered, and thousands turned out in Leeds Millennium Square, desperate to be with each other and sing out songs of triumph.

I was so pleased to celebrate the actual moment we went up with Andy, Katherine, and Mike, in Bishops Stortford last week. And on Saturday after the Charlton game, James would be home to crack a few bottles and let all the joy come out, having been stuck in London taking work exams over the promotion period.

While we enjoyed our success, fans of Championship clubs all over the country, and Wales as well, were biting their nails and getting their calculators out; there were just so many issues to resolve. Apart from us, of course. We were going up!

WBA were back in the driving seat for automatic promotion, knowing that if they slipped up, Brentford or even Fulham could still overtake them in the final game of the season. How gutting would that be for Albion fans. It had been us or them all season, and now finally we had pulled away and 'Brom were still sweating over a massive 90 minutes. They were playing QPR in their final match – one of the few teams in the league who had nothing to play for except professional pride.

Brentford entertain Barnsley, with both clubs desperate for all three points, as are Wigan and Fulham who meet in the North West. Elsewhere, Forest need only a point to be certain of a top six finish, something they were already celebrating in February after their 2-0 victory over us at the City ground. Cardiff are well placed, and even Swansea are still in the frame, though they will have to win well at Reading and hope the footballing gods conspire in some bizarre way to frustrate Forest or Cardiff.

At the bottom, Hull seem doomed, but Luton and Barnsley are still fighting and, along with Charlton who come to ER, are just about holding their heads above water. It will be a huge evening, and for the neutral and all Leeds fans, a fascinating end to the season. But it's one that just for once we can sit back and enjoy. Our match is not featured on Sky, who have chosen, not surprisingly, to focus on the race for second place. So I get ready to watch on LUTV while having the 'Soccer Special' on in the background with the sound down.

391

Bielsa has chosen to start with the strongest squad available to him, which means Meslier comes back in goal and Ayling, Cooper, Harrison, and Bamford return to the side. Phillips, Costa, Baradi, and obviously Forshaw, remain out injured, and it's an excitingly young bench with Shackleton, Roberts, Poveda, Davis, and Stevens all named. Struijk continues in Phillips' midfield anchor role.

Charlton, who have had a desperate season with all kind of ownership problems and injuries, have also found themselves since the 'restart' without their leading goalscorer Lyle Taylor, who turned down the opportunity to sign a contract extension to the end of the season. In refusing to sign, Taylor essentially put his own future ahead of the clubs, worried that an injury in one of the last nine matches could affect his chances of one last big pay packet and a move to a 'bigger club'. I have to say this must have been a hugely difficult decision for him to take, and one that has seen the player seriously criticised and called selfish for taking. But you only have to look at what happened to Gaetano Baradi at Derby, out for nine months with a knee injury, to see the dangers Taylor foresaw. That said, had it been me, I think I would have had to sign the short-term extension contract rather than let my teammates down.

So, this is our 46th match of a long, long season, and one that should have been played on 2nd May, before the pandemic took over and shook the world. It's a game I had hoped to be watching with my children, and on this occasion especially Kath, as we had watched together when we were effectively relegated after playing out a 3-3 draw with Charlton in our last home match of 2004. Of course, it wasn't to be; the pandemic saw to that. And that family celebration at ER will have to wait for a little longer, but it will be so sweet when it eventually happens.

With the pressure off, we start the game in fine style and push Charlton back from the off. It must be difficult for them to plan how to approach the game. They know that they can lose and still stay up, knowing that really only an improbable Barnsley win at Brentford can relegate them. The problem is that they don't appear to do anything other than form a guard of honour for us before the kick-off. At least Luton worked their socks off, and even Stoke held their own until nearly half-time, but Charlton just seemed caught in the headlights, and it was no surprise when we took the lead after 13 minutes. Charlton failed to clear a corner and the ball fell to White on the edge of the area who played it wide to Hernandez. The Spaniard's cross was headed clear but only back to White, who adjusted his body position and volleyed brilliantly past Phillips in the Charlton goal. The keeper managed to get a glove on the ball but was powerless to prevent it flying into the net. Some goal, some talent; we will have to try and keep him when all this is over.

On Sky, Matt Le Tissier is commentating on the goal, and it's not an exaggeration to say even someone as gifted as the former Southampton player would have been proud to have scored a goal of that quality. After turning the sound up to listen to Le Tissier, I decided to switch the TV off as the delay on the LUTV broadcast was spoiling my enjoyment of the game. I taped the rest of the Sky soccer special for later to see how everything eventually turned out. Hernandez, brilliant in his cameo roles since the restart, now cut in from the right and passed the ball through a defender's legs to find Dallas running free in the heart of the penalty area. The Irishman took a touch and then just toe-poked it past the keeper as he desperately tried to close the angle down. I got the feeling watching at home that if we wanted, this could become a cricket score. It's so frustrating not to be there to share in the success, especially after enduring all those 'nervy' finishes we seemed to specialise in at ER.

Ayling almost made it three when his fine strike from the edge of the area was just turned round the post by a diving Phillips, and the keeper also did well to deflect a Dallas shot for a corner, from which Charlton broke free and Doughty found himself suddenly one-on-one with Meslier. But with a clear chance to reduce the deficit, the midfielder could only pull his shot wide of the goal. There is no doubt he should have scored and it would have been a vital goal, dragging his team back into the game just before half-time. Meslier did well racing out of goal to confront the Charlton man and making things just a little more difficult. The young Frenchman has grown in stature since his league debut at Hull, conceding just five goals in 11 games, and must surely be offered a permanent contract when the season concludes. Charlton offered a little more in the first few minutes after the interval, and the substitute Aneke forced a good save from Meslier, who used his feet to save the forward's shot. But any hope the Londoners had of somehow getting back into the game was extinguished in the 51st minute when Roberts, on for Bamford at half-time and unmarked in the area, headed powerfully home from an Hernandez corner.

With the game clearly won, I take the opportunity to catch up on what is happening around the country and find most of the key matches are still evenly balanced. WBA, Brentford, and even Fulham are still in with a chance of automatic promotion, and improbably Swansea can still reach the play-offs, while Barnsley can still reach safety, which would be bad news for Charlton. I feel for all those fans desperate for a goal, a draw, a win, all watching the clock and praying for it either to go faster or slow down, wondering if they can dare continue to watch and whether they might 'jinx' their team if they left them in their moment of need. It's quite unbelievable to me that into the second half of the 46th and final game of the Championship season, there are so many issues still to be resolved.

One issue that is, however, very clear is that we are going to get our final three points of the season tonight, and when Struijk sends a brilliant raking cross-field ball to Poveda, the winger's simple pass is beautifully finished by the marauding Shackleton. It's a super goal and really the final meaningful action of the night, though Meslier does save well again from an Aneke header.

I know it may seem sacrilege, but with our game won, I can't help turning the TV on to see how everything turns out elsewhere. I am a Leeds fan obviously, but I'm also a football fan. I've been to most of the grounds in the Championship this season and watched all of the teams. I know their strengths and weaknesses, I've chatted with fans of clubs up and down the country, I know what they think about their own team and others. So, I'm really interested to see how everything finishes. And wow, what a finish there is as all the end of season issues are finally resolved.

Albion eventually secure the second automatic promotion place, playing out a nervy home draw with QPR, knowing with every second that passed by that if Brentford scored in the closing minutes of their game against Barnsley they would be overtaken by the West London club. And every Albion fan in the world would have had their hearts in their mouths when they heard there had been an injury-time winner at Griffin Park. Amazingly, it was scored by Barnsley, when Clarke Odour tapped in a Schmidt cross in added time. Quite unbelievable, but I am so pleased for Barnsley and their young team who have fought so hard against the odds in recent weeks and played some attractive football while doing so. Their win means 'Brom are promoted and Brentford, after such a good run since the season restart, have to settle for the play-offs. It also means Charlton, our visitors tonight, are relegated.

I feel sorry for Lee Bowyer and the Charlton fans. They have had to deal with so much on and off the field, and to be relegated with a goal in added time on the last day of the season must be tough to take. But perhaps not as tough to bear as all those Forest fans slowly beginning to realise that their side has thrown away a play-off spot at the last minute, losing 1-4 at home to Stoke, as Swansea triumphed by a similar score at Reading. They only needed a point tonight, and even with a loss, their goal difference should have made them safe. For Forest management, players, and fans, tonight is simply a disaster. I know exactly how they are feeling, but it's not difficult to track the seeds of their downfall when the whole lot of them celebrated far too early, like Lampard's Derby when they beat us at the City ground in February.

That night, Forest had closed in to just being one point behind us; tonight, as they hold their heads in their hands in abject dismay, and just 15 games later, they are 23 points adrift of us. A classic case of celebrating too early. In the next game, they showed disrespect to the competition and their opponents by resting key players and were defeated at home by lowly Charlton. You would have to say the management, left speechless at the end of the Stoke game, have much to rebuke themselves for when they review their input to the season and where things went wrong. I think I can help them just go back to the hugely premature celebrations on Saturday, 8th February, Sabri.

Elsewhere, Wigan – despite a tremendous run towards the end of the season – are relegated, following a 1-1 draw with Fulham. Without the 12-point penalty for going into administration, they would have finished safely in mid-table, and the draw is a disaster for their fans and all connected with the club. Players, coaches, and owners, all move on, but it will be the fans who suffer the anxiety of what waits for them in the future and through what is likely to be a miserable and painful close season.

Hull, as always seemed likely, are relegated with Charlton and Wigan, and in truth have gone down without much of a fight, unlike Luton – clearly inspired by the return of Nathan Jones –who reached an unlikely 51 points in preserving their Championship status. Perhaps it was the sheer emotion of Gerhart Struber that best summed up the passions aroused by this game of football. The Barnsley manager was rendered almost speechless in his post-match interview, so gripped was he with the emotion, pride, spirit, and sheer relief of his side's last-minute saving goal and consequent Championship survival.

So, in the end, a season that started for me on a beautiful August day in Bristol, finished nearly a year later watching the Charlton game in my front room, beaming signals from LUTV onto my laptop. And it finished with Leeds crowned Champions. Like most fans, I watched the presentation and scenes of joy from ER on the television. I knew fans would gather outside Elland Rd but just as at the beginning of this awful pandemic, the kids put the damper on me going, frightened that I would pick up the bug and become ill. In truth, I would have gone had it not been for the pain in my knee, which seems to be getting worse but for which, thankfully after a painful last week, I have at last got an appointment to see my doctor about. I just couldn't have made the walk down from Beeston to the ground. What a wimp I am becoming! But a few thousand did, and they got their reward when the players emerged from ER on an open-top bus to parade the trophy – this, after Angus Kinnear pleaded with the fans to stay away.

I'm not sure what to make of this. Apparently, it was done with the knowledge of the authorities, which is fine, but what of the fans who did as they were asked and stayed away? I must admit, I think this was unfair of the club, and though I personally would have struggled to get to ER, I know there will be thousands who would have wanted to be there sharing this moment of triumph with the players and each other. Our time will come, but sadly no-one knows exactly when this will be, and the real moment of excitement and celebration will have passed.

There are still the play-offs to come, and in the end those final places are taken by Brentford, Fulham, Cardiff, and surprisingly Swansea. I would have to say at this point I am hoping for a Brentford v Fulham final: A) because, in my opinion, they are the best two teams; and B) because they are the much better 'away' trip destinations. In the event, the final placings for the top six were as follows:

Leeds United......93
WBA...............83
Brentford..........81
Fulham............81
Cardiff.............73
Swansea...........70

In the end, we finished 12 points clear of Brentford in third and even closed down their better goal difference, and we were ten points clear of West Brom. It sounds a decisive clear and easy win, but it wasn't like that at all. And really, right up to that late goal for Huddersfield in their defeat of West Brom in the last-but-one game of the season, it was still possible that we could blow it. A defeat at Derby would have left us battling Charlton for that vital last point, and every Leeds fan in the world knows how badly we have dealt with such situations over the years.

Fortunately, we seemed to have learnt from the misery of last year, and following the disappointing home draw with Luton, we looked to have an inner steel and a real determination to see the season out successfully. And we absolutely did just that, winning our last six games on the bounce to be crowned at last worthy champions.

CHAPTER 22

AND IN THE END, HANDING
ON THE BATON

Brentford…1; Fulham…2
Tuesday, 4th August

So, now we know how it all finished, how a season like absolutely no other finally came to an end. Fulham beat Brentford, their West London neighbours, in a desperately dour, and from the neutrals' point of view, disappointing play-off final held at a near-deserted Wembley Stadium. In truth, I didn't really care which of these West London neighbours ultimately triumphed – both would provide a great 'away day', with Brentford in their new stadium and Fulham completing work on their new 'grandstand'. From my point of view, it's much better to head to London and a weekend with James than travel to South Wales, as would have been the case if either Cardiff or Swansea had managed to win the play-offs.

I realise as I jot down these thoughts about the play-off final that my work is done, and that I have at last achieved my ambition of writing that first book. It might not be very good, and it probably won't threaten the bestsellers, but it's my book and it's finished. A book that started out as a diary of our Centenary season and ended up as whole bunch of stories, loosely hung together by themes of football and family. I realise, too, that there are one or two constant threads running through this work that need tying up.

The Coronavirus changed everything. It changed the nature of this book; it turned the sporting world upside down; and it challenged the Government and NHS in ways they could never have imagined. Worse, far worse, as I write in early August, it has taken the lives of over 46, 000 people in our country. A truly disastrous figure that just a few months ago, back in March, we could surely not have anticipated. And people are still becoming infected and people are still dying. This evil illness has far from finished with us and no-one really knows, amid all the plans to try and return to some normality, when it will ultimately be beaten. Perhaps it never will.

I remember quite early in the 'lockdown', reading an article by Matthew Parris in *The Times*, in which the former politician argued that all the 'lockdown', all the closures of transport systems, entertainment venues, schools and offices, factories and businesses, were in place primarily to protect the elderly. Parris felt that while the actions taken to limit the spread of the virus were vital to protect the elderly and infirm, they would have an horrendous impact on the economy of the country, on the mental health of children denied their schooling, and of the younger generations forced to work in isolation in lockdown. Perhaps the most worrying aspect of Parris's article was the fear he expressed that this pandemic might just be the first of many, that while Coronavirus might be defeated, it could be followed in a year or so by another more virulent outbreak. The journalist essentially was asking the question: for how long can we close down our country? And can we keep doing it? I thought it was an incredibly perceptive and hugely troubling article. Just how do we react if this virus does not go away? Writing as someone who is 60-plus, I can see the sacrifices that the young are making to keep the older community safe and well, but I can also see that if pandemic is followed by pandemic, ultimately lockdown of the nature we have seen will be unsustainable.

At some point, the world will have to go back to work and some kind of normality, and those who are vulnerable will have to fend for themselves. There will be testing, there will be guidance and support, and there will be the need for people like me to make sensible decisions to protect ourselves. The horrible truth about all of this is that if it had happened 50 years ago, people would have put it down as some kind of 'Spanish flu' – the pandemic of 1918 that infected an estimated 500million people and killed between 20 and 50million people. And the world would have carried on.

The press and media, particularly the main news stations, had a field day with the virus and personally I felt they too easily politicised the pandemic, seemingly turning every news item into a criticism of the Government. I have mentioned this elsewhere, and certainly Boris Johnson's Government will be brought to task at some point. They clearly made mistakes, as any party would have done in such vastly challenging and quickly changing circumstances. It didn't help that Boris chose not to sack Dominic Cummings, who clearly breached the guidelines, even if I had the utmost sympathy for him escaping the disgraceful press pack that camped outside his house.

It seems to me that the media need to be more sensitive to the needs of the country as a whole, and to have a better understanding of those with views that might be different to their own. At times they seemed almost to be peddling their own 'culture change', a kind of silent 'big brother attack' seeping into our living rooms with the six o'clock news. My dad always used to say to me 'moderation in everything', and I think he was right. We have never needed it more than in the present troubled times, where the 'evils' of the extreme left and right seem to me to be equally as dangerous.

Hopefully with the advent of 'Black Lives Matter', society will look to create a better world where all people do indeed matter, and bigotry and racism can at last be defeated. It will need passionate, strong, courageous, and intelligent leaders for this to happen, and looking on the world stage, there seems a real dearth of such charismatic figures; sadly, no Bobby Kennedy, no Martin Luther King to be seen.

The virus impacted on all of us in some way, and for me one fairly minor problem in relation to the suffering of so many, revolved around trying to get an appointment to get my leg working again, without making me yelp in pain every time my knee had to bend. I had reached the stage where I couldn't drive because I couldn't get my leg into the car unless I could keep it straight – not an easy manoeuvre. Even before the virus, it used to take about three weeks to get an appointment to see my own doctor, and I was pretty pleased when, following our telephone call, Dr Vega invited me in and told me she would administer the cortisone jab I was now fairly desperate to have. Except that when she saw me and checked my knee, she was uneasy about giving me the jab, preferring instead to send me for an X-ray so she could be sure where to inject, and quietly suggesting that I might be looking at needing a replacement knee.

I was fairly despondent when I left the surgery, and things got even worse when the people I rang to book an X- ray appointment told me it would be at least six weeks before I got close. It's difficult to know what to do and say. So many people have died, so many are so seriously ill; I feel such a fraud as all I have is a gammy knee, but it's a bloody painful one. I head home and try to remember some of the exercises the physio gave me last time to help build the support up around the knee. I can't imagine six weeks of this, and after a really miserable weekend, I ring the surgery to try and get further advice. It's a 20-minute queue again, and at first when I get through all I seem to be getting is a bit of sympathy. But then – and I'm not sure if this was because I was whimpering down the phone – the receptionist tells me she will ask the duty doctor to ring me. That's as good as it's going to get, and the girl can't even tell me if the call will be today or maybe some time next week. But later that afternoon, one of the practice doctors, a Dr Ibrahim, rings me and chats with me about the problem. To be honest, he is brilliant and tells me to come into the surgery the next day and he'll look at the knee. And that's exactly what happened, and I quickly found myself sitting on the end of a trolley bed with Dr Ibrahim on my right, holding his needle, and a nurse on my left, holding a pad and plaster. I tell them I'm a coward and hope it won't hurt as much as last time when Dr Vega stuck it in my knee bone, but the doctor didn't aim for the painful spot, instead working on the other side of my knee and finding some soft tissue to put the needle in.

I started telling a joke – my usual way of trying to distract myself from what was happening to me. And as it was a different doctor and nurse, I told the one about the nun and the turf accountant again and turned away from the action to talk to the nurse. I knew it was coming, though, and soon felt a sharp sensation and then another like a scratch, so I figured he was perhaps giving some anaesthetic to ease the pain. The nurse leaned over with her pad, did a quick swipe round, and stuck a plaster on my knee.

'Is that it?' I asked. And it was. I couldn't believe it; the last time had hurt so much and didn't really work! I don't know if this will make things better, but it's worth a go and at least it didn't hurt much. I finished the joke before I left and was pleased that both of them laughed. Before I got home, I could feel the pain in my knee easing, and slowly and surely as the evening progressed, I managed more and more movement, at last free of the awful pain I had been experiencing. That night, the toast was Dr Ibrahim, and I dedicated a few beers and some red wine to his talent. The next day, for the first time in a fortnight, I was able to go cycling.

Of course, just like the players, we celebrated our Championship win, though I didn't go to any of the gatherings at ER or in the city, banned by the kids in case I picked up any infection that would threaten me or Andy, or particularly Eileen. James came home the weekend after the Charlton game, desperate to celebrate, and we had a great night going to the pub in Smeaton and meeting up with the Parkies, before heading home for supper and more celebratory drinks. It was a lovely evening that finished with him searching the house for whisky, which fortunately he was unable to find as I lay comatose and oblivious to his needs. I must say, as I read through these notes 'cold beers in the sun' seem to be mentioned with much regularity. This is because we really enjoy them, and they are usually the reward at the end of a long day. We are not – even with the stress of the promotion race – alcoholics, preferring to take the drink when we want to rather than because we have to. But honestly, who wouldn't enjoy a few chilled beers in the sun?

We had a 'Champions Zoom' night with the WhatsApp group and created a final Spotify playlist of songs that in some weird and wonderful way reminded us of supporting the club and memories of going to ER. These Zoom nights had kept us going through lockdown and we had created some great playlists, but I think the 'Champions' one was the best and we had a lively sing-song with everyone dressed up in Leeds colours. See what you think to our choices.

Give It Up; KC and the Sunshine Band
Dakota; Stereophonics
I'm Still Standing; Elton John
Double Barrel; Dave and Ansell Collins
Stop Crying Your Heart Out; Oasis
Two Hearts; Phil Collins
Just a Day; Feeder
2468 Motorway; Tom Robinson Band
Coming Home; Kaiser Chiefs
My Sweet Lord; George Harrison
Happy; Pharrell Williams
20th Century Boy; T Rex
Sweet Caroline; Neil Diamond
Tubthumping; Chumbawmba
Hey Baby; D J Otzi
Pump It Up; Endor
Glad All Over; Dave Clark Five
Greatest Day; Take That
Three Lions; Baddiel, Skinner, Lightening Seeds
Strings for Yasmin; Tin Tin Out
Ready to Go; Republica
Leeds, Leeds, Leeds; Leeds United football team

Some pretty good music there and some great memories of Elland Road. And that really is where I have to leave this work, by finally trying to sum up what Marcelo Bielsa and his team have achieved in this Championship-winning Centenary season. A season like no other, that started on a sunny August Sunday afternoon in Bristol, and finished almost a year later behind closed doors with our final victory over Charlton Athletic.

It was a season almost split into four parts in terms of results, with some strangely up and down performances in the opening flurry of games – the brilliance of our play at Bristol and Stoke being somewhat tarnished by the frustrations of needlessly dropped points against Swansea, Derby, Charlton, and Millwall. This unpredictable start was quickly forgotten when, following the defeat at 'The Den', we went on an 11-game unbeaten run which finished with defeat at Fulham, as we all got ready for Christmas. And the defeat at the Cottage clearly hurt, as we then managed only two wins in the next nine games, albeit the thrilling matches against Birmingham and Millwall. In this run of indifferent form, we lost at home to Sheffield Wednesday and Wigan, which prompted my email plea (unanswered) to Angus Kinnear to do something about the goalkeeping and striking situation before the end of the transfer window.

I did say at the outset of this book that the opinions expressed are entirely mine, based on observations I have made while watching the games home and away. I have no insider information, and I don't go on any of the social media platforms like Twitter. It seemed to me that without strengthening the team in these areas, we were seriously risking our chances of promotion. I still believe, even now looking back after we have been crowned Champions, that the club took a massive risk in the transfer window signing two players neither of whom were fit enough to come into the team and replace Eddie Nketiah. Goodness knows what would have happened had Bamford got injured before Tyler Roberts was fully fit. The truth is, in terms of player health – and especially Bamford's – we just got lucky.

We ended this third difficult stage of the season with the away draw at Brentford, which seemed to mark the low point for our keeper Kiko Casilla, who let a simple back pass from Cooper slide under his foot for Benrahma to score easily. I seem to have been harsh on the goalkeeper as I read through these notes, but so often he seemed to unsettle the defence and make unforced errors. It wasn't just me on the terraces who had his head in his hands every time we conceded a corner or free kick near the penalty area. To me, whatever success Casilla had enjoyed in the past, he was clearly struggling in his career at the moment, and I still can't understand why he wasn't taken out of the firing line to allow him to work on his game and regain some of his confidence. In the end of course, he was taken out of the team – banned for eight games as a result of alleged racist comments aimed at the Charlton player Johnathon Leko.

We left Griffin Park that night fighting to hold onto second place and slipping further behind West Brom as they stretched their lead over us at the top of the table. What we didn't know was that we were about to enter the most productive part of the season and a run of 14 fixtures that, as they concluded, would see us crowned champions, ten points clear of West Brom. It was the fourth part of the season, and at least at the start, the most nerve-wracking. Well, actually, the end was pretty worrying, too! I can still feel the tension of those two home wins against Bristol City and Reading, still see Nhaki Wells bearing down on goal only to shoot just over the bar, and in fairness Casilla blocking a last-minute shot by a marauding Reading defender. It was sheer agony being there, gripped by the theatre and a desperate need that I had inside me to see us at last, this time, after 16 long years, make it back to the Premiership. At times, I almost felt it might be better not to actually be there, tortured by every missed chance and every corner we conceded.

And of course, that's exactly what happened, after we stretched our winning run to five games with the 2-0 win over Huddersfield on 7th March. The virus hit and football was closed down until mid-June when, after a blip at Cardiff, we rallied and won our last six games. This included brilliant away performances at Blackburn, Swansea, and Derby, not to mention pretty impressive home wins against Fulham, Stoke, and Charlton. It was desperate that we couldn't be there to share the moment with the players, to hear ER once more rocking to the tune of *We Are the Champions* and *Marching On Together*. It would have been truly fantastic to have travelled to Derby as champions and celebrated for 90 minutes or more with the Derby faithful.

It had been my dream for two years now, given the revolution created by the appointment of Marcelo Bielsa; two years in which, win or lose, we had played such entertaining football; two years when I had driven up and down the motorway network at all times of night and day, following this team and our shared dream. And at last it had come to fruition. And yes it's gutting that we couldn't all celebrate together at a packed Elland Road, but we will do one day soon.

And when we do, what an emotional time it will be, with the deaths of Norman Hunter, Trevor Cherry, and Jack Charlton all occurring during recent months, and memories for me of great moments and celebrations of the past mingling with the memories of the current crop of highly motivated and successful players parading the Championship trophy in front of us. A Leeds United timeline that for me stretches from that first Boxing Day game in 1964 to the present day. A huge chunk of my life spent in this place, living the dream with these men in white, sharing in their despair and the joy down through the years, and realising just how many similarities there are between those players nurtured by Don Revie and today's Bielsa-inspired team.

Both football men through and through, both obsessive in their preparation, both driven to succeed, and both building teams with youth and skill, led by an older player still with the creative vision and talent to lead them to success.

For Bremner, Lorimer, and Gray, read Phillips, Harrison, and Shackleton; and for Bobby Collins, read Pablo Hernandez. For me, fortunate enough to watch both sides in action, it's hopefully history repeating itself.

In those early years of the sixties when Revie's team were promoted as champions from the old second division, no-one knew that they would turn into one of the greatest teams of their generation. A team that still dominates at ER with the strength of their achievements and whose legacy and memories are still alive in supporters like myself, who can see the seeds of something so special beginning to grow in the current group of players.

How respectful Liam Cooper, Kalvin Phillips, and the others have always been to those great legends of the past, who I am certain will be looking down from above as Bielsa's boys take to the field with their own Championship trophy. Happy to be handing on the baton of success and what it means to represent this massive club, to a group of players who have it in their grasp to write their own stories of victory in the coming years; to become legends in their own right. Legends of the very unique and special worldwide community that is Leeds United Football Club.

MOT

Adrian Taylor, August 2020

Lightning Source UK Ltd.
Milton Keynes UK
UKHW010631260122
397749UK00001B/110